LAW

&

ETHICS

FOR

CLINICIANS

LAW & ETHICS FOR CLINICIANS

JACQULYN K. HALL, B.S.N., M.ED., J.D.

JACKHAL BOOKS
AMARILLO, TEXAS

JACKHAL BOOKS
18 Nottingham Road
Amarillo, Texas 79124

Library of Congress Control Number : 2001118963

Cover photograph: Statue of Justice loaned by Cole Young of
Templeton, Smithee, Hayes, Fields, Young, Heinrich.
Stethoscope loaned by Texas Tech Internal Medicine Clinic.
Camera loaned by Tom Hale. Photo by the author.

LAW & ETHICS FOR CLINICIANS   ISBN 1-888856-00-9

Printed in the United States of America
Last digit is the print number: 9 8 7 6 5 4 3 2

To Hal

"And, when he shall die, cut him out in little stars,
and he shall make the face of heaven so fine, that
all the world will be in love with night,
and pay no worship to the garish sun."
SHAKESPEARE, *Romeo and Juliet*

PREFACE

This unique book is the essence I have distilled from years of learning and practice as clinician and lawyer, from experiences in sailing the Caribbean and Atlantic, and from living and studying history and philosophy in Europe--all the while observing clinicians and America close up and from a distance. This is a labor of love, written for clinicians who care for patients and who soon will care for me, to dispel their fear. They can lay down at last the tomes of ethics and law and get on with the work of caring for patients, certain in the knowledge that doing good patient care is lawful and right.

TABLE OF CONTENTS

Chapter 1:
Theories of Law and Ethics.

The student: "Who'll know about it, if I do [this bad thing that can't be detected]?" The teacher: "Who'll know? You'll know."
ROBERT ROSS, *Professor, Civil Procedure class, University of Missouri School of Law, 1978.*

CONTENTS

REFERENCES

Key concepts

law
ethics
statutes
regulations
case law
civil law
criminal law
federal law
state law
Internet
annotated statute
ultra vires
administrative law
procedural due
    process
substantive due
    process
Federal Register
Code of Federal

Regulations
moral reasoning
ethical practice
moral development
narrative ethics
ethics committees
Patient Self
    Determination
    Act
ethical decision
    making
applied ethics
non-normative
descriptive ethics
metaethics
general normative
    ethics
normative
    judgments

value judgments
prescriptive
    judgments
moral judgments
nonmoral
    judgments
skeptics
nihilists
eudaemonia
virtue ethics
 teleology
golden mean
casuistry
narrative ethics
paradigm case

What's in the book and why.

You have picked up or bought this book because you think you
need a book on law and ethics--or your teacher thinks so. You *could*
put it down or send it back after you read the next two sentences:
**All you need to do to be lawful is to be ethical. All you need to do
to be ethical is to treat patients the way you'd want to be treated.**

But likely you need proof of that statement, or need some specifics on law and ethics. Here they are.

This book was written for clinicians, not for lawyers. Lawyers don't need it. You need it, if you need proof that your good instinct for what is right, is right. You need it for a lawyer's assurance that what you instinctively know is right, is also lawful.

Here are all the ethics and law you need to know, in *general* terms. No book is adequate to give you specifics on the latest law. If you need that, you must find the current law by one of the methods outlined below.

The brief overview of the book below gives you some idea as to where to look for what. For more detail, look at the contents at the beginning of each chapter. To find a specific topic, look in the index. The goal is to help you find the information you need without reading the entire book. The names and citations of important legal cases are given, but it is my job to study the source material, distill it, and pass it on so you can use it. You should not have to consult the original sources to understand the law and ethics of clinical practice.

(The values listed below in parentheses, are the Latinized counterparts of the English language values.)

Chapter 1: Theories of Ethics and Law
Chapter 2: Do good (Beneficence)-- malpractice law
Chapter 3: Don't Harm (Non-maleficence)-- intentional torts and licensure law.
Chapter 4: Be Free (Autonomy)--law of consent, advance directives, and clinician autonomy.
Chapter 5: Be Fair (Justice)--due process, antidiscrimination law, and social justice.
Chapter 6: Be True (Fidelity: loyalty, confidentiality, veracity)--contract law, privacy, and whistle-blowing.
Chapter 7: Life--ethical and legal aspects of life surrounding birth and death.

The book uses the word "patient" in preference to some of the newer words used for that person, such as "client" or "customer." The Greek root of the word "patient" is *pati* or *pathi*, meaning "suffer" or "feel." The patient suffers, and we feel for her. This root also is the basis of the words em<u>path</u>y, sym*pathy*, com*passi*on, and <u>passi</u>on.

Those who argue for calling patients by some other term, say that the patients will be empowered by that new word. Clinicians who believe that changing the words we use for things or people, then will change our relationship to the things or people, should examine other cases in which this is done. For example, changing crippled to handicapped to disabled to challenged--changing graveyard to cemetery to memorial park--changing venereal disease to sexually transmitted disease--all changed labels but not the reality, not the attitudes of people. If there is something wrong with the relationship between clinicians and patients, we must change the relationship, not the label.

Call the patient your "client"? A client is one who is dependent on a person who is higher status--a patron. Call the patient your "customer"? Is that the extent and depth of the relationship that clinicians should have with their patients? It has been suggested (What's in a name, 2000) that those who wish to "empower" patients should heed the patients themselves. By a majority of 77% they want to be called "patient" (Ritchie *et al*, 2000). You might ask your own clients/ customers/ *patients*, which word they want used.

Regarding words used in the book, "clinicians" in is the title, and in the text, meaning professionals who care for patients. You know who you are. When you see the word "clinician," read "nurse" if you're a nurse, "physician," if you're a physician, "respiratory therapist," if you are--you get the idea.

Books written on the ethics and law of your profession alone are deceptively specific. The laws of various professions are very similar, because they all are based on the ethical values outlined in this book. Check out books written specifically for the law and ethics of your profession, to see if they are as helpful as knowing what you find here-- the law and ethics that apply to *all* clinicians. Remember to be skeptical of assertions made about specifics of law for any single profession--after you read this book, you will realize they very possibly are out of date.

Objectives of the book

After completing this book, you should be able to:
Predict that your practice will be lawful, when it is ethical.
State the areas of law that enforce the values of clinical practice:
> Do good
> Don't Harm
> Valuing Freedom
> Valuing Fairness
> Valuing Truth
> Valuing Life

Find specific current law if you need it.
Identify and define some basic theories of ethics, some concepts of ethics, metaethics, and moral deliberation

Features

Just as this first chapter on theory does, each succeeding chapter of the book will have the following features.

1) **Key Concepts** for that chapter are bolded the first time the concept is used, and most are defined in the glossary. Look over those concepts listed before you read the chapter-- first to see if you already know some of them, and second to get your mind prepared to learn them if you don't.

2) Questions about the material in each chapter are labeled **Think about it**. These questions are supposed to help you **think about** the issues raised, to stimulate your thinking. It is a good thing to make notes of your thoughts in the margin, to read later, or for the interest of your great grandchildren, or for the interest of the buyer of this book at your estate sale. The questions don't have answers listed anywhere, and your writer doesn't have all the answers, either. If you have some answers you'd like to share, send them to me in care of the publisher.

3) **References** are given in the text for that chapter.

The rules

Too bad we can't all just get along. But we can't, we don't, not all of us, not always, not ever. By the way, it would be a pretty dull world if we did. Ethics and law help people, especially clinicians and their patients, come within rock-throwing distance of each other and get along. At least some of the time.

Ethics and law are a system of conflict resolution. The system has developed from prehistoric times, through all the major religions and philosophies of the world. Here is the major premise of all of them: Treat others the way you would want to be treated. Dountoothers.

The Golden Rules

BUDDHIST: Hurt not others in ways that you yourself would find hurtful. *Udana-Varga 5:18*

CHRISTIAN: All things whatsoever ye would that men should do to you, do ye even so to them; for this is the law and the prophets. *Matthew 7:12*

CONFUCIAN: Surely it is the maxim of loving-kindness: Do not unto others what you would not have done unto you. *Analects 15:23*

HINDU: This is the sum of duty: Do naught unto others which would cause you pain if done to you. *Mahabharata 5:1517*

IMMANUEL KANT'S CATEGORICAL IMPERATIVE: Do only

those things that you would have everyone in the world do.

ISLAMIC: No one of you is a believer until he desires for his brother that which he desires for himself. *Sunnah*

JEWISH: What is hateful to you, do not to your fellow man. That is the entire Law; all the rest is commentary. *Talmud, Shabbat 31a*

TAOIST: Regard your neighbor's gain as your own gain and your neighbor's loss as your own loss. *T'ai Shang Kan Ying P'ien*

WICCAN: An ye harm none, do what ye will.

ZOROASTRIAN: That nature alone is good which refrains from doing unto another whatsoever is not good for itself. *Dadistan-I-dinik 94:5*

Good practice is good ethics is good law

The **law** is a minimum behavior standard. It enforces the higher behavior standard, the ethics. If you do good practice, as you learn to do it in your professional education, you automatically will be ethical. If your practice is ethical, it will be far above the lower standard of behavior--the law.

The golden rule, to treat others the way you want to be treated, is your guide to good behavior. If you follow it, you will stay out of legal trouble because you will be acting at a level higher than merely being lawful.

Ethics and law are found along a continuum of ways to solve conflicts between humans. The concept of a continuum is helpful in thinking about a number of concepts, from diabetes to ethics. At one point you can arbitrarily draw a line and say "here at this blood glucose level number, starts diabetes." You draw that line because at that point the condition starts to be pathologic.

The same thing can be done with law and ethics, but here the line is drawn exactly and arbitrarily when the law is written. There the ethical guide for behavior becomes legal, mandated behavior.

Remember that the law line is an arbitrary, human-constructed line. The law line changes, it moves up or down, every time the legislature meets, every time the bureaucrats issue a new rule, every time an appellate court writes a decision. Merely legal practice that is not at the higher ethical level, may not be legal either--after the law line moves.

The fine, bright line between ethics and law is fine indeed, and it moves (Hall, 1990). There is a difference between law and ethics (between what is mandated and what is desired). Law can be identified by its source. If it's not law, and it purports to be a guideline for human behavior, it's ethics.

Law usually seeks to control extremes of behavior. People together decide on certain actions that *must* be done--for example, parents must care for their children. Or they decide a certain action must *not* be done and, if done, will be punished–for example, parents must not abuse their children.

HUMAN BEHAVIOR CONTINUUM
(from higher ideal behavior to lower minimum standard of behavior)

       ETHICS   * (desired behavior)
                                 *
                                 *
                                 *
                                 *

LAW   LINE   * (mandated behavior)
                                 * (illegal behavior)
                                 *

-Credit is due Dr. Harold Werner for the original idea for this schematic. (Hall, 1996)

People together elect or authorize other people to <u>enforce</u> the law. The word force is important because force is implied in law--as contrasted to ethics, which seek to persuade and not force.

In statutes and paintings of Justice (as on the cover of this book), she is shown with a sword, used to enforce the law. She is blindfolded, to symbolize fairness or lack of bias. (But until the 1600s Justice was portrayed as clear sighted, in order to judge well.)

Justice has a scale in one hand, *weighing* the evidence, to see which side of the scale is heavier--who is guilty. In her other hand she has a sword--symbolizing her power to force people to obey the law, or to punish them if they disobey. Without force, there is no law. Without law, there is no justice--at least not until humans volunteer to behave a lot better.

To live together without fear, people can't allow force to be used by any people except those with authority of law. The authority to use force also extends to people who must use force to defend themselves.

On the continuum of human action seen above, ethics is higher behavior--desired behavior. We may wish that people would act ethically, but they will not be made to do so. If force can be used to order the act, and not mere persuasion, then that's law and not just ethics.

Adhering to the legal minimum behavior can be less than fully ethical, because law is a minimum ethic. Under the German law of the National Socialists of the 1930s, judges, lawyers, doctors, nurses, and other clinicians sanctioned and performed the torture and killing of patients. These acts were legal at the time but were unethical. Clinicians who say "It's the law--I don't have any ethical choice to make," should realize that clinicians in Nazi Germany said the same thing.

Difference between ethics and law:

	Words used:	Behavior is:	Written?
Ethics	words like *should* and *may*	desired behavior	may be written or not, by experts
Law	words like *must* and *shall*	mandated behavior	must be written, by people with authority

Natural law and positive law

There are two major philosophies of law-- **natural law** and **positive law**. Their differences are related to the issue we are considering, the difference between ethics and law. The difference between the two philosophies of law is illustrated by describing the focus of each.

Those who like the philosophy of positive law, focus on what the law IS. They believe that law can be determined and studied and enforced, without reference to ethics and morality. People who like the philosophy of natural law believe that what the law IS, cannot be considered without thinking about what the law OUGHT to be. They believe that law cannot be defined and enforced merely with scientific study, without reference to ethics and morality.

The difference is important. A natural law judge might say, "This law is not fair; I won't send this clinician to jail," while a positivist might say, "The law is clearly written and this clinician clearly violated it. Off with her head!" In another case, the positivist judge might say: "No technical violation--he's innocent," but the natural law judge would find: "It *should* be illegal--off with his head!"

Natural law or natural rights are said to be what the law ought to be, the "natural" God-given or evolved rights of people. This philosophical principle grew up as the influence of religion declined in Europe during the period called the enlightenment. Natural law replaces (and in many instances, it mirrors) the principles of religion, but it purports to be human law instead of God's law.

Natural law is not written, and so it can be discovered only by reference to what you believe is "natural." Remember this concept when you read about the philosophy of naturalism in Chapter 4. You will also see some reference to the "Is-Ought" distinction in that chapter. Notice the difference as it is used there, from its use in natural versus positive law.

This idea of natural law and natural rights was fully developed by the time of the US Revolutionary War. The writers of the US Declaration of Independence evidenced their belief in natural rights when they wrote

> "We hold these truths to be self-evident; that all men are created equal and endowed by the Creator with certain <u>inalienable rights</u>, among them life, liberty and the pursuit of happiness."

The emphasis above is added--inalienable rights means the rights can't be sold. That is another way to say natural rights, a reference to natural law.

The courts have used the concept of natural law when no written law was available to use, to mandate the result they desired or felt necessary. Natural law and natural rights are invoked when any group or person wishes to bolster their desire for some action with an appeal to law, especially when there is no written law mandating the action they want. They usually desire that some law be written, to replace the natural law.

The concept of positive law, on the other hand, has been used by the deconstructivist philosophers who assert that there is no moral or philosophical underpinning of the law, that it is merely the product of any given lawmaker's whim at any given moment. Thus they say the law deserves little respect, because it has no higher moral basis than a belch by the lawmaker.

Difference between ethics and law

Ethics can be defined as being the customs of a people. This is not a custom such as the custom of dress; instead it is a custom of ideal behavior that people should follow. Ethical behavior therefore is not instinctively known at birth, but must be learned as part of the culture. Students of Sir Karl Popper, the science philosopher, will recognize that this idea of ethics as custom, is part of his World 3. Popper's World 3 is the shared ideas and culture of people (World 1 is the physical world, and World 2 is the psychological world inside just your own head).

Humans likely have a genetic tendency to adhere to some principles of ethics, just as we also have genetic traits for language. But each generation must learn the specifics of ethical behavior, as we must learn language. To extend the analogy: Peoples speak different languages, but they all speak <u>some</u> language. Different peoples have different customs of ethics, but all have some codes of ideal behavior. Continue this line of thinking in Chapter 6 on ethical relativity if you're interested.

Ethics uses words such as *should* and *may*, while law uses words such as *must* and *shall*. The origin of the word ethics is from the Greek *ethike tekne,* meaning the moral art. In Latin the word becomes morals, and in English, character. Used in English, it means character and spirit of a people, or custom. The word ethics was commonly used in place of the word customs only a few decades ago (Cutter, 1893).

Relationship of values to the laws of clinical practice

Clinician ethics are based on values. Each value mothers some laws of practice that enforce the minimum ethic. These laws are identified specifically with each value in this book. The description of ethics and resulting law covers virtually all of the usual clinician's practice. The foundation of law is ethics.

Think about it.
What do you think of the idea that law is a minimum enforcement of a higher ethic?
Do you agree? Disagree? Why?
Give an example that supports that idea, or one that disproves it.

In this book's approach, the ethics are separated into values. For each value identified, the minimum law that flows from that value is discussed. The values discussed throughout this book are not exhaustive of all values held by people, but the following values are used often in professional practice. Each value is the topic of a chapter that explains the ethics and resulting law of that value.

Value: Do good (Beneficence). Beneficence is what clinicians call caring. Tort law, specifically malpractice or professional negligence, is the biggest area of law based on the value of Do good.
Value: Don't Harm (Nonmaleficence). Tort law and some other statutory laws enforce the ethical value to not harm others that all people have, including clinicians. The law enforcing Don't Harm includes the intentional torts of battery, assault, false imprisonment,

intentional infliction of emotional distress, and defenses to those acts.

Also enforcing the value of Don't Harm are those torts called quasi-intentional, now sometimes called economic dignity interests. These traditional torts of defamation (slander and libel), invasion of privacy, and some others, are discussed under Don't Harm, together with the defenses to those lawsuits.

The value Don't Harm is the origin of statutes that prohibit clinicians and others from maltreating people such as children, dependents, or old people. Other statutes require clinicians to report abuse that they learn about. Credentialing statutes and related statutory protection also are addressed under Don't Harm because credentialing law is a mandate not to harm the patient. The ethics and law of education for clinicians are enforced through credentialing law.

Value: Freedom (Autonomy). Consent law enforces the minimum of the autonomy value in clinical practice. Related laws are the advance directives--durable power of attorney and living will. Laws related to HIV/AIDS also are addressed under this value, that disease usually being a consequence of a freely chosen lifestyle. The law and ethics of transplant are grouped here also, as an issue of free choice to donate or not to donate body parts.

The freedom or autonomy of the clinician is a corresponding value, expressed in autonomous practice and its legal consequences. The giving of futile care is discussed under this value, because it's asserted that the autonomous caregiver should be able to make that determination.

Value: Fairness (Justice). The value of fairness under the law is important not merely because it's good to be fair. Without fairness in law there is no peace within a country. The discussions of law that enforces the value of justice include rights--limits on the power of lawmakers to control our lives. These are the rights to liberty, life, and property, enforced with due process and equal protection guarantees. Other "rights" are disputed, such as rights to privacy, to die, to abortion, and to life.

The assumption that law should be just, is so basic that it doesn't stir much ethical controversy. The idea of social justice does stir controversy, however, because it is an attempt to use the force of law to implement the value Do Good--different from procedural justice. Mandating social justice would change the economics of clinical practice, so some basics of economics affecting clinical practice are given. Labor laws and antidiscrimination laws also enforce the value Justice.

Value: Be True (Fidelity). The value *fidelity* includes keeping promises (loyalty), enforced in contract law and employment law. Enforcing the value of telling the truth (veracity) is done with laws that protect the public or other individuals by encouraging whistle-blowing.

Telling the truth also is enforced in requirements for informed consent and in requirements to protect the patient's contacts when the patient won't. Keeping the secrets or maintaining the privacy of patients (confidentiality) is required by case and statute law. That may conflict, however, with required reporting of certain patient conditions. All these are in the chapter on Be True–the difference is in to <u>whom</u> one is being true.

Value: Life. The value of Life is divided chronologically into two sections, titled A Time to Be Born and A Time to Die. One division concerns the issues surrounding the start of human life, and the other division is about the issues confronted near the end of human life. Some of the issues in each division have values and law in common.

A Time to Be Born covers the ethics and law of artificial insemination, in vitro fertilization, surrogate motherhood, stem cell research, abortion, and neonates. A Time to Die is about the ethics of dying, as well as the assumptions and myths of society that surround this action. The law and ethics that result are based on attitudes and statistics about old people, brain death, persistent vegetative state (PVS), quality of life, dehydration, cardiopulmonary resuscitation, suicide, euthanasia, and assisted suicide.

Values ≠ have conflicts–people do

When a conflict arises in the context of clinical practice, some say that these values are in conflict. They may say the patient's autonomy is in conflict with doing the best thing for her. But values have no voices, no thoughts

Think about it.
Can values be in conflict with other values?
People with voices express their values, so is it the case that some people with certain values, are in conflict with other people who have different values?

Most people don't have much internal ethical conflict about what they want to do. They prioritize their interests that may conflict and focus on one interest. At that point, they may be in conflict with other people who have differing interests. For example, some may want to let the patient with a living will die, to honor his autonomy. Others want to treat him, valuing his life.

Your own values might seem at times to be in conflict, for example if you want to honor the patient's autonomy, and also save his life. Using the *rules* stated above, to treat other people the way you want to be treated, usually helps resolve any conflict you have in your own mind.

In any conflict situation, and especially one labeled an ethics conflict, note who are the people involved, and then examine the interest (wishes, wants, biases) of each. If the society or the government is involved in some ethical problem, such as costs or system reform, remember that the society and the government are shorthand labels for a group of people, all with their own interests.

Law

I'd give the devil benefit of law, for my own safety's sake.

CHANCELLOR SIR THOMAS MORE, in Robert Bolt's play, *A Man for All Seasons*

Law is made by people with power to write law. If it's not written down so that people can read it, it's not a law.

Think about it.
If someone tells you "It's the law," what is your next question?
Might you ask, "Where is that written, I'd like to read it?"

If the writing is not authored by people with authority to make law-- legislators, judges, or law administrators-- it's not law.

Shortcut past the courthouse

The bad news: You cannot possibly know all the law you might ever need. Even your lawyer likely will have to look up the law when you ask her for help. They have all those big books, just to look up the law (now most of the law libraries are on CD-ROM). If even the lawyer doesn't know the specifics of the law until she looks it up, does the clinician have any hope to know it? You couldn't know the law even if you tried, because they're making new law in your state capital and in Washington, D.C.--even as you read this.

The good news: You don't have to know the specifics of the law. You can avoid legal problems if you practice ethically, far above that lowest level of behavior--the law. If you practice as you have been taught in your professional education, you will be doing good care, ethical care, and lawful care.

Sources of law

Law comes in three flavors: statutes, regulations, and cases. **Statutes** are written by the legislative branch--in the United States, the US Congress or the state legislatures. As an example, in most states the legislature has written a "living will" statute that mandates clinicians to respect the wishes of the patient about her care.

Regulations are the second of the three kinds of law, written by people in the executive branch of government (headed by the governor of the state or by the president of the country). Examples are regulations written by the people who work for the credentialing board--the administrative agency that enforces your licensure act.

Case law is the third source of law, written by judges after they decide the appeals of lawsuits. A lawsuit is the result when people in conflict with each other cannot compromise. Case law starts with a lawsuit, a trial, a decision by a jury or judge, then an appeal of the decision. The written decision of the appellate court is called a precedent.

That means it precedes, is binding on, future cases in lower courts under that appeal court's jurisdiction. That is, if the later case presents the same issue. This principle is called *stare decisis,* Latin for "let the decision stand."

Case law sometimes is referred to as "common law." And sometimes it is called "unwritten law" because it is written <u>after</u> the judges make a decision in a case. This is in contrast to the law that is written in advance of cases, the way statutes are written by legislators. But case law too is written--it must be, else it could not be used as precedent in other cases.

Constitutions may be thought of as "super statutes," that set up governments and limit their powers. Constitutions list rights, that limit future lawmakers' power to make law or to apply it. The people to be governed are the original source of constitutional power. They elect others to write a constitution, delegating their power to the government that is created by the constitution.

Law Source	Who makes law?	Lawmakers are called
Statutes (constitutions are "super" statutes)	Legislative branch of state or nation (the people "make" the original constitutions)	State legislators or Congressmen: called Representatives and Senators (power is delegated to the original constitution by citizens.)

Law Source	Who makes law?	Lawmakers are called
Regulations (rules)	executive or administrative branch of state or nation	Governor, President, bureaucrats
Cases (sometimes called common or unwritten law)	judicial branch of state or nation	judges, who review cases appealed after jury verdict

An easy rule to remember to distinguish law from non-law: Any written document that is not a statute, a regulation, or a case--is not a law. Law must be written. A document may be a writing used in enforcing law, such as standing orders, standards of practice, a patient's living will, or agency policy, but such writings themselves are not law.

Laws are statutes, regulations, cases and constitutions, written by people with authority to do so. Anything else is not law--that is the bright line between law and ethics. The problem (and sometimes the opportunity) is that unlike ethics, the law changes--the bright line moves. The legislators in each state make hundreds of changes to their laws every legislative session. Multiply those changes by 50 states, and don't forget the U.S. Congress.

Merely legal practice that does not reach the higher standard of ethical practice, is not safe practice, legally. What is ethics today may be made into law tomorrow. What you think is safely just above the law line now, may be dangerously below it--illegal--after the legislature meets and moves the line.

Solution? Practice up at the ethical level, far above the minimum behavior that could be mandated even if lawmakers move the line.

Classifications of law

Law can be classified in several ways. One division is between civil law, and criminal law.   Under **civil law** are classified such cases as malpractice suits. When the individual is considered to have wronged another private individual or organization, violation of civil law is charged. Civil law is divided further. One class of civil law is called torts (an old French word meaning *wrongs*)--such as malpractice suits. Another classification of civil law, is that of contracts (promises).

Criminal law includes things such as violations of licensure laws and failure to report abuse of children. Contrasted with civil law, violation of criminal law is charged when the individual is considered to have wronged the whole public. Crimes may be referred to as misdemeanors if the fine is less than $1,000 and the penalty is less than a year in jail. If the penalty is more than those numbers, the crime is called a felony. Criminal negligence consists of an act that is not intended, but that is so seriously negligent it is classed as a crime against the whole people. Thus, it is prosecuted under criminal law, with possible penalty of imprisonment.

Negligence that is not so awful may be subject to a civil lawsuit by an individual, with possible penalty only of money damages. Clinicians have been prosecuted for **criminal negligence**, for reckless disregard for human life, and for the similar crime of involuntary manslaughter. Usually a simple mistake will not suffice for a criminal charge. The act has to be so obviously wrong and negligent that it can be inferred that the clinician not only did wrong, but did not care. These prosecutions are similar to those in which very negligent or reckless drivers who kill are prosecuted for crime, even though they did not intend to harm.

The purpose in both civil and criminal law is to make the parties even or equal again. In a sense, this is an attempt to re-balance the scales that Justice holds, after the scales are used to weigh the evidence to see who has been wronged, and who is guilty. One person has been hurt, so the person who caused it must be hurt too.

Differences between civil and criminal law

	Wrongs are called:	Conflict with:	Loser may lose:	Standard of proof:
Civil law	Tort or breach of contract	Another individual	Property (money)	Prepond-erance of evidence (50%+)
Criminal law	Crime	The group (society)	Property (money) or liberty (jail) or life (execu-tion)	Beyond a reason-able doubt

Another division of law is between **federal law** and **state law**. Questions about whether the federal or state court has jurisdiction can be very complex. The distinction is presented here only so you can see that there are the two systems of law and courts. The states have power over most law that affects clinicians, in particular malpractice and licensure law.

Classification by federal or state law:

	Courts called:	Authority:	Highest court:
Federal law--made by federal lawmakers	Federal District Court (may be more than one in a state); Circuit Court of Appeal (11 in the U.S., each covers more than one state)	Over disputes involving federal law or US Constitution, or between citizens of two different states	US Supreme Court
State law-- made by state lawmakers	Varies; for example, district courts, courts of appeal	Over any matters, but if matter is subject to federal jurisdiction, one party may remove to federal court.	Usually the state Supreme Court

The good news about state power is that local control of law means people have more direct control over their lawmakers and laws. The bad news about state power is that 50 different laws are written on each of thousands of different subjects. That's why no book on law can tell you all the law. That's why the only way you can be lawful and right is to do good practice--do the right thing.

How to find the law

Sometimes, however, it's helpful to have the exact words of a law.

That is true if someone is using a law to try to change your behavior. It is especially important to get the words of the law that someone would use to force you to do something that you believe is unethical. In virtually every case, what looks like an unethical law turns out to be enforcement of a neutral law, in an unethical way.

Where to find the law:

Source of the law:	First place to Look:	Last, fail-safe source:
statutes	public library (look in the statute index), Internet, or your lawyer	your legislator, state or national: representative or senator
regulations	public library, law library, state or federal *Register* (a publication that lists all new regulations), the Internet, the organization that enforces the law (state or national), your employer, and/or your professional association	your legislator, state or national: representative or senator
cases	law library, Internet, or your lawyer	lean on that legislator again

For non-lawyers, statute law is easiest to find, regulations harder to find, and, case law hardest to find. Fortunately, most of the time you need only a statute.

Internet sites for law

The easiest place is to look for law is on the **Internet**, at home or at work or at a public library. Enter "law" into one of the search engines or use one of the sites suggested next. By the time this is printed the best sites that I can give you likely will have evolved, but try the following. Legal resources that charge for search time are www.westlaw.com, www.lexis.com, www.versuslaw.com and www.itislaw.com. Free sites include www.law.cornell.edu, and www.findlaw.com. The Library of Congress materials are at www.loc.gov, with links to http://thomas.loc.gov for information on legislation, current bills and the workings of Congress. The government printing office has the *Federal Register* at www.access.gpo.gov. Of course you know about free MEDLINE access at www.ncbi.nlm.nih.gov, and medical risk management articles are at www.pdr.net. Other sites for medical information are proliferating (Coomer, 2000; Mehta, 1999).

Statutes

The categories of statutory law discussed here do not cover all the statutes that may affect your practice. A book with all of those statutes would be at least a thousand pages long, specific to your state only, and would be out of date the moment it was written. If you are interested in specifics you can go to the library or Internet, find the state statutes and read some of the statutes specific to your state.

The clinician who does good practice will be lawful 99 percent of the time without knowing the statute language. The one percent of good practice that possibly is technically unlawful, will still be right. Even if you read *all* the statutes you still must do good practice, because knowing the law is not the same as doing lawful practice.

Statutes are the source of most law that affects clinicians. Credentialing (licensure), patient abuse laws, consent to treatment and refusal of treatment, Medicare and Medicaid reimbursement (source of much of your salary in former times), employment law--these laws largely are statutes, not cases or regulations. The clinician who finds the statute on a specific topic has found most of the law on that topic. Statute law is now the source of most law.

For much of the history of the United States, statutes were less important than law made by judge decisions. But that is changing. More law is now made by statute, by legislators sitting in state capitals and in Washington, D.C. They write prescriptions for behavior ("do it") and proscriptions ("don't do it").

Some experts say that making law by statute is a good thing. They point out that problems are solved more quickly by the legislature passing a statute, than if judges made a decision on a case. The advocates of statute law say it's fairer to have representatives of all the people make decisions about what the people must do.

Other people prefer less statute law, and would like more law made by judges instead, by case law or common law. The people who prefer that law be made by judges, worry that the majority in the legislature can act as tyrants, enforcing their will on the minority. Whichever side is right, application and interpretation of statute law always will require judges and juries to examine individual facts in particular situations to see if they fit the statute as written. No legislature can write a statute so specific that it will fit every situation without interpretation (see rules for analysis, below).

As you read statute law or hear of what sound like bad statutes, you may see that some statutes actually harm instead of help. That's because all laws have intended consequences <u>and</u> unintended consequences--consequences that can't be known until the statute is enforced. If the solution to a problem does not require a law, the best action is to not legislate. The problem may be better solved with private action than with state force.

Think about it.

In some instances, is it true that "no law is good law"?

Can you think of an example, or do you believe all law is good?

State law: Source of most clinician law

State statutes are the most important of the three sources of law for clinicians. Federal statutes are less important, because the states still have the power to govern most of the areas that concern clinicians. (This may not always be so, if power continues to be transferred from the states to the federal government.)

For example, the state grants your credential to practice--your economic base. The state says who can give or withhold consent to treatment for which patient. The state legislature defines the crime of patient abuse, and which diseases or injuries must be reported by the clinician. A state statute specifies how long an injured patient can wait to sue a clinician, where she can be sued, and many other conditions of malpractice liability. Some of these statutes also are discussed in Chapter 2, Do Good. You can find statutes using the processes given for how to find the law in this chapter.

To be enforceable as law, statutes of the state and federal governments must be published in some form so that the people may know their duties. State statutes can be located in a depository library, law libraries, the Internet, and from your lawmakers. In addition, most public libraries have a set of the state's statutes. Look in the index of the statutes for the subject you are seeking.

If you find a statute in hard copy, you must look under the same statute number in the supplement that accompanies it to see if the legislature passed any new law amending that statute. This supplement may be in a pocket at the back of the volume, and may be referred to as a "pocket part." In that supplement or pocket part, the legislature may even have repealed the statute or part of the statute you just found.

If you don't find any later law in the latest supplement, you know the original law is still effective as written--unless your state's legislature is currently in session, busy amending the law you just found. You can find current bills that are proposed to be passed into law, on your state legislature's Website.

Once you've found the law and determined that it hasn't been amended, you can interpret the law. See below for rules that some judges use to analyze statutes.

RULES FOR ANALYSIS OF STATUTES

Guidelines for analysis are used when the statute is vague, or when two statutes appear to conflict. That is--most of the time. The following guidelines are common:

1. Attribute plain and ordinary meaning to the words used in the statute.

2. Look at the general purposes (intent) of the legislation.

3. Identify the problem the legislature probably sought to remedy, and if possible the conditions existing at the time of enactment.

4. Interpret laws that amend existing statutes on the theory that the legislature intended to accomplish some substantive change in the law. A later written stature or amendment rules over an earlier one. For correct interpretation, you should get the **annotated statute** with dates of enactment and history of the legislation.

5. Try to harmonize the various statutes that are applicable--that is, interpret them so that both laws are given effect.

Administrative law

Situation: The state board of licensure in your state has made a rule that clinicians must have 15 hours of mandatory continuing education each year for relicensure. Jane Clinician did not document 15 hours of CE last year. The board has suspended her license to practice.

Think about it.

Can they do that?

Any legal proceedings that are not in a court that decides civil or criminal cases, nor in the legislature that makes statutes, can be classed as **administrative law**. This area of the law is only one of the three sources of law, but administrative law is very important to clinicians because credentialing is a part of it.

Administrative law includes all of the process used by regulators to make rules and enforce them. Your state credentialing board is an administrative organization, part of the state's executive branch of government. The rules and regulations that the executive branch makes to administer the statutes, are law also, enforceable in court and with police power, just as is any statute or court decision.

Rules are made by the executive branch of government, to carry out the aims of the statute law made by legislators. Rulemakers must not act outside the power that was granted by the legislators (in Latin, they must not act ***ultra vires***). In addition, rules must be made and enforced according to substantive and procedural due process (see below).

Each state has a procedure used to enforce administrative law. Sometimes this is written into a statute called an administrative procedure act. The act specifies what procedure must be followed in order that a rule can have the force of law. Many states set up a kind of judicial body, such as an Administrative Hearing Commission, to make decisions at a level just above the regulatory boards (such as your credentialing board).

Some lawyers specialize in representing clients in these areas–they practice only before boards and the administrative law judicial bodies. For example, if a hospital challenges the state agency's Medicaid reimbursement rate, the challenge will be heard in such a forum.

Regulators have two general functions. One is a rule-<u>making</u>

function, like the legislature's lawmaking function. In addition, regulators have a rule-<u>enforcing</u> function when they investigate, prosecute, and decide individual cases much as courts do. One example of their power is to deny licensure for failure to document mandatory CE–as in Jane's case. Both functions of administrative law, rule-making and rule-enforcing, require fairness.

Rules made by administrators are different from statutes made by legislators, in that rules must be made pursuant to some statute. That is, the board has no authority to make any rules that do not implement a statute. Jane can challenge administrative rules in court by alleging that the regulation was not authorized by the statute--that the administrator has acted *ultra vires*. Or she might assert that the board did not follow due process, either substantive or procedural.

Type of action of the Board	How you can challenge the Board
Rule-making function	Rule made is *ultra vires*, outside Board power Rule making violated due process, either procedural or substantive
Rule enforcing function	Board decision violated due process, either procedural or substantive

If Jane disagrees with the decision of her credentialing board to suspend her license for inadequate CE, her next appeal is to the administrative law court or commission. If she loses there also, she still has the option of appealing beyond the administrative law system to judicial court.

Think about it.

Was the mandatory CE rule that the state board of licensure made, ultra vires?

Here comes the lawyer's favorite answer–"it depends." The board might assert that its mandatory CE rule was not *ultra vires*, because the statute specifically gave them the authority to implement mandatory CE. Or they could assert that even without specific authority in the statute, the board has a broad duty to protect the citizens who receive care--and that this CE rule comes under that duty.

Jane might argue that the duty to protect the public is not so broad that it gives the board power to write any rule it wants, without the legislature having granted specific authority. Then an administrative commission court would give its opinion on which party is right. If Jane lost there, she could appeal to judicial court.

Due process

The Fifth and Fourteenth Amendments to the US Constitution, so important that they are set out below and again in other chapters, require that no person shall be deprived of life, liberty or property without due process of law--as a result of state or federal action.

No person shall...be deprived of life, liberty or property without due process of law... (Amendment V, US Constitution–limits the federales).

No state shall... deprive any person of life, liberty or property without due process of law... (Amendment XIV, US Constitution–limits the states).

Note that this protection is from government action, not from action by private individuals or businesses. Due process comes in two flavors, procedural due process and substantive due process.

Procedural due process

Questions of procedural law concern fairness in the process used, not in the substance of the law. Regarding the rule that requires CE, the fairness process questions are:

Was the rule published in a timely manner?

Were the people concerned, notified about the problem?

Was a hearing held on the matter?

Was the procedure that was followed, appropriate to the action taken?

If not, the rule may be overturned.

The board would not have violated procedural, rule-making due process when it made the rule about CE, if it complied with the procedures used to make such rules. As noted above, each state has a process that agencies must use for rule making and rule enforcing. For example, in rule-making due process, the board likely must publish the rule as proposed, hold hearings open to the public, allow time for comment, and then publish the rule again as finally adopted, in a state register of rules.

The procedural, rule-enforcing process will be specified by the administrative procedure act, and the rules adopted by its administrative agency. The board must comply with the state administrative procedure act, as well as the federal requirements of due process that arise from the Fifth and Fourteenth Amendments of the US Constitution set out above.

Your license is considered to be a property right, and your ability to work at an occupation is a liberty right. T r e a s u r e t h e s e amendments– someday they may be your only protection against big brother.

For fairness in rule enforcing, at minimum Jane must be:

1) given notice of the charges against her,

2) given opportunity for hearing on the charges,

3) given a right to be represented by counsel, and

4) guaranteed the right to unbiased decision makers.

Without those components of due process, the board can't lawfully discipline her credentials.

Substantive due process

Here, the fairness question is:

Did the administrative agency or board (or legislature) have some rational basis for their law?

The agency cannot act arbitrarily. As you can imagine, this challenge to a board's rule is tough to maintain because usually they can find some reason for their action or rule. The requirement of substantive due process is met if the board's act has a rational basis–that is, if the act had a reasonable relationship to the duty imposed on the agency by statute.

Substantive due process also can be used to challenge the constitutionality of statutes made by the legislature. The challenger will say that the statute doesn't meet the constitutional test set out in the Fifth and Fourteenth Amendments, seen above. For example, the challenger can say that there was no rational basis for the statute--that the statute doesn't meet the need that the legislature articulated.

The defender of the statute (usually the Attorney General, defending the Legislature who made the statute) can meet the rational basis test if the legislation has any reasonable relationship to the problem that the legislature sought to correct. If so, the rule or act will meet the substantive due process challenge and will be considered constitutional.

Jane, whose credential was threatened for not documenting her CE, might argue that there was no rational basis for imposing mandatory CE to protect the public. She could assert that no data exist that demonstrate that mandatory CE reduces malpractice, or that it reduces numbers of licenses disciplined for incompetence. That is, no evidence exists that mandatory CE increases competent practice, nor that it decreases incompetent practice.

Through her attorney Jane would argue that no data exist showing that mandatory CE has any effect on clinician behavior, other than to produce attendance at CE in the required minimum amount. Thus she would argue that the CE rule has no rational relationship to the goal of protecting the public. The effect of the CE rule is not to make safe clinicians, but to increase attendance at CE. She would argue that the mandatory CE rule is actually detrimental to the public, increasing the cost of care to the public through the lost time, cost of travel, food, lodging, and registrations required.

However, the rational basis standard is so low that the court hearing this case likely would decide that the minimal test of rational basis for the rule had been met, and the court would uphold the board in disciplining the clinician's credential. Even a requirement that clinicians swear that they have paid their state taxes, was upheld in Massachusetts as being reasonably related to their competence and safe practice (Holzer, 1991).

Finding the regulations

To be enforceable as law, regulations of the state and federal governments must be published in some form so that the people may know their duties. Regulations are harder to locate than statutes, but they can be obtained from depository libraries, law libraries, the Internet, and your lawmakers.

Federal rules

U.S. federal agency rules are published daily in the *Federal Register*, hundreds of pages long on some days. Again, note that it is impossible for anyone to know all that law, so some shorthand way of knowing the law is needed. Knowing the values and ethic underlying the law eliminates the need to know all the latest specifics.

But if you need the actual words of the regulation, you can find it at the local library that is a repository of federal documents. Each city or area has designated at least one library to keep a copy of all federal documents. Your branch librarian will know which library that is. In addition, other libraries and some medical libraries subscribe to the *Register*. If you know the date the rule was published in the *Federal Register* or the page number, you easily can find the text of the rule. If you don't know the date or page number, try the next step.

The *Register* comes with a cumulative monthly index, organized according to the name of the agencies that make the regulations. Most regulations of interest to clinicians come from agencies such as the Department of Health and Human Services and the Federal Drug Administration. Look at the list of agencies and identify which agency probably issued the regulation you want. The *Register* has an Internet site, www.access.gpo.gov.

Each year the new regulations are indexed and printed on a quarterly basis, into a new *Code of Federal Regulations* (CFR) under the proper area of the law. One-fourth of the CFR is reissued with changes incorporated in January, the next one-fourth is re-done in April, the third fourth in October, and the last in December. Then they start again. If the reference you seek has a particular CFR number, that's what you're looking for. You'll find the *Code of Federal Regulations* at law libraries, the local federal depository library, and at law sites on the Internet.

After you find the regulation you want, look back to the *Register* to see if there is a new rule that has modified the original code section, since the last CFR was printed. This is the same process as checking the statute supplement, for any addition made to a statute since its initial printing. (The date of printing the CFR is at the front of the Code.)

Check for the rule's CFR section and number in the index of *CFR-List of Sections Affected,* published each month in the *Federal Register*. You need to check each month since the Code was last printed. If your CFR rule has been modified, the index will give the date that the modification was printed in the *Federal Register*. Then go to that date in the *Register* to find the wording of the modification of the regulation.

State rules

State rules are handled in the same way but with many fewer rules than the federal government generates. The state will print a state *Register* with a list and text of new rules that have been written-- perhaps weekly or monthly. This goes to some libraries and subscribers. As with the federal rules, the newly published regulations are indexed and the code of state regulations is updated periodically. If you are serious about legal research, a lot of help is available from

Stephen Elias's *Legal Research: How to Find and Understand the Law*, Berkeley: Nolo Press, 1997--and from the ever-helpful law librarian, and the Internet.

With access to the Internet, you may be able to bypass the steps listed and access the regulations through the Internet law sources listed above. If you are involved in any dispute about a regulation, you still will want to find the current, certain, hard copy.

Case law

Much of U.S. and Canadian case law is inherited from England with its long tradition of judge-made law. The Magna Carta of 1215 (*magna carta* is Latin for "Big List") often is mentioned as the start of English law. But an important tradition long pre-dated that list King John was forced to sign, that granted fair treatment his nobles. The tradition of the tribes who settled England from Anglia and Saxony on the continent to the west (the Anglo- Saxons), was that their king or leader was merely first among equals.

This tradition accounts for the attitude of individualism and equality so prevalent in English-based legal systems. People are assumed to be autonomous equals--each person being as smart as any other about his or her personal affairs. This is the basis of freedom as many know it.

The various states in the United States of America (you remember that there are other "United States" in this hemisphere) used the case law of England as the base of their law. Most states adopted **inception statutes** soon after their statehood began.   Louisiana kept the continental law of France that it inherited.

Inception statutes say something like: "The law of England as of the year 1804 will be the law of this state." Then the legislature of the state and the judges of its courts begin to add on, extend, delete, and change the law as received from England.

The basis of statute law and case law in the United States is case law from England, so US malpractice law also is based on concepts first established in English case law. Legislatures have modified much of it by statute.

Case law is still important. The case (the controversy) is the actual application of a statute or common law principle on the subject. As noted above, legislatures can never make laws so clear and so specific that they can cover every conceivable situation in which people disagree. Judges, juries, and courts are necessary now, and will continue to be.

Statutes often are made deliberately vague in order to get them passed. If two sides on an a legislative issue are deadlocked, they may compromise on language that is vague enough so that both sides can claim that their interpretation is correct. Both sides can "win" at that point.

When a real conflict comes up, the people who are in conflict and cannot compromise with each other will bring their conflict to a court. A third party will settle their fight. When a statute is to be applied, the courts must decide what the legislature meant (see above for rules judges use to analyze the statute).

Think about it.

Is this system of conflict resolution better than having a duel or going to war?

The good news about courts is that they decide. The potential bad news about going to court instead of voluntarily compromising, is that somebody wins, but invariably somebody loses.

Anatomy of a lawsuit

To give you some idea of how a conflict between individuals becomes case law, the abbreviated outline is provided.

Two parties (for example, a patient and a clinician),

are in conflict, as in "You didn't tell me about the side effects" "Yes I did" [that's a malpractice case, patient sues clinician]. Or another conflict, "You owe me money" " I do not" [that's a contract case, clinician sues patient]. If they

cannot compromise, one may

file a lawsuit (that's the plaintiff).

The other answers (called the defendant). Then,

discovery commences (these are interrogatories [written questions] and depositions [spoken questions] under oath). If there

still is no compromise, then

the trial date is set, and a

potential jury is called. The jury is

selected after questioning (this is called *voir dire*-an Old French phrase meaning "To say the truth"). Then the

plaintiff's lawyer makes an opening statement (such as "We'll prove the clinician did not tell the plaintiff about the side effects.")

Then the defendant's lawyer makes an opening statement (such as "We'll prove she did instruct the patient about side effects").

The plaintiff's side may call an expert witness (who will say "The clinician's care breached the standard of care. . ."), and

the defendant's side calls an expert witness (who will say "The clinician's care did meet the standard of care. . .). Now, perhaps

the defendant presents supporting evidence (for example, documentation that says "patient was instructed. . ."),

then lawyers for both sides make closing arguments. Now

the jury decides and returns a verdict (for the defense, because she documented?).

Then the lawyers file motions and maneuver, and

the case is appealed, when

the appellate judges have the final say. Only this last decision is law, precedent binding on other lower courts in that jurisdiction.

People who sue didn't listen to Abraham Lincoln, who said to lawyers:

> *Discourage litigation. Persuade your neighbors to compromise whenever you can. Point out to them how the nominal winner is often the real loser. Fees, expenses, and waste of time. As a peacemaker the lawyer has a superior opportunity of being a good man. There will still be business enough* (Lincoln, 1850).

Lobbying

Unlike its ethical base, law certainly will change. It might as well change to be more efficient, gentle, tough, or whatever is more in accord with clinician and patient values and needs. Clinicians can influence changes in the law.

Statutes written by legislators can be influenced. Clinicians can run for office, vote for a particular legislator, or campaign for one. Clinicians can testify at hearings about proposed laws. Clinicians can support organizations whose lobbyists work to influence state and national law.

Clinicians who plan to be involved in the legislative process can obtain specifics about their state's process from the state clinician association or the League of Women Voters. The League fought for women's right to vote, finally winning in the 1920s after approximately 100 years of work. Changes in the law don't always come quickly or easily.

Clinicians too have lobbyists to tell them what they need to know about the legislative process. (Note: They're called *lobbyists* because they used to sit in the lobbies of the legislators' hotels and in the lobbies of the legislative chambers, waiting to talk to the lawmakers.) Lobbyists can explain exactly how a bill gets to be a law, at the state or federal level.

People who want a certain law passed almost always hire a lobbyist. Good lobbyists know the steps in the process, and where information or influence by clinicians can help. Lobbyists may know the procedure better than some legislators.

At the request of the members of a special interest (such as a clinician group) who have hired him/her, the lobbyist will write or have someone write a proposed law--a bill. The lobbyist solicits sponsors for that bill, trying to sign up influential members of the legislature and of the committee that first will consider the bill.

Think about it.

Did you know that as a clinician you were a member of a special interest group?

Do you doubt that?

More information

The lobbyist provides information to the legislators: why the bill is needed, and what it will do and how. State legislators do not have big staffs of people to gather such information. Even the federal legislators, who have more staff, can't possibly gather as much information on an issue as the many and varied lobbyists can provide.

The lobbyist's goal is to convince the legislators to vote for the bill and, to that objective, the lobbyist provides as much convincing information as possible. People who oppose the bill likewise have lobbyists who present information unfavorable to the proposed law.

Those special interests and their lobbyists maximize the information that the legislators receive to make decisions. Maximum information is the basis of the free market. Limiting information works badly, in markets or in legislatures.

This plural and maximal information input is the basis of the American legal system also, because judges and juries use information gained through the adversary system of law that exists in Britain and countries with British-derived law. Because people with different and opposing interests all furnish information, the largest amount of accurate information possible is obtained. The likelihood is increased that accurate and correct decisions will be made. Such decisions are more likely based on reality than if less information about reality were available.

The lobbyist also provides information on other bills, particularly on bills that the special interest group opposes. In this way the legislator, hearing of what sounds like a good law, may be informed of the harm to a special interest group's position. That knowledge minimizes the unintended consequences of that legislation. Killing a bill with potential bad consequences may be the best work lobbyists do.

SPECIAL INTEREST FAILURE TO LOBBY: A NEGATIVE EXAMPLE

The medical association in Massachusetts did not lobby against a law that forced physicians to accept minimum Medicare payment (called "assignment"). The well-intended consequence of the law was to provide cheaper medical care for the elderly.

Despite this good intention, the doctors' group knew that the result would be bad for doctors and thus eventually for their patients. But the association didn't want to be seen as a "selfish" special interest group, so they didn't lobby against this popular bill. Instead, they quietly challenged the law in court after its passage. Their court challenge failed.

The unintended consequence of the law was seen afterward. Doctors left the state or did not come to the state because of the law. There were fewer doctors to care for the elderly--the people the statute was supposed to help. The association didn't advance its members' interests at first, and the unintended consequence--foreseen but not acted upon by the medical association--was bad for all, patients and doctors.

Process

Your state's legislative process for making law may differ slightly from another state's, but in general it goes like this.

A bill (a wannabe law) is **introduced,**

gets **first reading,**

is **referred to committee.**

Then it may be **heard in committee** with testimony (perhaps from you?).

It may then be **voted out of committee,**

is **second read** in its house of origin (debated, amended, and voted on by the whole group).

It may be **finally passed** (third reading) by the house of origin.

Now it **goes to the other body** of lawmakers (Senate or House of Representatives),

to a committee there, and if voted out of the committee,

to the **floor of that second body** for a vote. If passed,

next it goes to a **conference committee** of lawmakers from both groups for final compromise.

If **compromise** is reached

it goes back to **both houses for final passage** (no amendments allowed),

then to the **executive** for signature (or veto!)

The law is really the product of committees. The above description is the best case scenario–most bills die in the original committee. If the governor or President signs the bill, now it's a law. If the governor or President vetoes the bill, the legislature still can pass it over the veto, by a supermajority vote (usually 2/3). Nurses overrode a Missouri governor's veto to obtain their autonomous practice act, the first override in that state in 138 years .

As noted above, your local League of Women Voters or legislator or professional association lobbyist can tell you about your state's legislative procedure and the status of any bill introduced that affects your practice. (Or you can get on the Internet and check the status of the bill daily on your state legislature's Website.) The lobbyist for your professional association also can tell you what can be done to help or hinder the bill, along with any other details you need.

Lobbying other venues

Rules and regulations made by people in the executive branch can be changed at the public hearings that must be held before the rules are adopted. Or, proposed rules can be changed during the time for public comment, after publication. Lobbyists for clinician associations influence the people who write regulations, too. Ultimately, a state's executive (the governor) and the US executive (the President), are responsible for regulations made by their employee administrators. Clinicians can work for the election or defeat of that executive.

Case law changes too. Clinicians change case law by bringing lawsuits as Missouri nurses did, to prevent the doctor's board in that state from stopping their practice. Their case affirmed the clinicians' right to practice, even to practice what the physician clinicians thought was medicine (*Sermchief*, 1983). Or clinicians can influence case law directly by sitting on a jury–don't pass up a chance to experience this exercise in citizenship.

Most simply and appropriately, clinicians can speak up. Your comments contribute to public opinion, and a distillation of that opinion is what lawyers, plaintiffs, defendants, and juries believe--and ultimately what judges will write into case law.

Speaking out creates public opinion, and may become the custom as ethics. Ethical behavior is the consensus/ consciousness/ conscience of what people think is desirable behavior.   Clinicians can sit on ethics committees in their community and organization. The *Quinlan* court actually mandated the use of ethics committees in some cases (*Quinlan*, 1976).

Clinician opinions are valuable because you know the reality of the problem facing your patients and yourself. The *Cruzan* case was not over for her clinicians when the patient's feeding tube was withdrawn (*Cruzan*, 1991). (In the aftermath of that Supreme Court case, clinicians were ordered to allow their patient to die of dehydration.) The case is not finished for the clinicians who cared for her as she dehydrated and died, nor for other patients and their clinicians as the patients are euthanized or as the patients live on.

The law and the ethics matter to patients and matter to their clinicians. Law can't be left solely to the lawyers, nor ethics to the philosophers–those are people who write abstractly about human action. Clinicians are the actors.

If you need more ethics theory than Dountoothers

> *The louder he spoke of his honor, the faster we counted our spoons.*
>
> RALPH WALDO EMERSON (1803-1882) *The Conduct of Life*

If you want to read more about or by the authors mentioned in these sections of each chapter, you may be able to find books or articles by them in your library, or in the following references:

Armstrong S, Botzler R (Eds.). *Environmental Ethics: Divergence and Convergence.* New York, NY: McGraw-Hill, 1993.

Arthur J (Ed.). *Morality and Moral Controversies* (4th Edition). Upper Saddle River, NJ: Prentice-Hall, Inc., 1996.

Beauchamp TL. *Philosophical Ethics* (2d Edition). New York, NY: McGraw-Hill, Inc., 1991.

Hall, Jacqulyn K. *Nursing Ethics and Law.* Philadelphia: W.B. Saunders, 1996.

Holmes RL. *Basic Moral Philosophy* (2d Edition). Belmont, CA: Wadsworth, 1998

Luper-Foy S, Brown C (Eds.). *The Moral Life.* Orlando, FL: Harcourt Brace College Publishing, 1992.

Shaw WH, Barry V. *Moral Issues in Business* (5th ed.). Belmont, CA: Wadsworth, 1992

In addition to the above references, there are *many* Internet Web sites for ethics. A few of the National Institute of Health (NIH) Web sites on bioethics:

National Bioethics Advisory Commission, provides access to Commission reports at http://www.bioethics.gov

NIH has a Web site on the regulation of health privacy at http://www.nih.gov/news/privacy

NIH has an Office of Science Policy site at http://www.nih.gov/icd/od/

An overview of some major aspects of ethics theory follows. Don't worry if the theory here and in other chapters is not completely clear at first studying. The clinician who completes a study of ethics must have been at least exposed to the terms covered below and in following chapters, and must have some rough idea of their meaning, in order to apply them to practice. If you are not studying this book to challenge a course in ethics or as a text in ethics, you can skip the rest of this chapter and the material with the same header in all other chapters. (You might just find it interesting for use in your own life, though.)

Or, you might need to know such terms if you happen to get into a room with an ethicist. Bad luck. Do not let such people snow you with fancy terms. Remind them that ethics is about figuring out what is the right thing to do, and ask how their term helps you do that. Bring up Sir Karl Popper, renowned philosopher of science. He refused to discuss definitions, finding them a waste of time and brain power.

If you like such esoteric discussions, maybe you'll want to go to ethicist school. You will encounter some of these terms and theories later in the book.

Once an ethicist makes a statement, he will seek to justify his argument--he will try to explain the justice, the foundation of his position. Most arguments look something like an algebra equation in their simplest form. They say that "X is true, therefore Y is true"--or, "Because X is right, Y is right." Ethical arguments usually are not stated quite that simply, as we will see.

Some ethicists believe that there are levels of justification of a position or argument, moving from lower to higher, starting at the low end with:

A **Judgment** about a single case or issue--for example, "Jane was right to kill the suffering patient in this case," and moving up to a more general level,

A **Rule** such as "Killing is right to prevent suffering," and on up to a more abstract level, to

A **Principle** like "Suffering is to be avoided when possible," and finally up to a very abstract overarching plane,

An ethical **Theory** such as "Pain is bad, pleasure is good." (See below)

Judgment ☞ Rule ☞ Principle ☞ Ethical theory

Theory of morality development

Though thinking cannot be observed, in some theories of ethics **moral reasoning** or thinking is distinguished from **ethical practice** or action. Some writers say this separation can be discerned through tests. For example, the question can be asked, "What do you think the clinician should do for the patient in this situation?" That would measure the thinking, the moral reasoning.

Then one could ask, "What do you think the clinician will do for the patient in this situation?" That answer could tell the interviewer about the ethical practice--the action--if the clinician knew and told the truth to both questions (Ketefian, 1989).

Some theories of ethics, such as Lawrence Kohlberg's (American, 1970's), propose that people develop morally over their lifetimes as they get older, more experienced, and more educated. Kohlberg's theory echoes the pervasive idea that people evolve from babyhood (Kohlberg, 1981). This is the same idea as Darwin's theory of evolution, the same concept as Piaget, Maslow, and all the Platonists. Kohlberg thought he could measure stages in development of ethical behavior from lowest ethical behavior to highest. This is an example of the human tendency toward creating hierarchy, toward ranking and elitism.

Kohlberg wrote that people develop ethically in stages that are invariable in sequence. People move from simple thought to complex moral reasoning. At higher stages, people use skills that were developed earlier, at lower stages. He constructed three levels of **moral development**, each having two stages. The three levels are:

1. **Preconventional reasoning**. Right and wrong depend one what Mommy (authority) says. For example, saying "I have to this thing because the law, or the organization policy, or the supervisor said 'this is what to do.'"

2. **Conventional reasoning**. Right or wrong comes from the family or group. The person wants to maintain existing social relationships or order. For example, saying "I do this thing because it's good for my family, my profession, my country."

3. **Postconventional--principled reasoning**. This person thinks above and apart from the herd and develops a conscience without referring to her own real situation.

The postconventional level may be classed with philosophies that espouse the intellect over action. At the highest level, reasoning alone and not emotion dictates the right thing to do. Justice is seen as the highest value to aspire to. For example, saying "I do this thing because it's good for the whole world, and I have reasoned for myself that it is the ideal right thing to do."

The testing required to measure these stages of ethical behavior is intensive and requires a specially trained interviewer, so it is expensive in both time and money to research Kohlberg's theory.

Think about it.

Might Kohlberg have seen differences in various people's ethical styles, not differences in the stages of ethical development in one person?

Might he have measured differences in the interests, values, or ways people decide, and then ranked the differences according to how he thought people should decide things?

When people take the same test time after time as his subjects (in the first tests, all men) did, they may seem to progress to higher levels as they learn more of the terms used or learn more what the interviewer expects or wants them to say.

Think about it.

What do you think of the idea that morality develops?

Do you agree that justice is the highest value?

Or do you think that any value women hold highest, is best?

Women who were tested under Kohlberg's theory of a hierarchy of moral reasoning never achieved the highest level of morality. Justice was identified as the highest value in Kohlberg's research, but on average women valued caring highest. (In this book, it would be called *doing good*). Because of that finding, Kohlberg's theory is challenged by feminists.

Carol Gilligan criticized the research on the ground that women were not used in the original research, and that when women were tested, on average they never reached higher than level 2. That is, women did not attain what was defined as the highest level of an adult (Gilligan, 1992). Women consistently cared more for family and friends and decided right and wrong on that basis.

Gilligan argued that the failure of women to advance to being concerned about the abstract ideal of justice for all, was the result of lack of focus on caring in Kohlberg's theory of moral reasoning. That lack of focus on caring in turn had been caused by the original exclusion of women from the research.

Think about it.

Might it be that women didn't agree with the test's definition of justice as social justice?

The idea measured by justice in such research is not always justice as defined as equal treatment under the law. Sometimes the word justice as used in ethics research actually means social justice--the idea of abstract equal outcomes for all. Whatever the reason, women in ethics research studies chose caring--relationships with individuals--over justice.

The finding of some researchers that women did value relationships and harmony over justice has broad implications. For example, the real relationships within the tribe (family) might be more important to women than the abstract ideal of democracy for the larger society.

Think about it.

Might such women be more tolerant of authority in the name of harmony, more ready to sacrifice individual freedom of others and their own freedom, for the sake of peace that would benefit the survival of their tribe?

If it exists, this genetic or hormonal preference in women for relationships and for the family may work to ensure the survival of the species. Women intuitively might support more intrusions into their lives--for example, socialist government programs--in order to have more benefits for more people. Women might value comfort, representing survival---food and shelter--over the abstract of freedom and equality.

Some evidence contradicts the idea that women's ethics are different, however. For example, in the 1980's some thought that having more women as judges would change the law, because women were thought to be more concerned with compassion than with justice. Suzanna Sherry's speculation in this area focused primarily on Supreme Court Justice Sandra Day O'Connor (Sherry, 1986).

However, contrary to Sherry's and Gilligan's beliefs, the evidence demonstrates that most women judges do not decide cases in a distinctively liberal feminist or feminine manner. It seems that other parts of women judges' backgrounds--such as their party affiliation and their prior professional history--matter more than whether they are men or women (Toobin, 2000).

Other research counters Kohlberg's theory that more education produces better moral reasoning. Women clinicians with more experience, even though they had less education, were better at making ethical decisions than those with less experience and more education

(Corley, 1992).

Feminist ethics

Feminist moral philosophy, still in its infancy, is described as being simply whatever is <u>not</u>, western male-dominated philosophy (that holds justice as the highest value). In contrast, feminist moral philosophy would hold relationships such as caring, doing good and being true, as the highest value. As noted above, when tested, women on average put a combination of the values Being True (Fidelity), Keeping Promises (Loyalty), Do Good (charity, caring) and Don't Harm (non-maleficence) on a higher level than justice.

Nel Noddings promotes an ethic of caring, based on a mothering model (Noddings, 1984). Some feminists have criticized any ethic of caring. They fear that caring can be exploitative, with the caring going in only one direction, from carer to cared for.

There is tension between using an ethics based on caring, and an ethics based on science, as foundation for clinical practice. The caring has emotion as a foundation, while science has intellect as foundation.

An example of the caring-thinking conflict was illustrated in a public information TV spot in the early 1990s, produced with the advice of the American Nurses Association. The goal was to get more young people into nursing and at the same time to have nursing be seen by the public as a thinking occupation. The punch line was "If caring were enough, anyone could be a nurse." In the eyes of many, that line effectively denigrated the value of caring, in order to elevate the value of thinking.

Think about it.
Do you agree that anyone (that is, everyone) is caring enough to be a clinician?

A caring ethic could underlie clinical practice. The symbol of caring differs from other metaphors for clinical practice, such as a religious calling or a duty to battle disease--said by feminists to be masculine metaphors that evoke images of separateness and adversity (Condon 1992). The caring metaphor is said to evoke images of people as parents, nurturers of the young, old, and ill. The image is one of humans connected, not disconnected--not of duty and a calling, but of caring, freely chosen.

A theory of caring is a valid part of the formal study of ethics. Knowledge about caring should give encouragement to clinicians who believe that the value of caring (emotion-based) is at least as important in their ethical decisions as the value of justice (reason-based).

Ethics committees

Ethics committees exist in most hospitals and other clinical practice organizations. Many hospitals and other organizations that care for patients instituted these committees in response to the Joint Commission for Accreditation of Health Organizations (JCAHO) mandate that the agencies it surveyed have some kind of ethics procedure for ethical problems.

JCAHO MANDATE FOR ETHICS MECHANISM
"...the right of the patient or the patient's designated representative to participate in the consideration of ethical issues that arise in the care of the patient:
RI.1.1.6.1 The organization has in place a mechanism(s) for the consideration of ethical issues arising in the care of patients and to provide education to caregivers and patients on ethical issues in health care" (JCAHO, 1993).

This JCAHO directive did not say that ethics committees were mandatory–for example, an ethics consultant could also serve as a mechanism and satisfy the mandate. But a cheaper and in some ways better method is to have an ethics committee (Ross, 1993)

The ethics committee usually includes staff of the organization (usually clinicians and administrators), community representatives, and perhaps a lawyer. Such committees write bylaws and procedures for the committee. They may set policy for staff to use in situations of ethical conflict, and they educate staff and the public about ethics.

The committees use the same process to resolve conflicts as do ethicists. Clinicians too can use the decision-making process for ethical issues in their practice. Below are some suggestions for such a process. Committee members ask questions, gather information, clarify interests (values), and act as mediator. If people who are in conflict can't agree after that, some committees will decide the issue for them.

The members of the committee may have no special qualifications in ethics, but they eventually may develop a consensus of opinion. In that sense they are making ethics, and those ethics may become law. Such committees were recommended in the *Quinlan* case, in which a young girl's ventilator was discontinued (however, she lived for years afterward with tube feedings). The court in that case mandated the use of ethics committees in "right to die" or withdrawal of treatment situations (*Quinlan*, 1976).

Some type of case review may be done by the ethics committee, in which the committee hears from some or all people involved. When recommended by a court of law, this case review by ethics committees is delegation of the court's decision-making power to informal courts of citizens who are closer to the situation.

Like the continuum from law to ethics, the formal law court gives way to a less formal committee, that often defers to the informal family/ patient/ clinician decision. Many believe that government or law or ethics all work better when decisions are made by people close to the problem.

Some have questioned whether ethics committees should themselves initiate investigation into cases, or should wait and be available to any patient or staff member who wishes to appeal to them. Some authorities prefer that an ethics consultation, face to face with the patient or family, be accomplished before the committee considers the matter. In that case, the patient is not necessarily present at committee decisions. Other writers insist that the patient must be involved when committees deliberate.   Some form of patient and/or family participation, somewhere, is indicated by the JCAHO requirements noted above.

Some authorities criticize any committee review of individual cases. They say the committee should be a forum for abstract discussion of ethical issues, not for advice on real cases. They believe that the committee should make policy and educate, but not do clinical analysis of cases. They believe that advice to the patient's family and clinicians should be given by an ethics consultant.

Some physician clinicians believe an ethics consultant should be a physician clinician who has an interest and skill in ethical decision making. Equally, some fear the authoritarian role that an ethicist might take on, and prefer the joint decision making, increased experience, and information that is available in ethics committee decisions.

Ethics committees may have some fear of lawsuit for their actions but lawsuits filed against committees are rare. In some cases like *Quinlan*, court-made law has required the ethics "court," be the ethics committee. In another example, the Texas Advance Directives Act (TX 1999) refers conflicts between clinicians and family over giving futile care, to the organization's ethics committee.

Patient Self-Determination Act

Federal law, the **Patient Self Determination Act** (PSDA), makes more work for ethics committees (New law, 1991). The act mandates that the organization have a policy to inform patients of their right to refuse treatment. The law requires the organization to decide whether it will honor advance directives.

The ethics committee should help decide whether the organization will participate in honoring advance directives, when they are used to end patient lives. The PSDA mandates that staff and community be educated about advance directives, and the ethics committee should be involved in that education also. The ethics committee may also recommend policy for HIV-infected workers in the organization.

Think about it.
Does your organization have an ethics committee? Ask your CEO why.
If not, ask her why not?
Do you know any of the people in your organization that are members of the ethics committee?
Are they ethical people? Is that important?

Ethicists and preferences

As noted, some organizations provide a mechanism for ethical discussion by employing or contracting for the services of an ethicist. "Ethicist" is a classification, as is "philosopher" (but philosophers usually are designated as such after their death!). In one sense, all people are ethicists because all have a philosophy and all decide every day on the right things to do. Living people who are identified as "ethicists" and "philosophers" usually work in a position in which that word is part of their title, or it is the subject they teach.

Authorities recommend that people who teach ethics have a degree in the field, profession, or area in which they are going to work--for example, in clinical practice--plus one year of ethics training. Or, as an alternative, the teacher can qualify with an advanced degree in philosophy, and one year in the clinical field of interest.

The person teaching ethics should be knowledgeable about the theories of ethics and philosophy, which is different from being ethical. Any of us can be ethical. But ethicists in clinical practice can ask questions, gather information, and help people see various interests in a case.

Think about it.
Considering that function, is it necessary to have a formal title as "ethicist"?

People formally labeled as "ethicists" are not likely to be conservative politically (Murray, 1988). As we all do, ethicists start with preferences. Human beings have built-in preferences, genetic and environmentally formed. Lawyers have preferences--when you enter her office to hire her, the lawyer has a preference for your position even before she hears any facts of your case. Computers too have built-in preferences--those of their human programmers. Remember this assertion that we all are *partial*, biased, when you read later about the idea that the bedrock basis of ethics is impartiality.

Judges too decide cases with their preferences. They hear the facts, decide the case on the facts, and then they find the written principles (law) to use as base for their legal opinion. Deep within their decision on the facts, they are applying unspoken, unwritten principles--the ethics with which they were born and grew up learning.

The preferences of ethicists can be detected by careful reading and listening. One ethicist described a number of cases that resulted in patient deaths as a positive thing. Then he wrote, "The *progressive* California decisions just cited were followed by a small number of extremely *conservative* rulings in New York, New Jersey, and Missouri." [emphasis added] (Raffin, 1991). His characterization of decisions that resulted in the death of the patient as progressive, while describing rulings that kept the patient alive as conservative (not progressive), reveals his preference.

Also about ethicists preferences, one description of Wesley Smith's book *Culture of Death* says that "an obscure cadre of intellectuals --bioethicists--has suddenly gained the upper hand in American courts and legislatures. . .[and] have quietly convinced many of our judges, hospital administrators, and doctors that some human lives have relatively less value, and therefore have less right to equal protection" (Smith, 2000).

Some distinguish the terms "bioethicist" and "medical ethicist." It is asserted that the study of medical ethics is not a value-free discipline, meaning that it has preferences that reflect the preferences that physician clinicians have.

Think about it.
*Does that imply that bioethics--different from medical ethics--has **no** particular values, that bioethics is a pure field of study, objective, without innate values?*

Decision process used by ethicists and clinicians

The clinician's first step is to be sure there is an ethical problem. Shorthand question for that: Is the issue about treating the patient right, or is the question about the right treatment for the patient? For example, *which* antibiotic to give is a medical question, but *whether* to give an antibiotic to a patient who can benefit by it is an ethical question.

Sometimes an ethical problem is really a practice problem or a labor relations problem. Suppose a patient refuses treatment and says, "Let me die." That may be the occasion for the clinician first to use her professional skills, helping the patient with depression and symptom relief. Only if that practice intervention is not successful will the clinician consider the ethical issue of allowing the patient to die. If there's a practice action to be tried, usually it should be tried before the issue is labeled an ethical issue.

Approaches to **ethical decision making**--other than the one recommended in this book--start with gathering of information about the case by seeking outside information. The different recommendation of this book is to do exactly the opposite: to start with the clinician's own values, the information inside yourself. See below for details.

As an example of the usual, outside information approach, one formula fits medical treatment to what the patient wants. That's rarely a problem because providers almost never treat a competent patient who doesn't want treatment. In contrast, the usual problem that raises ethical conflict is the situation in which there is no patient preference stated, because the patient is not competent.

Then the problem is to assess the quality of life for someone else, objectively. In fact, quality of life can be assessed only subjectively, by the person who decides whether life is worth living or not. The conflicts come from external factors, who may turn out to be daughters--one who wants to let her father die, and one who wants him to live.

Another approach to ethical decision making also puts heavy emphasis on considering medical decisions first. After considering those, the wishes of the patient are considered and other values are examined and ranked. In both of these decision processes, note that the ethicist starts with a value, implicit or unstated. Both processes start with the medical aspect of the patient's care--external information. Though it is never stated explicitly, by considering it first we can assume that the medical information is considered the highest value.

Specific techniques for ethical decision making are variants on the "gather information and assess" theme that is so familiar to clinicians as the scientific method. Other techniques simply apply their practice process--assessment, planning, implementing, evaluating--to the ethics process, again applying the scientific method.

A different way to approach ethical conflicts is to start with the clinician's own values--your internal information. This is the same advice parents give to children before they cross the street: A warning to stop, look, and listen--and add one more stop.

Stop, Look, Listen--and Stop Again

Process for ethical decisions

Stop. Suppose you are confronted with an ethical conflict--any conflict that involves values and is about the right thing to do. First, stop and realize this as an ethical conflict, then begin this process.

Think about your personal values and use them. Allow intuition, feeling, and emotion free rein and identify what you think should happen in this case--what you *want* to happen. Once this unconscious information is conscious, you can acknowledge that your actions in gathering data, looking, and listening, all will be from that point of view.

Admit your values, your preferences, to yourself first. The old cliches are helpful: Know yourself, to thine own self be true. One of the ancient virtues was prudence, portrayed in works of art as a woman with a mirror to see herself, to know herself first in order to act prudently. You will see in Chapter 2, that the standard of care in malpractice is what a reasonable <u>prudent</u> clinician would do.

Many sets of questions have been written for patients to use in identifying their own values, so that they can make decisions about their own care. It is just as important, possibly more so, for clinicians to explore and recognize their own values--the feelings used in giving care or not giving care to so many people. Below is a Values Assessment for Clinicians, adapted by the author from Rushton's values history for patients (Rushton, 1992). Clinicians who answer these questions may surprise themselves at what they learn.

Clinician Values Assessment: First Step in Ethical Decision Making

Describe your current health or illness status.

What do you plan for the future? (can make happen)

What do you hope for in the future? (can't make happen, but wish would happen)

What do you fear?

What is most important in your life now?

Is your life worth living?

What would make your life better?

What would make your life not worth living?

If you knew you were dying, what would be most important?

Where do you want to die?

How would you feel about life-sustaining procedures if you were dying? In a persistent vegetative state? If you had a chronic, irreversible illness? Such as diabetes?

How important are family and friends to you?

How important is your work?

How do you make decisions about your life? Your illness care?

What is your religion?

Does your religion affect your beliefs about death and illness?

Whom would you want to make decisions for you if you could not?

Have you informed your family, friends, or clinician about your values? Have you made an advance directive? Why or why not?

What would you do if you won the lottery?

___

Because we project our own values onto patients, we must be aware of our own preferences. Once you are aware of the influence of personal values in an ethical conflict, the easier part of the process follows.

Look and Listen. This part is easy for clinicians because they're used to gathering information, along with listening to overt and hidden communications. In looking and listening in order to make an ethical decision, clinicians look at the person and her condition, and listen to her wishes. They look for others who are interested, and listen to their wants.

By having admitted personal preferences before gathering data, the clinician is able to assess honestly whether she has all the information, or just the part she wanted to hear--the part that supports her preference.

Then STOP again. Separate your personal and professional interest from the patient's, the organization's, the family's interests, and other providers' interests. It may help to write down such assessments of interests, for your own private use.

At this point, the most important interests may become apparent. The more information gained about the conflict, the better, because more information yields a better outcome. (Or at least the result is more likely based on reality.) But be prepared to deal with the information sought. For instance, you may find the patient's living will--with a revocation of it at the back., signed and sealed. Or, questioned as to whether he wants intubation and ventilation, the terminal patient may answer "yes.".

Often this process of *stop, look, listen, stop*, is enough. Usually someone didn't hear or know some information--perhaps even you. The time involved in the process of gathering all the information may solve the problem because the patient may die anyway on the ventilator, or get better, or the relative may change her mind. You can help others in the case to work though the process in this stop, look, listen, stop again, method. At some point you may enlist the help of the ethics committee or consultant if needed.

Allowing time to gain information and reflect is always better than a quick decision based on inadequate information or on (sometimes unrecognized) personal preferences. Obviously you needn't create problems if they don't exist, there being plenty of problems without creating them.

There's no need to get a court order for treatment or non-treatment if the clinicians, patient, and family agree. Some hospital lawyers have not gone to court in years on an ethical conflict case for their facility. When the real conflict between people cannot be resolved with information, mediation, and persuasion--the courts exist as final venue for conflict resolution.

Think about it.

Do you use the ethical decision-making process that the author suggests? Why or why not?

Fear of courts

Some assert that courts are inappropriate places for making ethical decisions--that courts are inadequate to decide because they can't know the wishes of family and patient, and don't have the medical knowledge. But courts exist to resolve conflicts between people. Courts decide for people who cannot decide on an action among themselves.

The anger that some feel toward court interference in ethical decisions, in reality may be a preference for local, informal decision making at the bedside, in preference to formal decision making in a distant courtroom. When the court is asked to decide, however, conflict resolution at the bedside already has failed.

Much of this anger at court interference also may be a projection onto the court of what some actually feel toward the other people who will not agree. People who say that the court is meddling may really feel the other people in the conflict are meddlers.

Some people dislike court involvement in clinical practice simply because courts *decide*: Somebody wins and somebody loses. As lawyers know, people should stay out of court as long as possible, even when dealing with people who are thought to be meddling. They know that voluntary compromise means that everybody wins at least something they wanted. But in court, somebody may lose completely.

The court is a last resort for solving an ethical conflict that the parties cannot resolve themselves. Despite bad press, courts are remarkably good at this. Clinical practice issues are no more difficult to understand than any other area of human activity. The special area of ethics conflict expertise may seem mysterious, but engineering, finances, trusts and wills, all require expert testimony and evidence from families, just as do issues about clinical practice.

This endorsement of the judicial system as conflict resolver of last resort is the topic of the preceding section, the formal, written, and enforced part of ethics--the law.

Normative and non-normative ethics

Following is an ALGORITHM to help you see relationships between the terms of ethics theory. Look up the origin of the word algorithm sometime. Very interesting.

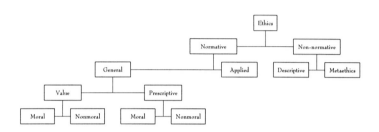

The little part in the algorithm labeled **applied** is where you use all of this material every day, for the whole of your professional practice.

Approaches to ethics are considered to be either normative or non-normative. That is, they either establish a norm--the root of the word normative--that says what certain behavior should be. Or, no norm for behavior is suggested—non-normative.

The classifications in the study of ethics under **non-normative** approaches are descriptive ethics and metaethics.

Descriptive ethics is the study of ethical beliefs of various cultures—for examples, describing some tribe's culture in National Geographic, or surveying clinicians to see if they would euthanize patients. Being in the non-normative area, descriptive statements don't prescribe what <u>ought to</u> happen, they merely describe what <u>is</u> happening –for example, "Jane is neglecting her patient."

Metaethics, the other subheading of non-normative ethics, is the philosophy of ethics. The theories of ethics you will study in this book are classed under the heading metaethics. Notice that the prefix, "meta" means outside of the thing it precedes--just as metaphysical means "outside" the physical world.

Under normative approaches to ethics, are classified general normative ethics, and applied ethics. This first chapter is about **general**

normative ethics--the theories of ethics that prescribe some rules for ethical action. Applied ethics are the subjects of all the other chapters of the book, with some ethical theories also included in those chapters that most pertain to the value of the chapter. For example, existentialism is discussed in Chapter 4, Be Free, because existentialists are said to value freedom above all other things.

First, look at the general heading in the algorithm of **normative judgments**. The words immediately give a clue that some norm is going to be used to judge something. Normative judgments come in two flavors, value judgments and prescriptive judgments.

Value judgments identify whether some thing or behavior is good or bad. As in, pain is bad. Note that these "values" are not up to the same elevated level as the principles or values that title the chapters of the book, such as Do Good, Don't Harm, and so on.

A value judgment says whether something is good or bad, not whether something is right or wrong. *Huge* difference. Something can be good--sex is good--and still be wrong in some situations. For example, in adultery. Something can be bad--pain and suffering are bad--and still be right in some situations. For example, when a soldier throws himself on a grenade to save his unit. Going further than value judgments, **prescriptive judgments** prescribe--note the root of the word--what people should do. As in, "Jane should not allow her patient to go without pain medication."

Of course, we often slide in the same breath from saying something is bad (a value judgment–for example, hitting patients is bad) to prescribing that we should not do it (a prescriptive judgment–for example, clinicians should not hit patients).

Value judgments and prescriptive judgments both can be considered either moral or nonmoral. Look at the algorithm to be clear about this. **Moral judgments** identify behavior that is determined to be moral, while **nonmoral judgments** do not. The value and prescriptive judgments described above, about pain and neglecting patients, are in the category of moral judgments.

A nonmoral, value judgment would be something like "pineapple pizza is good." A nonmoral, prescriptive judgment would sound like: "you should try the pineapple pizza." The prescription is that you should try pineapple pizza, but it's not a moral prescription--you still can be moral if you don't. Pineapple pizza is good, though.

Again, look at the algorithm to clarify how these terms are related. In ethics we almost always are talking about moral judgments, but nonmoral judgments such as those about pineapple pizza are described just to show you the difference.

Metaethics (the philosophy of ethics)

The term metaethics refers to study <u>about</u> ethics. Examples are study about how ethics originated, about why cultures differ on what is moral, about whether ethics is relative or absolute, or about the meaning of terms such as good and bad and right and wrong, and so on. Study about all the theories of ethics is classed under metaethics.

Metaethics is one of the <u>non-normative</u> approaches to ethics--see the algorithm again. In contrast, normative ethics seeks to decide and to say what behavior actually is right. Metaethics also is known as moral epistemology. Epistemology is the study of the origin of something. Metaethics is study about morality itself. That is different from studying about things that are classified as moral. An example of a normative question is "Is abortion wrong?" An example of a non-normative, metaethical question is "What is the basis of calling something wrong in this theory of ethics?"

Think about it.

Do you think it is useful to spend time to study the metaethics--the theories of ethics--or should one just apply whatever ethical framework she has, and forget about these questions?

Moral realism and antirealism

This is a part of the debate between cognitivists and non-cognitivists, that you will study again later in the book. Briefly, the cognitivists say that ethics can be known with cognition, with reasoning--and non-cognitivists say "not so." Along that line of thinking, some ethicists deny that any objective reality of moral statements can exist. That is, they assert that moral statements such as "killing is wrong" cannot be proven objectively.

In contrast, others argue that moral statements are real--that they can be proven objectively. Theories of ethics are asserted to be like theories in science, in that they describe realities that exist prior to human's thought about them, and prior to attempts to prove the theories of ethics. That would mean that ethics is a real thing, that ethics would exist even if there were no humans to be ethical or unethical.

J.S. Mill (British, 1806-1873), an antirealist, argued exactly the opposite. He asserted that there is no sound when a tree falls in a forest, unless a person is there to hear it. And as an analogy, Mill asserts that no good or right exists--no morality exists--unless a person is there to desire the thing.

A final pair of ethics designations, related to whether ethics are real: **skeptics** question whether an act can be judged right or wrong.

Nihilists, more extreme, absolutely deny that an act objectively can be judged right or wrong. Therefore they say people or societies can create their own right and wrong.

Moral deliberation

As noted above, some say that moral deliberation or reasoning can be distinguished from moral behavior. They say that moral reasoning is mental–it is what people think they should do. In contrast, moral behavior is the action--what people actually do that is moral.

Many philosophers have addressed the question "Why be moral?" Or asked another way, "What is the goal of being moral?" Both J.S. Mill and Aristotle believe individual morality is useful to set up conditions for the individual's good life.

The two might differ a little on what a good life consisted of, however. In general, the Greek philosophers believed a moral life contributed to the happiness of the individual. But Plato argued that individual moral lives were important for the overall good of the state. Thus the individual's morality was important only if it contributed to the state.

Think about it.
What 20th century system of government held Plato's view? Hint: Starts with a "C".

Immanuel Kant (Prussian, 1724-1804) believed the goal of morality was to cultivate people--individuals--of a good will. But G.J. Warnock believes that morality is important at the social level, for groups of individuals. Warnock argues that morality's purpose is to provide systems to resolve conflicts. Conflicts are inevitable because resources, information, and even human sympathy for each other, are limited. Warnock says morality can counter the bad effects of those limitations.
Think about it.
If we felt no sympathy for our patient, would we still care for her?
Do we give care because we are moral, or because we are sympathetic?

Moral judgment

Your judgment--for example, your decision not to cheat on a test–may or may not have the status of a **moral judgment**. Refer to the algorithm to see where this concept fits with the organization of ethics topics. In some cases, being moral may seem to go against our self-interest.

But if being moral produces a better world to live in, then it is always in the self-interest of the individual to be moral. The individual will benefit from living in the better world. If self-interest is defined broadly to include more than immediate gratification, being moral can't be against the individual's self-interest.

A longer view of self-interest can be contrasted with immediate self-gratification. A decision that involved immediate gratification might not be considered to have the status of a moral judgment. A long-range self-interest might be compatible with having the status of moral judgment.

For example, if you and everyone else cheat on tests, eventually the degree you get will be worthless. Your long-term interest is served by not cheating, so your decision not to cheat is a moral judgment. If you decide not to cheat mainly because you might get caught in the short term, your judgment may not rise to the level of a moral judgment.

On a larger scale, should nations be moral? In the U.S. and NATO war against Serbia it was said that Serbia was immoral in its behavior toward the Muslims in its Kosovo province.

Think about it.
In bombing them, was the U.S. moral in its behavior toward the Serbian people?
Or, by bombing them, was it assumed that none of the Serbian people were innocent?

David Gauthier discusses whether either of two nations should adhere to their agreement in which they promised mutual disarmament. He concludes that nations should be moral --keep agreements or promises (more in Chapter 6)-- because in the end it is prudent to do so. It is in their long-term advantage. Gauthier equates a moral system, or a reason to be moral, with advantage to the person who adheres to his promises. Gauthier says being moral is an advantageous thing to do. Later in the book you will encounter the ideas of John Rawls, who also discusses personal advantage when proposing his idea of justice.

William Frankena asserts that it is rational or sensible to be moral. In some measure his reasoning rests on a tautology. (A tautology is a circular argument that explains a thing in terms of itself. The conclusion also appears as an assumption. An example of a tautology: "the wine is good because it's wine.")

This is a logical fallacy called *petitio principii* (also described as begging the question or assuming an answer to a question). Frankena says that a moral human has self-respect, and self-respect is a moral attribute. In other words, he says one should be moral because it is the moral thing to do. (That's the tautology.)

Religion and ethics

Some would define ethics as being about doing the right thing according to one's religion. For as long as we can remember with history and undoubtedly before, human behavior has been guided by religion. Religions all give guidelines for behavior. You saw some above in "The Rules."

Think about it.
Were these guidelines developed by humans or given by God?
Does your answer depend on your religious belief?
Before reading this chapter, what was your understanding of the relationship of philosophy and religion to ethics?
Do you agree that religion is a part of philosophy?
That religion is the basis of ethics? Why or why not?

The words ethics and morals have similar origin. Though some writers try to distinguish ethics as being a guide for society, and morals a guide for the individual, both words mean the custom or character of a people. Many writers on ethics apparently prefer to use the word ethics instead of morals, perhaps because ethics sounds secular and the word morals is associated with religion. In Chapter 6 Be True you will read about "divine command" and see how some modern ethicists relate religion to ethics.

Ethics theory is inextricable from, and in many cases parallels, religious guidelines. Many of the world's major religions teach one major ethical principle, seen above in the "Golden Rules." At the end of this chapter, think about the philosophies and ethical concepts you have studied thus far. See if you find evidence of those principles of "treat others as you want to be treated," in all the ethical concepts mentioned thus far.

Virtue ethics

Virtue ethics, ethics of character, is another non-utilitarian ethic now making a comeback since first being described by Aristotle (Greek, 384-322 BC). Aristotle was a student of Plato's, but had a different philosophy. (Some say he merely re-worked Plato's philosophy--badly.) Aristotle strove for the middle--the golden mean or average. Only by acting within this golden mean, specific to each person's situation, could humans achieve a state of *eudaemonia*.

This word means something like well-being or happiness, but means something more than mere pleasure. Instead of focusing on <u>actions</u> as some other ethics do, virtue ethics emphasizes the person doing the act. The person's goodness, rightness, and character traits (moral virtues) such as honesty, kindness, and bravery are examined.

Think about it.
But is a virtue always moral? A virtue in a killer, might be ruthlessness.

The focus in this ethical theory is on being a virtuous person, instead of focus on doing moral acts. The assumption is that a virtuous person will act morally. Instead of prescribing rules for acts as do other ethical theories, virtue ethics seeks to identify virtues that characterize ethical persons. A virtuous person is said to have specific character traits, as contrasted with acting in a certain fashion. A person of good or virtuous character also would seem likely to do right, instead of wrong.

When we consider the person's motivation, we evaluate more than whether his act was right or wrong. We consider whether the motive for the act was good or bad. J.S. Mill thought analysis of motive was unnecessary if the act was good, that is, done for the greater happiness. This is the difference between ethics of being or thinking, and the ethics of doing or acting.

Some philosophers question whether virtue ethics is a separate philosophy of ethics itself, or merely an adjunct to other philosophies. That is, one could be a deontologist or utilitarian, and still be a virtuous person.

Think about it.
The problem: is it helpful to <u>be</u> a virtuous person, unless you also <u>act</u> virtuously?

As noted, Aristotle was the chief architect of virtue ethics. He considers that things move toward their natural ends or goals. Examining concepts from the point of view that they are destined to become something else, is **teleology**, a concept associated with the phrase "the end justifies the means."

In Greek, *teleos* means becoming. A contrasted idea is that of **deontology**, the idea that ethics arises from duty (the Greek word *deon* means duty).

Aristotle thought that ethics was a branch of *politikos*, Greek meaning politics. That is because ethics was part of the individual's learning to live with others in society. He believed that virtue could be cultivated, acquired and developed, by practice of right actions. Those actions were in the neighborhood of the **golden mean** (the mathematical middle). As an example, one is courageous when acting somewhere in the middle between foolhardy risk-studying, and timid flight.

Note the attention to virtue ethics in the best-seller by William Bennett, A Book of Virtues. Ten virtues were identified by Bennett as desirable to teach young people: self-discipline, responsibility, courage (those can be classed under the Value: Be Free); compassion (those classed under the Value: Do Good); friendship, loyalty, faith, honesty (those classed under the Value: Be True); perseverance, and work.

In the 1997 State of the Union speech President Bill Clinton called for character education for children, clearly supporting the teaching of virtue ethics. Clinton's 1998 State of the Union speech was given in the midst of allegations of his sex scandal (that he later admitted he had lied about).

Think about it.
Does the espousal of virtue ethics by a person who many believe was not virtuous, negate the validity of virtue ethics?

Casuistry

Toulmin and Wartofsky, advocates of **casuistry**, say this case-by-case basis is the only way to conduct ethics for clinical practice. In Greek terms, they say *praxis* (practice) is more important than *theoria* (theory). Pellegrino, in contrast, says that both theory and practice are necessary.

Casuistry is the basis of **narrative ethics.** This is the idea that simply narrating or telling stories about ethics cases and analyzing them, helps the person hearing the story see the right thing to do. People who use this narrative method often have a **paradigm case**, one that purports to set the standard. One example is to tell a paradigm case about a patient who wants life support discontinued, and it is done--that being the paradigm or standard for such cases. The problem is that real cases never fit exactly the facts of the paradigm case.

Narrative ethics seems to be more of a technique for discussing issues than an ethical theory or principle (Bowman, 1995). A related term is **contextual ethics**, referring to the need for ethical decisions to be made based on the context of the problem.

REFERENCES

Bowman A. Teaching ethics: Telling stories. *Nursing Education Today,* 1995; 15(1):33-38.

Condon E. Nursing and the caring metaphor: Gender and political influences on an ethics of care. *Nursing Outlook,* 1992; 40(I):14-19.

Coomer JS, Evans JF, McKeever M. Medical research: A lawyer's guide. *Texas Bar Journal,* 2000; 63(11):1062-1064.

Corley MC, Selig PM. Nursing moral reasoning using the Nursing Dilemma Test. *Western Journal of Nursing Research,* 1992; 14(3):380-388.

Cruzan v. Director, Missouri Department of Health, 497 U.S. 261 (1990).

Cutter E. Address on dietetics--Medical food ethics now and to come. *Journal of the American Medical Association,* 1893; 20:239-244.

Gilligan C. *In a Different Voice: Psychological Theory and Women's Development.* Cambridge: Harvard University Press, 1992.

Holzer HM. The physician's license: An Achilles heel? *Journal of Legal Medicine,* 1991;12:201-220.

In re Quinlan, 70 N.J. 101, 355 A2d 1647, *cert denied* (1976).

Ketefian S. Moral reasoning and ethical practice in nursing. *Nursing Clinics of North America,* June 1989; 24: 509-521.

Kohlberg L. *The Philosophy of Moral Development: Moral Stages and the Idea of Justice.* San Francisco: Harper & Row, 1981.

Lincoln A. Lecture notes, 1 July 1850. *The Harper Book of American Quotations,* New York: Harper, 1988.

Mehta N. Searching the Internet for medical information: Practical tips. *Cleveland Clinic Journal of Medicine,* 1999; 66(9):543-553.

Murray TH, Director, Center for Biomedical Ethics, Case Western Reserve, in Physicians, journalists, ethicists explore their adversarial, interdependent relationship. *Journal of the American Medical Association,* 1988; 260: at 757.

New law creates challenges for hospital ethics committees. *Medical Ethics Advisor,* December 1991, pp. 148-150.

Noddings N. *Caring, a feminine approach to ethics and morals.* Berkeley: University of California Press, 1984.

Raffin TA. Withholding and withdrawing life support. *Hospital Practice,* 15 March 1991, pp. 133-155, at p. 141.

Ross J, Glaser J, Rasinski-Gregory D, Gibson J, Bayley C. *Health care ethics committees: the next generation.* Chicago: American Hospital Publishing, 1993.

Rushton CH. Advance directives for critically ill adolescents. *Critical Care Nurse,* June 1992, p. 36.

Sermchief v. Gonzales, 660 SW2d 683 (Mo. 1983).

Sherry, S. Civic virtue and the feminine voice in constitutional adjudication. 79 *Virginia Law Review* 543 (1986).

Smith WJ. *Culture of Death.* San Francisco: Encounter Books, 2000.

Toobin J. Annals of law: Women in black. Female judges are more compassionate than men, the theory goes. Not in Texas. *The New Yorker* 10/30/00, pp 48-55.

Texas Health and Safety Code Ch. 166 (Vernon Supp. 1999). (See http://www.capitol.state.tx.us/statutes/he/he016600.html#he001.166.001.)

Chapter 2: Do Good.

"They shall lay hands on the sick, and they shall recover. ."

MARK 16:18, *New Testament*

CONTENTS

Key concepts

beneficence	negligence	agency
malpractice	statute of	Captain of the
duty	limitation	Ship
standard of care	malpractice	borrowed servant
breach	insurance	sovereign
causation	claims made	immunity
foreseeability	occurrence	governmental
but for	tail	immunity
substantial factor	punitive damages	joint and several
res ipsa loquitur	vicarious liability	liability
damages	*respondeat superior*	contribution
contingency	corporate liability	indemnity
contributory	agent	Good Samaritan
negligence	apparent or	alternative dispute
comparative	ostensible	resolution

mediation	code of behavior	extrinsic values
arbitration	axiological	act utilitarianism
negligence per se	deontological	rule utilitarianism
enterprise liability	utilitarianism	teleological
documentation	hedonism	paternalism
profession	intrinsic values	
codes of ethics		

Beneficence in clinical practice

In English words, the value discussed in this chapter is simply Do Good. A Latin-derived term for this important value is **beneficence**. Translated: *Bene* in Latin means "good" in English. The root of *ficence* in Latin is "do" or "make." Clinicians act for the good (the benefit, the health) of another--the patient. Beneficence is another way of describing what clinicians do: Caring.

Doing good for other people, specifically for patients, is a major value of clinical practice. People who are not clinicians, generally are not mandated to "do good" for others, but they are mandated not to harm. Laws usually do not force people to Do Good, even at a minimal level. For example, laws rarely even require people to stop at the scene of an accident except when they were involved in the accident.

Even professionals in clinical practice are not mandated to do good, unless they are being paid to do so. But when professionals obtain an education, certification, and accept pay for giving some care (for doing good), the mandate applies. Professionals accept the ethical duty to do good to other people, and the law enforces a minimum level of that higher ideal.

Think about it.
Do you agree that beneficence, above all values, characterizes clinical practice? Why or why not?
Which other value do you believe might be the most important to clinicians, and why?

Law enforcing the value: Do Good
Torts: negligence and malpractice

Malpractice is the law that enforces that minimum level of doing good. To most clinicians, lawsuits are the most feared manifestation of law. In reality, discipline of your legal credential or license is more dangerous–see Chapter 3–but the perception is that malpractice lawsuits are worse.

This chapter introduces several legal terms if you happen to need them, though clinicians seldom need to know many legal terms about malpractice. You are unlikely to be sued if you do good practice.

Malpractice (professional negligence law) originally was made by case law, but in all states part of that law has been modified by statute. To read the details of your state's malpractice law statutes, look in the index of state statutes in the local or central library under such headings as Malpractice or Professional Negligence or Tort, or use the Internet as set out in Chapter 1.

Torts, a French word for <u>wrongs</u>, may be done accidentally (negligently), or intentionally, or with degrees of intent in between. Tort law is subdivided into negligence law and other divisions, and negligence law in turn is subdivided--with malpractice law being one of the divisions.

Various torts and the degree of intent involved are shown below.

TORT LAW SCALE OF INTENT

Negligence (Malpractice)	Quasi-intentional Tort (Defamation, Invasion of Privacy)	Intentional Tort (Battery, Assault, False Imprisonment)

☜Less Intent   More Intent ☞

At the left or "accident" end of the intent scale, torts are described as being caused by negligence. Some association with accident is implied--but accident with a cause. Someone is at fault. Negligence law includes car wrecks and falls in supermarkets. **Malpractice**, a subdivision of negligence law, is the term for some negligent practice by a professional, that causes injury to the patient or client.

Further to the right on the scale are the intentional and quasi-intentional torts, discussed in Chapter 3, Don't Harm.

Anyone can sue you, anytime, for anything.

"Oh, he might sue us!" You have often heard that concern. You will be better served to get past that worry, or resign yourself to be forever worried. Just because someone can sue, doesn't mean they can win. Four things are necessary:

They can sue, but they can't win a lawsuit for malpractice against you, unless four criteria are met.

You, the clinician
1) had a <u>duty</u>, and you
2) <u>breached</u> the standard of care, and
3) that breach was the <u>cause</u> of the patient's
4) <u>injury</u>.

Again, not everybody who sues, wins. You must have had a duty to care for the patient--that is, he was <u>your</u> patient--and you must fail to act as a reasonable clinician would, doing something that breaches the standard of care. Further, that failure must be the cause of some actual injury to the patient.

Duty

The person sued must have had a **duty** to the person who sues. The person suing must have been your patient. What if a visitor slips and falls on an icy entryway to the clinician's office? There was no professional-patient relationship. But the office might have a duty that any business has, to keep its premises safe. If you're a clinician with an independent office, you may have the same duty.

Questions that help determine whether you owe a duty to the person injured, follow. Was this person actually your patient? Did the incident happen on the your unit, in your office, in the cafeteria, in your backyard, or did you give the person some free advice over the backyard fence?

If you are not acting in the capacity of a clinician–that is, not getting paid to practice, representing yourself as able to give professional care at that point--the law seldom imposes a duty to do good for another person.

The law does impose a duty on everyone, clinician or not, paid or not, to avoid harming other people if possible. The law of negligence in the area of car wrecks, dog bites, or icy steps is about failing to avoid harm to others. The law of negligence in the area of malpractice is about failing to do good for them.

The duty to do good is imposed only on people whose job or other situation requires doing good--for example, a clinician. Even without a protective statute, courts almost never award damages against a volunteer or Good Samaritan who had no duty to care.

For example, Good Samaritan statutes (see below) generally do not protect professional paramedics from lawsuit, because it's the paramedic's job (duty) to rescue. But in general, the public has no affirmative duty to do good. The parents of a baby who is run over by a truck usually cannot sue the bystander who stood idly by and let it happen.

However, a few states have passed laws that say that citizens have a duty to rescue others if the potential rescuer is at no risk to herself. Such laws contradict thousands of years of tradition, that say that citizens don't owe each other a positive, legally enforceable duty to do good (beneficence). Historically and in general today, people owe each other merely the negative legal duty not to harm (non-maleficence).

But once you take a job representing yourself as being willing and able to do good in a professional capacity, you have a legal duty to do so. For example, if you work in a free immunization clinic for no pay you still represent yourself as a clinician, with some assurance to the public that your practice will be good. This is also the situation in giving free advice to your neighbors, if you know the neighbor will rely on your advice alone. If harm and a lawsuit resulted, the court would consider the circumstances and might find that you had no duty of reasonable prudent care to your neighbor because you were not paid for the advice.

Malpractice law holds that even when working for pay, you have a duty only to a <u>foreseeable</u> plaintiff. If you can't foresee that someone could hurt by your action, there is no duty to that person. Usually this is not an issue in a malpractice case.

Foreseeability might be an issue in a lawsuit brought by a family member who witnesses harm to a patient and sues for her *own* injury–the upset she feels as witness. You can foresee that the patient might be harmed by your negligence, but it's unlikely that you could foresee, for example, that the patient's relative would be so upset at the patient's harm that the relative would have a heart attack.

As noted above, usually there is no duty to act for the good of another or even to rescue her, unless you assume that responsibility, by such action as working as a clinician. However, if you negligently put someone in peril, you may have a duty to rescue the person so endangered.

Also, if you put someone in danger, you are liable for injury to the person who acts to rescue the endangered person. It can be foreseen that an accident might produce a volunteer rescuer, so if she's injured at the scene of an accident that you caused, she also can sue you.

As another example of duty, airlines, bus companies, and innkeepers have a special duty to protect passengers and guests. Clinicians may have a duty to control a third person, if you have charge of the person and you know there is a need to control her. This could be an area of liability for clinicians who care for the mentally ill.

The duty relationship to the patient is harder to establish without person-to-person contact. For example, a consulting clinician who spoke by telephone with the ER clinician about a patient, but who never spoke personally to the patient, may not have a duty to that patient. Clinicians whose practice is almost entirely by telephone or Internet, however, may have a duty to the patients they advise directly by those media. It easily can be foreseen that the person spoken to might be harmed by bad advice given by the professional (Kupchynsky, 2001).

Standard of care

If you had a duty to the person injured, the second requirement the plaintiff must establish to prove liability for malpractice is that you **breached** that duty. The definition of breach is failure to act as a reasonable, prudent clinician would act in that circumstance. This is an old value--Prudence was one of the four main values of the ancient Greeks. Failure to act in accord with accepted practice is evidence of the breach. If you need a reason, that's a good reason to keep your practice current with continuing education.

Think about it.
Why should clinicians be held legally responsible for a breach in the standard of care, if they did not intend to harm?

The law holds professionals accountable for practice at a certain level, a **standard of care**. That legal standard is this:

> **To give the care that a reasonable prudent clinician would give in similar circumstances.**

You do not have a legal duty to be an excellent clinician, just a reasonable prudent one.

The reasonable prudent clinician standard is objective, not subjective. That means your own personal age or tiredness or particular stupidity is no excuse. Clinicians are judged according to what they *should* be and do as a reasonable, prudent clinicians, not according to what they actually are.

The law stands you up in an abstract reasonable prudent clinician's shoes, not the dirty shoes run over by the portable x-ray machine as you looked in disbelief at the administrator who said you were needed to work another 12 hours in addition to the 12 you just finished.

Contrasted with the law's unconcern for your personal plight, the law does require that you consider your patient's particular characteristics. If you know a patient has certain physical handicaps or mental conditions, you are expected to be careful of them. The standards in a lawsuit--objective standard for clinicians, subjective standard for patients--may seem unfair, but the patient is sick, helpless, and has an expectation of safe care.

You, the clinician, are assumed to have options, while the patient does not. Your bad work situation is not the patient's fault. Clinicians have worked in such conditions by choice ever since the Thirteenth Amendment to the Constitution abolished slavery.

Evidence of breach

Evidence of a breach of the standard of care can come from various sources. For example, in testimony by an expert witness, she might say that in her opinion, your behavior was not that of a reasonable, prudent clinician (Popp, 1992). Another evidence of the standard of care against which the your behavior could be measured is organization policy. This is a good reason to know policy and make sure it conforms to what actually is being practiced.

Equipment instruction books too can be introduced to establish the standard of proper use and care of equipment. You must know how to use equipment that ordinarily is employed in your practice, and you must see that it is in good working order. It's your task to make sure the equipment is safe for the patient, as far as can be determined, and to refuse to use equipment that doesn't work. If a faulty electric bed causes a fire or shocks the patient, the jury will not be sympathetic to an excuse that the maintenance department was overworked and so the clinician didn't report an unsafe condition. The patient deserves safe care.

Other standards that could be used to establish breach of the standard of care are those of your professional association. Such standards usually are written in general terms so they may be difficult to apply to a specific situation, but plaintiffs might seek to hold clinicians to such vague statements.

Still other standards are set by specialty organizations. If you practice new and unusual procedures you should look for, and adhere to, any such guidelines done by specialty organizations (Murphy, 1993). Be aware of your professional association's general practice guidelines and recognize that they too can be used as the standard of practice in malpractice actions (Audet, 1990).

Standards for professional care established by the Joint Commission on the Accreditation of Health Organizations (JCAHO) might be introduced to prove breach. Use of their standards in a lawsuit could hurt you worse than bad marks on their survey ever could. (Surveys rarely result in an organization being decertified by the JCAHO.)

Standards of care can be evidenced by some of the documents developed in quality improvement programs, such as critical pathways and total quality management documents. Such documents have many names-critical paths, practice guidelines or parameters, clinical guidelines, clinical protocols or algorithms, anticipated recovery paths, clinical outcomes, collaborative care tracks, key processes, outcomes management, program evaluation, service strategies, standards of care (!), target tracks, and uniform data systems.

Critical pathways and protocols may be used by lawyers for the plaintiff to prove that they were not followed and so the standard of care was breached. Clinicians should recognize the potential liability that may result (Lumsdon, 1993). If you don't adhere to the pathway, this could be evidence of malpractice (Woolfe, 1993).

Meeting the standard is evidence of some quality of care. But be careful: Such written statements all describe what should happen to the average patient, and almost never describe what should happen to the individual patient.

If you use standing orders or protocols or critical pathways or similar tools in your practice, they can be used as evidence to establish breach of the standard of care. If individual circumstances indicate the need to deviate from the pathway, do it and document the reasons. Clinicians don't have to follow such guidelines if there is good reason to deviate, but you should document why the guidelines were not followed.

Statutes themselves can be very weighty standards of care. Consider a statute that prescribes a certain behavior that is intended to protect the class of person who has been harmed--that's exactly what your credentialing statute does. Violation of such a statute may lead to a charge of what is called in legal terms, ***negligence per se.***

Example of Texas regulation used by plaintiffs in malpractice cases, to show the standard of care:
"[The RN shall] 4) accurately and completely report and document:
(A) the client's status including signs, symptoms and responses"
22 Tex. Admin. Code §217.11, adopted to be effective September 1,

Under the theory of *negligence per se*, if the practice act in your state says that clinicians shall observe the patient, and you fail to do so, the statute itself can be admitted as evidence of the standard of care that should have been met. The statute establishes both the duty and the standard of care.

In some states such evidence of violation is a *conclusive* presumption, meaning that no other standard of care is needed. The plaintiff wouldn't need an expert witness to show the standard of care. But the opposite evidence, showing that you complied with the statute, is not conclusive presumption that you took due care.

Your state's credentialing law could be used to show the standard of care that you should attain, even though no violation of that standard has been charged by the licensing authority. This use of the law is quite common, because credentialing provisions are often general and vague.

Your profession's Code of Ethics also might be used as a standard in law cases, though as ethics it should be seen as an ideal behavior, not a minimum required by law. The standard of care for non-physician clinicians who practice medicine (for example, some physician assistants and nurse practitioners) may be the behavior required of a reasonable, prudent physician, regardless of whether the clinician has a medical education (Hirsh, 1991).

If you are a defendant, any of these evidences of standards (for example--expert witness, agency policy, association or JCAHO standards) also can be used in your defense, to help establish that your actions were in accord with good practice.

Professional journals and textbooks are admissible in some states as another source of the standard of practice applicable to malpractice suits. The law's standard of care is never higher than the professional standard of good practice, so keeping up with what is good practice also keeps you above the standard of practice required by law.

Many clinician journals regularly update the latest legal cases and statutes that apply to clinicians, describing the standard of care in some cases. These articles are interesting and helpful, but not a substitute for knowing that the basis of the law is ethics and good practice. The changing cases and statutes are merely variations and examples of the principle (we love to say it): Good practice is lawful and right.

Causation

Another requirement to establish liability for malpractice in addition to duty and breach of the standard of care, is **causation**. That simply means that the patient's trouble must result from your action--your breach of the standard of care. Note that even if the case turns out badly–if the patient does not get well or dies–you are not automatically liable. You are liable only if you did not act as a reasonable prudent professional would, thus you breached the standard of care, and in turn that breach <u>caused</u> the patient's damage.

Causation is established when the patient's lawyer proves
(1) the patient's injuries would not have occurred, but for the clinician's failure to act as a reasonable prudent clinician; and
(2) the clinician could foresee that failure to act in such a way would result in injury.

This is another application of the concept of **foreseeability**–the question of whether or not you could anticipate that the breach of the standard of care would cause a problem. The exact kind of injury needn't be foreseeable. Foreseeability was mentioned above with duty (to whom you could foresee you had a duty), and it is discussed also regarding intentional torts, in Chapter 3.

In malpractice cases, the damage itself is usually foreseeable from the breach. For example, the breach of prescribing too much insulin can be foreseen to cause low blood glucose and it's foreseeable that the patient might suffer damage as a result. It's questionable, however, whether it's foreseeable that the low blood glucose would cause the patient to shoot her husband, making the prescriber liable for the death. (That is a criminal act anyway, possibly classed as an intervening intentional cause, thus relieving the prescriber of liability.)

The "**but for**" test of causation is really a test of what is the proximate (close) cause of injury. "But for" the occurrence of the first event-- the breach of the standard--the second would not have occurred. Several states have adopted this test (Doerhoff, 1994).

Substantial factor

A lesser or looser legal level of the standard of causation is used in some states. In those states, liability exists if the clinician's failure is even a **substantial factor** among other factors causing the injury. If there are joint causes of injury, for example if two clinicians both are negligent, you may be liable if your act was even a substantial factor in the injury.

If alternative causes of the injury are alleged, each defendant must prove his or her negligence was <u>not</u> the proximate cause. For you, the defendant clinician to win, there must be no connection from your negligent act to the plaintiffs injury. For example, say you prescribed too much insulin and your patient was parked in front of his house in his car in shock when a drunk driver crossed the street and ran into him.

Your breach might not meet the higher "but for" standard–but it might meet the lower standard of being a "substantial factor" in the patient's injury.

An example of another extension of the causation theory occurs when you the clinician fail to assess for, or fail to suspect, or fail to report, obvious child abuse in a minor patient in the office or the emergency department. Your failure may produce civil liability in addition to being a crime.

If the child returns to the abusive situation and is injured or killed, you could be sued for the injury or for wrongful death. The failure to assess and report may be considered negligent--a breach of the standard of care, and a "substantial factor" in the child's death. Your failure was not the direct cause of the death--the abuse was. But the breach might be considered a substantial factor in the death.

Intervening forces

Intervening forces that were *foreseeable* do not exculpate the negligent person. If the negligence was an indirect cause of the injury, for example, if a person slightly injured in a car wreck dies as a result of later malpractice, the person who caused the wreck still is liable along with the negligent clinician. Foreseeable intervening forces are sequelae that can be predicted from a situation, such as medical malpractice, negligent rescuers, predictable reactions to an event, subsequent diseases, actions of people protecting property, and even subsequent related accidents.

Think about it.
If you fail to treat the patient's diabetes and he develops complications years later, would the intervening force of the patient's aging process exculpate you?
Is aging foreseeable?

On the other hand, the negligent defendant will not be held liable for unforeseeable intervening forces that cause harm. Two things that are not foreseen or anticipated as a result of a negligent act, are criminal acts (such as the example above of the hypoglycemic patient who killed her husband)--and intentional torts done by third persons. Note that both are *intentional* acts of a third person, not accidents. Intentional abuse of a child is a crime too, but the act can be foreseen from the pattern of past abuse.

Loss of chance

Some states allow a theory of causation called loss of chance. This theory allows the patient/ plaintiff to recover damages if the clinician's negligence caused him to lose a chance of cure. An example is a patient who dies of a brain tumor, negligently undiagnosed at a point when (at best) the patient had a 30 percent chance of recovery. The damages for the patient's wrongful death are calculated, and the survivor who sued is given 30 percent of the calculation. In states that do not allow this loss of chance theory, the patient must have had at least a 50% chance of survival even if correctly diagnosed, for a wrongful death lawsuit based on misdiagnosis to succeed.

Res ipsa loquitur

A peculiar version of proving causation in some states, is *res ipsa loquitur*. This Latin phrase literally means the "thing itself speaks." The thing--the injury, the incident--tells its own story and proves negligence. Under other theories of causation, the plaintiff must prove that one or more specific defendants were negligent.

The classic example of *res ipsa loquitur* is the situation in which the patient goes to the operating room for a hysterectomy and comes out with a dislocated shoulder. No one knows (or will admit) what happened. The patient can't prove specifically who injured her--who was negligent--so the theory of *res ipsa loquitur* presumes that anyone with an opportunity and control of part of the procedure could have been negligent.

In this example, any and all of the operating room staff will share negligence. In the real world, the employer's liability insurer will pay-and possibly the clinician's personal insurer, if there is one.

In *res ipsa* states, the burden is on each defendant to show innocence, or else share the blame. In other states, however, if more than one person is a defendant, the plaintiff still has the burden of proving which one caused the damage.

Damages

The fourth requirement for liability in a malpractice case is that the clinician who 1) had a duty, 2) did breach the standard of care and 3) did cause the fourth requirement--4) **damages** to the patient. To succeed in a lawsuit, the patient must have been injured by the breach of the standard of care. Most states require the patient to have been physically injured, not merely emotionally damaged. Usually it is not a problem for the plaintiff to prove physical injury and damages, because the patient and her current clinician or expert witness can testify as to injuries.

If the patient can't prove injury, no liability exists--even if the clinician had a duty to the patient and breached it. For example, if you breach the standard of care and give a patient the wrong medication, if the patient is not harmed by the breach there is no liability.

As a practical matter, the patient must have considerable damages in order to get a lawyer to represent her. In the U.S., malpractice lawyers for the plaintiff work on a **contingency** basis. That means they get paid a percentage of the damages, contingent on the plaintiff winning. Such cases are expensive to bring to trial and win, and defendants win about 90% of the time. A patient who has not been injured seriously is unlikely to find a plaintiff's lawyer willing to take the case.

The lawyer usually can't take a malpractice case unless it is likely to result in victory and enough damages to pay for time and expenses. Small damages usually are not sued on, because the cost of prosecuting a small claim exceeds the possible recovery.

Other systems for paying lawyers exist. In Britain, the payment to plaintiff lawyers is not contingent on winning. Instead, they are paid by the hour, either by the patient or a taxpayer-paid legal aid system. The loser of the lawsuit, whether plaintiff or defendant, must pay the lawyer of the winner.

The advantage of that system is that it increases out-of-pocket costs to the patient-plaintiff, thereby discouraging frivolous lawsuits. The disadvantage is that poor people with injuries due to malpractice may not be able to get a remedy for the wrong done to them.

Damages may include pain and suffering, loss of income, medical bills, and other economic damages. Damages can be sought and awarded for past, present, and prospective injury. They can be special damages, for specific expenses incurred as a result of the harm, or they can be general damages.

You saw above that foreseeability is a factor in determining whether there's a duty to a particular person, or whether it's foreseeable that the breach would cause the some injury. But once duty is established to a particular person, and foreseeability that the breach might be the cause of some kind of injury, it doesn't matter that the clinician couldn't have anticipated the specific kind of injury that resulted from the act. Whether the damage was foreseeable is not an issue in determining the *amount* of damages, either.

Damages include interest that accrues on the monetary damage award from the date the award is made by the court, but damages do not include interest on the award all the way back to the date of injury.

Specific amounts usually are not awarded for attorney fees. Instead, attorney fees are paid by the plaintiff as a percentage of the total amount of damages awarded. The percentage paid to the attorney is set by a private contract with the client, and usually increases with the amount of work needed to recover the money. In many areas of the country, the attorney gets about 1/3 of the amount if the case is settled before trial, about 40% if the case is won after a trial, and about 50% of the amount of the award if the trial verdict was appealed and had to be defended at the appellate level.

Punitive damages, sometimes called exemplary damages, are a way to punish. They enforce the values Don't Harm and Do Good, by providing a penalty for people who do harm with a large degree of recklessness or even with intent. Punitive damage amounts are not related to the amount of injury of the patient, but are levied by the jury and judge to make an example-- to punish--in order to deter really bad behavior.

Such damages are not for unintentional behavior, so they rarely are awarded in negligence actions. The exceptions are in cases where the defendant was grossly negligent, exhibiting what sometimes is called "willful and wanton" behavior.

For example, if you commit an accidental medication error and report it, your patient who is harmed by it may sue for negligence. Even if you lose the case, no punitive damages will be awarded.

But if you commit an accidental medication error and intentionally do not report it in order to cover it up, that action would be classed as intentional or at least willful and wanton. If serious damage resulted, the jury or court might be provoked to award punitive damages.

In some states, a statute limits punitive damages to 3 or 4 or some other multiplier, times the actual compensatory damages. In such situations, if the actual damages were $1 million, the maximum punitive damages would be $3 or $4 million.

The plaintiff has a duty to **mitigate damages**--that is, to prevent further damage when possible. An example. If your patient gets bad advice from you that causes injury to his leg, he can get damages. But he will not receive damages that occur after he calls back and then ignores your advice, letting the injury deteriorate to the point where amputation is necessary. He can recover damages only for the original injury.

In most states, the plaintiff's damages are not reduced by "**collateral sources**" such as insurance that reimburses the patient's costs. That means the patient can recover the cost of medical care needed as a result of the malpractice, even if insurance already has paid for it. The reason for this policy is that the defendant should not be helped, nor the plaintiff hurt, by the plaintiff's foresight in providing personal insurance or other protection.

Damages for lost earning potential and for anticipated medical expenses can be shown at trial by experts. In some states, damages for pain and suffering are limited to a certain dollar amount. By the way, the plaintiff's lawyer calls it "pain and suffering" while the clinician's lawyer calls it "non-compensatory damages."

Think about it.
Why would the plaintiff's lawyer and defendant's lawyer characterize this concept differently?

Damages for nonphysical, psychological pain are harder to prove. In some states, such damages cannot be awarded unless the injury was caused intentionally.

Defenses to malpractice

The obvious defense to malpractice is to deny one or all of the four elements that are necessary to establish liability for malpractice. The patient/plaintiff has the burden of proving all four conditions above-- duty, breach, causation, injury. The professional/defendant can defend by denying that any or all of those conditions are met. Further, in some states the plaintiff/patient will lose the suit or have damages reduced if it is proved he contributed to his problem. This is called **contributory negligence**.

Contributory negligence

Until the last few decades, one of the principles of tort law was that any negligence on the part of patient-plaintiffs was a defense to a suit for malpractice against a clinician. For example, if the clinician misapplied a cast or failed to warn the patient to check her toes for circulation, the clinician committed malpractice. If the patient also was negligent, however--for instance if she noticed symptoms and failed to seek attention for them--the patient would have been contributorily negligent. That is, she was negligent and contributed to her own injury.

Under contributory negligence theory, no matter how bad the malpractice of the provider, any negligence contributed by the plaintiff was a good defense for the provider. This doctrine has been modified by case or statute law in most states into some form of comparative negligence.

Contributory negligence was imputed from the actual negligent person to the person who was vicariously liable–that is, the one who was liable only as a result of law, not personally. If the employer sued someone, he would have his employee's contributory negligence imputed to him. A partner in a business who sued would have her other partner's negligence imputed to her.

A person in a joint venture who was sued would lose, if another in the joint venture were contributorily negligent. But husband and wife are not in such a vicarious relationship, nor are child and parent, nor car owner and driver, except when the state passes a statute to create the relationship.

Comparative negligence

People didn't like the outcome of contributory negligence theory, because the plaintiff who was only a little negligent still lost completely. So various states changed the law. For example, Texas established comparative negligence by statute in 1973 with what is called the proportionate responsibility code (Tex. Civ. Prac. 1999).

As an example, the patient whose initial injury was due to malpractice, and who was told to call or come back for attention if his wound became red, hot, swollen, and painful, and didn't--still is partly to blame. He still is negligent. But in comparative negligence states he doesn't lose all, as he would have under contributory negligence. Instead, the damages due to him may be reduced, proportionate to his own percentage of fault. If he's 50% to blame, he gets only 50% of the award of the court. This is called **comparative negligence**.

The theory of comparative negligence is relatively more favorable to the plaintiff/patient. In states with that system, the clinician still could be assessed liability, even if there is some negligence on the part of the patient. The amount of damages is established, the percentage of each party's fault is decided, and judgment is given accordingly. Under the original contributory negligence principle described above, a patient who was at all negligent would lose all.

As an example of a judgment under comparative negligence, assume you failed to instruct your patient properly about his medication, but the patient also was negligent in not reporting that he had a reaction. The jury set his total damages at $20,000. If you and the patient each were found to be 50 percent at fault, you pay $10,000. Under traditional contributory negligence case law, if the patient was at all negligent he lost everything.

Such a change in the law of your state may have been made by statute, found in the statute index or on the Internet. If the change from contributory to comparative negligence was made by the court (judges) in the state, the section on "History" in the annotated statutes on malpractice will describe the case and decision establishing comparative negligence in the state. Any lawyer you consult in your state should know if the state has a system of comparative negligence. Refer back to "How to find the law" in Chapter 1.

Think about it.

Is comparative negligence theory a good policy?
Would contributory negligence theory be better for you?
For your patients, in the long run?

Statute of limitation

Another defense to malpractice is the **statute of limitation** that limits the amount of time after his injury that the patient has to file a lawsuit. If the patient waits longer to sue than the time specified in the statute, the case is automatically lost. Such statutes are written so that people who intend to file a lawsuit will do so relatively quickly, while evidence is fresh and available. The statute also limits the time that potential defendants must live under the threat of lawsuit for their past acts.

Most states have set the time limit to sue for professional negligence (malpractice) at from two to five years. In a particular state's statute, this limitation of time to sue may be shorter for suits against clinicians than for suits against other people. Depending on what the state statute says, a person injured in a car wreck might be able to wait almost five years to sue the other driver, while a person injured by an operation may have only two years to sue the clinician.

The statute may say the time limit for suit starts to run:
(1) at the time of the injury, or
(2) at the time of the discovery of the injury, or
(3) at the date when treatment ceased.

Or the statute may specify some other variation the state legislature devised.

Two years from the date of discovery to sue may be a long time to bring suit. The patient may not discover the injury for many years, and then she has two more years from that date of discovery to sue. For example, the patient with a retained sponge or hemostat may not discover the injury until years later, at a subsequent surgery.

If the injury is concealed from the patient--for example, if the clinician fails to inform the patient of a complication that she knows about-- the time available to sue will not start until the patient actually discovers the injury. That concept is "tolling the statute" or delaying the start of the running of the time available to sue.

Deliberately concealing the possible existence of malpractice is called fraudulent concealment. That act carries penalties of its own, not least of which is that juries tend to punish clinicians who engage in such behavior, even if it develops that they were not actually negligent.

Another statute passed by many state legislatures modifies

malpractice case law, by requiring that plaintiffs must give the defendants a notice of intent to sue before filing a lawsuit. That notice also tolls or suspends the running of the statute. The hope was that the parties would have time to settle disputes informally without the necessity of a lawsuit, but this seldom happens. The time limit for giving notice of intent to sue may be significantly shorter than the statute of limitation, in particular against taxpayer-supported defendants.

A state statute usually specifies how long a minor has to sue. In traditional case law, the minor could (or even had to) wait until he was no longer a minor. He could be (or would have to be) 21 years old--later lowered to age 18–then he could sue. Some states have changed this case law by statute.

If the patient cannot point to any one incident that is the particular malpractice, then the end of a course of treatment--the treatment that is the basis of the malpractice--may become the starting point for the running of the time of limitations. For example, patients with chronic diseases, in which complications can be prevented by careful early treatment, may not know of malpractice until complications develop.

One example is the patient with diabetes. It now is known that complications can be greatly reduced by early and aggressive control. The clinician who sees the patient, and who tells him not to worry about his blood glucose--"anything below 200 is fine"--might face liability in ten years if the patient loses his eyesight then as a result of the clinician's unconcern.

A two-year statute of limitations probably will not begin to run until the patient discovers the complication or the course of treatment ends. Clinicians carefully should document efforts to educate patients, particularly those patients who continue to be non-compliant with treatment suggestions.

Wrongful death

In a wrongful death lawsuit, the relative or dependent of the patient who died, sues for his or her own loss that was caused by the malpractice of the clinician. This lawsuit is brought when a patient dies of the malpractice committed.

Wrongful death lawsuits did not exist at common law--the law we inherited from England--but legislatures in the various states have created it. The time limit to bring a lawsuit for wrongful death may be different from the time limit for other actions brought as a result of malpractice.

The specifics of how much damages can be awarded and the time limit to file a wrongful death lawsuit differ from state to state. You can find your state's wrongful death statute in your library or on the Internet.

Think about it.

What might be the reasons for a limitation on the plaintiff's time to
sue? Memory? Fairness? Can the result be unfair?
Is life always fair? Should it be?
How would you define fair?
Refer back to this answer after you read the Chapter 5 on Justice
to see if your answer agreed with some of those definitions.

Consent as a defense

Contrary to the belief of many clinicians, a signed consent to a procedure is *not* an automatic defense in malpractice action. Just because the patient signed a form saying that she understood the risk of a hysterectomy included a nicked ureter, does not mean she consents to your negligently nicking her ureter. A valid consent <u>would</u> be a defense, to a lawsuit brought on the grounds of a "negligent" failure to inform her of the risks of the procedure.

A suit alleging that the clinician was negligent in not informing the patient of the risks of the procedure would be classed under negligence law. In that case, showing a valid informed consent would be a defense. Consent also may be a defense to a different kind of tort, a charge of battery--classed as an intentional tort and discussed in Chapter 3.

The extensive listing of risks of the procedure in a consent form is done to inform the patient of risks, and to defend against that lawsuit of "negligent failure to inform the patient of risks." Listing the risks does not shift the burden of assuming the risk onto the patient. If this were so, clinicians could merely list, as one risk on the consent form, "risk of negligent care" and presto, there would be no grounds for lawsuit from negligence.

That is not the law. Consent is good to get–see Chapter 4, Be Free, for a complete discussion. But consent is not a defense to a malpractice lawsuit unless the negligence charged is something like "negligent failure to inform the patient of risks." When the patient signs the consent form with the risk listed, she is not consenting to, nor assuming the risk of, your negligence.

Malpractice insurance

Many clinicians carry some type of **malpractice insurance**. But many clinicians don't have enough assets to attract lawsuit. If that's your situation, even being found liable for a lot of money in a malpractice lawsuit would merely prompt you to file bankruptcy. You would keep substantial assets such as home equity, car, and retirement account--the specifics depend on the current federal bankruptcy law and the law of your state.

If you are a clinician with a lot of assets, you likely work with a financial planner to protect those assets with various kinds of trusts, plus buying malpractice insurance.

Two kinds of malpractice insurance are generally available for clinicians to buy--occurrence and claims made. **Occurrence** malpractice insurance covers the clinician for any event that occurs while the policy is in force.

Claims for malpractice are likely to be made some years after the injury. **Claims made** insurance must be kept in force--paid for--all during that time. Depending on the time limits of the statute of limitations in your state, you may need to keep the premium paid for up to five years after the injury to the patient. In the case of minors you may need insurance coverage until the patient's 18th birthday, plus the length of additional statute time limit to sue.

In some states the statute does not start to run--that is, the time limit to sue does not start--until the patient discovers the injury. That could be years later, for example at a subsequent surgery. Clinicians who retire often carry "tail" coverage that protects them from claims filed later, for events that happened during their working years. See below.

To help you assess whether you need personal malpractice insurance, ask your risk manager:
1) if the organization has malpractice instance that covers you. Then ask her
2) whether the policy covers employees as individuals,
3) whether the insurance is occurrence or claims made, and
4) what are the limits of coverage.

For most clinicians, lawsuits are unlikely. True, about 1300 of 10,000 physician clinicians are sued every year-- but some individuals account for several of those suits per year. As an example of other professions' risk of liability, only about 5 out of 10,000 nurses are sued each year. Other non-physician clinicians rarely are sued, are even more rarely found liable, and if so the average damages are low (Faherty, 1998).

Your employer's malpractice insurance almost invariably would cover you adequately. As is the case when you buy any kind of insurance, malpractice insurance may be indicated if your economic situation warrants protecting large assets, or if buying it will increase your comfort level.

Type of insurance:	Covers:	Cost:	Availability:
claims made	claims that are made while the insurance is paid for	cheaper	usually available
occurrence	events that occur while the insurance was paid for	more expensive	may be unavailable for high risk clinicians
tail	events that occur after the work is ceased	cheaper	usually available

More insurance means more lawsuits

The biggest worry is not the liability–it is rarely found and usually small except for physician clinicians. The more likely event, still uncommon, is that you would have to hire a lawyer to defend a suit that has no merit, filed because other clinicians have bought liability insurance and the perception was created that all clinicians have deep pockets.

Buying malpractice insurance increases the expectation of plaintiff lawyers that all clinicians have their own insurance in addition to that of their employer. Thereby, all clinicians are converted into relatively "deep pockets." As more clinicians obtain insurance, the possibility is increased that clinicians will be sued as individuals, in addition to a vicarious liability suit being filed against their employer.

The insurance company's lawyer, whether hired through the employer's policy or your own insurance, is selected by and paid by the insurance company, not by you or by the employer. Some physician clinicians hire their own attorney and pay privately, in order to protect their own interest. Unless the you pay out of pocket and choose your own attorney, the insurance company will choose the attorney.

The advantage to having your own policy of malpractice insurance is that your own insurance will pay for your own attorney if a suit is brought. If you are covered only by your employer's insurance, the attorney hired by that insurance company may be less interested in your separate liability, even though they have an ethical and legal obligation to be.

In extreme cases, the employer's liability insurer might even find it helpful to their case to characterize your actions as illegal. That might free the employer of responsibility--see *respondeat superior* below. In such situations their lawyers have an obligation to notify you that a conflict of interest exists, and that you should have separate representation.

If you or your employer have claims-made insurance, it is necessary to have coverage continue after you stop working there or retire. **Tail insurance**, as it is called, covers claims made after you leave, on occurrences that happened while you still were working. A problem: organizations go out of business. Your risk manager should know if the employer's policy covers the employees after the organization closes, or what arrangements are made for that eventuality. For example, if an employer went bankrupt, injured patients might have only the individual clinician to sue, to recover damages for injury.

Clinicians generally need tail coverage only for the time period of the statute of limitations in the state. After that, a patient alleging negligence cannot sue successfully. Some kinds of practice, for example surgery and pediatrics, might require a longer tail coverage. Tail coverage is proportionately cheaper than for coverage of current risks.

Insurance usually will not cover the punitive damage part of a liability judgment. There is an ethical reason for the legal and contractual policy of not covering punitive damages by insurance. If insurance covered the "punishment," the individual or organization wouldn't really feel any pain for having harmed the patient.

Insurance rarely covers fines that are levied as punishment for crime, because a crime usually is deemed to be intentional. The insurance company covers only for unintentional acts--negligence--not for something done deliberately. Discipline by the licensure board is not a malpractice action in civil court, so your malpractice insurance policy will not cover costs or attorney fees in licensure matters, unless the coverage is specified in the policy.

Most clinicians need little if any malpractice insurance as protection. However, there is an ethical question as to whether clinicians have a duty to carry insurance or else have enough assets to protect patients who might be harmed by their practice. Every patient of a clinician is at some risk, because every clinician risks doing harm to the patient in the course of practice.

Because clinicians are human and humans make mistakes, there is no way to prevent some degree of malpractice. People who accidentally hurt others are not considered evil, but in this society they are held responsible for their actions.

Think about it.

Do you agree the ethical clinician buys malpractice insurance, not to protect herself, but to reimburse the patient against the risk of causing harm?

Or is risk a part of the human condition, a cost of living as a human being?

Is it good for people to be insured for all risk in their lives?

Does the existence of car insurance make people less careful drivers?

An alternative to buying extra malpractice insurance exists. If your employer already covers you, you can spend the money for an "umbrella" coverage policy for yourself, family, home, and car liability. Check with your insurance agent--such a policy may not cover you at work, but it needn't if your employer's policy does. Remember that your personal insurance coverage and your employer's insurance coverage, both, are exactly as reliable as is the insurance company.

General tort law
Vicarious liability

Vicarious liability is another way of saying "those who benefit, bear responsibility" or "the deep pocket loses." Vicarious liability enforces responsibility on one person or entity, for the actions of another. In clinical practice, application of the principle usually results in liability of the employer organization for the actions of the employee clinician.

The Latin phrase for the employer's legal liability for their employees is ***respondeat superior,*** meaning that the superior responds or pays. This does not mean that the *supervisor* clinician is responsible for the acts of all employees under her supervision. The supervisor is liable under this doctrine only if she is actually the employer who pays salary, hires and fires, and reaps profit.

Vicarious liability law is important to individual clinicians because vicarious liability lawsuits are more numerous than lawsuits against individual clinicians. Vicarious liability cases set the legal standard of care that will be applied when clinicians are sued personally. Most of the malpractice law has been written in vicarious liability cases.

The individual clinician also may be interested in the legal theory of corporate liability, a form of vicarious liability. That is because the corporation is may be liable to the clinician, for a wrong done to her.

Vicarious liability can be applied to find the employer liable for the clinician employee's negligence, even if the employer had hired supervisors doing a reasonable job of supervising. All that is necessary is to find that the clinician is engaged in some lawful activity on behalf of the employer, and that the clinician is liable.

Under *respondeat superior* theory the employer is automatically liable for that negligence, too. Once the employee's negligence is established, the employer bears strict liability. That is, the employer needn't have been at fault.

Corporate liability

Organizations always have been responsible for the acts of their agents. An **agent**, either an employee or independent contractor of the organization, works on behalf of the organization, her **principal**. Hospitals too have become responsible for the acts of their employees and agents, as other organizations are.

The idea of "**corporate liability**" on the part of clinical practice organizations sounds new. But when analyzed, corporate liability is found to be merely an extension of existing theories of law, to organizations that care for patients. The old theories of agency law and *respondeat superior* law are clothed in the new term, "corporate liability."

The employer can be found liable also under the heading of corporate liability for negligent hiring--failure to check out skills, references, and licenses, at the time of hire. The employer also is liable for negligent supervision of clinicians. All these are considered to be under the theory of corporate liability, though in essence they are variations of the very much older idea of *respondeat superior* (Hall, 2000). The actual negligent hiring is done by an employee of the organization, so the organization is liable under *respondeat superior* for that employee who hired--but it is called corporate liability.

These theories called corporate liability may be used also if there is difficulty in proving that the clinician was an employee. Corporate liability has been used successfully in suing organizations for the acts of clinicians who are considered independent contractors. In reality, this is merely the old law of **apparent or ostensible agency.**

If a clinician appears to act on behalf of the organization, the organization may be liable whether or not the clinician actually has authority to act. This theory is called ostensible or apparent agency. The organization is liable for permitting the clinician to appear to have authority, regardless of whether the authority is actual or not.

For example, the organization may be held liable for the acts of a temporary hire who is not a formal employee with the organization. This happens because the temporary employee apparently--to the patient–has the authority and status of an employee of the organization.

Negligent supervision

The theory of liability for negligent supervision is different from negligent staffing, discussed below. A supervisor may be liable for the acts of workers if her supervision is negligent. For example, the supervisor may be liable for negligently assigning an assistant to care for a patient on a ventilator, if the supervisor knows or should know the assistant never had training or experience with such patients. Unlike the theory of *respondeat superior* imposed on employers, supervisors of clinicians are not automatically liable under the law for all the acts of all the people under their supervision.

You may feel responsible if someone under your supervision is negligent, and management may hold you responsible. However, the law will find you liable for negligence and hold you legally responsible for damages, only if you have been negligent in supervision in some way.

The standard:

whether you acted as a reasonable and prudent supervisor would act in similar circumstances.

Reasonable and prudent supervisors do not stand over people, nor do they do all their work for them. Reasonable and prudent supervisors do assign people work that they can do, and make checks on the quality of the work done.

Supervisors are liable for making assignments–that is, assigning enough staff to do the job, assigning competent staff, staff who are able to care for those particular patients, and allowing adequate time to do the job (see the discussion of the "four rights" of delegation, in Chapter 3).

When alerted to a problem, supervisors must respond appropriately. This is most important when allegations of sexual harassment are made. The supervisor must teach and inform staff appropriately, ascertain that staff complied generally with policies and procedures, verify that training was adequate, provide for student supervision, and report conditions that could injure patients, such as inadequate staffing levels--to senior management.

Captain of the ship and borrowed servant

In former times, some physician clinicians were liable for the acts of others under their supervision. This was the "**Captain of the Ship**" doctrine, and it was used to get to the physician clinician's pocket for negligence committed by others. It was considered a necessary legal fiction, in the days when hospitals were charitable institutions and were immune from *respondeat superior* liability for their employees.

The same was true of the "**borrowed servant**" doctrine. In this legal fiction the physician clinician was held to have "borrowed" the charitable hospital's employee and thus as putative employer was liable for her negligence under the theory of *respondeat superior*. Both of these theories have been less used, since hospitals now have lost charitable immunity status and are liable for their employees under *respondeat superior*.

Negligent staffing

In this variation of vicarious liability, the organization is responsible for damage to patients from unsafe staffing. It might be called direct corporate liability, but again the organization is responsible for a breach by its employee or agent. That individual failed to employ or assign adequate staff, and the legal theory that applies is either *respondeat superior* or agency law.

This responsibility is levied because the organization represents to patients that they will provide safe care in return for payment. Organizations take the money, and then must deliver care or face liability. If harm comes to the patient as a result of lack of staff, damages can be awarded. Lawsuits can succeed against organizations that have been repeatedly informed of lack of staff, whether so informed by employees or credentialing agencies (*Texas Health Enterprises*, 1999).

If clinicians and managers communicate their concerns about staffing properly, they as individuals should not be liable. Whether clinicians cease to work for such an organization is an ethical issue for them, and they may have a higher duty than the minimum ethic imposed by law. The law will hold the organization liable for inadequate staffing if the patient is injured and sues, and depending on the circumstances, punitive damages may be justified.

Neither individual clinicians nor supervisors are held responsible for poor staffing if the harm to the patient is not due to the clinician's own negligence or the supervisor's decision to assign inadequate staff.

The credentialing board of the clinician may, however, hold the clinician accountable for inappropriate delegation--see the discussion of unlicensed assistive personnel (UAPs) in Chapter 3.

The clinician and supervisor are liable for any malpractice they personally commit, regardless of staff available. It is not the patient's problem that clinicians have too many patients or unskilled assistance. It is not the patient's problem that the organization has too few clinicians or hires unskilled people.

Clinicians are responsible for meeting the objective standard of the practice of the reasonable prudent clinician. The standard is not subjective-it is not the standard of the "reasonable prudent clinician with too many patients" or the "reasonable prudent supervisor with too few skilled clinicians."

If there is a danger to patients, the clinician or administrator's duty is to communicate that fact to the level of management who can deal with the problem. Clinicians must tell administrators that staffing is inadequate-every time it happens, and in writing. The supervisor must do something with that information--investigate, assess, and if needed, either supply more staffing if that's within her authority, or inform the next level of management.

Survival of lawsuits

Torts for injury to property and person will "survive" the death of the plaintiff because they are for past harm. That means that the malpractice lawsuit can commence or continue after death. In most states, suits for defamation, invasion of privacy, and malicious prosecution alleging harm to the person's reputation generally do not survive because such suits can be pursued only by the person who was injured.

The ethical principle here is that the reputation died with the person, or at least the emotional feeling about his reputation did. State statutes specify which suits survive, so if you have a question about your state's law you should read its specifics. You can find the statutes in the local library, using the index under Survival, or on the Internet.

Immunities from lawsuit

Immunities from suit for family members, charities, and governments--to the extent they still exist--enforce the ethic that protecting the potential defendant is more important than holding the responsible party liable in specific situations.

Sovereign immunity

The clinician who works for the government may be protected from some lawsuits. In olden days, kings and queens could not be sued because the sovereign was thought to be ordained by God, Who could do no wrong. So neither the sovereign nor God was responsible for wrong. As a practical matter, enforcing a judgment against the sovereign was difficult, and **sovereign immunity** was good policy from the government's point of view.

That viewpoint continued as kingdoms evolved into non-monarchies, and sovereign immunity evolved into **governmental immunity**. In recent decades the policy of governmental immunity, too, has been abolished or limited in application, but governmental immunity still can have meaning for clinicians who work for organizations run by local, state, or federal governments.

In many states, clinicians who work for the state or local government have limited liability for malpractice. The organization's liability is limited, too. Some state employees may be covered by a liability insurance pool. You can get information from your organization's risk manager about a state liability insurance pool if one exists in your state.

Clinicians who work for the federal government--for instance, for the Department of Veteran's Affairs (VA)--have immunity from lawsuit for *negligence* they commit, but they can be sued for wrongs they do intentionally. Under the Federal Tort Claims Act, all federal organizations can be sued for negligence and for intentional torts, but their employees cannot. This protection from liability probably has some effect on clinicians who enjoy it.

Think about it.
Does immunity from lawsuit reduce responsibility?
Does immunity from suit reduce the practice and cost of defensive medicine?
Does the immunity improve practice, worsen it, or have any effect at all?

Governmental immunity may protect government workers and officials for what are called discretionary acts, but not for ministerial acts. This means acts of managers and officials that are labeled discretionary policy decisions, are immune. However, the ministerial acts of lower level employees who carry out automatic functions of the job (such as clinical practice) may not be immune from suit, and the organization can be sued for such acts.

Sometimes acts that can only be done by government, such as police work, are immune, but government functions that are proprietary are not. Proprietary functions are those that could be farmed out to private business, such as trash collection.

If you work for a government (taxpayer-paid) organization, check with the risk manager or management as to whether the organization and/or you are protected from suit by governmental immunity in your state law. You can find the statutes in the local library, using the index under Immunities, or on the Internet.

Joint and several liability

The legal concept of **joint and several liability** holds that all tortfeasors are held equally liable. (In old French, tortfeasors means wrong-makers.) Each defendant is liable for the whole of the patient's damages, if the other defendants can't or don't pay their share.

Under the theory of joint liability, three defendants who are jointly liable each owe one-third of the judgment. But assume that two of the codefendants are "judgment proof"--lawyer talk meaning a judgment against them can't be enforced, that the money can't be gotten from them. Defendant number three (you?) now is severally (or severably) liable. The defendants with no money available are "severed" and the one with money is liable alone, owing the plaintiff the whole bill.

If the third defendant doesn't have insurance (you?), enforcing the judgment may <u>not</u> take all her money, the oldest child, and 50 percent of all her earnings from now on.   Your lawyer may advise the plaintiff's lawyer that, unless there's agreement reached for less money, you might declare bankruptcy.

The plaintiff's lawyer may then offer to settle. That is done because depending on your financial status and state limits in bankruptcy, the plaintiff might not get much unless he makes a deal with you for what is affordable. The clinician who declares bankruptcy, depending on your state's law, might be able to keep a car, the equity in her house, personal things, pensions, some bank account, and be free of debt--including the entire malpractice judgment. Bankruptcy is a last resort, but it can be useful if the worst happens.   Non-physician clinicians do not lose a lot of money in lawsuits, and airline mechanics are not the main target when the plane crashes, for the same reason.

In states with comparative negligence, the jury may assess each defendant's degree of fault. If this is done, the clinician may not be jointly and severally liable. She is liable only for the percentage of the judgment that the jury assessed her individually.

Variations of joint and several liability laws have been enacted by creative state legislatures. For example, in Texas, clinicians were not jointly and severally liable if their percentage of liability is less than ten percent, and if that amount is less than the percentage of liability assigned to the patient. Such formulas are hard to remember, even for lawyers, and they are not worth worrying about until verdict time in a malpractice case.

Texas changed the rule in again in 1995, another instance where knowing the law is difficult if not impossible for clinicians, and the law should not be your standard of practice anyway. Good practice will be ethical and lawful and usually will avoid a lawsuit.

Contribution and indemnity

These concepts are related to joint and several liability and to insurance law. In the legal principle of **contribution**, one codefendant has a claim against another if he paid more than his correct share of the judgment (as could happen with joint and several liability, above).

This rule may be changed in states with comparative negligence. There, the loss may not be joint and several, but instead may be exactly the percentage determined by the jury for each defendant. Co-defendants who commit intentional torts, cannot force the other to contribute. The ethical value underlying that law is that people who intentionally do acts that injure others, don't deserve fairness between themselves.

If the patient recovers for clinician malpractice under a vicarious liability theory, the employer who has been held liable then can sue the employee. The employee would indemnify the employer for any loss suffered as a result of her malpractice. In contrast to contribution, the legal theory of **indemnity** shifts the entire loss, not just a share.

Employers rarely sue for indemnity because (1) clinicians don't have much money for the organization to recover, (2) the employer's own liability company likely also insures the clinician under the organization policy and would have to pay itself; and (3) such suits are not good public relations for recruiting clinicians and patients.

Good Samaritan laws

As part of a general fear of lawsuits, clinicians express concern about being a **Good Samaritan**, about stopping to aid at accidents. They say they fear the person aided will sue them. Such suits happen no more often than when clinicians are at work--indeed, they are far less common. But the fear remains.

The story behind the name.

The Good Samaritan story from the New Testament is about the poor fellow who had been mugged on the road to Jericho. Lying there bleeding, he was bypassed by a judge--symbol of a formal legal system that should help such people. He was also ignored by a priest--symbol of the formal ethic/ religious system that should help such people.

Finally, he was aided by a member of a rival gang, the Samaritans--

symbol of the private, informal, voluntary, instinctive, human response to do good for another person. It was not the Samaritan's job to help anyone, much less a member of another gang, but he did. Hence the term "Good Samaritan" (as opposed to the usual Samaritan), for one who stops to aid a stranger, enemy or not (Luke).

The story illustrates that one needn't be an ethicist or a lawyer or a paramedic to help out on the road.

Think about it.
Do you believe that clinicians have a moral, not legal, duty to act when faced with emergency situations?
Is fear of legal recourse an excuse for failing to provide first-aid care?
Might the fear of lawsuit voiced by some, be an excuse for doing something the ordinary Samaritan doesn't want to do anyway? (Castledine, 1993)

In response to the fear of suit, legislatures in many states have modified the case law on malpractice to insulate clinicians from the extremely rare lawsuits by the rescued. You can find you state's statute on Good Samaritan protection in the statute index or on the Internet.

In such statutes, the general rule is that clinicians will be held liable for gross (great) negligence. Clinicians will not be held liable if you are not negligent, of course, nor will you be held liable even if you are ordinarily negligent. In the usual practice situation, clinicians who are ordinarily negligent, who do not act as a reasonable and prudent clinician, lose the lawsuit. If they are similarly negligent at the side of the road, they won't lose the unlikely suit because of the Good Samaritan statute protection.

Instead of being held to a standard of ordinary negligence like the rest of the public, the clinician can be ordinarily negligent in a volunteer emergency situation. But you still may be liable if you are grossly negligent. As noted above, Good Samaritan statutes generally do not protect professionals who are paid for emergency or prehospital care from lawsuit, because it's their job to rescue.

Clinicians who stop at accidents rarely are sued, and even more rarely lose the suit. There's no legal duty to stop, except in a handful of states in which laws mandate anyone, including clinicians, to rescue persons in danger. These statutes run counter to centuries of legal tradition and are likely to be unenforceable.

If clinicians decide to stop, they can't rely on the Good Samaritan statute to immunize their acts completely from suit. They simply shouldn't do procedures they aren't skilled in, and should rely on good judgment and common sense as always. Good practice is lawful and right.

Think about it.
Are these Good Samaritan laws good policy?
Should clinicians be excused from responsibility for bad actions, even if they are doing it for good motive?
Is this question related to whether clinicians should be held liable at all, if they don't intend harm?
How about the car wreck, where you didn't intend to harm but ran a red light?

Tort reform

Much of the drive for changing the system of tort law is based on misconceptions, mistakes, myths, and untruths. Here are some truths: Lawsuits usually are won by defendants. Poor people are less likely to sue for malpractice than wealthier ones. Frivolous suits usually are dismissed. Median awards are much lower than the highest awards would indicate.

Some believe that malpractice lawsuits are not adequate to help the people who are injured by clinicians. It is estimated that only one in ten of the people injured by malpractice, sue. On the other hand, some people who sue are not even injured--estimated to be as high as one-third of them.

Statutes have been passed by state legislatures and Congress, seeking to reform the system of tort law that includes malpractice law.

These statutes variously:

1) limit amounts of damages,
2) cap non-economic damages available for pain and suffering,
3) limit availability and amount of punitive damages,
4) limit attorney fees,
5) penalize frivolous suits,
6) change methods of resolving conflict such as alternative dispute resolution, or
7) presume no breach of the standard of care, when practice guidelines are met.

The last reform idea in the list would limit liability for clinicians who use and adhere to guidelines. If clinicians use established guidelines–also called checklist, protocol, or critical pathway--the injured plaintiff then must prove that the clinician unreasonably deviated from the guidelines.

Alternative Dispute Resolution (ADR) has been tried as a substitute for malpractice suits with some success. ADR includes **mediation**, in which parties voluntarily try to settle their conflict with a helper. The outcome is not binding on the parties. In some states the malpractice statutes give the judge in a case the power to require the parties to try mediation before proceeding to trial (Berry, 2001).

Arbitration is another variation of ADR in which the parties agree to abide by a binding decision by judge-like decider. These tools of ADR also often are used in collective bargaining disputes.

Some of these varieties of tort reform were tried in the 1970s when malpractice insurance for physician clinicians became very expensive. In some systems the patient-plaintiff was required to submit the case to a panel of physician clinicians and others before going to court. Some reforms put a cap on damages, especially non-economic damages (pain and suffering). Many states have required various proofs of the legitimacy of a lawsuit for malpractice, before the court will allow the suit to be filed or go to trial (Grant, 1994).

Some of those legislative solutions were found contrary to the federal or state constitutions, being limits on the citizen's right of access to the courts. The Seventh Amendment to the US Constitution limits federal tort reforms in this way:

> **"In suits at common law where the value in controversy shall exceed twenty dollars, the right of trial by jury shall be preserved."**

State constitutions have such guarantees too. You can find the text of the your state constitution in the front or back of the set of state statutes at the library, or on the Internet.

Attorney fee reform

Hoping that limiting lawyer fees will decrease lawsuits, some have proposed reforms of tort law that limit lawyer contingency fees. Some lawyers charge 40 percent of the award for cases that go to trial, and 50 percent for cases that are appealed, because of the expense of prosecuting such cases. Some reformers have pushed for limiting the lawyer's maximum fee to 15 percent. But Rand Corporation studies found that restraints on lawyer fees don't reduce the number of suits filed (Danzon, 1993).

Oregon repealed its 33 percent cap on contingency fees, when that state found the cap didn't make any difference in the numbers of suits.

Studies have shown that number and size of awards are reduced by shorter statutes of limitation, and by ceilings on damages awarded for pain and suffering. Consumer advocates say the downside of such reforms is that poor patients then are less likely to get a remedy for injury.

Enterprise liability

One proposed reform of malpractice law would be to make the organization responsible instead of the clinician. This is called **enterprise liability**. This situation exists to a degree in the Veterans Affairs system, and under corporate negligence doctrines. Some believe that if the organization is liable, as in enterprise liability reform, the organization then would find errors and correct them. They believe errors are largely preventable.

Think about it.
Do you agree that most or even all errors are preventable?
Do you believe the organization can prevent them?

In enterprise liability reform, individuals sue the organization instead of the clinician. So the public's attitude toward different types of defendants, matters. Studies of attitude show that the public is more likely to believe the individual's version of a story than a defendant corporation, and they are likely to believe that a corporation being forced to pay $1 million in a legal dispute is just a slap on the hand. These attitudes might make it difficult to get juries that are willing to be fair to corporate defendants.

In reforming malpractice law, liability of the enterprise is substituted for the clinician's personal responsibility for his actions. The enterprise already is vicariously liable for the acts of its employees under the theory of *respondeat superior,* and also directly liable under the theories of negligent hiring, supervision, admission to staff, and others (Crane, 1993).

The difference: the professionals would be relieved from liability and all risk is put on the employer organization. The hope is that then clinicians would practice less defensive medicine, in which they are thought to waste money by ordering tests and treatments as defenses to potential lawsuits.

But some studies indicate that this "defensive medicine" factor represents only a small part of the cost of clinical practice, and that clinicians use the specter of lawsuits to justify the ordering of tests and procedures that they would order anyway. It's asserted that clinicians learned to practice the defensive way, and that the real cause of inflation in costs is the belief of clinician and patient alike that the care is free. That belief exists because the costs are paid for indirectly, with money from the taxpayers or premium-payers.

Existing enterprise liability

Because of market trends and court rulings, enterprise liability already is an informal reality. The liability will fall on whoever has the ultimate authority and accountability for the delivery of care. Because health maintenance organizations (HMOs) control more of the market and employ more clinicians than ever before, HMOs more often are sued.

Many of the physician clinicians in United States have affiliated with HMOs, some being actual employees. In these situations, the HMO is vicariously liable for the employee's act under the theory of *respondeat superior.*

If the clinician is affiliated with the HMO by independent contract, the contract may say that the HMO furnishes malpractice insurance or pays legal costs and damages. Non-physician clinicians usually are employees of the HMO, so the enterprise automatically is liable for their acts.

Dozens of state court decisions have found the insurance plan and provider liable for clinician acts, even if the clinician is not their employee nor their independent contractor (agent). Under the theory of ostensible agency, the HMO is responsible for negligence when patients believe its clinicians act as agents of the HMO.

The courts say that HMOs must meet standards of care. If the HMO were not held liable for breach of the standard of care, it would be able to cut costs by hiring cheaper clinicians--presumably less competent. California cases that held the insurer liable demonstrate that the insurer is the HMO, and vice versa.

In these cases, clinicians still are named as codefendants, a difference from a formal enterprise liability program. But the employer organization has more money and always will be sought as responsible. It is harder for such defendants to win even when they are not negligent (Medical plans, 1993).

Because it would increase HMO liability, a system of enterprise liability also would increase HMO supervision and intervention into clinician practice. That is one reason some clinicians oppose any enterprise liability plan. Although some clinicians might welcome any proposal that exculpates them from liability, some assert there remains an ethical problem.

Think about it.

Would relieving professionals from responsibility for their actions strike at the very heart of "professionalism?"

Must clinicians who would be autonomous, also must be responsible?

If clinicians want authority, must they also have the duty?

Would removing responsibility for their actions produce. harm?

Would relieving professionals from responsibility for their actions injure the assumption that the clinician is an adult professional who is responsible for her actions?

Has relieving professionals from responsibility for their actions done that for government-employed clinicians who are immune from suit?

Think about it.

Do we need tort reform? What are problems with ideas given?

"We must never make our professions immune to suit for damages we cause by our negligent act for two reasons. If we cause harm we must pay, and the fear of a suit serves as a deterrent to negligence and causes us to strive toward at least the standard of the reasonable clinician under the circumstances" (Cazalas, 1978)

Avoiding lawsuits

How to win friends, influence people, and reduce the risk of lawsuit in your practice:

Above, you saw the four requirements for the plaintiff/patient to win. Many more people file lawsuits than win, and defendants win most of the time. But lawsuits are costly even if you win. If it was your action that prompted the suit, whether or not you are legally liable you may lose your job. Observe the following algebraic formula, please, and save yourself a lawsuit or two.

Mad (ANGRY)

Most people who sue are mad. They can't win their lawsuit unless they meet the four criteria described above (duty, breach, causation and damages), but anyone can file suit. With good relationships, you can do something to prevent those people from going away mad. You can't make everybody happy, but you can be honest with your patients and exhibit compassion for them.

Most patients who sue are hurt. We can do everything in our power to prevent that hurt by good practice. Only one person in 10 who could sue for malpractice, does--so a lot of hurt patients don't sue. Likely they're not mad at their clinician.

The hurt patient, who for some reason also is mad, may sue. See the overlap of the circles below? Only patients who sue and who *also are injured* have even the potential to win a lawsuit against you.

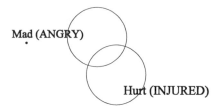

But even if patients have a bad outcome, they cannot win if you practiced as a reasonable prudent professional. Some patients would have a bad outcome no matter how good your practice.

The final, worst part of the equation is to add fault. If the patient is mad he might sue. If he is hurt in addition he may sue, might win. What if, in addition, you have done a dumb act--that is, failed to practice as a reasonable prudent professional?

Then that <u>mad</u> patient, <u>hurt</u> by a <u>dumb</u> act is in the area in the center, where all three circles overlap. All that added together is that likely he will sue, and now he can win. Solution? Practice as a reasonable prudent professional.

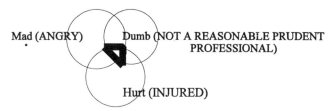

Venn diagram: mad patient, hurt patient, dumb act by professional

Now for the good news:

Look at the areas on this diagram that do not overlap another circle. See from the circle labeled "dumb" that not all negligent acts result in injury, or make patients mad. You know that truth from your observation of other clinicians. We are only human and we make mistakes. Fortunately, most do not hurt the patient (or if they do, he's not mad enough to sue us).

From the circle marked "mad" you see that not all mad patients are hurt. Nor are they mad because of negligent acts--malpractice. Some other dumb act such as rudeness may have done it. Either way, the patient can't win even if he sues.

From the circle marked "hurt" you see that not all injured patients are mad, nor did their injury come from negligent acts. Likely the patient won't sue if he's not mad, and even if he does he can't win, if his hurt wasn't caused by a dumb act.

Bottom line–you can reduce the risk of lawsuits. Minimize the number of mad patients in your practice with compassion. Avoid hurting your patients at all costs. Don't do dumb things in your practice by being competent.

Think about it.
Could we avoid a lot of malpractice suits with "treat people the way you'd want to be treated"?

Final bit of motherly advice from one who has advised many clinicians:

> No matter how hard you try, sometime during your career, you actually will do a dumb act. That act may cause harm to a patient who is mad (or it will make her mad) resulting in a lawsuit and judgment against you. Get over this possibility, NOW.
>
> Anticipate the prospect, determine not to let it ruin your career and your life, and prepare psychologically and financially.
>
> If you have the resources that will attract lawsuit, buy adequate insurance and arrange your finances with trusts for retirement, children's education, and offshore trusts, with a good money advisor and attorney.
>
> Most of all, vow <u>now</u> not to allow this possible side effect of your life of good work, ruin your life of good work.

Hot button areas for lawsuit

The most common allegations of negligence cited in malpractice suits overall are:

- **medication errors,**
- **poor history or assessment,**

- poor physical exam,
- failure to consult a specialist or physician clinician when appropriate,
- faulty diagnosis,
- anesthesia problems,
- failure to provide any care,
- complications of cesarean sections, and
- negligence in manual delivery of infants.

Failure to monitor is the number one reason for report to the National Practitioner Data Bank (Faherty, 1998). In some way, all of the above are failures to maintain a minimum standard of practice. All demonstrate the thesis: Good practice is lawful and right.

From another source, the commonest clinician malpractice suits were for :
- medication and treatment errors,
- lack of observation and timely report on the patient,
- use of defective technology or equipment,
- infections caused or worsened by poor care,
- poor communication of important information,
- failure to intervene to protect the patient from poor care.

All these are legal problems that can be avoided by adhering to minimum ethics and practicing just average clinical practice.

Regarding medication errors, note that the JCAHO has identified five "high-alert medications" with the greatest risk of causing injury, specifically insulin, opiates and narcotics, injectable potassium chloride concentrate, intravenous anticoagulants (heparin), and sodium chloride solutions above 0.9 percent. Special care is indicated with those medications, using the JCAHO report standards (JCAHO, 1999).

The JCAHO has mandated that accredited organizations must report "**sentinel events.**" These are occurrences that signal problems with safety or quality of care such as surgery done on the wrong body part. The formal definition is:

"an unexpected occurrence involving death or serious physical or psychological injury or risk thereof."

Some risk management or quality improvement departments examine such sentinel events by using what is called "root cause analysis" to find the root (not the proximate) cause of the problem.

One technique for doing that is to ask "why" up to five times

(Williams, 2001).

For example:

✓ The nurse gave KCl, IV push and killed the patient. **Why?**
✓ Because the KCl label looks like that of another drug. **Why?**
✓ Because the pharmacy company is unaware of the problem **Why?**
✓ Because there is no policy to inform them of problems of this kind. **Why?**

Think about it.

What might help avoid the problem?
Can you can think of some other answers to the "Why" questions?

As for the infections caused or worsened by poor care, bacteria found under the long fingernails of two nurses in a neonatal ICU was the source of infection contributing to the deaths of 16 babies. You shouldn't need to read it again--you know that short fingernails and clean hands are cheap and effective to prevent physical injury to your patient's health, and to prevent lawsuit injury to your economic health.

Witnessing in court

Advice on testifying as a defendant or witness:

✓ Talk to your lawyer about what is likely to be asked of you. The other attorney will ask "Have you talked to your lawyer about your testimony?" Your answer is "Of course."
✓ Practice Q&A with your lawyer.
✓ Tell the truth, the whole truth, nothing but the truth. You'll be sorry if you don't, regardless of what you've seen elsewhere.
✓ Read all statements that you are asked to sign and make sure they are accurate.
✓ Understand the questions that you are asked--don't hesitate to say "I don't understand."
✓ Think before answering--say "I don't' know" if you don't.
✓ Don't accept the other lawyer's statement as fact. She'll ask, "When your colleague left the patient, you'd agree that was malpractice?" Your answer "But I don't know that she did that."
✓ Don't argue--it makes the jury think you're argumentative.
✓ Don't volunteer anything. Tell the whole truth in answer to the question, but don't add anything even if you believe it will help your side. It may *not*.
✓ Look at the judge and jury when you sit down and when you answer questions.

✓ Be courteous, always--doesn't cost a dime.
✓ Be cooperative, same cost as above.
✓ Take your time, this may be your only experience at this.
✓ Correct mistakes if you recognize them--the jury will respect you for that.
✓ Don't guess. This is not an exam.
✓ Don't assume, as in accepting the other lawyer's statement is true.
✓ Don't chew gum or candy. Please. There are old uncool people on juries who will lose respect for you.
✓ Don't smoke during a deposition, even if they say your can. The other lawyer will respect your self-control, even if she smokes. Especially if she smokes.
✓ Do dress neatly and conservatively, in a blue suit (Fitzgerald, 1992). There's some research evidence for this!

Documentation

Documentation is discussed in this Chapter 2, Do Good because it often is the issue in malpractice lawsuits, and often "lawsuit" is the reason given for documenting. Good documentation is part of the standard of care as evidence and part of good practice. The plethora of books and articles explaining documentation and the need for it, show the concern of clinicians about the subject. Documentation is more important than a way to deal with lawsuits, however.

Reasons to document:
(1) Documentation is required by law–in state licensure statutes and in case law malpractice standards (Blackwell, 1993).
(2) Documentation is necessary for reimbursement and accreditation.
(3) Documentation is needed for the continuity of care of the patient.

Documentation is a part of avoiding lawsuits, because adhering to the standard of care means documenting appropriately. Good documentation is a part of good care.

The standard for documentation is that your charting or documentation should be an

<u>**accurate and complete record of the patient's condition and care.**</u>

The primary reason to document about the patient is number 3 above--to make a record that you or a subsequent clinician can refer to at the next encounter with the patient in hospital or office. Documentation insures continuity of care. It enables the clinician to compare the patient's condition from encounter to encounter. This is an essential part of diagnosing the patient's illness and of evaluating the outcome of treatment.

Other reasons to document have gotten more attention, especially the use of documentation as evidence at a trial. Evidence that is written, aids credibility. For example, a witness who testifies in 2001, "I did instruct the patient about the procedure," who also documented the instruction back in 1997, is more likely to be believed.

The jury assumes that the testifying clinician is tempted to remember the most favorable version of events--it's human nature. If the clinician's version is documented, too, the jury will assume that the clinician had no reason to lie in the record, because the record note was made prior to the lawsuit, perhaps even prior to the incident/accident.

The common saying, "not documented, not done," is not accurate in a legal sense. Clinicians can testify as to what was done (Hall, 1994). But lack of documentation may create a presumption that the care was not done. For example, a blank flow sheet in an outpatient's chart, or a shift without any notations about the patient's condition, looks as though the patient got no assessment or care.

The presumption can be overcome, but overcoming it will require testimony. The clinician who does not document appropriately must be able to remember and to testify to what she did this morning--even five years from now.

Worse for the clinician who documents poorly is that some cases draw the inference that poor record keeping itself is an indicator of poor care. Some experts for the patient-plaintiff have so testified. Whether it's true or not, that's the expert testimony, and that's the inference. The reasoning: if notes are sloppy, probably so is the care. Expert witnesses for the patient-plaintiff may use poorly kept notes as support for a conclusion that the patient is poorly monitored by staff (*Maslonka*, 1980).

Example:

No observation was charted for seven hours, of the toes of a patient whose leg was cast. The first note after seven hours was that the toes were noted to be "dusky and cold." This allowed a jury to conclude that failure to document indicated failure to observe; that breach of the standard of care led to liability for amputation (*Collins*, 1974).

Example:

Vital signs were ordered hourly on a postoperative patient but they were not recorded hourly. Instead, they were recorded every six hours. The patient's temperature rose in one period from 101.4 to 105.2 with resulting brain damage. The failure of the record resulted in a judgment that reasonable post-op care was not given (*Robert*, 1978).

Another legal reason for good documentation: the Board that credentials you requires adequate documentation of your practice, as noted above. Failure to document might result in loss of lawsuit (money). Worse, it might result in loss of your license (work, money, career, prestige, and so on).

Another reason to document is the important economic reason--to prove to a third party payer (insurance company or government) that the procedure that was charged for, actually was done. Government auditors have also heard the mantra "not documented, not done," and they have modified it to read "not documented, not paid."

Documentation need not be long and wordy. Short, simple words and sentences are best. The patient's name, the date, and the time must be on every document. Files get mixed with others and lost. The outcome of a lawsuit--or more important, the patient's life--may hinge on finding that information fast.

Most important: Do not, ever, falsify a record. Of course you can correct errors with a line through and "error" written above. Using the word "error" is not an admission of malpractice. It is merely using the correct word for what has been done--an error in writing, not an error in care. Make sure you can still see what's written underneath, to avert suspicion that you've covered up something.

But if you actually falsify the record--for example, destroy one record and substitute a different one--you run the risk of charges of fraud in addition to liability for whatever you tried to cover up.

Different kinds of documentation, for example, computerized, voice-activated, negative-only, flow sheet, and so on, all will be accepted as lawful if they meet the standard:

an accurate and complete record of the patient's condition and care.

Incident Reports

Incident reports are made to help analyze problems and solve them, so that errors are not repeated. Incident reports may or may not be discoverable in a lawsuit, depending on your state's law at any given time. A good guide for documentation is to assume that anything you write will someday be read on the evening news. It'll keep you honest and accurate and conservative in your statements.

Keep notes and disposable work sheets made during your practice, recording your own notes about patient conditions and assignments, as an aid to your memory or even evidence of an incident if needed in a future lawsuit or licensure action. Date and sign the notes and keep them in a separate chronological file–someday you may be glad you did.

Documentation do's and don'ts

Lists of "do's and don'ts" of documenting all are based on the standard for documentation: **an accurate and complete record of the patient's condition and care.**

Do document:
✓ Legibly-"legibly" means so that other people can read it. The patient-plaintiff's expert who examines the record and can't read your handwriting, may advise filing a lawsuit because she can't tell whether you were negligent or not.

(A Texas court held a cardiologist and a pharmacist liable because the physician's handwriting was hard for the pharmacist to read, resulting in a medication error. The cardiologist wrote Isordil 20 mg q6h for angina. The pharmacist filled the prescription with Plendil, same dosage and instruction, but Plendil's maximum dosage is 10 mg qd).

✓ In ink--black used to be required but now it's not so important. Check your organization's policy. Not in pencil, because...? Right, because the writing in pencil can be changed. You should go to law school. Naah.
✓ The date on every page and time with every new entry.
✓ In every blank. Draw a line in those not used.
✓ Corrections to errors with a single line, signing your initials and date and time.
✓ With signature after all entries, lining through empty spaces.
✓ Using standard abbreviations.
✓ Without defaming (writing an untrue fact that would damage the reputation of) the patient or other clinicians.
✓ Efforts to protect the patient.
✓ Patient responses to your practice.
✓ The patient's symptoms in his own words, with your observations.
✓ What has been done-not what didn't get done.
✓ Late entries, as needed, but dated and timed at the time actually written.

Document and keep your own personal notes. If the information is not pertinent to the patient's condition or care, do NOT write it in the patient's record. For example, put in your own notes: "The patient's brother visited, hair uncombed, unshaven, clothes torn and dirty. Seemed agitated, said to me "You're trying to kill my sister.""

Write and keep your own narrative of any worrisome event such as the one above, signing and dating it. The legal terms for such writings are Present Recollection Refreshed, or Prior Recollection Recorded. Keep these notes in your own files at home, to be used in court later if needed.

Documentation Don'ts...
Don't:
✓ Retaliate in the chart.
✓ Destroy and rewrite, or erase, white out, or write a late entry dating it as though it were made earlier.
✓ Add to a printed document such as a consent form, unless the patient initials next to the addition.
✓ Add anything after the patient signs. If needed, write a new document and get another signature.

If you need more ethics theory than Dountoothers

(If you want to read more about or by the authors mentioned in this section, you may be able to find books or articles by them in your library, or in the references listed in Chapter 1.)

Professional ethics

The idea of **profession** is a concept, a construct, with definition and meaning often subject to individual interpretation. The traditional professions of law, medicine, clergy, and military, first were formalized in England. These honorable occupations were needed for the younger sons because under the system of primogeniture, the oldest son inherited the farm.

There are said to be three qualities exhibited by a profession:
1) organization of the clinicians of the occupation,
2) learning by the clinicians of the occupation, and
3) a spirit of public service, altruism, on the part of the clinicians of the occupation--as individuals and as a group (Pound, 1953). In that interpretation, earning a livelihood is of lower priority.

Think about it.

Might it be that economics--earning enough to survive--underlies all of the professional's ideals?

Is the basic self-interest of all people (including professionals) the provision of enough necessities of life to survive?

People who work in occupations that don't fit the traditional or sociologist definitions, seek to mold their occupations to those definitions. Being a member of a profession is valued. People labeled as professional are seen as more educated, thoughtful, wise, wealthy, trustworthy, or more powerful than the non-professional person. In the history of clinical practice, the early professional role model was medicine.

Think about it.

Ask yourself which came first, the idea of profession or the attributes? Did certain occupations first gain higher status, then its members become defined as "professional"?

Professionals are organized

All occupational groups that seek professional status, organize themselves into formal associations. To contact your profession's state association, call the information operator in your state's capital or largest city and ask for the state association office for your profession. Or use the Internet.

If you haven't joined your occupation's association, you likely can learn about it online. Most professional associations have Websites. If you are a clinician whose occupation is not yet formally organized, its first step toward professionalism will be to form such an association.

The American Medical Association (AMA) and American Nurses Association (ANA) are two of the oldest organizations of clinicians in the U.S. Many other specialty organizations represent smaller numbers of clinicians of those professions as well. The associations for professional clinicians write codes of professional behavior for the members of the profession.

Codes of Ethics of the AMA and the ANA are examples of such codes. Those codes have sections suggesting that, to be ethical, the clinician must work for improvements in the profession and in the community. One way to do that is to work through the association(s) of clinicians. The codes for nurses and physicians can be found on their Websites, and codes for other professions can be found in their literature or from the professional organizations on the Internet.

Codes of ethics

One obvious difference between the ethic of the professional and the ethic of the nonprofessional is that professions usually have a written ethical code of behavior. The professional obligations are formalized, somewhat agreed upon, written down, and taught. This does not imply that nonprofessionals have a lower standard of behavior, but they may not have standardized, formalized, or written **codes of ethics**. The code of behavior or code of ethics is a series of statements about what behavior or ideals are expected of a person in that occupation.

Some writers distinguish between codes of ethics that they consider to be ideals, and **codes of conduct**, that they consider to be behavior. But the ideals of people can be observed only from what they do, their conduct. Behavior is evidence of what the clinician believes. The two concepts really are the same. If the individual behaves badly, whatever she said was her ideal obviously didn't help.

Codes of ethics or conduct of different occupations differ in detail, but they have some values in common. They echo the values that are the titles of the chapters of this book--the mothers of the law. The codes stress Do Good and Freedom for the patient. The codes discuss Be True (Fidelity) to their occupations, and to the improvement of their profession.

Through promises to maintain competence, codes promote the value of Do Good and Don't Harm the patient. Codes say the clinician should promise to Keep Secrets of the patient and to Be True and Be Fair to the patient. Codes may hint at Do Good in the form of social justice. Underlying all, as always, is the value of the Life of the patient.

Who writes codes of ethics?

The professional association of the particular occupation writes its code of ethics. It might be that the most politically active people in the occupation--not necessarily the most ethical--write the code. Even if "experts" in ethics help write the code, it could not state what every member of the group thinks is ethical behavior.

The code is necessarily a compromise between what most of the group thinks are the most important ethical attitudes of members (code of ethics), or behaviors of members (code of conduct).

If a code mandated behavior, it would then be written law and clinicians would be forced to follow it. Instead the code is a guide, some suggestions for action in situations that clinicians often encounter.

As guides for behavior, medical oaths such as the oath of Hippocrates are similar in some ways to codes of ethics. An oath is a personal promise by an individual to behave in a certain way, while a code is a group promise or ideal way to behave.

Writers of ethics textbooks have not always advocated written codes of ethics for clinicians. One said:

> *A written code usually includes concessions to dogmatic, well organized, highly vocal minorities, and the more liberal* [original use of the word] *members of the profession ought to keep clear of such commitments. Once a code is adopted, it is very difficult to get it changed, because of inertia if nothing else.* [material in brackets added] (Densford, 1946; p. 181).

Densford did, however, suggest some "good rules" for clinicians to follow.

Think about it.
Are suggestions of some "good rules" for clinicians to follow, close to a code of ethics (or behavior)?

As noted above, clinician codes evolve, as evidenced in the 2000 year old Hippocratic Oath. The codes change as the relationship of clinicians to society changes, and as the attitudes of society change. The ANA revises its Code of Ethics--in the year 2001, they were on the 11th draft (see the latest draft or new code at www.nursingworld.org).

Think about it.
What if the society in general endorses euthanasia and genocide, as did the leaders and clinicians of Germany in the 1930s and 40s? Should the profession's code change to echo that endorsement?

You can get a copy of your profession's code from your professional association--most have Websites on the Internet.

Think about it.
Do you agree that there is any ethical basis of professional codes of ethics?
If you do not agree that the values suggested are the bases, what do you believe codes of ethics are based upon?

Professionals are educated

Despite the requirement for a profession that its members be educated, even physician clinicians didn't begin to have a "long" education until about the start of the twentieth century. Changes in medical education had commenced even before a report was issued then, stating that there were a lot of quacks calling themselves professionals. Medicine gradually lengthened its education and set standards for its clinicians.

This lengthening and standardization of education still is seen as the route to professionalism for most clinical occupations. Independent or solo clinician job structures are preferred because they provide independence from, hopefully leading to equality with, the physician clinician--although increasing numbers of physician clinicians work as employees and not as entrepreneurs.

Non-physician clinicians seek to work in teams, making them to some degree independent of, equal to, and as professional as, the physician. Team care also may improve the care of their patients. Workers in clinical practice seek autonomy in their practice, just as the physician has, or is thought to have, or had. Physician clinicians too have lost freedom, through managed care, quality review, payment review, peer review committees, and state medical boards--not to mention the ultimate review, malpractice suits.

Such review of practice within a profession is not a new idea, however. In the late 1300s the medical guild (union) of Florence in Italy required that "bad cases" be reviewed by a committee of the guild. This was an extension of the control of the law to voluntary peer review, much like professional review committees today function to control practice without the formality of law.

Occupations that want to become professional, seek to increase the thinking part of the jobs and to decrease the portion of time spent doing technical things. However, the technical procedures done by physician clinicians have been more highly valued than thinking activity, and paid more under Medicare and insurance reimbursement.

Practice in caring for patients is a continuum from unpaid, amateur care done by family volunteers, to people who are paid to care-- professionals. The word *amateur* originally meant one who did something for love, not for money.

Clinicians are taught to do more complex procedures for patients, based on some knowledge of science. Still further along the continuum are the artificial distinctions of clinical practice aide to technician to professional clinician. All are engaged in some form of care.

CARE CONTINUUM--by complexity and scientific knowledge required, not by intensity or quality or importance of care.

Care by family	Care by generalists	Care by specialists
☜LESS COMPLEX		MORE COMPLEXITY☞

Professionals are altruistic

Most sociologists mention as one of the most important characteristics of a profession, that the professional puts the patient or client first before her own self-interest. That may be a poor description of the way it works. The clinician's interest in being a good clinician or professional actually may be a form of self-interest. That interest may precede other self-interests such as eating, going home early, or making a lot of money.

Being defined as "professional" has not kept lawyers and physicians from making a lot of money. On the other hand, neither will being described as a "profession," make the occupation into one that earns a lot of money. Teachers, clergy, military people, all are called professionals, but they do not make a lot of money.

More education does not cause an occupation to make a lot of money--the market does that. The market tells us, based on what is paid to clinicians, how much people value the occupation. You don't have to agree that they're right--but that's the reality.

If it weren't, different pay for different jobs would not exist, in the fairly unrestricted market for clinicians that exists in the United States. Through the market, people pay more money for professional baseball and basketball players than they pay for physicians. They don't pay the players for their education.

Professional employee conflicts

Clinicians experience conflict when they are employed and professionals. As managed care organizations limit care to decrease costs, the ethical and sometimes legal conflicts for clinician employees increase. Whether you are technically an employee or an independent contractor--and why that matters--is discussed further in Chapter 6. In this section on professional ethical conflicts, an "employee" can mean an independent contractor or a person in a partnership or a corporation. Only the entrepreneur is apparently independent.

Even among self-employed people, the relationship of the clinician to the payer looks increasingly like the traditional employee-employer relationship. The patient seldom pays the clinician directly--the payer usually is the government or insurer or HMO.

Earlier in clinical practice the clinician saw herself, and was seen, as an employee, a contractor, or a servant---of the patient. With payment of the bill by either private or government insurers, the clinician is not directly responsible to the patient, but to the sometimes anonymous third-party payer (3PP). In effect, the unseen 3PP directs much of the work.

The patient- 3PP- clinician relationship

Without third party payment:

Patient ☞$ to
Clinician ☞Care to Patient

With third-party payment (3PP) from insurance or government):

Patient ☞$ to
THE MIDDLE MAN--3PP ☞$ to
Clinician ☞Care to Patient

In any work setting, there is some conflict between the interests of the employer and those of the employee. The usual differences are pay for work, hours of work, and conditions of work. Different from other employees, clinicians and their employers may be in conflict about professional ethics and standards of practice.

The clinician's potential conflict with the employer about ethical standards is not unique to clinical practice. Other professionals such as engineers have a professional standard, perhaps different from their employer's, to build good and safe buildings and cars. Lawyers who work as employees have a standard of professional responsibility, not just to their employer, but also to their clients. But now in clinical practice, not only the employer but also the other "boss," the 3PP, has something to say about what the clinician does, to whom, and how.

The professional employee and organization policy

Employers of clinicians have policies or standards on a number of ethical and legal issues. For example, the employer probably has policies on numbers of patients each clinician will care for, confidentiality of patient information, living wills and other advance directives; policies on no-code orders; policies on reporting child abuse, elder abuse, and all other reportable conditions such as gunshot wounds; policies to follow in organ donation; required pre-op pregnancy checks, ICU selection, determination of death, code blue policies; and more, no doubt.

Any of these policies may have ethical and legal implications for the professional clinician who tries to follow the policy. Some of the policies probably were made with the help of the ethics committee of the organization, and some with the help of the legal counsel. Discussion of their specifics is impossible here, but you should be aware of them and know their content generally.

After reading this book you should be able to analyze the values expressed in the policy--whether it enforces the value(s) do good, don't harm, be free, and so on, or a combination of values. In addition, you should be able to identify the interests of the people likely to be affected by a policy in a given situation.

Employer policies are not law, but they can be used as standards of practice in lawsuits or credentialing actions, to measure your practice performance. It is possible that the policies are not even ethical by the your personal or professional standards.

Think about it.
What if the policy requires resuscitating newborns no matter what their birth weight, and you believe that policy is not ethical?
What if the policy requires not resuscitating babies under a certain birth weight, and you believe that policy is not ethical?

In some instances, you may face a decision of whether to follow policy and keep your job--or, as a professional and human being, to adhere to what you see as the right, ethical, behavior. You may keep the job and work to change the policies that you see as being unethical according to your personal and professional standards.

Think about it.
What would you do about a policy that prescribes CPR for all patients found unresponsive, regardless of the patient's prior condition and wishes, or regardless of the clinician's professional judgment about whether CPR can succeed?

Clinicians will experience professional conflict when they find unsafe practices where they work. These can include short staffing, long hours, working without training in the specialty required, use of unprepared help, patients' rights violations, and even poor physical plant, maintenance, and equipment (Yocke, 1992).

You may work with your peers to set up committees for broad problem areas, using the existing workplace and professional grievance systems. Or you may work with the appropriate credentialing board (hospital or clinician credentialing board) to solve the problem (Rushton, 1993).

Professionals: not necessarily more ethical

Clinicians have an ethical interest and a legal mandate to do good for their patients. Other workers may not have that ethical and legal duty. Clinicians, unlike other workers, are expected to prioritize their own interest in doing good, above some other of their interests. That prioritizing of professional interests does good for their patients. The professional who puts the patient first is valuable to the society. Professionals can be relied on to act in their own professional interest, and that usually coincides with the patient's interest.

But people classed as professionals do not necessarily have a generally higher ethical or moral sense than other people. Other occupations also have self-interests that are beyond immediate gratification. The factory worker too has some concern for, and obligation to, her fellow human to make products that are as safe as possible. Some groups of auto mechanics have a written code of ethics.

The ethical and legal obligation not to harm other people pre-existed the concept of the professions. All humans are expected to feel some obligation or duty toward other people, at least enough not to harm them.

The professional assumption is that when the interest of the client/ patient/ customer conflicts with another self-interest of the professional, the professional will put the other self-interest second. The professional is putting a professional work interest first. The professional still acts out of self-interest, and it benefits the patient, too.

PROFESSIONAL'S SELF-INTEREST IN DOING GOOD

=

PATIENT'S INTEREST

Both professional and patient benefit. The patient's need for care is met. The professional's need to be a good clinician or help others-- whatever the professional's self-interest in doing the job–is met.

Professionals prioritize their own interests so that their work interest in doing a good job comes first most of the time. Usually the work interest in doing good comes first more of the time for professionals, than for nonprofessionals. That is what is implied by "professional." Any other implication, that professionals are better or kinder or more ethical than others, is difficult to prove.

This ethical standard is more pronounced in clinical practice. The people the clinician serves could be injured or die as a result of the clinician's act, or failure to act. But mechanics, too, have such responsibility. I hope the mechanic is a "professional" and puts my safety, and his interest in doing a good brake job, ahead of another interest such as leaving work early.

Utilitarianism

The ethical theories of utilitarianism, teleology, consequentialism, and axiological theories all are related to the value of this chapter-- beneficence. These theories look to what is the greatest good or benefit--the value is beneficence--to groups of people.

Caveat: (Latin for "beware"):

The theory of utilitarianism says that the right action is the one that produces the greatest good (utility) for the greatest number. But before taking "utilitarianism" too seriously as an ethical theory, remember that some authorities do not believe that it is an ethical theory at all. At most, they say utilitarianism is a way to do "cost-benefit" analysis after a real ethical theory has been used to determine what is the "good" desired.

The only theory of morality described as axiological, teleological, or consequential, is utilitarianism. (More about teleological and consequential, later). If utilitarianism cannot be a theory of morality, then there is no morality that is "teleological" or "axiological" or "consequential." Critics say that utilitarianism is not a system of morality, because at best utilitarians merely apply some other moral theory, one that does state what is good. For example, what is "good" in society might be justice, or material goods, or happiness.

Utilitarians must assume that what is good, already is known and agreed upon. Utilitarians can provide only some technique to distribute that known good(s), to the greatest number of people. This technique of distribution usually is some form of socialism. The prior knowledge of what is good that utilitarians use, must come from some deontological theory of morality. Otherwise, immediate disagreement about what is "good" would result, when utilitarians start to redistribute the "good(s)."

End *caveat*.

Axiological theories are contrasted to **deontological** theories of ethics. A deontological system of ethics is exemplified by duties (in Greek, *deon* means duty) and by rules to follow, such as Christianity's "do unto others as you'd have them do unto you" or Kant's "do only those things that you would have everyone do."

Think about it.

Is clinical practice somewhat a deontological system, with rules to follow about assessing, planning, implementing?

Or is it more axiological?

In axiological ethics, what is "right" is described in terms of what is valued. What is "right" is not what a duty or rule says--as a deontological ethic would. Remember from Chapter 1 that people who look at the value of an act are looking at whether it is good or bad, not whether it is right or wrong. In axiological ethics, evaluation of the situation is necessary to determine if it is good (or pleasurable, or whatever is defined as good). Note that the root of the word evaluation is value. If it is found to be good, then it is considered to be right.

Think about it.

In clinical practice, do we evaluate each situation to see what is right?

In **axiological** ethics, what is right is determined by the value of the consequences. Under utilitarianism, an action is morally right only if it contributes some good more than it produces "non-good" or harm. It's sort of a cost-benefit analysis. It's called **utilitarianism** because all actions are judged by the principle of its utility (usefulness) in producing the desired effect.

When applied to societies, the principle is known as the "greatest good for the greatest number." It underlies much thinking and action in current U.S. society and in others.

Think about it.

Is utilitarianism the underlying philosophy of collectivist governments-- of socialism, of communism, of fascism?

(The fascists in Germany were National Socialists--their shortened German name was "Nazis.")

The problem when utilitarianism is applied to a profession such as clinical practice: what is "good"? Most utilitarians considered pleasure as the highest good. This concept also is known as **hedonism.** J.S. Mill and Jeremy Bentham (English, 1748-1832) were utilitarians. Mill acknowledged that certain pleasures are better than others. For example, he thought it better to be an unhappy Aristotle than a happy pig. But Kant thought a "good will" was the highest good, and W.D. Ross thinks it is knowledge.

Think about it.
Would your professors agree with Ross?
Do you?

What is determined to be the highest good, matters. The lawmaker who is a utilitarian might pass laws that maximize virtue or knowledge as the greatest good. Your world would look much different if she thought pleasure or material goods were the greatest good, and passed laws to maximize those "goods."

Think about it.
What would the clinician utilitarian see as the highest good? Her own pleasure?
The patient's health? The patient's life? The patient's pleasure? The patient's autonomy?

Another problem with utilitarianism is related to value. Remember that utilitarians look to the value of the consequences of an action to determine whether it is right. (You remember that this use of the word "value" to decide what is right, means something like "worth," not the way we use it for example, in Value: Do Good, as the right thing to do.)
Value can be **intrinsic**--inherent qualities, inside themselves. Hedonists believe the only intrinsic value of a thing is the pleasure it gives. Or the value of things can be **extrinsic**--relational qualities, valuable for what they do for us. Hedonists believe all extrinsic values are valuable only to the extent they promote pleasure. For example, a car has intrinsic qualities in that it is red, or big, or shiny; but its extrinsic value to us is that we can travel in it, have pleasure in it, feel good about ourselves driving it.
Other problems that arise with utilitarianism:
The morality of some acts, such as telling truth or keeping promises, does not seem to have immediate utility for the individual. That is, the acts may not produce immediate good for the truth-teller, yet they still are the moral thing to do--even for utilitarians. Some

rights and freedoms such as right to life and freedom of speech may be violated by utilitarianism.

For example, it is not of great utility for the whole society to have a baby with anomalies born and saved, but it's important to the baby. To save the life of a patient who is poor or old, who will not pay taxes or otherwise contribute to society, is not useful to the larger society. To tax some people is useful for the whole society, but violates the freedom of the taxpayer who is forced to pay the tax, or go to jail.

Think about it.
If it's good for the majority, should all smoking be banned? All drinking? All sex?

Another example: The concept of justice is not always of utility to the whole society. It is not particularly useful to the whole group, to give a person accused of murder many avenues of appeal. It is of benefit to the accused. The great utilitarian J.S. Mill answers this criticism of utilitarianism. He believes rights and justice for individuals should be defended, because in some way those rights and justice promote the "general utility."

It is argued that utilitarianism would require individuals to calculate, for each action, whether it would be better for the whole. Mill answered that criticism, too. No, he said, individuals need only answer
1) whether their act is better for themselves as individuals, and
2) whether the act is not violating the rights of other people--the others'
 "legitimate and authorized expectations."

Think about it.
If you are a clinician utilitarian deciding whether to agree to work overtime, how do you answer questions 1) and 2) above for yourself, your patients, your employer?

It's argued that utilitarianism ignores the value of keeping rules such as"don't lie, don't steal." That argument can be met by assigning some *value* to keeping the rule. (Remember, utilitarianism measures the *value* of the consequences of an act to determine its rightness.) Then the ultimate value of the consequences also includes some weight or value for keeping moral rules.

Think about it.
Does that change utilitarianism into a deontological, rule-based ethic?

Ethical theorists identify two kinds of utilitarianism. **Act** utilitarianism is defined strictly by the first description above: maximize goodness. No evaluation of rights, or rules, is done. The other kind of utilitarianism, **rule** utilitarianism, says that following good rules has some value to add to the equation of what is the greatest good. In doing this, the rule utilitarian sounds more like a deontologist. She would answer that she is still a utilitarian, because she is considering the consequences of following the rule. If she looks at the long-term consequences of following some moral standard, she's still a utilitarian, but a rule utilitarian.

Consequentialism

The doctrine of consequentialism holds that the rightness of an act is determined by its consequences or outcomes.

Think about it.
Is it right to lie to the patient if the consequences, the outcome, is good for him?

In contrast, nonconsequentialists generally argue that rightness is not determined by consequences. They believe that the rightness of an act can be separated from its consequences.

Think about it.
Is it always wrong to lie to the patient, even if the consequence, the outcome of lying, is better for him?

There are stronger and weaker forms of consequentialism. In the weaker form of consequentialism, consequences are relevant to rightness of an act but they are not by themselves decisive of the right act to take. That is, evaluation of consequences is necessary but not sufficient to make the decision about what is right.

This kind of consequentialist will look at outcomes, but may not make her decision based only on that. For example, the outcome of aborting her child may be more freedom, but that freedom may not determine her action.

In the stronger form of consequentialism, the consequences of the act determine the "rightness" of the act. The consequences "decide" what is the right thing to do. The adherent to the stronger form of consequentialism merely looks at the outcome, more freedom, and makes her decision to abort.

Teleological ethics

Teleological ethics are related to consequentialism. The root of the word *teleos* is Greek, meaning "becoming." Teleologists look to the outcomes of the action to determine its rightness or wrongness. In evaluating the rightness of an act, teleologists look for the "locus of the good"--where the good effect is located. And they look for the relevance of bad results--what are the bad consequences. Finally, they examine what the effects on specific groups (not individuals) will be.

Teleology also is contrasted with deontology, described above as doing something because it is one's duty (that is, because some rule derived from the duty says it's right). In contrast, under the concept of teleology, one does not act because it's her duty, but only to get certain results.

Teleology might assume that, whatever the end, it is a result of some deliberate process. For example, the fact that people have noses is assumed to be the result of noses being designed, planned or evolved for some reason, not just being a random mutation that survived.

Remember the root of the word, suggesting that teleologists believe things are in process of becoming. Teleology, like consequentialism and axiological ethics and utilitarianism, is exemplified by the phrases "the end justifies the means" and "the outcome excuses the process."

A teleologist would find an action "right," if on balance, its bad consequences were no worse than its good consequences. If leaving work early (a semi-good consequence for the clinician) produced no worse consequences than leaving the patients with warm water to drink (a semi-bad consequence for them) then her action would be right.

If the good consequences were not just equal to the bad, but were greater than the bad, --for example, if the clinician left work early for an interview for a better job that she got and she wouldn't have gotten otherwise--with her patients suffering only a little pain--then the act would be more than just "right," it would be "obligatory."

With this theory, an action could never be "obligatory" and at the same time not "right"--because "obligatory" encompasses the condition of "right." Because the good consequences are greater, the act would be both obligatory and right.

Think about it.

Do you think more clinicians are utilitarians, or do more clinicians adhere to some deontological ethical theory?
Are you a utilitarian? Why, or why not?

Some ethical algebra:

Add the concept of consequentialist ethics (look to the consequences) together with axiological ethics (look for the good). Together they yield teleological ethics, another name for utilitarianism.

Consequential (look at outcomes and consequences)
+
Axiological (look at values of those consequences)
=
Teleological ethics--Utilitarianism (utility).

Paternalism

The discussion of paternalism is related to the idea of doing good, because paternalism implies that the clinician knows what is good, what is best, for the patient--as a father would. The Latin root of the word, *pater*, means father. This principle is understood as justifying the restriction of liberty of some in order to do good for, or to limit or prevent harm to, the person himself.

Paternalism is associated with less freedom, less choice, with someone making decisions for another. Thus in the current milieu of increased freedom--or at least increased focus on it-- paternalism is out of favor. Ironically, at the same time, interference by the government to "protect" the individual, even against his will, has become more prevalent. The idea of government as parent or father is prevalent also.

Think about it.

Is the state justified in forcing a cyclist to wear a helmet to protect the person from his own inability to protect himself—his inability to voluntarily wear a helmet?

If we didn't protect people from their own folly by paying for their injuries through taxpayer financed insurance, would we have any right to enforce the helmet law?

If taken to extremes, the state would be justified in forcing people to stop behaviors, to protect (do good for) the people against illness that results. Those behaviors include smoking (lung disease), drinking (cirrhosis), using injectable drugs (HIV/AIDS), having promiscuous unprotected anal sex (HIV/AIDS), and eating too much fat food, such as potato chips (heart disease).

Remember the distinction in Chapter 1 between bad versus good, compared to right versus wrong. Smoking is bad for us, so some to say it is wrong morally. The determination that a behavior such as smoking is bad produces the determination that it is wrong. Then right behavior is prescribed or even mandated with law. Bad behavior (smoking) automatically is conceptualized as being wrong, too.

A value judgment that you read about in Chapter 1, is made when we say smoking is not good. A prescriptive judgment is made when people say you ought not smoke. If the judgments are enforced by law, they represent a minimum moral value--they have risen to the level of a moral judgment.

When smoking is illegal, it also appears to be immoral. If homosexual activity by consenting adults is not punished by law, it may appear to be more moral than smoking. Drinking alcohol can be analyzed by the same standards. The act of owning and driving a vehicle that uses excess amounts of fuel can be analyzed this way--any human action can be. It's easy to go from value judgment--"that's bad for you/for us/for the earth" to prescriptive judgment-- "you ought not do that"--all the way to legal mandate: "you cannot do that."

J.S. Mill thought the state did not have the right to impose behaviors to protect the person from his mistakes. Some believe that great utilitarian would think differently, if he knew the extent to which the state already has assumed fatherhood for the people who become ill and don't have the money to pay for the consequences of their own choices. The whole "society" pays for much risky behavior, and some argue they should have the power to control it, in order to protect themselves from excess cost.

Paternalism often is encountered in medical ethics, where it implies decision-making by a professional or clinician instead of the patient. The clinician says that she knows what is good for the patient, and what the patient should do. In reality, sometimes the clinician did know better, but the concept has been so disparaged that some beneficial paternalism has been discarded.

In some cases patients are asked to make decisions that they are ill-equipped to make. Some patients might be happier (and possibly healthier) having the professional clinician make the decision. As an example, consider the issue of screening for breast cancer.

Women who are between 40 and 50 do not have clear guidance as to whether they should have regular mammograms. Some clinicians exhibit paternalism when they insist that patients *must* have preventive screening such as mammograms.

Mammograms find some breast tumors earlier, hopefully making them easier to treat. But they also find more false positive tumors that require investigation, with potential morbidity and mortality from that. If you have a mammogram and breast exam for 10 years in a row, you have a 50% chance of having a false positive result (Sox, 1998).

Over many years, women screened for breast cancer were compared with those not screened. There was one less death from breast cancer in the screened group, but six additional lives were lost to other causes compared to the unscreened group (Gotzsche, 2000).

Some clinicians encourage patients to "get the facts" and make their own decisions, when the facts are elusive and contradictory. Studies show that screening a whole population with breast self-examination and mammograms does not decrease mortality from breast cancer in the population (see discussion in Chapter 7).

Think about it.

Can facts make judgments? Or should the clinician be a little more paternalistic?

Do you think patients or people in general might be better off if a little more paternalism were imposed by people who know better? Or would you argue for less paternalism?

Does your answer depend on how you feel about government? About how much professionals know?

About the ability of people generally to make good decisions? About how smart you are?

REFERENCES

Audet AM, et al.. Medical practice guidelines: Current activities and future directions. *Annals of Internal Medicine,* 1990; 113:709-714.

Berry DB. The physician's guide to medical malpractice. *Baylor University Medical Center Proceedings*, 2001; 14:109-112.

Blackwell M. Documentation serves as invaluable defense tool. *American Nurse,* July/August 1993, pp. 40,41.

Castledine G. Ethical implications of first aid. *British Journal of Nursing,* 1993; 2(4):239-241.

Cazalas MW. Nursing and the law. Germantown, MD: Aspen, 1978, p. viii.

Collins v. Westlake Community Hospital, 12 N.E.2d 614 (Ill. 1974).

Crane M. The malpractice reform idea that won't go away. *Medical Economics,* 1993; 70(14):27-34.

Danzon P, head economist, Wharton School, Wall Street Journal, 12 October 1993, B5.

Densford KJ, Millard SE. *Ethics for Modern Nurses.* Philadelphia: Saunders, 1946; p. 181.

Doerhoff DC. Supreme court adopts 'but for' causation rule. *Journal of the*

Missouri Bar, January-February 1994, p. 5.

Faherty, B. Medical malpractice and adverse actions against nurses: five years of information from the national data bank. *Journal of Nursing Law,* 1998;5(1):17.

Fitzgerald WB. Checklist for the witness. *For the Defense,* July 1992; 1823.

Gotzsche PC, Olsen O. Is screening for breast cancer with mammography justifiable? *The Lancet,* 2000;335:9198.

Grant JA. Florida's presuit requirements for medical malpractice actions. *Florida Bar Journal,* February 1994, pp. 12-19.

Hall JK. Liability specific to nursing. Vicarious liability for nursing negligence. Chapters in *Nursing practice and the law: avoiding malpractice and other legal risks.* M. O'Keefe, Ed. Philadelphia: F.A. Davis, 2000.

_____ No substitute for good practice. *Nursing 1994;* 24(12):4.

Hirsh HL. Medico-legal considerations in the use of physician extenders. *Legal Medicine,* 1991;127-205.

JCAHO. Accreditation Manual for Hospitals, Patient Rights, 1993, p.106.

JCAHO. High-alert medications and patient safety (1999). Retrieved June 19, 2000 from the World Wide Web: http://www.jcaho.org/edu

Kupchynsky RJ, Camin CS. Legal considerations of telemedicine. *Texas Bar Journal,* 2001; 64(1):20-31.

Luke 10, New Testament

Lumsdon K, Hagland M. Mapping care. *Hospitals and Health Networks,* 20 October 1993, pp. 34-40.

Maslonka v. Hermann, 414 A.2d 1350 (N.J.App. 1980).

Medical plans take on greater liability. *Wall Street Journal,* 18 October 1993.

Murphy S. Legal issues for nurses: IV conscious sedation. *Texas Nurse,* January 1993, pp. 8-15.

Popp PW. Experts in malpractice litigation-What about nurses? *Legal Medicine,* 1992:165-178.

Pound R. *The lawyer from antiquity to modern times: with particular reference to the development of bar associations in the United States.* St. Paul, MN: Western, 1953.

Robert v. Chodoff, 393 A. 2d 853 (Pa. Super. 1978).

Rushton CH, Hogue EE. Confronting unsafe practice: Ethical and legal issues. *Pediatric Nursing,* 1993; 19(3):284-288.

Sox HC. Benefit and harm associated with screening for breast cancer. *New England Journal of Medicine,* 1998; 338:1145.

Tex. Civ. Prac. & Rem. Code Ann.§33.001 (Vernon 1999).

Texas Health Enterprises Inc. d/b/a Kern Manor and HEA Management Group Inc. v. Geisler, No. 2-98-026-CV (TX Ct. App., 2nd Dist., June 24, 1999).

Williams PM. Techniques for root cause analysis. *Baylor University Medical Center Proceedings,* 2001;14(2):154.

Woolfe SH. Practice guidelines: A new reality in medicine: III. Impact on patient care. *Archives of Internal Medicine,* 1993; 153:2646-2655.

Yocke JM, Donner TA. Floating out of ICU: The ethical dilemmas. Part I: The ethical case. Part II: The case analysis," *Dimensions of Critical Care Nursing,* 1992; 11(2):104-107.

Chapter 3: Don't Harm.

"I never wonder to see men [and women] *wicked, but I often wonder to see them not ashamed."* [material in brackets added].

JONATHAN SWIFT, *Thoughts on Various Subjects*

CONTENTS

Licensure and registration
Endorsement and reciprocity
Compact licensure
New categories of diagnosers/prescribers
Unlicensed assistive personnel
Discipline
Contacting the state credentialing authority
Common provisions
National Practitioner Data Bank
The ethics and law of clinician education
Mandatory continuing education law
Competence
Institutional licensure
If you need more ethics theory than Dountoothers
Ethics theory related to the value Don't Harm
Non-cognitive theories

REFERENCES

Key concepts

non-maleficence
primum non nocere
general intent
specific intent
intent
motive
battery
assault
false imprisonment
intentional
    infliction of
    emotional
    distress
negligent infliction
    of emotional
    distress
trespass to land
conversion
quasi-intentional
    torts
defamation

slander
libel
slander *per se*
invasion of privacy
strict liability
malicious
    prosecution
intentional
    misrepresenta-
    tion
abuse
neglect
qualified immunity
Nuremberg Code
Belmont Report
Institutional
    Review Boards
land ethic
sentient
licensure
registration

compact licensure
endorsement
reciprocity
discipline
competence
performance
mandatory
    continuing
    education
a priori
a posteriori
maxims
categorical
    imperative
good will
cognitive
non-cognitive
prescriptivism
emotivism

The ethics mothering the law

The Latin term for the value Don't Harm is **non-maleficence**. *Non* means not, *mal* means bad, and *ficence* means to do or make. Another Latin term, ***primum non nocere*** (pronounced "preemum non no-cherry"), is your mandate to "first, do no harm."

Clinicians understand immediately–you help patients if you can, but at least you avoid making them worse. The things you can do to people, however, make this easier said than done. Considering the iatrogenic or provider-caused illness that exists, just coming into the hospital or being a clinic patient is a risky business.

The self-interest you have in doing no harm is the same interest you have in doing good (beneficence). You feel good, you are seen as good, and you adhere to professional values. Not harming patients enhances your self-esteem as a valued member of society. If clinicians don't hurt others, they in turn are less likely to be hurt by others.

Clinicians who don't harm others, avoid breaking laws that are made to punish harm. If you do hurt other people, criminal prosecution could cost your liberty or even your life, and civil lawsuits could cost you psychic pain and money.

From both values, of doing good to people (beneficence) and doing no harm to people (non-maleficence), come the mandates for the clinician to provide competent care. Professionals are mandated to keep their skills current and to practice competently.

Most of the codes of ethics for professionals hold competent practice as an ethical value. Those competency clauses in codes are based on the values of doing good for, and doing no harm to, the patient.

The malpractice suit results when the values of do good and don't harm are not upheld. The patient is compensated if the clinician fails to do good. Through lawsuits, the clinician who "intentionally" does harm is punished. Specific intentional torts are explained in the section on law in this chapter.

The duty not to harm others is required of all people, not just clinicians. This is different from the duty to do good to others, that is required only of clinicians and other who voluntarily assume the duty. The ethical duty to do no harm is the base of all criminal law. The civil law also enforces the value, Don't Harm, through liability for wrongs (torts) that are done intentionally.

This duty not to harm is essentially a negative duty. Criminal law such as laws punishing murder, theft, rape, assault, and battery enforce this basic human value. Particular crimes that clinicians are more likely to encounter, such as child and adult abuse, are discussed in the law section of this chapter.

Law enforcing the value, Don't Harm

The ethics and law of not harming patients are obvious to good clinicians. As noted, all people, not just clinicians, have a duty not to harm other people, enforced in all the criminal laws against killing, stealing, lying, hitting, and abusing. Criminal law was developed so that individuals and families and tribes would not go to war for revenge of a wrong. Instead, the citizens yield their quest for revenge to law--a neutral third party to judge guilt and to punish.

Enforcing criminal law cannot "unharm" the victim. But it can make things even again between wrongdoer and wronged, by harming the guilty one equally. When law fails to do this, people get their own revenge. They are said to "take the law into their own hands." They literally take the law, in this case the act of revenge, back out of the hands of the neutral third party (the police and courts) who have failed them.

There is another side of the "do good unto others" presented in Chapter 1 as a principle found in many religions. The other side is to "do evil to others who have done it to you." You recognize that principle in the Old Testament "eye for an eye, life for a life." All statutes that contain a penalty for violation (a fine or jail time) are based on that premise of doing harm to one who has done harm to another.

Such **criminal law** includes credentialing law discussed in this chapter. Other examples are laws against abuse of dependent people--children, old, and disabled. Those laws usually require clinicians and others who work with such dependent people, to report abuse to some organization that can help.

Intentional torts

You have now a basic knowledge of one kind of tort, malpractice--discussed in Chapter 2. There are legal differences between malpractice (a negligence tort) and intentional torts.

Torts that are totally or partly intended by the actor are different from the failure to do good--punished by malpractice suits as detailed in the preceding chapter. Those acts of malpractice are considered to be *un*intentional–they are more or less accidental or negligent.

The first difference between unintended and intended acts in their legal effect, is that damages usually are automatically awarded if an intentional tort is found. In contrast, in a negligence action the patient must prove damages.

Another difference: expert witnesses usually are needed to prove the breach of the clinician's standard of care in negligence or malpractice, but experts usually are not needed in intentional torts. Expert witnesses are allowed to testify as to their opinion in negligence cases, only to aid the jury in an area in which the jurors aren't competent. The jury does not need an expert's opinion on whether or not the defendant intended an act or injury--they have expertise in that facet of human nature. Final difference: punitive damages are not usual with negligent torts such as malpractice, but are more likely to be awarded with intentional torts.

You needn't have an intent actually to injure someone, to be held liable for damages under the civil side of the law of intentional torts. Civil liability for intentional torts (unlike criminal liability) requires only that you <u>intended to perform an act, knowing the result of the act with substantial certainty.</u> For example, if you withdraw food and water from a patient you may not intend to kill her. But if that act does kill the patient, and you knew with substantial certainty that death would be the result, you can be held liable for an intentional civil tort.

That standard of intent is called **general intent**. General intent can be presumed from the fact that you did the act, and that you knew in advance what the result of your act would be. That presumption of intent is made, because the law can never know or prove with certainty, what is in your mind.

The criminal standard of intent needed to convict you of a crime (with possible penalty of loss of liberty) is higher than the civil standard of intent needed to find you liable (with possible penalty of loss of money). To convict you of a crime may require specific intent. In **specific intent**, <u>you must have intended to accomplish the result of the act, not merely intended to do the act</u>. An example showing specific intent could be the act of removing food and water, plus a statement made to a colleague that you wanted the patient dead.

Kind of Intent:	Kind of liability	Possible Penalty	Require-ment	Presump-tion:
General intent	Civil liability for intention-al torts	Money damages	Intended to perform an act, knowing the result of the act with substantial certainty.	Presumed from the fact that you did the act, and that you knew in advance what the result of your act would be.

Kind of Intent:	Kind of liability	Possible Penalty	Require-ment	Presump-tion:
Specific intent	Criminal liability for crime	Loss of liberty or life	intended to accomp-lish the result of the act, not merely intended to do the act.	None, must be proven from act and circumstan ces.

Intent and motive can be distinguished. **Intent** is <u>what</u> you meant to do. For example, my intent was to give the patient a substantial dose of morphine. **Motive** is <u>why</u> you did the act. For example, my motive in giving morphine might be to relieve pain, or it might be to kill the patient.

Motive is not relevant to whether you intend an act--to what you did. Either you intended to give the morphine, or not. But your motive may be relevant to whether you are prosecuted and punished for what you did. For example, if your motive in giving the morphine was only to relieve pain (and that would be obvious from the size of the dose), you would not be prosecuted for killing.

Intent: what act you meant to do.
Motive: why you did the act.

Children are presumed to have the intentional will required to commit intentional torts under civil law. The age at which the child is considered responsible and can be sued, depends on state law. Children are sued, because some have assets in their name or their parents' insurance covers their actions. Children usually are not presumed to have the requisite intentional will to commit intentional crimes under criminal law, however.

Regarding intent, people who are **incompetent** are in about the same legal position as children. They too may be presumed to have the intentional will required to commit intentional <u>torts</u> under civil law, but not to commit intentional <u>crimes</u> under criminal law. Age is not a factor as long as the incompetent person is at least 18. As is the case with children, the incompetent person may have assets that can be accessed by lawsuit or they may be covered by insurance for their acts.

Below, several of the kinds of intentional torts that clinicians encounter are discussed. The tort law scale of intent seen in Chapter 2 is repeated here, to reinforce the distinction between intentional and unintentional torts.

TORT LAW SCALE OF INTENT

Negligence (Malpractice)	Quasi-intentional Tort (Defamation, Invasion of Privacy)	Intentional Tort (Battery, Assault, False Imprisonment)

☜Less Intent		More Intent ☞

Battery

The civil tort of **battery** is defined as harmful or offensive contact to the person, with intent to contact, and caused by the person who is the defendant in the lawsuit. Merely touching the person without his consent is a technical battery. In the context of clinical practice, battery occurs when surgery or some other procedure is done on a patient who has not consented specifically to that procedure.

The contact can be direct or indirect. Indirect contact, for example, would be setting up a machine that will hit the patient, or contact with her clothes, purse, or bed.

The patient needn't know of the contact–for example, it is battery to do an unconsented pelvic exam while the patient is under anesthesia. The patient doesn't have to prove special damages, but the more direct and harmful the contact, the more damages. Consent is a good defense to lawsuit for battery–that's one good reason to get the patient's consent before doing a procedure on him. The various kinds of consent are discussed in Chapter 4, Be Free.

Assault

The intentional tort of **assault** in civil law, is defined as fear of immediate harm from a battery. Assault is one step short of a battery. Unlike battery, the plaintiff suing only for assault must have been aware of the assault. If he isn't aware, he can't be afraid. An immediate threat to the person is required for a lawsuit for civil assault to succeed.

It's not enough to threaten future harm or violence to another person, but gestures with the words make the threat immediate. For example, to say "I'm going to kill you" is not an assault unless the intended victim believes you will do it immediately. It's not a good thing to say, to anyone, in any case.

Striking or threatening another person usually is unethical, and unlawful. Extreme situations however, might require self-defense. No clinician anticipates violence, but the stress of work and handling combative patients, particularly those who must be restrained, can provoke violent situations.

In the midst of a crisis, try to envision how the situation could look to a jury (law problem) or to a respected peer (ethical and possibly law problem). Rarely should patients need to be physically subdued. Care of patients is not a contest for control.

Time and careful observation will allow many patients to calm themselves. If immediate restraint is necessary to protect the patient or staff, only people who are trained in using physical force should do so. Restraining the patient may expose the clinician to potential liability for battery or for false imprisonment.

False imprisonment

The intentional tort of **false imprisonment** is defined as confining a person to a bound area by force. This includes even threat of force to the person or her property, and includes acts or words reasonably implying force. Saying to the patient "You will not be allowed to leave the building until you pay your bill," might be considered false imprisonment.

False imprisonment includes failure to provide a means of escape when the defendant (you, the clinician, are the defendant) has the means to provide escape. False imprisonment includes situations when the plaintiff (the patient) is under the your control and can't leave without your help. An example of this is the situation in which the patient is wheelchair-bound, and you won't provide a wheelchair.

Moral pressure, or future threats to detain the person, are not sufficient to produce liability. Saying to the patient that he shouldn't leave without paying his bill, is not false imprisonment. In a situation analogous to victims of rape, the plaintiff needn't resist a forceful imprisonment to recover damages. Any duration of false imprisonment produces liability, but the duration of time the person is confined affects the amount of damages given.

The plaintiff must have known of the confinement, unless it causes injury. For example, a patient who is confined without cause in a mental hospital, but who is drugged and unaware of the confinement, would have to prove some injury it caused. (That likely would not be difficult.) No confinement occurred if the person was aware of any reasonable means of escape. Like the other intentional torts, there usually is no requirement to prove specific damages in order to establish liability, but damages are higher if injury can be shown.

Lawsuits involving the use of restraints on incompetent patients will probably allege negligence instead of false imprisonment. Regulations about restraints established by state agencies and by JCAHO can be used to establish the standard of care that clinicians should meet in those negligence cases. Be aware of those rules and regulations, don't violate them, and document your practice. You can anticipate most guidelines by applying the Dountoothers rules from Chapter 1–pretend the patient is your mother. Or pretend she's you, because that's coming sooner than you think.

Clinicians of psychiatric and emergency care can follow that same ethic and act on the value that the patient should not be harmed if at all possible. The result will be that the patient will not be restrained without good reason. That's the "false" part of false imprisonment–the patient is restrained without good reason. The "good reason" to restrain is for the safety of the patient who is a danger to himself or to others.

If your practice is with patients who must be restrained involuntarily, such as psychiatric or emergency practice, you should read your state's statutes on involuntary commitment. These are found in the index to the state statutes, and on the Internet. Even without knowing the details of the law, you know the principle. Protect the patient, and protect those the patient might harm, but only to the extent necessary, and you'll be ethical and thus lawful.

Defense to false imprisonment

As with all the intentional torts, consent is a defense also to the intentional tort of false imprisonment. An example of consent: the patient who commits herself to an institution consents voluntarily to be imprisoned as necessary. Necessity--the need to protect the patient--also is a defense to a lawsuit alleging false imprisonment. The clinician can defend by establishing that the action was reasonable to protect the patient from danger to himself, and that another reasonable prudent clinician in the same situation would have done the same.

Note in Chapter 4 on autonomy, that necessity is an ethical justification for limiting the patient's autonomy (freedom). It should then come as no surprise that it's a legal justification as well.

If the patient is incompetent and in danger of falling when getting out of bed without help, false imprisonment liability is not a worry. The patient needs protection from harm. How this is done--whether restraints are necessary and safely applied--are malpractice questions of negligence law, not questions rising to the level of the intentional tort of false imprisonment.

You have a duty to reasonably protect the patient from falls, but you will be liable for damage from improperly used restraints. As always the solutions are determined case by case, using good judgment and documenting your thinking and action.

First, restrain yourself while you assess whether some other solution will work. Document the reasons for your action. Don't use restraints unless you determine they are necessary. Apply them according to the standards mentioned above--in accord with your organization policy, according to the regulations on restraints established by your state health agency and according to JCAHO guidelines (available from your risk manager and from the JCAHO Website).

Intentional (and negligent) infliction of emotional distress

The tort of **intentional infliction of emotional distress** is outrageous conduct that makes the patient/ plaintiff experience severe emotional distress. In legal terms, general intent (not specific intent) suffices in this tort as in all the intentional civil torts. As noted above, in contrast to civil liability, some crimes require specific intent. Conviction would require proof that the clinician intend to accomplish the result of the act, not merely intend to do the act.

For example, if as a joke you intentionally tell your patient she is HIV positive, she can sue successfully in civil law, even if you didn't intend the result that she be upset. General intent suffices--to intentionally do the act with knowledge that such an act could cause the distress. You cannot defend by saying that you had no intent to actually make the patient distressed.

Different from other intentional torts, the person who sues for intentional infliction of emotional distress must prove damages. That is because the causation of the injury is more difficult to see than an injury, for example, from battery.

In contrast, **negligent infliction of emotional distress** is not an intentional tort, so the rules of negligence malpractice are applied. This tort is more likely in clinical situations than the intentional tort. An example of negligent infliction of emotional distress might be if you tell the patient she is HIV positive when she is not, because you negligently misread the lab report. For you to be liable, she must establish duty, breach, causation, and damage.

Think about it.
From your knowledge of malpractice law, do you think the patient in the last example could win a lawsuit?
Why or why not?

Other intentional torts

The other intentional torts seldom are encountered in professional practice, but they may be important in your private life. If a situation involving one of these torts arises in private life, you should seek legal advice.

These torts generally protect property or punish harm to it. They enforce the value, Don't Harm, because harming your property harms your ability to survive. The other intentional torts include **trespass to land**--entering property without permission. Land occupies a special place in law and human thinking because it was--and though dimly realized it still is--the source of food and thus the means of survival.

The intentional tort of **trespass to chattels** includes any action done to another's personal property--that is, anything movable--without permission. The origin of the word chattel is cattle. The word was later applied to human slaves and still could be applied to people who are made slaves today, for example Christians in the Sudan. Chattel is the general word for all personal property that is not land.

Conversion, another intentional tort, is defined as acting to exercise dominion and control--as though an owner--over another's chattel. This tort is the civil equivalent of the crime of theft. But instead of (or in addition to) the police prosecuting the thief, the owner of the property can sue the thief in civil court to recover the property.

Defenses to intentional torts

As noted earlier, consent is a defense to all the intentional torts.

This is different from malpractice law in which consent is <u>not</u> a defense, except to the charge of negligent failure to obtain informed consent. As you will see in Chapter 4, Be Free, consent can be express (written or spoken) or implied (apparent or implied by law).

For example, if the patient alleges the intentional tort of battery--that she didn't consent before a procedure was done–your defense is the written consent form and/or testimony that she did consent to the procedure. Consent can be exceeded, however. For instance, a consent for a pelvic exam does not extend to consent to pelvic surgery (*Schloendorff*, 1914) The law of consent enforces the value placed on the freedom of the individual, her power over her body.

Self-defense can be used as a defense to an intentional tort, as well as a defense to criminal charges. Saying you were defending yourself can excuse an act that would otherwise produce liability for battery and assault. To be excused for the act that otherwise is wrong, such as striking a patient, your assertion of self-defense must be based on a reasonable belief that attack by the patient was imminent. The person asserting self-defense needn't run to avoid the attacker, but he won't be excused for retaliation after the attack.

The self-defense exculpation may be allowed even if you injure a third person while defending from the attacker–if you swing to defend yourself and hit a colleague, for example. Defense of another person, perhaps a colleague, is justifiable if you personally had a reasonable belief that an attack on her was imminent.

Defense of property has different rules from defense of yourself or defense of another person. To defend your property and have a valid defense for the action if you later are sued, you first must have asked the person to stop bothering the property before taking any action. You may use only reasonable force to defend your property. Deadly force to defend property will not be excused, unless you also are defending your life or another person's life, or preventing forcible entry into your home.

Related to the idea of self-defense is necessity. Necessity is a general defense to intentional tort liability. As noted, defense to a suit for false imprisonment of a patient is that the act was necessary--in that case, to protect the patient or another person. The person defending on necessity grounds will allege the act was needed, either to do a public good or a private good.

Even if you are excused from liability because your action was necessary, any damage you do in accomplishing the public or private good still must be paid for. The classic example is the situation of tying your boat to a private dock if a storm makes it necessary. You are excused from a lawsuit for trespass, but you still must pay for any damage you caused to the dock.

The defense of necessity has arisen in the context of clinical practice and ethics. Some anti-abortion demonstrators, charged with trespass on private property of abortion clinics, have sought to defend on grounds of necessity–the necessity to save fetal lives. Statutes that make such trespass a federal crime, also have eliminated that defense.

Quasi-intentional torts (injury to economics and dignity)

Quasi-intentional torts also are called injury to economics and dignity. They are considered to be on a middle area of intent between intentional torts and unintentional torts (negligence). Check the Tort Law Scale of Intent above if you need to clarify this.

Defamation

Quasi-intentional torts such as defamation also clearly enforce the ethical value of don't harm (non-maleficence). The ethic underlying defamation is relevant to clinicians when it is stated, "Don't harm other professionals." In the context of clinical practice, suits by clinicians against each other or their employers are more likely than defamation suits by patients against clinicians.

Defamation is an injury to the person's reputation that results from an untrue statement made to a third person. If the statement is true, it is not defamation. **Slander** is spoken defamation, and written defamation is **libel**. Telling the lie to the third person is called <u>publication</u> of the defamation. An example of publication could be writing an untrue remark that injures the reputation of the patient or another person, in the patient's record.

Making the statement only to the person spoken about, isn't considered publishing the defamation to a third person. But a letter is considered published to a third person if, for example, the writer of the letter knows the recipient's secretary will see it, too. As noted above, writing something defamatory in a patient's record, that you know others will see, might constitute publication of the defamation.

The statement may not clearly damage on its face–that is, if it is taken out of context. To say "Jane is blue" is not defamatory on its face. But the statement may be damaging in the whole context in which it was made. That context is termed the <u>innuendo</u>. For example, if everyone knows that being "blue" means one is a criminal, the innuendo is that Jane is a criminal

The statement may not directly identify the plaintiff, but the person may be recognizable in the context of the situation-- known as the <u>colloquium</u>. To say merely "The Nighthorse is a terrorist" is not defamatory on its face because no person is identified. But if everyone knows that John Jones is the Nighthorse, it is defamatory.

The plaintiff who is a public figure will have a harder time winning damages for defamation than we anonymous folk would. That is because public figures are presumed to tolerate some notoriety and defamation, as a consequence of their fame. News organizations that are sued for defamation thus are less likely to lose than other defendants are.

The laws that protect the freedom of the press enforce the value we place on truth in the society. Punishing every misstatement of the media might result in self-censorship of the press and result in less information to the people. In some cases this policy outweighs the need to punish those who defame.

Think about it.
Do you agree that the press should get a break in defamation suits?
Or should they be held to an even higher standard than private individuals who are accused of defamation?

British libel law makes it much easier for the plaintiffs to win suits against the media. For example, the British defendant publisher has the burden to prove that a statement he has printed--alleged to be defamatory--is true. In the United States, the plaintiff has the burden of proving the statement that was published, is false. The British legal system makes the loser of a lawsuit pay for the winner's legal fees, as is done also in their malpractice lawsuits. That means many potential plaintiffs who might sue for defamation are reluctant to sue even if they might deserve to win, for fear that they literally can't afford to lose the lawsuit.

No proof of actual injury is necessary if the defamation is made in writing (libel). If libel is established, damages are automatic but automatic does not necessarily mean large damages. The amount of damages depends on how widespread the publication and how clearly the statement is damaging.

Damages also are automatic if a spoken defamation is any one of the following four lies. In legal terms, these are called **slander** *per se*--slander all by itself, without any additional proof of damages.

Slander *per se:*

1. The person has a loathsome disease. This category used to include leprosy and cancer. Now, alleging the person is HIV positive might be slander *per se*.
2. The person is guilty of a felony.

3. The person's reputation in a profession or business is injured, as in, "She's a terrible clinician. I have seen her hit patients."
4. A woman is "unchaste." This statement seldom is sued upon any more, because a reputation for being "unchaste" is not as injurious to women as in the days when virginity and fidelity were considered more important.

The third item above is important for clinicians. First, due to intemperate statements, you could be made a defendant in a lawsuit by a colleague or patient.

Second, you could be a plaintiff if your reputation in your profession is damaged by some untrue statement. A Missouri case held that Kennedy could sue Bailey for libel that was recorded in a deposition for a malpractice suit against Kennedy. Kennedy's patient had changed to Bailey and then sued Kennedy.

Patient's wife said in deposition, that Bailey told her and her husband that Kennedy did an unnecessary procedure, only for "monetary" purposes (MD can sue, 2000).

Here the ethical mandate of this chapter, "first, do no harm," means not to harm patients or coworkers or employees or employers. Employees too bring lawsuits, against employers for alleged defamation made in the context of discharge. This topic is discussed in Chapter 5, Fairness.

Defense to defamation

Truth is an absolute defense to a charge of defamation. If the plaintiff can't prove the statement you made is false, or you, the defendant, can prove the statement you made is true–for example that your colleague indeed did hit a patient--then your statement is not defamation. Another defense to defamation is to prove that your statement was opinion and not allegation of fact. You are free to give your opinion that "She's a terrible clinician." That's opinion, not fact. But if you add the fact statement "She does unnecessary procedures only for the money" or "She hits patients," you had better be able to confirm that.

Of course you know that you can stay out of legal trouble for defamation by not making such statements in the first place--good ethical behavior. And if you knew those statements to be true, you would be obligated to do something other than just gossip about it. You would have an obligation to report it to an authority such as the credentialing board, who can stop the behavior.

Invasion of privacy

The quasi-intentional tort **invasion of privacy** also enforces the ethical value of don't harm. In addition, a lawsuit for invasion of privacy enforces the ethical value of keeping secrets (confidentiality).

One example of invasion of privacy is using your face, picture or name for advertising without your permission. But the invasion of privacy class that is most applicable to clinicians and their patients is called <u>disclosure of private facts</u>.

A "private fact" in terms of tort law could be disclosure of the patient's diagnosis, treatment, prognosis, or just about any fact known to you because of your special relationship to the patient. The fact must be one that a reasonable person would find private. For example, though the patient's address is not generally known, it probably is not a private fact.

In the past, disclosure of the fact that the patient has delivered a baby and is not married has produced legal liability on the part of the clinician. Changing morals might make disclosure of some private facts like that, less actionable.

Implied in the idea of invasion of privacy is that the fact is private and that disclosure is embarrassing. If people no longer keep such facts private it means they are not embarrassing. Remember that ethics is mother to the law. Changing ethics may mean some facts no longer are private (shameful) and thus their disclosure has no legal consequence.

As is true in other intentional torts, the patient needn't prove damages in order to recover in a lawsuit for invasion of privacy. As always, however, if no injury is proven the recovery will be small. More penalties for failure to protect patient privacy may result from a federal law, the Healthcare Insurance Portability and Accountability Act (HIPAA) discussed in Chapter 6.

Defense to invasion of privacy

Unlike the situation in defamation, the fact that the statement is true is not a defense to a lawsuit for invasion of privacy. For example, even if it is true that the patient is HIV-positive, if you make her status public she can sue you. That you did not intend the invasion of privacy (breach of confidentiality), is not a defense. Nor is it a good defense that you acted in good faith, nor that you lacked malice.

In that respect, analysis of this tort is more like a **strict liability** analysis. In strict liability torts, the plaintiff need not prove you were negligent <u>or</u> intentional in disclosing the private fact, only that your action revealed something that should not have been revealed. See strict liability analysis, below

As is always the case in intentional or quasi-intentional torts, if the patient consents to the disclosure he can't sue for invasion of privacy.

That's why you request the patient to consent to the release of information, before you release her information to a third party.

In addition to consent, another defense to an allegation of invasion of privacy is necessity. If disclosing the information is necessary, the patient can't win a suit against you for doing it. In the case of the HIV positive patient, it may be necessary to the patient's care to disclose his status to another clinician.

Depending on your state's statute, it may be necessary to disclose the patient's HIV status or some other condition–for example, infection with tuberculosis, to the state health department or to the patient's partner. The ethical mandate is to not harm your patient by disclosing. But if greater harm to others might result from keeping the secret, you may have qualified immunity from liability by disclosing facts that will prevent that harm to them.

You will have qualified immunity when reporting your patient's condition to one who needs the information to care for him--for example, to a colleague who also cares for the patient. Your state statute index or Internet site will reveal your state's statutes about specific conditions that you may or must disclose, and to whom.

Other quasi-intentional torts

Other quasi-intentional torts are malicious prosecution and intentional misrepresentation. **Malicious prosecution** is not often encountered in the area of health law. To succeed, the person bringing the suit (defendant in the first suit) must first win the prosecution (lawsuit) brought by the bad guy, then prove that the bad guy had no reasonable grounds to sue in the first place, then prove that the bad guy had a bad motive for bringing the suit against you. As you can see, such suits are difficult to win.

Suits have been brought for a similar tort, for malicious reporting to a credentialing board. A clinician in Corpus Christi, Texas, won a jury award of $20 million, charging malicious reporting to the his credentialing board and to the National Practitioner Data Bank. He also charged slander and interference with his relationship with his patients (Lawsuits, 2000). If you report a colleague to his credentialing board in good faith--that is, if you have some reason--you should be protected from lawsuit. Malicious reporting to a credentialing board, however (reporting without any basis to do so), might produce liability.

Think about it.
Do you think it is a good thing or a bad thing that malicious reporting should have potential consequences?
Why good, or why bad?

A suit for **intentional misrepresentation** succeeded in a California court. A medical technician sued the patient who had not revealed a positive HIV status. A jury gave the technician $102,500 in damages for the mental anguish of worrying about whether HIV had been contracted from the patient. A judge upheld the award at the trial court level, saying that the patient has no obligation to tell the provider his HIV status--but when he intentionally concealed it, he was liable when the worker suffered harm (Law notes, 1993).

The tort of <u>negligent</u> misrepresentation differs from intentional misrepresentation. As you noted already from the phrase, negligent misrepresentation is non-intentional and so would follow the legal rules for negligence--requiring duty, breach, causation, and damages as discussed in Chapter 2. Using the HIV positive patient as example: if the patient did not intend to mislead the clinician, but negligently forgot to tell him, the negligence analysis would apply. Intentional misrepresentation is an easier action to punish than negligent.

Strict liability

In a lawsuit brought under the theory of strict liability, people who engage in an activity are automatically liable when someone is harmed as a result of the activity. The person sued needn't be negligent to be liable, but is liable for harm done by performing the act (even if done very safely). The mandate not to harm is so strong in some situations that even if no negligence is present, having someone harmed produces automatic liability.

The subdivision of strict liability law that applies most readily to clinical practice is product liability. For example, if a product is found to be unsafe, the manufacturer and seller may be liable even if they did not act negligently nor intentionally. Clinicians who sell products should seek legal advice on the legal exposure that may produce.

Statutes prohibiting maltreatment

Clinicians are included in the general ethical mandate not to harm, enforced by many criminal statutes. In addition, clinicians also are specifically mandated to report harm they know about.

Without knowing specific laws, you can assume that the ethic, Don't Harm, will be enforced in criminal law and civil lawsuits that prohibit and punish **abuse** of people who are unable to defend themselves--such as children, dependent elderly, and disabled persons. And without knowing specifics, you can assume that the law will require you to report known or suspected abuse of dependent persons to some entity that can help.

These statutes also may make the act of **neglect**, failure to provide necessities for a dependent person, equivalent to abuse. This definition of abuse is of particular concern to clinicians in nursing home and home health practice.

The penalty for a crime such as abuse or failure to report abuse will be some classification of felony or misdemeanor. The index of statutes or Internet under Felony or Misdemeanor will reveal the statute that specifies the amount of jail time and/or fine that will be imposed in your state for either type of crime.

The civil law too enforces the ethic of reporting harm. For example, suppose a child is injured by an abusive parent, and you, the clinician in the emergency department or clinic or hospital, have reason to know the child is abused. If you do not report the situation, and if the child is injured subsequently, she can sue you for those injuries.

In similar fashion, if you fail to report a situation in which a nursing home patient is dehydrated through poor care, you could face a criminal charge for failure to report neglect, and civil lawsuit for injury that followed your failure to report. Even if no statute required a report, your failure to report abuse that you suspect might be considered negligence if you are sued in civil court.

Look for applicable abuse statutes in the index of your state's statutes under Abuse--Children, Adults, Minors, Disabled (or Challenged, or whatever euphemism your state uses). You can find the statute there or on the Internet. Or, you can assume that abuse of dependent patients is a crime and that reporting it is mandatory.

If you have reason to believe a dependent patient has been abused, you will not err in reporting it to people who can help. As mentioned earlier, the label for that protection from legal liability for ethical behavior is **qualified immunity**. You have qualified immunity from liability when acting to protect the patient. There is qualified immunity from a suit for invasion of privacy if it is necessary to reveal a secret.

You also have a duty to adults who are not dependent and who appear to have been intentionally injured, for example by a violent spouse or partner. The phrase "intentionally injured" is more specific than abuse. Loose definitions of abuse such as "ignoring your feelings" may contribute to the trivialization of a very serious wrong. This is similar to the effect of including in the category with aggravated assault and rape by a stranger, the act of "date rape."

Your duty toward patients who have been intentionally injured by a partner is to ascertain the cause of their injury, to treat the injury, and to offer the patient referral for the cause of the injury. Unlike the situation of dependent patients, you should not report the patient's injury without the patient's consent unless your state mandates it. If you encounter such patients often in your practice, you should check the requirements of your state's statute in the statute index or on the Internet (Hall, 2000).

Required reports

In addition to reporting abuse, state statutes require reporting of certain diseases, injuries, and crime. In general, the rule is that any condition of the patient that could harm public safety must be reported. Examples of required reporting are communicable disease (for instance, tuberculosis or AIDS); results of tests required by the state (for example, phenylketonuria [PKU] in newborns); and evidence of crime (for example, gunshot wounds, some injuries from violence).

You can get your own state's requirements from the organization's risk management department, in the statute index or on the Internet law sites by subject. The local public health department or your state's professional association also should be able to supply you with the reporting requirements for your state.

You have a professional (ethical) and legal duty to protect the patient's confidentiality, but that duty is qualified. Your patient's condition may be reported–his confidentiality breached--only as necessary to protect the public or the patient, and only to the people authorized as responsible for the protection of the public or the patient.

Federal laws enforcing the value don't harm

The ethic of not harming patients is enforced by many federal statutes, one of which is the Emergency Medical Treatment and Active Labor Act (EMTALA), 42 U.S.C. 1395. That statute requires any hospital with an emergency department (ED) to stabilize the patient who is in the emergency department, before transferring her to another hospital. An inelegant way to state the law's mandate is

"don't dump the patient."

The hospital must provide an appropriate screening exam to see if a medical condition exists that needs stabilization. The patient is not "in" the ED merely when in contact by car phone, or by radio contact in the ambulance--but if she is on the property, in the vehicle, the patient is "in" the ED.

The EMTALA provides remedies, one being that the patient can sue for tort in federal court. This is important, because malpractice lawsuits usually are restricted to state courts unless the parties are from two different states. The government can assess fines against the providers who violate the law, they can be excluded from future Medicare and Medicaid payments, and the organization can lose federal building funds and its tax-exempt status, because it is not providing community benefit.

Dumping the patient was thought to be motivated by the patient's inability to pay, and the EMTALA sought to prevent that harm. But court decisions have found that the dumping does not have to be motivated by the patient's inability to pay. That means that a charge of dumping can't be defended by explaining that the transfer wasn't because of the patient's insurance status.

Regulations have been written to flesh out the requirements of the statute. If you need it, you can find the statute and regulations at a library that has copies of the US Code and Code of Federal Regulations, or on the law sites on the Internet.

Federal law also enforces the value of Don't Harm by encouraging clinicians to report information about medical devices that harm patients, under the Safe Medical Devices Act of 1990. If a medical device causes or contributes to the death, serious injury, or serious illness of a patient, the Food and Drug Administration (FDA) and the manufacturer of the device should be notified--both should have Websites.

Because the FDA regulates the medical devices industry, patients can't sue the manufacturer by alleging failure to warn of possible injuries from the medical devices. This is an example of federal law that is interpreted by the courts to be the only remedy in a field of law. Such law completely preempts state law remedies of the same kind.

Federal laws that are based on the value of not harming are too numerous to list here. When and if you encounter them you will recognize their ethical base. You know that by doing good ethical practice you will protect your patient from harm and meet their minimum mandates.

Non-maleficence in research

The values most important when protecting subjects of research from injury, are don't harm (non-maleficence) and tell the truth (veracity).

Nuremberg Code

The **Nuremberg Code** is the cornerstone of current research ethics and law (Permissible medical experiments, 1946). It was written as a response to clinicians who tortured and killed subjects of research during the National Socialist (Nazi) regime. The rules of the Nuremberg Code still are used today. They include the following:
1) voluntary consent of the subject is essential,
2) experiments must be designed using results of animal research and

knowledge of the condition,

3) the risk to the subject should never exceed the potential humanitarian importance of the problem,

4) only qualified persons should conduct the research,

5) the subject must be free to end participation at any time, and

6) the researcher must terminate the experiment if there is cause to believe that continuation will cause injury, disability, or death of the subject.

Put very simply, the Code countered the Nazi assumption that allowed the Nazis to do such awful experiments--the assumption that *the research was more important than the subject.*

Earlier German codes

Even earlier than the Nazi years, rules regarding human experimentation existed in Germany to guide researchers. A Prussian edict of 1900 barred non-therapeutic interventions without voluntary consent of the subject, and prohibited experiments on minors and other vulnerable or incompetent persons unless the research was for their benefit.

In 1931 the Reich Health Office issued guidelines that forbade experimentation on dying persons or experiments that would put anyone under age 18 at risk. That law was characterized as being very strict. The Nazis protected even animals; a German law passed in 1933 strictly protected the rights of animals from experimentation that might cause them injury or pain.

Think about it.

If the guides were in place, how could researchers do experiments on people who had never volunteered, experiments that killed people with simulated high altitude tests, that froze people to death, and that injected children with live tubercle bacilli, to cite but a handful of relatively benign examples?

The logic of the researchers is clear from their actions. They did not do experiments on healthy Aryan Germans, so the language of the rule was interpreted as prohibiting such research on those people. But neither the researchers nor their society in general considered Jews, Gypsies, Poles, Slavs, Russians, or handicapped Germans to be *people,* who would be protected by the rule. Some reasoned that because they were to be killed anyway, their lives might serve a purpose in research.

Declaration of Helsinki

This standard for ethical research was promulgated by the World

Medical Association in 1964 and after several revisions, was under revision again in 2000. The document allowed for consent to research to be given by proxy for persons who are incompetent to give it personally–such as children and mentally incapacitated persons. Similar to the Nuremberg Code, the Declaration asserts that absolute priority must be given to the subject, over the interests of science and society.

The Belmont Report

Continuing the history of attempts to protect subjects of research is the **Belmont Report.** Like the Nuremberg Code, this ethical standard for research was issued in response to an ethical disaster in research--this one in the U.S.

Starting in 1932, the United States Public Health Service conducted a 40-year study in Tuskegee, Alabama, on men of color who had contracted syphilis. The subjects deliberately were denied treatment that became available during the study, in order to observe the long-term consequences of their disease without treatment.

Think about it.
Why didn't the Nuremberg Code, well publicized during part of the research period, act to protect these subjects from harm?

Certainly, quoting that Code, "continuation. . . [of the research would] cause injury, disability, or death of the subject. . ." and it did. The actions of these researchers is evidence that, like the German investigators, they felt that these subjects were not *people* deserving of the protections of the written ethical standard of the time.   The researchers shared the attitudes of the larger society, just as did the German researchers in their time.

American regulation of research

US regulations governing research first were issued in 1974. The current regulations governing protection of research subjects are at 45 CFR 46. US law mandates a type of ethics committee, an **Institutional Review Board** (IRB) to protect both animal and human research subjects from harm. The power of IRBs is delegated by the Congress to the people on boards in each organization, not to government regulators. This avoids the necessity of the government agency making decisions on the safety of all research subjects. As with ethics committees, there is delegation from a formal national government body to a less formal local body, the IRB of the organization (Agich, 1989).   IRBs review the consent of subjects to research in studies that are funded or supervised by the federal government. In contrast, consent for treatment that is not experimental may never be reviewed, unless a malpractice suit is filed as a result of the procedure.

Consent to research upholds the same value as consent to treatment–namely, the autonomy of the subject. Voluntary consent is the base of ethical research. If the individual cannot legally consent to the research, as in the case of children or incompetent persons, utmost care should be used to assure that the subject's interests are protected. The subject's consent (or assent) should be sought, in addition to the consent of the person legally responsible.

Despite laws and ethical guidelines, the ultimate responsibility for ensuring ethical research practice rests with the individual investigator and the people who do the research. The IRB and the researcher who adhere to the ethical mandate Don't Harm, ensure that people at risk of coercion or undue influence actually will not be harmed.

Women in research studies

Federal law and regulations require that women be "appropriately" represented in medical studies. Research protocols that automatically exclude pregnant women may be in violation of such law. Many research protocols have automatically excluded pregnant women, whether or not the protocol is thought to be harmful (teratogenic) to the fetus. This automatic exclusion from study may be considered discrimination on the basis of sex, because only women may become pregnant.

After inclusion of women in research, the next policy change is the change from a policy of presumed exclusion of pregnant women from protocols, to a policy of presumed opportunity for inclusion. (Hall, 2000). Federal rules mandating this situation became effective in 2001 (Federal, 2001).

Ownership of tissue

Controversy has arisen over who owns the products of research. In one famous case, the subject had consented to research but said he had not granted ownership of his cells to the researcher. The material developed from his tissue became valuable, and this case gave compensation and interest in the potential profits to the man whose tissue was used in the research (*Moore*, 1988). Research subjects should be made aware if there is potential for profit from their participation in research, and their consent sought.

Think about it.
Should the subject share in the profits because they originated in his body?

Or should they go to the researcher who did the work?
Or should the profits be distributed to the poor?
Think about this issue again after you read about the concept of "desert"
    in Chapter 5, Justice.

Animal and environmental research

Experiments on animals raise some of the same issues that apply to
people who are labeled less than human. Read the section on moral
standing in Chapter 7 and determine whether you believe animals have
moral standing.

Think about it.
If animals had moral standing, would researchers need their permission
    to do research on them?
If so, how would we know that the animal consented? Did not consent?
Can we project onto them what we think they would do, if they could tell
    us?

Some ethicists argue that it is permissible to do research on fetuses
that are scheduled to be aborted, and on stem cells that are to be
discarded, because they are going to die anyway. They say that we can
assume that the fetus who knew her death was inevitable, would want to
have her short life serve some purpose.

Think about it.
Can we make the same assumption about animals that are subjected
    to research?

Other ethical research issues arise when the environment is
threatened in order to provide illness treatment. That was the case when
taxol, needed for treatment of breast cancer, was obtained from a rare
yew tree. Subsequently, taxol was synthesized and the yew was
protected. Related issues are apparent when a threat to the environment
is seen to cause illness, such as air and water pollution.

A new area of ethics theory is environmental ethics. Aldo Leopold
wrote about the **land ethic.** His followers believe the main criterion for
moral standing, discussed in Chapter 7, should be ecosystem integrity.
Carried to extreme, that would mean that the ecosystem is more
important than any of its components--people or animals or vegetation.

True believers in the land ethic say that being **sentient**–capable of
experiencing pain–is not the criterion for moral standing. Trees probably
are not sentient, nor are rocks. Of course, the definition of sentient could
be modified from "capable of experiencing pain" to "capable of being

damaged."

The enormous consequence of this position is that neither humans nor animals would have rights if they were in conflict with the ecology. Too many humans or rabbits or trees for the ecosystem? Too bad for the humans, rabbits or trees. Of course, for millennia when humans have come into conflict with their environment, *they* have said "too bad."

A classic illustration of the land ethic is the position of some scientists who object to researcher Jane Goodall who spent money on raising orphan chimps. They argue that the money it cost to maintain the individual orphans could be used to improve the environment for all chimps. That objection about spending money on the orphan chimps is an example of the attitude that the collective is more important than the individual.

Think about it.
Are these land ethic utilitarians?

By the way, Goodall thinks that the chimps not only are sentient but can reason (Miller, 1995). A similar effort to raise orphans was attempted for gorillas (McRae, 2000).

The foregoing discussion has major implications for resource use. The question asked is, for whom do the "resources" exist–for humans, animals, or for "themselves." Some assert that the earth/ecosystem as a whole has direct moral standing, that it has rights.

If so, there is a moral obligation to honor the rights--no automatic right of humans to dig minerals, or to take oil from the ground, to raise grain from the soil, or to eat any animals. Perhaps there is no right to kill any living thing, no right to abort any fetuses or to euthanize any people in "vegetative state."

On the other hand, there might be a moral obligation to reduce the population to levels that won't damage the ecosystem. Animals that have been developed for human use--for example, all domesticated sheep, cattle, fowl, and so on–might require eradication so that the original or natural state of the earth is returned. For those who would return the Earth to a natural condition, there is a huge problem.

Think about it.
What is the Earth's original or natural condition–as it was after the last ice age, or before the last ice age when Wisconsin was under glacier? When the gomphotheres roamed Kansas?
Is the original or natural condition of the Earth, the one existing before humans emerged, or after humans became dominant?
And with which humans?

Some Australians wish to rid their continent of animals that are not indigenous there. But the humans are not indigenous--they came to Australia only about 40,000 years ago. They came to North America only about 13,000 years ago or a few millennia earlier (depending on which archeologist you read).

Credentialing
Purpose and effect

During the 20th century, the various states instituted a system of credentialing for clinicians, intended to protect the public from those who were unsafe. Though licensure is only one form of credentialing, the word licensure often is used in discussions about credentialing. People are credentialed in order to certify their capability to practice with patients without doing them harm. The ethical base of the credentialing law is the duty to do no harm.

In theory, the system of credentialing should protect the public by ensuring that clinicians are safe. The only people who can do certain dangerous acts are people who have met certain tests--who have certain education and skill. Lawmakers create credentialing systems because they assume that the public cannot judge the clinician's ability for themselves. This is in contrast to situations where the public can judge, such as when they employ mechanics and other workers.

The system of credentialing restricts the voluntary market relationship between clinician and patient. Only people who are credentialed may do certain work, so the patient can hire only those credentialed people for that work. Economists see this as a state-enforced monopoly by people who provide a service. Credentialing is very beneficial to the people in the credentialed occupation, because it restricts their competition.

The monopoly is justified if the safety of the public--the prevention of harm to them--is valued more than the freedom of the uncredentialed person to practice, or the freedom of the patient to choose an uncredentialed clinician. Credentialing replaces the market as the information-gathering function for the individual. Instead, the state functions as the market does in other situations, inquiring about the education and ability of the clinician.

Because the US Constitution did not grant the power to regulate practice to the federal government, the power to credential is retained by each state's government. The power to regulate clinical practice is among those that the Tenth Amendment reserved to the states. For this reason, each of the 50 states has different credentialing laws and may credential different occupations as it sees necessary.

In the latter half of the 20th century many different types of workers were credentialed in the different states. This seldom was done at the request of the public or their lawmakers--almost always being done through the efforts of people in the occupations. Some see the resulting confusion of laws and bureaucracies as wasteful and ineffective to protect the public. In the 21st century, it is projected that credentialing restrictions will decrease, with more occupations cross-trained in several skills. The hoped-for result would be workers able to do several kinds of tasks.

Licensure and registration

Legally enforced credentialing generally is called licensure or registration. The most restrictive status is mandatory credentialing--**licensure**. Licensure requires the clinician to be licensed in order to do certain kinds of practice. No one, other than the person licensed, is permitted to do that particular practice. Sometimes an incorrect distinction is made between "mandatory" and "permissive" licensure. Using the term *licensure* implies that it is mandatory. "Permissive" licensure should be classed with the less restrictive status of registration.

The next less restrictive level of state-enforced credentialing is **registration**. Registration does not restrict the practice of an occupation as does licensure. Instead, it restricts the use of a certain title to a person who has proved certain qualifications to the state agency. Laws that register or title clinicians, designate only that the title is protected. The law says that certain people with certain education or competence are registered (or certified) and that they have a protected title. Only the use of the title is prohibited to others, not the practice of what they do.

From the public's view, the purpose of registration law is to inform the public that this person has certain qualifications. From the clinician's view, the purpose of registration is an economic one-- that people will choose the titled over nontitled clinician.

Titling and registration laws are considered steps toward the goal of the more restrictive status of licensure. Registration laws are permissive credentialing--the clinician may be registered, but is not mandated to be registered, to do the work.

As a historical note, for example, registered nurses are called "registered" because initially they were listed on a central registry that checked their credentials and sent them on cases. They were required to register every year.

When nurses sought and obtained legal protection of their title, they still were considered "registered," but now with the state. More recently all RNs have been licensed, restricting the practice of nursing to certain persons, and not merely the title of "registered." Though now licensed, nurses still are known by the name of the old system--"registered."

Less restrictive of practice and freedom to contract than state registration, is a system of voluntary credentialing. This usually is done by a private organization that tests and approves of people seeking to be certified as meeting certain criteria of education and examination.

The language of credentialing law is vague, because it must be. If the practice of various professions were strictly defined and restricted, then for example taking a blood pressure might be considered to be part of "diagnosing" and thus violate the medical credentialing statute. Because of that vagueness, it is very unlikely that an uncredentialed person will be prosecuted for actually doing the practice of a another kind of clinician. More usual is prosecution for falsely advertising oneself as a licensed person--using the title "doctor" or "MD" or "RN" or "RT" without being licensed.

Some state credentialing boards use certification by private associations as a requirement for credentialing as a specialist. In some occupations, the state may rely on the testing by a private group, such as the respiratory care association or the nursing association.

When a state agency allows a private group such as the clinician association to certify the clinician's qualifications, the agency lends state authority and responsibility for credentialing to a nonpublic entity. This is true when the agency uses any test not made by the state, even the NCLEX (the acronym for the basic licensure test for nurses, used in all states).

Nonlegal credentialing is voluntary (not mandated by law). When physician clinicians obtain credentials as specialists (for example, as board-certified), they use a private process regulated by private organizations, not a legal one. Other clinicians who get additional certification such as nurse certification, also use private credentialing.

The actual effect and value of certification may be questioned, however. One study of certified clinicians revealed that 65% of them felt "more competent, " but only 4% fewer errors were reported, only 2% fewer work related injuries, and 1% reduction in discipline by credentialing boards (Cary, 2001).

☜More restrictive status	Less restrictive status ☞		
RESTRICTIONS ON FREEDOM TO PRACTICE, MOST TO LEAST			
Licensure (restricts practice to the person licensed)	Registration (restricts use of a title to the person registered)	Titling by state organization (restricts use of title-- police enforced)	Credentialing by private organization (restricts use of title but not police enforced)

Endorsement and reciprocity

As noted above, some types of credentialing are more likely to create monopoly than others. Any type of required credentialing may decrease movement of clinicians from state to state, interfering with a free market. When a clinician moves to a new state, that state's credentialing agency has the task of ascertaining whether her credentials in the original state meet their criteria for credentialing.

One method of ascertaining credentials to a new state is **endorsement**. In this process the clinician's original state of credentialing endorses her application for credentials to the state where she wants to practice. The term **reciprocity**, however, is properly used only if two states have a reciprocal agreement to honor one another's credentials. Reciprocity exists, for example, if Alabama credentials Florida clinicians on condition that Florida in turn credential Alabama clinicians.

This arrangement is common in lawyer licensing and other occupations. It may be useful for new kinds of clinicians such as physician assistants and nurse practitioners, whose credentialing requirements are not the same in all states.

Compact licensure

Compact licensure is another solution to the restriction of credentialing that limits movement of clinicians from states where they are licensed, to states where they would like to work. Compact licensure is similar to the idea of reciprocity. It was begun for nurses in the late 1990's in the states including Texas, Arkansas, Delaware, Maryland, Iowa, Nebraska, North Carolina, South Dakota, Utah, Wisconsin, and Mississippi. Idaho and Arizona joined as of 2001.

Those states had a compact (an agreement) to license clinicians who were licensed in any of the other states. This idea may be used by other clinician professions in the future. The status of compact states for nurses is located at the National Council of State Boards of Nursing Website, www.ncsbn.org.

New categories of diagnosers/ prescribers

New categories of workers have joined physician clinicians as diagnosers and prescribers–for example, nurse practitioners, physician assistants, advance nurse specialists, and clinical pharmacists. This is a result of economic pressure in recent years, exerted to break the licensure monopoly of physician clinicians.

This move has yielded credentialing of still more categories of workers. All these clinicians function to some degree as physician clinicians did in the past. In many states, they can prescribe some medications under certain conditions. See more discussion in Chapter 4, under the topic of freedom for the clinician.

The credentialing of so many categories of workers in clinical practice has left those who are not licensed or registered or credentialed, almost as the minority. At one time such workers were called "aides," but the prevalence of the disease HIV/AIDS has made that term unusable. A term used to replace "aides" is "unlicensed assistive personnel" (UAP).

Unlicensed assistive personnel

As noted in Chapter 2, the clinician sued for malpractice of the UAP may not be liable, unless the delegation somehow was done negligently. But her credentialing board may hold the clinician accountable and thus subject to discipline, when she delegates part of her practice to a person not licensed. Each state's board will have regulations on the subject if the clinician is responsible for delegated acts under the credentialing law. Those regulations should be available from the board or on its Website.

As an example of a profession's definition of delegation, the council of state nursing boards defines delegation as "transferring to a competent individual the authority to perform a selected [practice] task in a selected situation. The [clinician] retains accountability for the delegation" [material in brackets added] (Hansten, 1998). One author suggests using a "four rights" approach for appropriate delegation--right task, right person, right communication, right feedback (Hansten, 1992).

"Certified" assistants to clinicians are not technically UAPs because their certification functions as something of a credential. The cautions about careful delegation to them apply equally, however.

Pew Commission on Credentialing

Many predict that credentialing will be much less prevalent in 21st century. The powerful Pew Commission on the Health Care Professions (*Pew*, 1995) advocates such change. They say licensure fails to protect the public, increases cost of care, requires that 50 states credential hundreds of occupations, is ineffective to protect public safety, and is restrictive of health care reform.

They recommend replacing licensure restrictions with less restrictive forms of credentialing, with cross-training of workers, and with testing for competence. The ideas are sure to be popular with states that are trying to save money on clinical practice, and with managed care companies trying to cut costs by using workers more flexibly.

A follow-up study (*Pew* 1998) found that despite major changes in today's health care environment, most boards that regulate medicine, nursing, pharmacy, and other professions, do not require health professionals to periodically demonstrate their competence. Legislatures have not forced regulatory boards to set standards for continuing competence, leaving that role to the private sector. The report contends that this raises major quality of care issues, and may be putting consumers at risk.

The Taskforce asserted that minimal standards that prevent the most egregiously incompetent health professionals from practicing are not enough, that law "must ensure that every patient receives quality care." The report builds on the 1995 recommendations and says that policymakers should focus on three broad areas for improving how health care professionals are regulated:

1) health professions boards and governance structures,

2) scopes of practice authority, and

3) continuing competence.

Regarding each area:

1)   Revamping professional boards within each state will be a major step, according to the report, because these are "the key to the current professional regulatory scheme." Although these boards are charged with consumer protection and are required to have open meetings, their processes are generally unknown to the public, according to the Commission. A persistent lack of coordination among the individual boards within a state or among the states has led to under use of professionals, turf battles regarding scopes of practice, limited professional mobility, and has restricted access to care for patients.

2)   The report criticizes scope of practice laws, describing them as "a source of considerable tension" among health professions that leads to

costly and time-consuming turf battles that clog legislatures around the country. The Commission says that more empirical evidence is needed to help legislators decide whether new or unregulated disciplines should be regulated and whether currently regulated professions, such as nursing, should have expanded practice authority.

3) The Commission calls for major changes in how the health professions are regulated. Specifically, the Commission recommends that all health care professionals be required to meet specific competency requirements throughout their careers, not with just one credentialing exam at their entry into practice.

The Commission also recommends that individual health professional boards increase representation of public, non-professional members to at least one-third of the members of the boards, in order to ensure that the professional board is more accountable to the public. The Commission recommends that states implement nationally uniform scopes of practice for all the professions.

Discipline

Under current credentialing statutes, clinicians who harm are punished for violations of the law. Below under common provisions are listed some reasons your credential can be **disciplined**. The discipline might be a warning, probation, suspension, termination, or non-renewal. Many credentialing statutes require those who are credentialed to obtain a minimum amount of continuing education, and to prove that they have done so or else risk discipline.

An investigation of your credential is serious. A malpractice suit can cost you money, but a credentialing problem can cost you a career, a livelihood. Consider any credentialing board investigator to be an arm of the police, because he is. Consult your personal lawyer prior to providing any records requested or answering any questions. Your intent is not to thwart the law, but to ensure that any and all of your rights are protected.

If you receive a discipline from a state credentialing board, you can contest the board's decision by filing for a review in court, just as you could contest any decision by an administrative agency. The board must comply with your right to due process and the state's administrative procedure act (Jordan, 1994), discussed in Chapter 1.

Due process is guaranteed in the US Constitution in both the Fifth and Fourteenth Amendments of the Bill of Rights, discussed in Chapter 1 and again in Chapters 4, 5, 6, and 7. Due process includes at a minimum: notice of charges, the right to defend against the charges, and unbiased decision makers.

Your state will have a some kind of administrative procedure act, that specifies just what procedure the licensure board must follow to investigate, to prosecute, and to judge a complaint that is filed. Decisions of administrators may be wrong, so you will have access to an appeal to the court system after final board action.

Contacting the state credentialing authority

Because each state's laws are different and subject to change every legislative session, no book can't tell you what is in your own state's law. Even a list of the credentialing board locations and phone numbers or Website of each state, rapidly would be outdated. But you easily can contact your state's credentialing board and find your credentialing law.

Most credentialing boards have Websites and email addresses, so start with a search on the Internet. If that is impossible or unsuccessful, call information at the state capital or larger cities and ask for the phone number. From that office you can get the name of the executive director and the address of the board. During the call, ask for an annotated copy of your credentialing law and regulations, or write to the state credentialing board at the address you obtained.

Common provisions

When you get your copy of your state's credentialing statute, notice the titles to its various provisions. Credentialing statutes generally
1) establish a board,
2) define the practice that is credentialed,
3) prohibit practice that is uncredentialed,
4) set minimum qualifications for credentialing and minimum curricula for schools of clinicians,
5) provide for examinations for credentialing, and
6) list exceptions from the requirements for credentialing.
7) Perhaps most important to the individual clinician, the law will set out reasons the board can discipline the clinician's credentials.

Relative to heading #7, most credentialing laws list "unprofessional conduct" or "professional misconduct" as one possible reason for disciplining the credential. As example, conduct that has been considered by nursing boards to be professional misconduct include advising a patient of a cancer treatment alternative that the patient's physician clinician opposed (*Tuma,* 1979) and giving patients needed and ordered morphine from another patient's supply (Headlines, 1993).

A nurse lost her license for "unprofessional conduct" because, after much deliberation, consultation, and an independent assessment, she did not report her coworker for misappropriating drugs (Fiesta, 1990).

As an example of a credentialing board's use of "unprofessional," the Texas nursing board defines "unprofessional." The Board then says that the rules they made are intended to protect clients (nurse newspeak for "patients") and the public from "incompetent, unethical, or illegal" conduct of licensees. The Texas board does have authority over illegal conduct, and incompetent conduct should also be illegal.

However, it should be noted that un*ethical* conduct does not necessarily fall to the lower level of incompetent or illegal practice. Ethics covers higher optional actions than the minimum legal safe practice. If you are ethical you will be legal, but if you do not reach the higher level of ethical behavior you still might have exceeded the minimum legal standard.

The Texas board says the purpose of the definition and rule making about professional conduct is to identify behaviors of the nurse that the board believes are *likely* to "deceive, defraud or injure clients or the public." Note that unlike malpractice law, your act may violate the credentialing law even if it does not injure the patient. The patient may be, often is, entirely unhurt by an act that the board considers is *likely* to injure him. Some bad behaviors are listed in such a rule, but others that are not on the list also can be punished. For example, most credentialing boards have the power to discipline a clinician's credential because of failure to blow the whistle on a colleague (Tex. Admin. Code, 2001).

One of the liabilities of having a credentialing law is that state legislatures may use such laws for purposes other than protecting the public. For example, they may impose a tax just on your occupation, a tax you must pay in order to stay licensed. In an extreme example, a license can be lost for neglecting to file a state income tax return, characterized as a crime of "moral turpitude."

As noted in Chapter 1, a nurse in Massachusetts challenged the state's requirement on the renewal application form, that nurses swear they have filed state income taxes. The Massachusetts Supreme Court ruled she had to swear to that for license renewal, even if it appeared to have nothing to do with safe nursing practice (Holzer, 1991).

You are still practicing your profession even if you are conducting some or all of your practice by telephone or on the Internet. Thus your credentialing board has power to regulate that practice as well as your practice in person (Kupchynsky, 2001).

National Practitioner Data Bank

Federal law enforces the values, Do Good and Don't Harm, by collecting and making available information about "bad" clinicians. The National Practitioner Data Bank (NPDB) is the result of a federal law, the Health Care Quality Improvement Act. The Data Bank collects information about clinicians in one place, so that those who harm patients can be tracked.

The Data Bank was created to remedy the problem that state boards and employer organizations could not readily find out that a clinician had been in trouble in another state. The perceived need was for a national bank of data on these people.

Such law has negative implications for the ethics of confidentiality of records--not those of the patient, but those of the clinician. The law creates a federal repository of data on malpractice payments and adverse actions taken against the clinical privileges and licenses of certain clinicians (not all--check the Website for current occupations covered). Disciplinary banks have existed before (Milazzo, 1990) but this one is national. A change proposed by the Clinton Administration would have made all the data in the bank available to the public. The bank has a Website at http://bhpr.hrsa.gov/dqa/DataBanks.htm.

Think about it.
Might patients want to know the clinician's secrets, kept by the federal government?
Should they have access?

The NPDB mandates specific reporting requirements. In general, money paid out on a malpractice action is to be reported, whether settlement preceded trial, or was the result of a verdict. Discipline by the employer that affects clinical practice also must be reported. An example of this could be a medication error that resulted in supervised administration. Further, adverse action against the clinician by a state board or professional association must be reported.

Organizations must inquire of the Data Bank before admitting clinicians to staff. If clinicians associate with hospital or nursing homes as consultants, those organizations likely will have to check the Data Bank before affiliation. State boards can get full reports of prior data on individual clinicians who may have been subject to discipline.

Clinicians are to be notified when reports are made and will be given the opportunity to correct errors, if any, in the reports (Birkholz, 1991). As noted, the Data Bank requires insurance companies to report when they pay money on a claim. Many states have statutes that require insurers to report not only when money is paid, but also when a malpractice claim merely is filed against the licensee (Mo. Rev. Stat. 383.000 et seq. 1994). This practice can result in continuing investigation by the clinician's licensure board, even if the malpractice claim was deemed frivolous and dismissed by the court.

A related data bank is the Healthcare Integrity and Protection Data Bank (HIPDB) created in 1996, which collects information on providers who defraud and abuse the federal system of payment for clinical practice (for example, Medicare, Medicaid). The Website for that data bank is the same as for the NPDB--http://bhpr.hrsa.gov/dqa/DataBanks.htm.

The HIPDB also defined and created new federal crimes for fraud (charging the government for unnecessary services) and abuse (charging too much even though the service was necessary). Some states have passed similar laws, that make defrauding the state government a crime.

The ethics and law of clinician education

Credentialing laws require clinicians be educated to a level of competence, and require them to maintain that competence. These laws enforce the ethical values of do good and don't harm. Credentialing law may mandate the minimum educational level for clinicians. The standard for clinician entry into practice usually is education, rather than competence, skill, or knowledge, because education is more easily measured.

Setting standards for practice is not the same as "standardizing" education. Law may require that all clinicians prove they can achieve some standard, either in competence or knowledge. In contrast to that, "standardizing" fixes the way that clinicians are taught, so that only people educated under the standardized format can enter the occupation.

Mandatory continuing education law

Mandatory continuing education (MCE) attempts to protect the public by preventing harm from incompetent clinicians. Many states require mandatory continuing education by clinicians to renew their credentials. Unfortunately, there is little if any connection between MCE and competence. No evidence exists that states with MCE have increases in clinician competency. In MCE states, no evidence shows a decrease in malpractice case filings, settlements, or verdicts, nor fewer disciplines by state boards, nor are patient outcomes improved. Legal challenges to mandatory CE laws have been unsuccessful, except when private groups are delegated to manage CE. Predictably, attendance at continuing education programs does increase under MCE.

Think about it.
If mandatory CE does not guarantee competence, how can it be done?

Competence

Testing the **competence** of clinicians measures their ability in advance of practice–an example is the credentialing test you must pass before entry to practice. In contrast, testing the **performance** of a clinician is an ongoing assessment of her ability during practice. The purpose of credentialing law is to insure competence, to protect the public.

Maintaining competence does not issue directly from "going to courses." Competence is learned and maintained, not only from formal courses, but from informal experience self-sought and self-taught. This voluntary action is the essence of true education. As noted above in the information about the Pew Commission, the direction of policy makers and lawmakers may be to require competence and continued monitoring of clinician performance.

This could be done by requiring all clinicians to re-test periodically, as physician clinicians must re-take specialty boards. Or some kind of practice monitoring could be done, with patient encounter records submitted to reviewers. Credentialing boards have considered requiring work-related CE, and considered requiring a minimum number of hours of work in the field of licensure (Continued competency initiative, 2000). One wonders whether the public will believe that merely practicing one's profession assures competent practice.

Institutional licensure

Proposals have been made for alternatives to licensure. Some include licensing of other kinds of clinicians, or changing the licensure laws to license only institutions, or dispensing with licensure altogether.

To solve the problems of proliferation and restrictions of licensure, the solution called **institutional licensure** has been offered at different times in the past. Economists, planners, and some hospital managers advocate that the state not grant licenses from the government for each kind of occupation.

Instead, they recommend that only institutions be licensed. The qualifications of who does what would be decided within the organization. In such a scenario, the monopoly benefit of licensure would continue for organizations. The monopoly benefit of licensure for clinicians, would end.

Clinicians of occupations that are licensed oppose this solution, because the power to decide safe clinicians would rest with the employer. Clinicians fear that employers would not have the same interests as do professionals–in particular, the professional's interest in professional care, the professional's interest in the patient, the professional's interest in quality of practice. Employers surely would not have the same interest as the clinician, in the clinician's economics.

If you need more ethics theory than Dountoothers

(If you want to read more about or by the authors mentioned in this section, you may be able to find books or articles by them in your library, or in the references listed in Chapter 1.)

Ethics theory related to the value Don't Harm

The philosophy of Immanuel Kant (Prussian, 1724-1804) is most closely related to the clinician's mandate not to harm other people. Kant's basic belief was that people should be respected as persons. That respect would give them standing not to be harmed by another person. People should be treated as important in themselves, not used by others for their own goals.

Kant believed that *a priori* knowledge was possible. That means that he believes you could know something through reasoning, not just by experience. In contrast, knowledge gained after observing the fact of experience, knowing something through the senses, is called *a posteriori.*

Think about it.
Would that make Kant a cognitivist? Answer that question after studying Chapter 5.

Immanuel Kant's name is associated with the **Categorical Imperative.** That is the idea that you should judge every act you do, by whether you would choose the same behavior for everyone in the world. Another way of saying Kant's categorical imperative is "Do only acts that you would be happy to have all other people in the world do."

Think about it.
Will you think about Kant's imperative, the next time you throw a soda can out the car window or see someone else do it?

The word "categorical" means unconditional, mandatory, irrespective of desires or preferences, absolutely necessary, "not permissive." For Kant, there would be no evaluation of the consequences of following the rule–unlike the utilitarian process.

The word "imperative" has roots in the word that means command, from imperial, as in Emperor. The moral imperative would have us all moving toward "a dream of fulfilled human potential to attain a supportive community of peace, justice, and freedom in a sustaining natural environment," a utopian ideal. Advocates of that utopia believe humans need an ideal, something more than the material world to live and strive in.

Think about it.
But what if the ideal is imposed, an imperative for people who do not share it?

Kant described not only the categorical imperative but also other "duty-based," "non-consequentialist" concepts. Kant believes it is not right to base the morality of our acts on whether they produce pleasure (as utilitarians do), because we can never know for sure all the consequences of our acts. We never can know whether or not our acts truly will produce happiness.

For Kant, the **"good will"** is the only intrinsic good. The "good will" is a good mind, a good intent. In contrast, the intrinsic good for utilitarians generally is pleasure. Kant asserts that persons are rational beings, born with the ability to reason to determine what is good. His position is contrasted with a more non-rational concept of being ruled by desire for pleasure (prioritized by utilitarians).

Think about it.
What would Kant think about a patient in a persistent vegetative state, thought to be without reason or cognition?
Would she be a "person" and deserving of respect, or not?

Kant believed people operate on a set of subjective principles that they set for themselves, even if they are not aware of them. Even before we encounter an ethical problem, we have principles that guide our behavior. A word Kant used for these principles is **maxims**. He believed that every time we choose an action, we are acting on a previously formulated maxim. An example: "In this kind of situation, I will choose this sort of act." "When I am asked to document something that did not happen, or not to document something that did happen, I will refuse."

Another philosopher associated with *a priori* reasoning is Renee Descartes (French, 1596-1650) (pronounce it "Day-<u>cart</u>"), whose name you will see associated with the idea that one can be sure of something by reasoning alone. The maxim that he believed proved his existence was "I think, therefore I am." (I know that I reason, therefore I know I exist).

Non-cognitive theories

Some theories of ethics are labeled **non-cognitive**. These non-cognitive theories are used to justify ethical statements--all theories of ethics are. They have particular relevance for this chapter, based on the value of non-maleficence, of not harming patients. You will see the connection as we describe them.

These non-cognitive theories of ethics have developed since the 1950's. They are, predictably, counter to the cognitive theories that also are used to justify ethical statements. In Chapter 4 on Autonomy you will see the **cognitive** theories--intuitionism, contractarianism, and naturalism.

Unlike the cognitive theories, non-cognitivists believe that moral truths are not logically thought out. They believe that moral truths cannot be proven as true or false. This is an extension of the idea of the deconstructivists, that there is nothing real, true, or enduring–that everything is relative, nothing is absolute. Obviously these people are ethical relativists. You will read about ethical relativists in Chapter 6.

One non-cognitive theory is **emotivism**. Emotivism developed as a reaction to problems that some see in the cognitive theory of intuitionism. Intuitionism, the idea that some call merely very fast reasoning, is the idea that you intuitively know the right thing to do.

In contrast, emotivism theory holds that a moral attitude is not reasoned. An attitude such as "harming patients is bad"--the value that is the basis of this chapter--arises from whether people approve of some an act, or not. Only your emotion--the pleasure or pain you feel at considering the act such as harming your patient--determines its morality. The morality of an act is not determined by your logical reasoning about it. In this theory, morality becomes a set of desires, rather than a set of principles determined by reason. You hear a topic and you instantly react: "Abortion, yes!" or "Abortion, no!"

Emotivists can engage in discussions about morals, but the discussion is not based on reasoning. They wouldn't change their reasoning as a result of the talk, because their ethical attitude isn't based on reasoning. They might change their emotion. Argument with emotivists is based on providing further facts that will make the emotivist change or modify his emotion about an issue.

It wouldn't affect him to reason with him, for example, to say that "sometimes we must harm–amputate the foot-- in order to help the patient, that is, to save his life." But it might affect the emotivist if you showed him a picture of the patient's gangrenous foot because it might increase his emotional reaction of disgust. That emotion might make him more likely to agree that "harming" by amputation was the right thing to do--another connection with this chapter on Don't Harm.

Think about it.

Do you think this is a valid moral theory that some thinkers have constructed?

Do many real people make moral judgments like that?

*If your first emotional reaction to sex is "good," do you automatically
think sex is right--moral--in all situations?*

After emotivism, ethicists and philosophers developed another non-cognitive moral theory-- **prescriptivism.** Prescriptivism still is not a philosophy of reason, meaning the proponents of the theory don't believe reason can be used to find ethical truths. Under this theory, moral language is said to be prescriptive--that is, language prescribes some behavior. Moral language either commends or condemns some action.

This theory still was non-cognitive, still from the position that there were no provable moral truths--only mere statements that prescribed some action. The Latin *primum non nocere* is the statement of prescription of this chapter.

Note that non-cognitivists believe that normative ethics–that is, statements of right and wrong-- are not cognitive (not reasoned). Look back at the algorithm in Chapter 1 if you need to clarify normative from non-normative ethics. The non-cognitivists believe that normative statements merely are emotional. In contrast to that position, non-cognitivists do believe that discussing the philosophy of ethics-- metaethics-- is a cognitive discussion.

Non-cognitivists assert that normative ethics, such as statements such as "abortion is wrong," come from the non-cognitive, emotional part of the brain. That is the part of the brain that they believe decides what is ethical. But they assert that philosophers (they) can have reasoned cognitive discussions about ethics. They, non-cognitivists, can talk about questions such as "what do we mean when we say something is 'wrong,'" by using the reasoning part of their brains.

Think about it.

Are these non-cognitivist positions consistent with the data from neurology research that shows thinking is not clearly distinguished into areas of "reasoning" and "feeling?"

Evidence from studies shows that a person whose "thinking" is not a mix of reason and emotion, that is without emotional components such as love, fear, and hate, is demonstrably sociopathic.

REFERENCES

Agich G. Human experimentation and clinical consent. In Monagle J, Thomasma D, (Eds.) *Medical Ethics.* Rockville, MD: Aspen, 1989.

Birkholz G. Implications of the National Practitioner Data Bank for nurse practitioners. *Nurse practitioner,* 1991; 16(8):40, 42-43, 46.

Cary AH. Certification of RNs: results of the study of the certified workforce. *American Journal of Nursing*, 2001;101(1):44.

Continued competency initiative for all nurses. *The Florida Nurse*, December 2000, p. 22.

Federal rule promotes inclusion of pregnant women in clinical trials. *Clinical Trials Advisor*, 2001;6(4):1.

Fiesta J. Safeguarding your nursing license. *Nursing Management,* 1990; 21(8):20-21.

Hall JK. The doctor's legal responsibility to the intentionally injured patient. *Panhandle Health*, January 2000:15-17, update of original publication August 1993:36-7.

____. Research with pregnant women and fetuses: update on the ethics and the law. *Journal of Nursing Law.* 2000;7(3):7-18.

Hansten R, Washburn M. How to plan what to delegate. *American Journal of Nursing*, 1992;92(4):71.

Hansten R, Washburn M. *Clinical delegation skills: a handbook for professional practice.* (2d ed.) Gaithersburg, Md: Aspen Publishers, 1998.

Headlines. *American Journal of Nursing,* 1993; 93(3): 9. Conversation with Ray Linder, Director of Labor Relations, Montana Nurses Assn., 1 September 1995.

Holzer HM. The physician's license: An Achilles heel? *Journal of Legal Medicine,* 1991; 12:201-220.

Jordan DRE. Licensing issues at the administrative hearing commission. *Journal of the Missouri Bar,* January-February 1994; pp. 23-29.

Kupchynsky RJ and Camin CS. Legal considerations of telemedicine. *Texas Bar Journal*, 2001; 64(1):20-31.

Law Notes. *Wall Street Journal,* 23 June 1993, p. B5.

Lawsuits resolved in favor of physicians and patients. *Action, Texas Medical Association*, November 2000, pp 1-2.

McRae M. Central Africa's orphan gorillas. *National Geographic,* 2000;197(2):84

MD can sue for slander 3 years after statement, 14 MLW. 324, 358, 3/27/2000.

Milazzo VL. Disciplinary data banks are not new. *National Medical-Legal Journal,* 1990; 1(2):2.

Miller P.   Crusading for chimps and humans.   *National Geographic*, 1995;188(6):102-129.

Moore v. Regents of the U. of California et al., 88 Dailey Journal D.A.R. 9520 (Cal. Ct. App., 2d Dist., Div. 4, 1988).

Permissible medical experiments. *Trials of War Criminals before the Nuremberg Military Tribunals under Control Council Law No. 10: Nuernberg, October 1946-1949. 2.* Washington, D. C.: U. S. Government Printing Office, pp. 181-182.

Pew Health Professions Commission Taskforce on Health Care Workforce Regulation. *Strengthening consumer protection: Priorities for health care workforce regulation.* The Pew Foundation, 1998.

Pew Health Professions Commission Taskforce on Health Care Workforce Regulation.   *Reforming Health Care Workforce Regulation: Policy Considerations for the 21st Century.*   The Pew Foundation, 1995.

Schloendorff v.   Society of New York Hospitals, 211 N.Y. 125, 105 N.E. 92 (1914).

Tex. Admin. Code, §217.13 (Vernon Supp. 2001).

Tuma v. Board of Nursing, 100 Idaho 74, 593 P2d 711 (1979).

Chapter 4: Be Free.

> *"The only freedom which deserves the name is that of pursuing our own good in our own way, so long as we do not attempt to deprive others of theirs, or impede their efforts to obtain it."*
> **J.S. MILL, *On Liberty***

CONTENTS

If you need more ethics theory than Dountoothers
- *Autonomy*
    - Limits on autonomy
        - *Harm as a limit on autonomy*
        - *Offense to others as a limit on autonomy*
        - *Paternalism as a limit on autonomy*
        - *Legal moralism as a limit on autonomy*
        - *Necessity as a limit on autonomy*
    - *Kant on autonomy*
    - *Cognitive theory*
        - Intuitionism
        - Contractarianism
        - Naturalism
    - *Egoism*
        - Psychological egoism
        - Ethical egoism
    - *Existentialism*
        - De Beauvoir
        - Sartre
    - *Structuralism, Deconstructivism*

REFERENCES

Key concepts

autonomy	**DNR**	intuitionism
consent	mental health	*prima facie*
implied consent	directive	contractarianism
express consent	Patient Self-	naturalism
consent by proxy	Determination	naturalistic fallacy
minor	Act	egoism
emancipated	transplantation	psychological
incompetent	futility	egoism
incapacitated	harm	ethical egoism
ward	offense	existentialism
guardian	paternalism	structuralism
advance directives	legal moralism	deconstructivism
living will	necessity	
durable power of	heteronomy	
attorney	cognitive theories	
out-of-hospital		

The ethical value: freedom

The Latin-derived word for freedom is autonomy. The word **autonomy** comes from the Latin--*auto* means "self," and *nomy* means "control." Other words that convey somewhat the same idea are power, liberty, and choice.

The individual's autonomy--freedom to act–is not absolute. Laws enforce, protect, but also limit the individual's power to decide and to act. The philosophy underlying the value of freedom is individualism, as contrasted with the philosophy of collectivism.

Think about it.
Does anyone have complete control over him- or herself?

Some clinicians would always value the patient's autonomy--or their own autonomy--first. That means autonomy would win over doing good, not harming, being fair--over life itself. Others believe that, depending on the situation and the person, any one of the values can be most important at any given time.

Remember the discussion in Chapter 1, that when values seem to conflict in reality it is not the values in conflict. It is the people who are in conflict. If values seem to conflict in your own mind, go back to the value in Dountoothers–treat other people as you'd want to be treated.

Law enforcing the value: Be Free
Freedom for the patient
Consent

Implementing the value autonomy means that patients can refuse to follow your orders, may refuse treatment, and may choose to follow lifestyles that cause them higher risk of illnesses--smoking, drinking, eating fat foods, promiscuous anal sex, and/or abuse of injectable drugs. You may inform them of the consequences of their behavior--indeed, the law probably would hold you to the standard of informing them fully of their risk.

But after you have informed them, you will not be held responsible either morally or legally for the consequences they choose to risk. If they are competent adults, honoring their autonomy means you cannot force them to behave in any different way. You are their advisor, not their parent, not their policeman.

The US Constitution has a guarantee of freedom -- not all countries do. The Fifth and Fourteenth Amendments of the Constitution protect the "life, liberty and property" of the people, against taking by government without a good reason. Note that life and property are protected in addition to liberty.

No person shall...be deprived of life, liberty or property without due process of law... (Amendment V, US Constitution–limits the federales).

No state shall... deprive any person of life, liberty or property without due process of law... (Amendment XIV, US Constitution–limits the states).

Think about it.
Is the right to keep private property you own, related to having liberty?
Are people free if they can't earn, and own, and keep property--their means of survival?
If people can't keep their own property, the means of survival, might they be dependent on others–the government or charity–for their very lives? If that were so, could they ever really be free?
Are the three rights--to life, liberty, and property--all related?

State laws that enforce the patient's freedom, include 1) laws of consent, and 2) laws of advance directives. In reality, advance directives too usually give or withhold consent to treatment, to take effect in the future.

**CONSENT =
CON (with) & SENTIRE (feeling)**

The word "**consent**" is derived from two Latin words, *con* meaning "with" and *sentire* meaning "feeling." The origin of the word shows that the measure of consent is whether the patient feels in agreement with someone else, the clinician. Because a competent adult is considered to be the "owner" of her own body, she may give or withhold consent, to what is asked of her. This autonomy over our bodies reached the level of a fundamental right under the US Constitution, in the Cruzan decision by the Supreme Court (*Cruzan*, 1990). More in Chapter 7 about that.

Exceptions to the patient's power to give or withhold consent are made in certain circumstances. For example if the patient is not competent, or if someone else might be harmed by her refusal (for example, her fetus), her power to withhold consent might be curtailed. Some general rules for consent follow.

Consent is the defense to a civil lawsuit for battery. As you saw in Chapter 3, the act of battery may be as benign as touching the patient without her consent. But consent is not a defense to a criminal charge of battery. One cannot consent to being beaten, a non-benign touching. The law requiring informed consent enforces a minimum of another value, Telling Truth.

Consent is a process of agreement, not a piece of paper with a signature.

Beware (be wary) of relying too much on written, signed forms. True consent is a continuing process, an agreement between the patient and clinician on a procedure--not merely a signed form. Patients often do not understand what they are signing, and even if they sign a form, later they may deny that they were fully informed of the dangers of the procedure.

Remember, the patient can change his mind. If there is any question as to whether the patient has understood and consented to a procedure, err on the side of caution. Delay the procedure, and explain more fully to the patient to make sure nothing is done without his full consent.

Two categories of consent are recognized--implied and express consent. **Implied consent** is not expressly spoken or written out. In such cases consent may be implied by the patient's condition. One place for this kind of consent is the emergency department, but consent can be implied in the outpatient situation if action is necessary.

Consent is implied if failure to act immediately would result in death or serious harm to the patient's health, no matter where that occurs. For example, if a patient is in cardiac arrest, consent to do cardiopulmonary resuscitation (CPR) will be implied. Consent will not be implied, however, to do elective surgery.

Consent also may be implied by the patient's act, by his coming to a place where treatment is given. Consent for some kinds of care is implied by the fact that the patient came to the clinician or sought treatment. The act of coming implies that the patient wanted the kind of care usually given in the place where he sought care.

In the past, consent for outpatient care was implied--the clinic patient rarely was asked to sign a consent. But express consent forms are becoming more common in outpatient offices, as a result of the fear of litigation.

Express consent is just that--expressed, either in writing or speaking. A spoken consent is just as valid as a written one, but it is harder to prove in court years later, if that is necessary. Evidence presented by testimony of the clinician that the patient spoke his consent, plus evidence of a written consent, will carry more weight with a jury than the testimony alone. Written consents have become the standard, so that failing to have the patient sign one might constitute evidence of failure to obtain any consent.

Some states have specific consent forms for specific procedures or situations, and use of those will protect against a lawsuit for negligent failure to obtain informed consent. The management of your organization will know the details of those statutes and consent forms, or you can find the consent statute in the index of your state's statutes or administrative code or on the Internet. The patient's living will also may be evidence of express consent to certain treatment–or express withholding of consent to certain treatment. It is necessary to read the details of the document.

One variation of express consent is **consent by proxy**. Consent by proxy still is evidenced by verbal or written expression, but in this situation one person gives consent for another--she becomes proxy or stand-in for another. This happens when a parent consents for a minor, or a guardian/surrogate consents for an incompetent ward (see discussion of incompetence below).

Kind of Consent	How Evidenced
Implied	Act or condition of patient
Express	Verbal or written by patient
By Proxy	Verbal or written by proxy

Minors

People under 18 usually cannot consent for themselves. The parent of the **minor** or the child's guardian can consent to treatment for him. If the parents are divorced, the parent with custody should be asked to consent. The parent or guardian has the power to consent or refuse for the child, only if the decision is made in the child's best interest.

If you think the decision made is seriously against the child's best interest, you may have a responsibility to intervene. The child is your patient, the parent is not. Your ethical duty and legal responsibility is to do what is needed to be an advocate for the child's best interest. Under some state laws, if you suspect that a minor has been abused the child may be examined without the parents' permission.

Some minors have become **emancipated** or freed, so that they are able to consent for themselves. They include minors who are married, minors who live independently from their parent, or minors who are in the military. The mother who is a minor generally can consent for herself and for her child, but this may not be true of the father who is a minor. Your state's statute will specify who qualifies as an emancipated minor in your state, and if you frequently practice with adolescents you should read the statute.

Some states have statutes that allow minors to consent for themselves to certain kinds of treatment, for certain conditions. Such treatment includes treatment for sexually transmitted diseases (STD) including HIV/AIDS, consent to abortion, consent to treatment for drug abuse, for treatment during pregnancy, and so on.

By the way--"sexually transmitted" in the old days was called "venereal disease." The origin of venereal is Venus, because the connection to the worship of the goddess of love was noted early after the poster boy of venereal disease, syphilis, was taken to Europe from the Americas. The name VD was changed to STD, to reduce the stigma of the label.

Think about it.
Did it work? Is the stigma reduced?
Can you change the reality of the thing by changing its name?

If you need specific information about your state's law on minor consent, you may be able to get it from the emergency or pediatrics department of your local hospital, your statute index at the public library, under "minors" or "consent" or some of the conditions or procedures to be done, or on the Internet as detailed in Chapter 1.

Consent and refusal for incompetent patients

Patients who are incompetent may not be able to consent for themselves. A three-part test for competence is below--not the specific legal definition in your state's statute, but a general guide to help you decide whether your patient is competent to give or withhold consent to a procedure or treatment.

TEST FOR COMPETENCE TO SIGN A CONSENT:

1) **Can your patient understand information about the procedure, including alternatives?**

2) Can your patient think and decide and communicate her decision about the procedure?

3) Can your patient understand the consequences of her decision?

If the patient "fails" any one of the three parts, she's unable to consent for herself.

Think about it.

What if your patient passes parts one and two of the competence test, but not part three?

For example, she says "Yes, I understand that surgery is one alternative, and I've decided not to have it." Is she competent without part three?

Suppose she says then, "No, I don't think my leg is gangrenous; I think that black part of my foot will clear right up if I go home"?

SHE FAILS.

Note that it is the clinician, not the court, who makes the initial determination of whether the patient is competent to make a decision. You make it every time you allow a patient to give or withhold consent to a procedure--you don't let her consent if you think she's not competent.

The patient in the example above may need a guardian, in which case you should contact your organization's social service department. Or she needs some member of the family to consent for her. Some states have statutes that specify which members of the family can consent–find out from the organization's surgery department, from the statutes in your local library, or the Internet as described in Chapter 1.

Mentally ill patients can give or refuse consent to treatment, to the extent that they have decisional capacity–see the criteria above. Patients with exacerbations of chronic mental conditions may have completed a mental health advance directive that consents to certain kinds of treatment, discussed later in this Chapter.

Shorthand test for competence: If your this patient were your mother would you let her give consent for surgery?

The clinician who will perform the procedure is responsible for explaining the procedure to the patient, and ascertaining her consent (*Nevauex*, 1983). Non-physician clinicians may be responsible for obtaining the patient's signature on the consent form and for signing the consent form as a witness to the patient's signature. As witness, your signature does not mean that you affirm that the patient consented, you merely are witnessing that he signed. However, as a clinician you have a duty to be an advocate for the patient.

If you believe the patient is not fully informed, it is your responsibility to bring that fact to the attention of someone who can remedy the situation. A Texas case held that nurses were responsible, when they failed to explore their patient's misunderstanding of the surgery to be performed. She thought there was merely to be an examination, but the surgery listed on the consent form that she actually signed said "hemorrhoidectomy" (*Urban*, 1993).

To be valid, consent must be informed–unless the patient refuses the information. The patient can waive his right to receive information he doesn't want to hear, about a procedure he will undergo. The reason he doesn't want to hear the information should be explored. Document the reason and ask the patient to sign a written waiver of his right to receive information. In such a case, the patient is not giving informed consent, but that is done at his request.

Informed consent standards

The old standard for informed consent was "What does the reasonable clinician tell the patient about the procedure?" The newer standard for how much and what information the patient needs, is: "What would a reasonable person in similar circumstances need to know to make an informed decision?" The standard shifts from clinician-centered to patient-centered.

Failure to inform the patient to that standard could leave you open to a lawsuit for negligent failure to obtaining informed consent. That is a malpractice tort in which the rules of negligence from Chapter 2 apply-- not an intentional tort of battery in which the rules from Chapter 3 apply.

The practical difference in law: before, an expert witness clinician could testify to the standard, as to what the reasonable clinician would tell her patient. Now, the jury doesn't need an expert; they can use their own standard as "reasonable people in similar circumstances" to gauge whether the patient had enough information.

People who are dependent on others, such as the minors discussed above, have less autonomy. Thus they have fewer powers to consent or to refuse treatment for themselves under the law of consent. **Incompetent** patients are considered unable to make rational decisions in their best interest. Generally they cannot lawfully give or withhold consent to treatment for themselves. Some statutes use the term

incapacitated instead of incompetent, and if so there is no legal difference.

People who have been formally judged by a court to be legally incompetent are called **wards**. The person who is made responsible for the patient is called the **guardian**. The guardian has the power to give or to withhold consent for his ward. The standard by which the guardian's actions are measured, is:

What is in the best interest of the patient/ward?

Some state statutes give family members authority to decide for patients, even if the patient has not been judged to be incompetent in court. If the patient has not had a guardian appointed and she does not fit any of the specified circumstances in the statute–or if there's no state statute written on the subject–then case law may determine who consents to or refuses treatment.

Your organization's risk manager or attorney will have information on your organization's policy. You can find the statute if your state has written one, by looking in the index to statutes in the library or on the Internet. Your organization's policy regarding who consents for incompetent patients is based on statutes and case law. If there is no law that governs, follow the standard of acting in the patient's best interest. Back to the Dountoothers standard in Chapter 1–treat the patient the way you'd want yourself or your family member treated.

In such situations, the reasonable, self-interested question of the organization and clinician is: "Who can successfully sue me and for what?" If your patient receives care that a reasonable clinician would have done for the patient's benefit, the answer is probably no one, for any reason.

Specific consents and refusals

As mentioned above, some state statutes specify the consent forms to use in certain procedures. Usually these are consents for commonly performed surgeries. The signed paper creates a presumption that consent was informed. Failure to use the correct form might result in the opposite presumption.

Special consents forms must be used when providing immunizations. The Center for Disease Control writes federal rules (42 CFR 110) specifying what information must be provided in consent forms from patients being immunized against diphtheria, pertussis, and tetanus (DPT); measles, mumps and rubella (MMR); and polio.

Consent to participation in research is a special consent, overseen by a board with power delegated by the federal government through regulations. (The Institutional Review Board and other legal and ethical research concerns are covered in Chapter 3, Don't Harm.)

Withholding consent to treatment

Withholding consent to treatment is considered differently in law from giving consent to treatment, because giving consent is seen as life-affirming and withholding consent is associated with ending life. Exceptions to the power of a competent adult to withhold consent to treatment may be made, if the interests of other people are affected. An example of that is the situation in which the father of children refuses a transfusion.

The presumption sometimes is made by clinicians that the patient who refuses treatment is incompetent. For example, one surgeon described her patient: "He must be crazy. He refused to let me treat him." While clinicians must assess the competency of their patients, considering the patient incompetent merely because he refuses treatment could lead to abuses. Treatment should never be forced on patients without 1) a careful determination of the patient's status as incompetent, and 2) assessment of the treatment's status as necessary.

If the patient leaves a medical organization against medical advice (AMA), that act negates any consent to treatment that was implied when the patient came to the organization for care. Patients who are not competent may require forced protection (restraint) if leaving would endanger them.

The psychiatric commitment law in your state gives the clinician a limited ability to act without the patient's consent, but the law prescribes a process that must be followed. In general, to forcibly keep a patient against his will requires that it done in the interest of the patient or of other people. That is, it must be evident that the patient is incompetent and if allowed to leave he would be a danger to himself, or dangerous to others.

A quick assessment for competency to leave against advice, is the familiar "Is the patient competent to give consent to surgery?" If not, the clinician must contact the proper authority within the organization for the procedure to follow to protect the patient.

Even if the patient is considered competent to leave AMA, the same contact to authority must be made. The patient should be asked to sign a release form, stating that his discharge is against the advice of the clinician. Remember that the patient leaving against advice is still your patient until he is out of your care.

Emergency and psychiatric departments should maintain policies regarding patient refusal of treatment, that enforce good ethical standards and the applicable statutes of your state. The text of such statutes can be obtained from the local branch library's set of state statutes, indexed under Mental Health, Involuntary Commitment, or similar words--or on the Internet.

Advance Directives

It is an error to say or write "advance<u>d</u>" directives. There is no "d" at the end of the word. There are no "basic" directives, so logically there will be no "advance<u>d</u>" directives. **Advance directives** are merely directives, made in advance of something happening. They are made by people who worry that they will become incompetent and unable to give or withhold consent to treatment for themselves.

Kinds of advance directives

ADVANCE DIRECTIVES COME IN (AT LEAST) FOUR FLAVORS:
(Texas specific--your state may differ)

Kind of Directive	Says what?	Who decides incompetence	Revoke while incompetent
Living Will	Says **what I** want, *if* incompetent and terminal	Clinicians	Yes
Durable Power of Attorney for Health Care	Says **who** decides what I want if incompetent (not necessarily terminal)	Clinicians	Yes
Out-of-Hospital DNR	Says (usually) **"don't resuscitate"** to EMTs (signed by physician)	Not applicable	Yes
Mental Health Declaration	Says I **want** certain treatment if incompetent	Judge	NO

All except the OOH DNR must be made *while* the person is competent. All except the OOH DNR take effect only *after* the person is incompetent.

In legal theory, advance directives are a presently given or withheld, consent to future treatment. In practice, advance directives almost always withhold consent to some treatment that is anticipated to be given in the future. Advance directives include living wills (written or spoken), durable powers of attorney for health care, out of hospital do-not resuscitate (DNR) orders, or mental health declarations. All these advance directives have been written into statute law since the 1970's, so you may anticipate that others kinds will follow.

In general, an advance directive must be made by a competent person, and takes effect only if and when the patient becomes incompetent. The directives have force only if they were made by competent people who had capacity to consider their own best interest at the time the directives were written.

Advance directives must be made, and signed (if written) by a person who is able to consider information, to make decisions, and to know the consequence of those decisions. The rough guide for competence is the same as given above--whether you would consider the person competent to give or withhold consent for surgery.

History

In 1967 the Euthanasia Society (now called Choice in Dying) produced a document that they described as a way to soften resistence to euthanasia. That document is the **living will**. Law journals and state statutes recognized the document starting in 1969. Most of the states have written statutes that request or require clinicians to honor the wishes of the patient for treatment as written in the living will--if the patient becomes incompetent and terminally ill or in an irreversible condition. (Watch that definition in your own state's law carefully--diabetes is an irreversible condition).

The trend in the law is to make the use of advance directives and withdrawal of treatment easier. One rationale for that trend is the myth that old people will not or cannot die--discussed in Chapter 7.

Many states have another statute that patients can use to designate a person to give or withhold consent to treatment for them if and after they become incompetent. That written designation is called a **durable power of attorney** (DPA) for health care. In the DPA a person is named who can give or withhold consent to treatment if the patient cannot--an **agent** for the patient (this person also is called the "attorney in fact" to distinguish her from "attorney at law"). In this situation, the patient is called the **principal**. The DPA laws originally were written to give power to someone to manage the patient's finances, but the laws have been expanded to include health decisions.

Other kinds of advance directives are provided for in some state statutes. The **out-of-hospital DNR** (OOH-DNR) is an order by an authorized clinician (usually a physician) to prehospital clinicians who give emergency care. The order says to <u>not</u> give certain care (usually resuscitation) when clinicians are called to the patient's aid outside the hospital. If you work in this area of care, you must know your statute's specifics. The OOH-DNR may be effective even in the emergency department of the hospital.

A **mental health directive** or declaration is written by a person who currently is competent, but who anticipates a period of incompetence or incapacitation because of recurrent episodes of mental illness. That person can write a directive consenting to certain kinds of treatment (usually psychoactive medication, electroconvulsive therapy, and emergency mental health treatment) in the event she becomes incompetent again.

Living wills for kids.

Some state laws provide that parents can make advance directives for their children. These documents in effect order that the child be DNR in case of arrest.

Names vary.

Terms used for the living will and DPA may vary from state to state--for example, Texas law calls the living will a "Directive to Physicians and Family or Surrogates" and calls the DPA a "Medical Power of Attorney" (Texas, 2001)

Needn't go to court.

Refusal of treatment for the incompetent person rarely requires court action to interpret the patient's advance directive. As you will see discussed in Chapter 7, courts that have considered the patient's wishes have used the "substituted judgment" and the "best interest" standards to determine what should be done for the patient. These actually are the same standard.

Also in Chapter 7 you will see explanation for the reason that some courts have required clear and convincing evidence that the patient would wish to withhold consent to treatment in such a situation. That standard has been required instead of the lower "preponderance of the evidence" standard, or a higher "beyond a reasonable doubt" standard-- necessary to convict in criminal cases.

Spoken living wills are valid.

Informal, spoken directives are valid and have been upheld in court cases. Written directives are preferred by lawyers, because they usually are better evidence in court than verbal testimony. Even if the directive does not meet the statute requirements, it tells the decision maker of the patient's wishes.

An advance directive, whether written or spoken, formally or casually made, whether the patient is terminal or not, should be followed if following it will be in the interest of the patient. It shouldn't need saying, but often clinicians fail to do it: Read the directive.

Find it at the library.

The specific statute on advance directives for your state can be found at the local branch library, indexed under headings such as death or Medical Treatment, or on the Internet.

Yet another advance directive.

Another kind of advance directive can be used if guardianship appears to be likely in the future. In that case, the person who anticipates becoming a ward can request in advance that a certain person be named his guardian, or that a certain person not be named his guardian.

The PSDA.

The federal law discussed in Chapter 1 encourages the use of advance directives and hopefully enforces the autonomy of the patient. The **Patient Self Determination Act** also is called the Danforth Amendment, after the senator who sponsored it. The law requires that agencies receiving Medicare money:

1) ask patients if they have advance directives,
2) inform patients of their rights to refuse treatment under state law; and
3) educate staff and the community about those rights.

Failure to comply with the law could cause the organization to lose its Medicare funding. The purpose of the PSDA was at least in part concerned with the economics of care. Advance directives are seen by some as devices to allow patients to die without expensive treatment, so as to save money on care.

Cautions about advance directives

Not all agree that advance directives are beneficial for patients or even that they enforce the ethical value of autonomy. For example, providers don't follow the advance directive in about one-fourth of cases. They are more likely to deny treatment that was requested in the directive, than to give treatment refused in the document (Danis, 1991). Despite years of encouragement, only eight to 15 percent of Americans have written some kind of advance directive.

Think about it.
Have you written an advance directive?
If so, what kind? Why?
If not, why not?

Other negatives of advance directives:

Such documents may be required by state statutes to be copied into the patient's record, creating more paperwork. Advance directives may expose providers to penalties, and advance directives may be contradictory as to the patient's later wishes. The majority of people who have advance directives say they don't want them followed exactly (Sehgal, 1992).

Some clinicians assume that an advance directive on a patient's chart means the patient would prefer to be DNR in an arrest. Some providers may assume that the existence of a directive means the patient doesn't want treatment to save her life, even if her prognosis is good.

Americans of color are less likely than other Americans to have advance directives and they are less likely to donate organs. In part, this may be because they see advance directives and organ donation as taking away their hard-won autonomy and right to good care.

Another argument against using advance directives is that giving or withholding consent to treatment *in advance*, violates the principles of informed consent. The patient who gives or withholds consent in advance of the need for treatment, cannot have full information about a situation that occurs later. Advance directives could allow the past interest of the person--for example, her interest in being in control of her future--to harm her present interest in living, once she becomes incompetent.

As with the requirement for informed consent to treatment, caregivers who suggest advance directives to a patient, or who assist a patient to prepare them, must fully inform the patient of the potential consequences. Those consequences include the assumptions of some caregivers that the patient with an advance directive would not want treatment to save her life.

Some criticize advance directives because they seem to make the patient responsible for his own death. The provider can rationalize that "It's not my decision to terminate care--the patient wanted it this way."

Clinicians have a legal and ethical duty to protect their patient if the surrogate decision maker does not act in the patient's best interest. The clinician can assess that best interest by using her duty to do good for the patient, to do no harm, to preserve the patient's autonomy, and to value the life of the patient. If all other assessment fails, see if the surrogate is treating the patient the way you'd want to be treated--or the way you'd want your father or mother to be treated.

Advance directives about money (wills)

Another aspect of autonomy is the person's freedom or power to make a will that determines who inherits her property after death. Living wills and other advance directives are about your life, but "real" wills are about your property. Clinicians who hear patient questions about wills should understand and communicate one basic legal fact: the patient needs a will.

If you don't make a will, someone else (the state legislature) already has made one for you, parceling out your children and your property. If you die intestate (without a will), the court will apply state law that decides who gets what.

It's unwise to try to answer the patient's specific questions about wills, other than the fact that most people do need a will, and that they should seek an attorney's help to make one. The will "kit" available in the bookstore and on-line is cheap to buy, but it might be very expensive if you make a mistake and your will is held invalid.

In general, clinicians should not witness the patient's will, in order to avoid claims of undue influence later. However, if no other witness is available and it seems necessary, you can sign as a witness, document the patient's mental status and document any circumstances such as who was present and what was said.

Think about it.
Have you made a will?
Why? Why not?

Transplants

Transplantation is discussed in this chapter on freedom, because the value most important to the donor of the body part is autonomy. That autonomy represents the donor's power over her own body after death (or her family's power over the body). The value most important to the recipient of the body part is fairness in the distribution of body parts.

Organ transplantation usually requires a brain-dead, ICU maintained body. But tissues for transplantation (corneas, skin, bone) can be taken from dead, nonmaintained bodies. The term body parts covers both organs and tissues for transplant

At the point of death, the power (autonomy) of the person over her body is transferred to her family. Her wishes about what happens to her body usually should rule over the feelings of relatives, but the strong feelings of relatives may prevail. Laws that enforce control over the body after death include consents required for autopsy and consent to donation for body parts or of the whole body.

Federal regulations mandate that institutions that receive funding from Medicare, must ask families for permission to use transplantable body parts. Proposed laws would mandate that body parts automatically be donated, unless the patient expressed an objection in advance of death.

Transplants also involve economics. Transplantable body parts are in short supply. Some suggest that body parts should be distributed to the highest bidder or most advanced transplant center. Some believe they should be equally available through a waiting list. Most agree that body parts should be available under a fair procedure of allocation.

US statutes make it illegal to pay the donor for body parts--different from some other areas of the world. Some propose a law that would prohibit transplanting body parts that are donated in the United States, to non-U.S. residents. Growing nonrejectable body parts in pigs could provide enough body parts, but this may raise issues of animal rights and of cross-species infectious diseases.

Some transplants are paid for by taxpayers through Medicare and Medicaid, so fairness in the form of social justice might dictate equal outcomes for all. Federal law, the National Organ Transplant Act (NOTA, 1984), mandates fair allocation of organs. A government study concluded, however, that the allocation system of body parts violates that law by denying the parts to sicker patients, and makes some patients wait longer than others. The study said that the needs of transplant centers were favored over the needs of patients.

Federal law set up a network to which all organ procurement organizations must belong if they are to receive federal money. That network is the United Network for Organ Sharing (UNOS), operated under federal contract. The number of people waiting for transplants grows faster than the number of organs available. A single area-wide waiting list means the next patient on the list would get the next organ, instead of distributing organs to the next hospital on the list. Federal law says patients should be prioritized by medical criteria, not social criteria or economic status.

A similar ethical issue of the 70's was the agonizing decision about who would receive (then scarce) kidney dialysis. Congress was asked to help decide. They decided that the taxpayers would pay for dialysis for *everyone* who needed it. So much for asking Congress to make hard ethical decisions. Now the End Stage Renal Disease program (ESRD) costs enormous amounts of Medicare money, and many believe there are patients on dialysis whose conditions are medically inappropriate.

There are said to be fewer organs to use for transplant because fewer people are involved in automobile crashes, and in motorcycle accidents without a helmet. Those events sometimes result in head injuries but little body injury, allowing the patient to be declared brain dead so organs can be taken.

Think about it.

Who should get a new heart?

The oldest, the sickest, the most valuable to society, the most able to benefit from the organ, the most irresponsible, the richest, the poorest?

Do we worry about fairness to the person, about benefit to the person, about the good of the society, about the utility of the person to the society?

If you are asked whether a certain patient should have priority for a new heart, what is your first question?

Does your first question determine in part, what your philosophy and criteria for decision are?

Such as, How old? Sex? Medical condition? What will it cost? If the patient is over 65, will Medicare pay? Should it?

Should Medicare pay if the patient is a multi-millionaire?

What if the patient is older than the age of life expectancy?

What if the patient is a brilliant scientist on the trail of growing new hearts from hPSCs? (Stem cells, see Chapter 7).

What if the patient is an illegal alien from Mexico?

What if the patient is a legal alien from Saudi Arabia with millions to contribute to a new transplant center?

What if the patient is a 60 pack-years smoker (the equivalent of a pack a day for 60 years)?

What if the patient says "I'm not going to quit smoking"?

What if smoking doesn't have anything to do with heart disease, just increases the microbe population in your mouth, and that actually causes heart disease?

What if we find that people who eat potato chips have the same risk of heart disease as smokers?

What if the patient is your mother?

You have been at this kind of questioning long enough to know that none of the above questions have hard and fast answers--the answers *depend*, on your attitude, on the society's attitude. You know also that those attitudes will determine the ethic, and the ethic will determine the minimum behavior mandated in the law. You can analyze the values underlying--autonomy, beneficence, justice, fidelity--and the ethical philosophies including utilitarianism.

Transfusion of blood is a transplant issue too, although the issue is not so controversial because donation of blood does not require a dead body. Live people donate blood, so usually there's no serious shortage of the "transplant." But ethical controversies do exist.

For example, religious groups such as Jehovah's Witnesses object to receiving blood. The law will protect their autonomy to refuse except in extreme cases. If the life of the person needing the blood supports the life of another--for example, a pregnant woman or father of children who need support--the law may override their autonomy to give or withhold consent to treatment Even in those extreme cases, good communication and alternative treatments may avoid the need to seek a court order to treat.

The discovery of the HIV virus in the blood supply created the need to protect the public from harm as well as to tell people the truth. These ethical values, enforced at a minimum level by law, were violated in scandals uncovered in Germany and France, in which HIV-infected blood was given to patients while bureaucrats knew of the infection. The cover-ups by officials were discovered and the people responsible were prosecuted, but not before many people were infected.

Think about it.
What ethical Rule mentioned in Chapter 1 (if the officials had adhered to it) would have prevented that outcome? (Hint: starts with "D.")

Autopsies

The ethics and law of autopsy incorporate autonomy issues. State statutes dictate that an autopsy must be performed under some circumstances of death--usually death from violent, suspicious. or unknown causes. In those conditions, consent for autopsy cannot be withheld.

The state statute on autopsies also specifies who can give or withhold consent for an elective autopsy. If you need it, that law can be obtained from the organization where autopsies are done, or in the local library's statutes indexed under Autopsy, or from the county coroner or medical examiner's office, or on the Internet.

HIV/AIDS autonomy issues

Human Immunodeficiency Virus/Acquired Immunodeficiency Deficiency Syndrome (HIV/AIDS) is discussed as an autonomy issue, because the issue is one of freedom for the person who engages in the risky behaviors that cause most infections. The issue also is one of freedom for the clinician who cares for the patient--because the clinician's life conceivably might be endangered by caring for this patient.

The ethics and law around HIV/AIDS and tuberculosis (TB) recreate controversies that have surrounded communicable diseases throughout history, diseases such as leprosy and bubonic plague. The conflict today is often between the autonomy of the patient to behave freely and to have care when needed, versus the autonomy of the clinician to exercise judgment in her practice.

Whether patients will be held responsible for behavior affecting their health is relevant also to people with diseases other than HIV/AIDS. The issues relate also to smokers with lung cancer, alcoholics with cirrhosis, and other illness in which freely chosen behavior is a causative factor.

A majority of individuals infected with HIV/AIDS, or at risk of the infection, are in that condition as a result of freely chosen behavior. HIV infections leading to AIDS have occurred overwhelmingly in two populations--promiscuous homosexual males and injecting drug users. Both groups engage in the risky behavior that allows transmission of the disease. Only a small percent of the people who are HIV positive, were not engaging in behaviors that are known to be risk for the disease.

Data show that it is far easier for a man to give the disease to a woman through intercourse, than vice versa. Men who have heterosexual intercourse with prostitutes have less risk of getting infected by the prostitute than the prostitute's risk from the customer who is infected. Even considering that fact, transmission of the virus by heterosexual non-anal intercourse is very difficult. Data indicate that people who are not promiscuous, and who do not abuse injectable drugs, have little risk of HIV infection--regardless of their sexual orientation, color, ethnic background, or sex (Padian, 1991; Stewart,1995).

But in future this sometimes fatal disease likely will be concentrated in groups now considered minorities. Already 30% of gay men of color are HIV positive, while only 7% of gay Caucasian men are infected and 1% of gay Hispanic men. This fact will intensify ethical and legal conflicts about the control and treatment of HIV/AIDS. A sizeable minority of Americans of color even now believe that AIDS is an attempt at genocide of their people.

Efforts to educate young people with high-risk behavior have been unsuccessful to prevent HIV/AIDS (Stiffman, 1992). Education apparently is not the answer for the subgroups that engages in such risk behavior.

Laws could prohibit such risky destructive behavior that hurts society. The hurt is the cost of care of people with HIV/AIDS, to all taxpayers. And laws could prohibit acts that hurt other individuals. The hurt in that case is infection of the sexual partners of HIV/AIDS-infected people, who will be infected if their partner does not inform them of the infection. The standard for such laws is discussed below.

Under the Americans with Disabilities Act (ADA), HIV-positive clinicians are considered to have a disability. That means that HIV positive clinicians must not be discriminated against because of their condition, and can bring suit if they are (Nurse, 1999). In addition, if all clinicians were required to be tested for HIV as has been proposed, then the value of fairness might require that all patients be tested as well. Lawsuits with HIV/AIDS as the issue are frequent and will continue to make law in this area.

Much misinformation has been promulgated about this disease. For example, projections for great increases in the numbers of women infected with AIDS, and for an epidemic of heterosexual AIDS in the United States as has occurred in Africa, have not materialized. The conditions in Africa and the U.S. are very different, physically and socially.

Statistics

Statistics used in descriptions of all diseases and especially HIV have large effect on ethics, law, and public policy. For that reason the use of statistics by advocacy groups must be critiqued carefully--see the headline below.

STATISTICS ARE SLIPPERY

Imagine a headline:
WOMEN FIVE TIMES AS LIKELY TO BE NEW HIV INFECTED.

Suppose the data show a 50 percent rise in women infected, and *"only"* a ten percent rise in the numbers of men infected last year. Think carefully about what that means. If few women are infected at present, the proportionate rise in *rate* of infections will be greater in women. For example, if two women in a population are infected this year, and next year three women are found to be infected, there has been a 50 percent rise of infections in women in that group (1 new case + 2 old cases). This statistic sounds alarming, but only a small number of women are infected.

In contrast, if 50 men of a population are infected this year,, and 55 men are found to be infected next year, the rate of increase is only ten percent (5 new cases + 50 old cases). But in that example, five times as many men (5) as women (1) are newly infected that year. The totals: 55

men are now infected, and three women. The headline is comparing a ten percent *increase* with a 50 percent *increase,* but the actual numbers sound much different. Read statistics carefully.

Tuberculosis

Tuberculosis (TB) is the leading single infectious cause of death worldwide. Untreated TB leads to death in an average of five years-the same average prognosis originally was given for HIV/AIDS. TB is related to HIV/AIDS and autonomy, because ninety percent of active cases of TB are reactivation, often in patients with HIV/AIDS. TB control statutes still in effect are available to control patients who will not practice infection control. For laws that interfere with patient freedom, for example, TB and mental health laws, the standard is:

Is the patient a risk to self or society, and is there a less restrictive choice?

TB is more dangerous to clinicians and the public than is HIV/AIDS, because it can be contracted by being in the same room with an infectious person. Some have worried that TB may become a new plague, because the incidence of disease falls and then rises again.

The ethical and legal questions for clinicians about duty to care for the patient versus duty to care for one's self, are the same in HIV and TB as they were for the clinicians of the middle ages who confronted patients with plague.

Some clinicians, reluctant to care for HIV/AIDS patients, may find that the law enforces the duty to care for all patients. Clinicians may refuse to compromise their own safety and ethical standards, but they have a professional responsibility to ensure that the needs of patients are met at least on an emergency basis.

Whether the clinician has a duty to care for all patients and to what extent, depends on a combination of the clinician's ability, the requirements of the patient, and the degree of risk. Clinicians may consider the risk of caring for some patients depending on the degree of risk to themselves, their families, and their personal ethics. If the risk is minimal or low, the legal duty of the clinician is high. The more actual risk, the less compelling the ethical and legal duty.

Specific (and varied) state statutes provide for informing patients about HIV testing, obtaining consent, reporting HIV-positive patients to the proper authority, and for informing partners. These statutes and rules change frequently.

For example, Texas requires clinicians to test pregnant women for HIV, syphilis, and hepatitis B not only during pregnancy but also at delivery, unless the patient refuses (HIV/STD rules, 2000). Your organizations's infection control department, risk manager, the local library, or the Internet will have information on your state statute's specifics. The statute will be indexed under HIV/AIDS, or the spelled-out forms of the words.

Suicide

The ethics and the law of suicide, euthanasia, and assisted suicide are based on the value put on being free--of having power over one's life and death. Some believe a person's right to die extends to the right to kill oneself under some or any circumstances. Some even argue that the freedom to suicide extends to the right to be killed by clinicians.

Mental health clinicians long have assumed that people who want to kill themselves are in some degree mentally ill or at least depressed. Such people have been rescued, restrained, and treated for depression. The clinician's question is whether such patients need help to live, or to die.

The issue of suicide is treated in Chapter 7, Life. But note that the ethics and the law of suicide, euthanasia and assisted suicide, and living wills, all are in some manner enforcement of the value put on Be Free, of having power over one's life and death. The value placed on Life is the counterbalancing weight to the value of being free--free to be dead. In some situations for some people, the value of living does not outweigh the value of dying.

Freedom for the clinician

The issues raised above about caring for HIV/AIDS and TB patients show that not only patients, but clinicians, too, need autonomy. Laws that enforce the value of the freedom of the clinician, include the Constitutional Amendments discussed above, and conscience clauses. These clauses in state statutes protect the clinician from being fired, if she refuses to participate in specific procedures that violate her morality such as euthanasia, abortion, and executions.

Conscience clauses

Some states have "conscience clauses" that allow clinicians to refuse to cause death in nondying patients (that would protect the clinician to refuse an assignment to aid in an execution as well). The law also may allow clinicians to refuse to assist in abortions. Some of the state laws on the subject have to do with life-sustaining treatment of competent patients who have expressed preferences for future treatment, when those patients are dying. Most state legislatures have not considered the situation of the clinician asked to cause death, for example, by dehydration in incompetent, nondying patients.

If they exist in your state, conscience clauses may create more of a legal liability for clinicians who do participate in causing death. Such clinicians then have no exculpation if they assert that they had no choice but to assist.

Conscience clauses enforce the value of autonomy of clinicians who might otherwise be threatened with loss of their job if they refuse to assist in causing the death of patients.

In those statutes, the legislatures often protect clinicians from participation in causing death--even in patients who are dying from other causes and who voluntarily request that food and water be withheld. Evidence of a legislature's concern for clinician ethics and personal morals is the "conscience clause" in Missouri's Elder Abuse Act:

Refusal to honor health care decision, discrimination prohibited, when.

404.872.

"No physician, nurse, or other individual who is a health care provider or an employee of a health care facility shall be discharged or otherwise discriminated against in his employment or employment application for refusing to honor a health care decision withholding or withdrawing life-sustaining treatment if such refusal is based upon the individual's religious beliefs, or sincerely held moral convictions (Elder, 2000).

Clinician rights to refuse

In other areas of clinician freedom, the law is changing because the ethic underlying is changing. For example, freedom is the value apparent in medical ethics cases when the patient wants one thing and the clinician wants something different. Autonomy is important not only to the patient, it is valued by clinicians for themselves, too.

Think about it.
Must the clinician provide care that is considered to be useless, just because the patient or surrogate asks for it?
Must she care for patients whose diseases endanger her?

Can she assert her own autonomy and assist patients to commit suicide?
Can she assert her own autonomy and <u>refuse</u> to assist patients to commit
*   suicide?*

Before you were a clinician, you were a human being with ethics and rights. After your training, you still have power over your ethics and actions, just as you did before. The Fifth and Fourteenth Amendments to the US Constitution, cited in various other chapters, apply to you just as they do to your patients. You have the right to refuse to do any procedure or action that seems wrong to you.

If you do, you may lose your job, depending on whether your state has a conscience clause statute and whether it applies in the situation. But you can never say that you were forced to do an act. That is because the Thirteenth Amendment to the US Constitution forbids slavery. So whatever you do, you do it because you believe it is the right thing to do in the circumstance. You are not being forced to do it. It is your choice to do or not.

Because of the variety of occupations that use this book, it is impossible to discuss the legal issues of autonomous practice of all the professions. But in general, the ethical value of autonomy, mothers the law of all occupations.

Nurse practitioners and physician assistants are the most visible examples of the clinicians who have gained some legal autonomy from physician control. However, all clinicians <u>including</u> physicians must make constant efforts toward independence when it benefits their patients.

History

The ethics and law of clinician autonomy can be better understood and predicted by knowing the history of independent clinical practice. The distinction between professional and nonprofessional clinical practice is a cornerstone of modern practice, but clinical practice is recognized as a continuum of activity that all human beings do for each other.

For example, Florence Nightingale wrote that every woman is at some time in her life a nurse (it might be added, so is every man). She wrote "Notes for Nurses" for lay persons who some time in their lives inevitably would care for another person. The "Notes" were not written for people who care for the sick as their paid work.

In the long process of human economic development, divisions of labor developed in which people began to pay specialists to do patient care work, instead of doing it themselves for their families. Clinicians were "professionals" in the sense that they worked for pay. This differentiated them from people who cared for the family or friends for no pay.

Only later did clinician work come to include a specialized body of knowledge and other attributes, constructed to distinguish professions from other kinds of work. The payment for clinical practice is the basis for imposing a legal duty on clinicians to do good and to prevent harm.

Many professionals still are similar to their amateur counterparts except that they are paid, making the activity their vocation instead of their avocation. Examples of these are professional athletes and professional artists.

CARE CONTINUUM--by complexity and scientific knowledge required, not by intensity or quality or importance of care. (The continuum showing quality and importance of care might well run from right to left!)

Care by family ☞ Care by technicians ☞ Care by professionals

Simply caring for people who were sick likely preceded the attempt to cure those people with magic and its successors--science and medicine. The knowledge that clinical practice is such an old activity makes it easier to understand the autonomy of that practice in the modern era. All along, clinicians including physicians have been autonomous, working sometimes with and sometimes without other clinicians.

Starting in the 1930's, more clinician work moved from the home to the hospital. The Depression of that decade speeded the development of hospital alliances such as Blue Cross and physician alliances such as Blue Shield. These payment plans (insurance) let people pay small amounts monthly to have large amounts available to pay providers when and if needed. The increased technology that developed and was accelerated by WWII in the 1940s, meant that care was better done in the hospitals than the home.

Now clinicians were in closer proximity to each other and more likely to have supervisors. They now had a legal and ethical duty to the employer as well as the patient, and more legal supervision by others.

The wage and price controls of the war years made employers unable to give pay increases to recruit scarce workers. In place of that they gave a new benefit, health insurance. The system of getting insurance through the workplace, accelerated. The clinician now added a fourth legal relationship--to the third-party payer--in addition to her existing duties to patient, other clinicians, and employer.

The majority of clinicians in all areas of clinical practice are women, so the history of women in the society affects the history of clinicians too. Economic needs dictate the success of movements, and with them, clinician autonomy. When economics dictate or allow the attitude that women not occupy jobs, women are seen as better off at home with the children.

The 1950's economic need was for women to be primarily homemakers, because returning soldiers from World War II needed the jobs that women had held during the war. The economics and lower tax structure of the time allowed one worker to earn enough money to support the average family, so fewer women needed work outside the home.

Women clinicians who did work, were perceived to be subordinate to men (for example, to physicians, then almost all men). This dependence was enforced in law, in practice acts that said that clinical practice was done under the supervision of the physician.

Another women's movement in the 1970s and 1980s resulted from the renewed need for women to work outside the home to maintain family standards of material consumption. The clinician credentialing laws then were duly amended in the 1970s and '80s to echo the more independent role of women clinicians. References to physician supervision were deleted.

In 1971, the American Medical Association proposed that nurses become "physician assistants" to relieve the shortage of doctors. Organized nursing declined the invitation, so PA programs recruited paramedics returning from the Vietnam War. Another war created another economic need and opportunity.

Originally programs for nurse practitioners and physician assistants developed as intensive, nonacademic, one-year certificate programs, for clinicians who had a basic education and experience in clinical practice. More recently the programs have moved into academic settings and award a master's degree on completion.

The law has changed again, now to provide legal cover for non-physicians for some medical practices such as prescribing drugs. The non-physician clinician who does medical practice has supervision, by administrative agency or physicians, or practices in collaboration with physicians.

Studies show that alternative providers (in this case nurse practitioners and physician assistants) give primary care as competently as their physician counterparts, for less money. But the patients of these providers are screened for complexity, and the more complex, difficult, and thus expensive cases are referred to the physician or specialist.

The trend toward giving care under managed care organizations (MCOs) may make the controversy over independent clinicians moot for the immediate future. MCOs make clinicians *including* physicians, more dependent, more like employees.

The downsizing of hospitals and predicted return to more out-of-pocket payment by the patient could have two results: More care is and will be given in the patient's home, and the clinician will be paid directly by the patient. The earlier ethic, law, and economics may return, in which the clinician's primary relationship and responsibility is to the patient. (See Medical Savings Accounts in Chapter 6.)

Negligence liability for autonomous practice

In a democratic society, each individual has power over him or herself (autonomy). The law of clinician practice recognizes that autonomy. The other side of the autonomy coin is responsibility, the payment for the autonomy. The clinician has autonomy to act, and as a result must act responsibly. The clinician has responsibility for acts if they harm, or do not help as intended.

Freedom that leads to responsibility is the reason for allowing malpractice lawsuits against clinicians. That concept of responsibility is challenged by ideas of tort reform that would make the employing enterprise liable in place the clinician.

When the clinician is acting in the capacity of physician, the clinician's standard of care is the same standard of care as a physician's (Hirsh,1991). Whether this is an appropriate standard may be questioned, but the public sees the primary care clinician as they have in the past--as a physician. So the standard of care is the same, even if the care is given by a non-physician.

Prescriptions by non-physicians

Most of the states have granted legal authority to some non-physicians, to prescribe some drugs. In some states, nurse practitioners, physician assistants and clinical pharmacists have authority to prescribe without the direct supervision of a physician. In most states, those clinicians may prescribe only in collaboration with a physician.

Until the 1930's, patients could buy drugs directly from the pharmacy, without an intermediary. The physician "prescribed"--meaning recommended–and the patient took the recommendation to the druggist who compounded the drug and sold it. The law that prevents patients from buying some drugs without a prescription has roots in the ethics of Don't Harm--protecting the public. But the effect of the law is to decrease the patient's autonomy and to increase cost.

Economic efficiency is enhanced by eliminating artificial barriers to the ability of the individual to work. One author has proposed a two-part proposal for reform of prescribing law. One part would be to pass an "authorized prescriber" statute, requiring a provider who wants to prescribe drugs to pass an examination on pharmacology and prescribing.

The second part of the proposal would eliminate the prohibition against "unauthorized practice" in the various statutes that credential providers (Hadley, 1989). For example, anyone could do medical practice, but they couldn't prescribe drugs without the "authorized prescriber" status.

Others propose to enhance patient choice in drug therapy and decrease cost, by eliminating the requirement of prescriptions for patients to obtain medications. Patient freedom also would be enhanced by eliminating restrictive credentialing of all providers, allowing patients free access to the provider of their choice (Hall, 1993). This is essentially the situation now with alternative remedies.

The question of whether clinicians can write prescriptions independently, increasingly is moot. Insurers, governmental agencies, and health plans issue drug formularies that limit all prescribers to medications listed within that formulary. As medicine becomes more regulated, so will the people who practice it.

Abandonment

The value that is related to the idea of abandonment of the patient is freedom--the freedom of the clinician to choose whom he will care for. That freedom of the clinician means that the clinician does not have a duty to care for patients indefinitely if he considers the patient to be a danger to himself--see the discussion in HIV/AIDS above. Nor does the clinician have a duty to care for the patient if he believes he cannot help the patient because of a personality or behavior conflict.

However, the clinician's autonomy to choose to care or not, is not absolute. Assuming there is a clinician-patient relationship established, the clinician has a duty not to abandon his patient. The civil law (malpractice lawsuit) and criminal law (credentialing statutes) both enforce that higher ethical duty not to abandon.

The duty not to abandon also could be discussed under Chapter 6, Be True, because one of the values enforced by the law of abandonment is the ethic of being loyal to the patient, of not abandoning him. Concerns about terminating the relationship with the patient also are discussed in that chapter.

You can anticipate from the underlying ethical values that the clinician's legal duty not to abandon the patient means she will care for the patient who needs care, until another clinician can be found or until care can be continued in some other way. For example, leaving an assignment without notifying one's supervisor or arranging for care of one's patients, is at least unprofessional conduct under some credentialing law (Owen, 2000). It also might result in liability for malpractice if it caused harm to a patient.

Some clinicians who work in poor or even unsafe conditions of practice may want to leave their work and/or resign to make a point to management, or because of worry that they are jeopardizing their license. Failure to provide the full period of notice specified in the personnel handbook might bring employer sanctions, but it should not be considered abandonment.

However, leaving patients without immediate care probably would be considered abandonment. That act would expose the clinician to malpractice liability if the patient were harmed by his leaving, or to discipline by his credentialing board even if the patient was not injured. Instead, the clinician should provide for the care needed immediately by patients. The person and organization responsible for the unsafe situation should be informed, in writing, and the clinician should make plans to terminate the relationship with the employer in orderly fashion.

Patient demands

The clinician's exercise of freedom (autonomy) may conflict with the patient's freedom. The clinician has an interest in doing what is seen as the best practice. The clinician is interested in using her best judgment, doing her best work, and being free personally. The clinician has a professional interest in maintaining integrity--the word means wholeness. Clinicians won't do just anything their employer asks them to do. They are free professionals.

Think about it.
Will clinicians do whatever the patient asks them to do?
Would they assist in removing the patient's healthy leg, because the patient who is a beggar wants more sympathy?
In removing the patient's breast, because the patient believes she might get breast cancer? If she has no relatives with cancer? If every woman in her family has developed cancer?

(In a study of 639 women who had bilateral mastectomy for fear of cancer, only 18 fewer women died of breast cancer than a similar group who did not undergo mastectomy. (Prophylactic, 1999)

What will clinicians do for the patient who requests abortion?

Sterilization? In vitro fertilization? Male circumcision? Female circumcision? Cesarean?

(These usually are procedures patients want, not always procedures that are medically necessary for life and health.)

Cosmetic surgery is the classic demand for medically unnecessary care. The majority of these procedures are patient initiated and most would be considered not medically necessary.

Some clinicians assert that patient power to demand treatment should be limited to treatment that the clinician has decided is medically necessary--that the clinician can decide when treatment is futile. But that argument is compromised by actions of other clinicians who assist with and perform treatment done at the demand of the patient and not of medical necessity. Examples of such patient demands may be cosmetic surgery, abortion, sterilization, fertilization, or cesarean sections done for patient convenience.

The difference between clinician autonomy to decide futile care, and clinician acquiescence in patient demands for unnecessary procedures, may depend on <u>which</u> patient demands the care. The patient who wants elective procedures probably is up walking, talking, paying taxes and paying her own bill.

The patient who wants what the clinician considers futile treatment just to live a little longer, likely is old and sick and not valuable to the society. And the taxpaying clinicians are actually subsidizing the care they give that patient.

Conflicts arise between people who value patient autonomy and people who value patient safety (preventing harm). Examples are the lawsuits and controversy over the danger (or nondanger?) of silicone breast implants. Over the last four decades, one million women in the United States, and more in foreign countries, have had the implants. The Food and Drug Administration disapproval of the implants at one point, illustrates again the value of patient safety (doing no harm) prioritized over the value of patient choice (autonomy). The lack of availability of implants became a problem for reconstruction surgery in breast cancer patients.

Think about it.
Should the patient be free to choose breast implants, at slight risk, if she knows the risk and voluntarily assumes it?

Plastic surgery is not limited to facelifts, or nose reconstruction, or breast implants. In some areas of the world, and in the U.S. among some peoples from those areas, clinicians are asked to do what some call female genital mutilation. Others call it female circumcision, or female genital surgery.

The procedure involves a partial or total cutting away of the female external genital organs and the clitoris with razors, ceremonial knives, or blades--often under nonhygienic conditions without anesthesia. If the patient or her family want the procedure done, it may be asked whether female circumcision different in kind, or only in degree, from much other plastic surgery.

Think about it.
Do patients have the right to mutilate themselves?
Do they have the autonomy to ask clinicians to do it for them?
Does the clinician have freedom to refuse to do it?
Do parents have the right to give consent for female circumcision, considered unnecessary by some?
For male circumcision, considered unnecessary by some?

Futile treatment

The issue of the clinician's autonomy to refuse to give "futile" treatment is a problem of definition--that is, when is a treatment futile? The issue is about doing and paying for care that does not return people to full function. In practice, **futility** is asserted only in cases of patients who are not competent, when withholding treatment will end what is perceived as poor quality of life. You will read more about this concept in Chapter 7.

Withholding or withdrawing such care may be appropriate, but use of the word futility may mask the reality of the reason for the action.

Futility means different things to different people. Some consider treatment futile, if it merely keeps the patient alive. Some consider treatment futile if it merely returns the patient to consciousness. Some think that treatment that doesn't return the patient to a meaningful quality of life, is futile. Some might consider the care futile if it doesn't fully return the patient to the life she experienced before the illness.

Another phrase used for futility is "medically inappropriate" (treatment that will not work). That is, the treatment won't accomplish what it is supposed to do. An example would be performing CPR on a patient who is brain dead.

Some distinguish futile treatment from treatment that is "inadvisable." Inadvisable treatment is treatment that is "not worth the effort," or treatment that restores the patient to a state in which "we ourselves would not want to be like that." Some believe that the drive to define and use futility in clinical practice has gone out of style--others disagree (Helft, 2000).

One writer raises the question about a definition of futile care as "medically inappropriate:"

"What does 'medically inappropriate' mean...? [S]ince laetrile's clinical ineffectiveness is a technical medical fact about which doctors are supposed to have professional expertise, it is professionally appropriate for doctors to refuse to grant a patient's request to have laetrile prescribed for cancer. But [in the *Helga Wanglie* case] the parties to the dispute do not disagree about whether maintaining Mrs. Wanglie on a respirator is likely to prolong her life; they disagree about whether her life is worth prolonging. This is not a medical question, but a question of values .... It is as presumptuous and ethically inappropriate for doctors to suppose that their professional expertise qualifies them to know what kind of life is worth prolonging as it would be for meteorologists to suppose their professional expertise qualifies them to know what kind of destination is worth a long drive in the rain" (Ackerman, 1991).

In the *Wanglie* case mentioned above, Mrs. Wanglie's clinicians sought a court order to have her removed from a ventilator because they believed that treatment was "futile." She had expressed her wishes to have such treatment to her husband--a verbal living will. The court allowed the treatment to continue, and she died shortly after that decision (*In re Helga Wanglie*, 1991).

One can assume that there are four reasons for limiting treatment of the patient:
1) refusal of the treatment by the patient,
2) the quality of life of the patient,
3) the cost of the treatment, and
4) futility of the intervention.

Who decides to limit treatment differs, depending on the reason to limit treatment.

Using the reasons to limit treatment given above,
1) Refusal of treatment is decided by the patient or surrogate.
2) and 3) Quality of life and cost of treatment are decisions that the patient and her society may decide.
4) Of the four reasons given to limit treatment, the only one that the provider can decide is to limit (not offer) treatment because the treatment is futile, that is, not indicated.

Clinicians should not offer treatment they believe to be not indicated. Nor should they fear to discontinue treatment that is not indicated, especially if it will not cause the patient's death.

Your writer encountered a case in a VA hospital in which the clinicians felt they could not discontinue a ventilator--though the patient was capable of breathing well without it. The family *mistakenly* thought the patient needed the ventilator and wanted it continued, and the clinicians did not explain the medical situation but merely continued the ventilator. What we had was a massive failure to communicate.

An economic or money value also underlies all these futility cases. Although not immediately and openly stated, sooner or later will be heard: "All the money it's costing," or "It's not fair to spend all this money on these old people, when it could be spent it on prenatal care for the babies," or "No wonder our health insurance premiums are going up," or "Look at the bill for the hospital and taxpayer in this case."

Considering the cost of care always is appropriate. Money issues should be confronted openly, not hidden under other considerations of "futility", "clinician autonomy," or "best interest of the patient." That is because the money issue is not one for the clinician to decide alone. The discussion about futility is turning from whether treatment is futile (useless), to whether the patient's life is worth the cost (useless).

Think about it.
Are we asking whether the treatment is futile, or whether the patient's life is futile?

One writer has said that he has a practical, arbitrary benchmark for stopping care: "highly improbable." He defines a "highly improbable" chance of success as a chance of less than one in 100. Remember that such a number or estimate of a procedures effect is an average, determined from a population of patients that may be different from the individual patient.

Think about it.
Can the clinician consider life-saving treatment "futile" if its chance of success is less than optimal?
Can the clinician consider life-saving treatment "futile" if its chance of success is less than average (50%)?

Some British clinicians may consider treatment futile if the patient isn't compliant with what the clinician thinks is correct behavior. In England, thoracic surgeons have refused to do lung transplants on smokers.

In another case, 47-year-old Harry Elphick didn't get coronary bypass surgery because he smoked 25 cigarettes a day. He quit smoking, but died of a second heart attack before tests and surgery could be performed He was buried on the day his catheterization was scheduled. Doctor Colin Bray, his cardiologist, said that refusal was the policy of Manchester's Wythen-shawe Hospital, and that smokers on *average* benefit less from bypass than non-smokers (Schmidt, 1993).

Whether the patient's life is valued, and whether the patient's freedom is respected by the clinician, should not depend on whether the patient agrees with the clinician. If the patient and/or family don't agree with the clinician that treatment is futile, then whose judgment, whose autonomy, whose life, wins? In some cases such as the *Wanglie* case, the clinician has asked a court to force the professional judgment and values of the clinician, on the patient.

Freedom to choose does not mean freedom only to refuse the treatment offered. If the patient is not also free to choose to have or continue a treatment that is offered, he doesn't really have a choice. Clinicians should be certain that they are not offering a "choice" that really offers only one option.

For example, freedom of choice in abortion does not mean merely "free to refuse abortion," nor does it mean only "free to choose abortion." If the patient is offered a true alternative of refusing treatment, be sure that the patient understands that it's a choice, and that the other alternative (treatment) actually can be chosen.

A guide: If you offer a procedure you believe will be futile, and you expect only a refusal, don't offer it in the first place.

Incompetent patients

When caring for a competent patient the word *futile* is not used. Instead, the clinician says to the competent patient and family, "There's no other treatment we can do" (for example, in cancer care). If there were another medical treatment possible, it would be tried.

The word futile is only used when the patient is incompetent and treatment is possible, but quality of life is questioned because of the incompetence. If treatment were <u>not</u> possible, it would not be suggested. If quality of life is good, any possible treatment is considered to be worth it.

The clinician who says that treatment is futile means that the contemplated treatment indeed might work, but the incompetent patient's quality of life is not perceived to be worth prolonging. If the family of the incompetent patient does not contest the clinician's assertion of "futility," the clinician will have made the decision.

Futility never is decided solely on medical grounds. The decision is based on the values of the clinician and the family--both judging the quality of life for another person. In many cases the decision not to treat is appropriate, but using the word *futility* may cloud the reality of what is being done.

Also note that life-sustaining treatment for an incompetent person is characterized as futile only if withdrawing the treatment results in ending the person's life. If stopping a treatment will not result in death, the treatment is not characterized as futile. For example, stopping an antibiotic that's not working is not characterized as stopping futile treatment, but only as discontinuing ineffective therapy.

Consider a patient receiving an antibiotic for an infection. If the antibiotic will return the patient to an active life in the community, the therapy is not characterized as futile treatment. If the drug will return the patient to a vegetative state in the nursing home, however, it may be characterized as futile--considering the patient's quality of life. If the patient will not die without the treatment, the word futile will not be used to characterize the treatment. To summarize:

Competent patient (good quality of life assumed) + treatment possible = **the word *futile* is not used.**
Incompetent patient (poor quality of life assumed) + treatment possible + death results without treatment = **the word *futile* is used**

Clinicians increasingly use quality of life criteria to justify their decisions about futility. Quality of life also is defined and discussed in Chapter 7. Futility almost always is shorthand for a decision not to treat an incompetent patient, that will result in the patient's death. For many reasons it may be the right decision, but few reasons of those reasons have to do with the actual autonomy of clinicians not to give futile care.

Assisted suicide

If patients have a "right" to die, then perhaps they have a right to kill themselves. Further than that, efforts have been initiated to give people the right to demand assistance from clinicians in killing themselves. Such an initiative was approved by the voters in Oregon in 1994. As with suicide, perhaps this is the ultimate in autonomy for the patient. But the autonomy of the clinician could be threatened by participation in patient suicides.

The individual clinician, and perhaps her whole profession, should have the right to refuse to act contrary to personal and professional ethics. The same questions are asked about assisted suicide as are asked about the patient's right to suicide. Some say that people who want to die are mentally ill--at least depressed. Again, the clinician must ask whether such patients need help to live, or to die.

The issue of assisted suicide is discussed in Chapter 7, under the topic A Time to Die. But the ethics and the law of suicide, and of causing death in patients by euthanasia and assisted suicide, are all enforcement of the patient's value of being free--of having autonomy over one's life and death. The patient's power over life or death, however, may be in conflict with the clinician's power over the ethical practice of her profession.

If you need more ethics theory than Dountoothers

(If you want to read more about or by the authors mentioned in this section, you may be able to find books or articles by them in your library, or in the references listed in Chapter 1.)

Autonomy

The principle of **autonomy** requires that actions taken should be those that are freely chosen. That means that the choice should not be made for us by someone else. In Greek, *autos* means self; and *nomos* means governance. The word originally referred to the city-states of Greece, that governed themselves.

If you can control yourself, you are not controlled by someone else. You are free, at least relatively--you have liberty. Liberty is a strongly held value in this society, and in all countries whose governments originated in western Europe. Closely related to liberty, autonomy, and freedom is the philosophy of individualism. Focus on the individual also is a characteristic of the countries whose governments originated in western Europe--more so than in countries with a more traditional tribe or family focus as found in parts of Africa and Asia.

Think about it.
Is our emphasis on individuals and freedom in the West necessary, or

could we change to be less autonomous?

Western societies have been more open and dynamic– characterized by mobility of the individual, physically and in levels of status. These societies are contrasted to the societies of the East that earlier were more closed, more static. In the West, people who are quite different from each other--from different tribes--must live in proximity. Often they do not share values and traditions. This is a different situation from people in more traditional countries. To succeed in Western open societies, people must be more free--more individual--to differ from each other and with each other.

Writers on autonomy say that three conditions are necessary for an action to be characterized as autonomous:

---

1) You intend to do the action. That is, you don't do it automatically or accidentally.

2) You understand the intended action. That is, you know what is being done and the conditions accompanying--you actually know what you are doing.

3) You act freely, without control by another person or thing.

Notice how many of the concepts in these criteria for ethical behavior, are enforced in clinician law. For example, the whole basis of holding someone liable for an intentional tort is that he intended to do the act (Number 1 above). Another example: one criterion for the patient's competency to give or withhold consent to a procedure, is that the patient understand what is to be done (Number 2 above). Another example of law enforcing this ethical value: the basis for a valid consent is free consent by the patient without coercion or pressure (Number 3 above).

Limits on autonomy

The last condition given above for an autonomous act is most important–that the act be done without external control. Control can range in degrees of strength from persuasion, to manipulation, to coercion, in which some kind of force or threat to the person is implied. The clinician who honors a patient's request to withhold treatment is honoring the patient's autonomy-- his control over himself.

It is asserted that some external control over the autonomy/ liberty of individual persons is necessary in order for people to live together. That is, external control over individuals is needed for society to exist.

Think about it.
Is society a real thing, or just a handy expression to describe a group of individuals? What would happen if "society" ceased to exist?
Would the individuals automatically disappear too, if the "society" they are a part of, disappeared?
The Greek, Roman, Mayan, Aztec "societies" disappeared, but the people are still there . . . ?

Harm as a limit on autonomy

The principles used to limit the autonomy of the individual can be examined, to see if the limits can be justified. **Harm** is almost universally recognized as a justification for limiting liberty. The principle of harm is understood as justifying the restriction of liberty of some, in order to limit or prevent harm to others.

J.S. Mill in *On Liberty* argued that the prevention of harm to others--physical harm, or actual harm to another's interest such as his liberty--is the only just reason for making laws that interfere with liberty. Critics argue that his definition of harm is too vague. They worry that many laws could be justified to limit liberty, merely by saying the acts were harmful.

Think about it.
Is harm from second-hand smoke a reason to limit smoking?
To prohibit smoking indoors? Outdoors? In the smokers' own homes, if they have children? If they don't?
Does the harm to conservative causes justify removing Democrats from the ballot?
Does the harm from sports utility vehicles justify banning their sale?

Offense to others as a limit on autonomy

Another principle for limiting autonomy is **offense** to others–this is "injury" that falls short of actual harm. Note the difference between harmed, and offended. "Offended" may include being disgusted or merely bothered. The example of the offense principle most often encountered is that of limiting the liberty of individuals to produce and purchase obscene materials.

J.S. Mill would argue that unless some actual harm can be shown to result from pornography, that it is in the realm of private behavior and should not be interfered with even if it is offensive to some. The counter argument is that obscenity or pornography actually is harmful--to the dignity of women, to children who might view it, and because adults who view it may be inspired to harmful acts.

Even if offensive behavior is harmless, it may be argued that limiting it is beneficial to the whole society, perhaps because less conflict will result. Therefore limiting acts that are merely offensive is justified on utilitarian grounds, even if individual liberty is curtailed.

Think about it.

How much offense justifies limiting free speech?

If I am offended at hearing arguments for Republican candidates, does that offense justify forbidding their freedom to make commercials?

Paternalism as a limit on autonomy

Another principle for limiting autonomy is **paternalism.** We justify the restriction of liberty of some people, in order to prevent or limit harm we judge would come to the person himself. This ethical principle is at the base of all laws that allow involuntary commitment to mental institutions, and the base of the law that permits appointment of a guardian for people who are not competent to care for themselves.

Legal moralism as a limit on autonomy

Legal moralism is another principle used to justify the limiting of autonomy. The autonomy of some is limited, in order to prevent harmful or immoral behavior. This is behavior that may not cause harm or not even offense. But the justification is made that the whole society is better off, if less immoral behavior occurs. Homosexuality is said to be an example of such morally wrong behavior without victims. Mill might argue that if no one is harmed, such behavior should be a private matter and not regulated by law, even if it is offensive to some.

Proponents of legal moralism say: In a democracy the majority rules in legal matters, and that should be true with morals too. In the *Paris Adult Theater* case, the Supreme Court noted that governments can impose certain moralities that the majority sees as part of a "decent society." In addition, societies are said to be able to limit autonomy, when the acts of the individual threatens the society order itself. See the above questions regarding whether the "society" and the "people" are the same thing.

H.L.A. Hart attacks the limiting of freedom on the grounds of legal moralism. He distinguishes between 1) positive morality–the consensus in the society of right and wrong--and 2) critical morality, the morality that criticizes positive morality and social institutions. He's worried about using positive morality to limit freedom, but he is in favor of critical morality. (He would be--he's a critic of positive morality and social institutions.) Utilitarians probably would defend the use of legal moralism if the laws it produced were useful to the society.

Necessity as a limit on autonomy

Think about any assertions you hear that seek to justify limits on liberty by arguing that the limits (usually laws) are a **necessity**. That is the argument that the police must make people do something they would not otherwise do–that the law is needed, necessary.

Think about it.
What would be the consequences if that particular law did not exist?
If there were no law mandating people to drive on the right --or left, in Britain and its former colonies except the U.S.-- would people drive in the "wrong" lane?
Do people drive on the right lane because it's a law, or because they'll get hit head-on if they don't?

The custom of everyone in a country driving on one side of the road or the other, pre-dated the law mandating that action by a long time. Whether you believe many laws (limits on liberty) are necessary, or you don't, is a philosophical attitude. Your attitude may depend on your reaction to authority--that is, whether you think people are able to control themselves, or whether you think they must be controlled.

That attitude in turn may depend on whether you think that people are as smart (self-controlled) or dumb (not) as you are. From research on identical twins raised in different environments, it is known that one's attitude toward limits on authority is at least in part genetically determined.

Kant on autonomy

Immanuel Kant, the philosopher you have encountered in earlier chapters, believed that these choices made by autonomous persons are not totally your personal choices to make. He believed the moral person is always a reasoning person. She will reason and choose what is right, universal, consistent, and respectful of other persons.

Kant says that a person who is a slave to desire and not reason is acting according to **heteronomy** and not autonomy. From the Greek, *hetero* means other than self, and *nomos* means control. Together, the words mean "under the control of others." Kant did think people should respect the autonomy of others, and his famous categorical imperative was stated in Chapter 1 as one of the golden rules--act only as you would have all others also act, judge every act you do by whether you would choose the same behavior for everyone else in the world.

Kant's autonomy would be classed as "moral" autonomy rather than "individual" autonomy. That is, autonomy doesn't mean doing just anything the individual wants to do. You can't respect another's autonomy unless you have respect for him, at least as another human being. Kant believed that people must be able to reason in order to be able to act autonomously.

Think about it.
Does a person without reasoning capacity, or with diminished capacity, have autonomy?
Is brain function the basis for limiting autonomy?

Cognitive theory

All ethical theories are used to justify an ethical argument or position. Three of those ethical theories are related to Kant's emphasis on reason (and not on emotion) as the basis for ethics. They are called **cognitive theories** because they assume the cognitive abilities of human beings, their ability to reason and act logically. The cognitive theories include intuitionism, contractarianism, and naturalism.

Cognitive theories were the major trend in ethical thinking during the first half of the 1900's. The development of thinking on ethics after the cognitive theories were popular, was in the opposite direction-- toward the non cognitive theories of emotivism and prescriptivism, discussed earlier in Chapter 3.

Don't imagine that the cognitive theories are outdated just because they are over 50 years old. Nearly every day you will hear someone express an idea that you can identify as based on one of these theories. For example, decide which of the theories below fits the statement "I don't know much about art, but I know what I like when I see it." Hint: the theory starts with an I.

Intuitionism

The word **intuitionism** has different meanings in ethics vocabulary.

First meaning: When speaking about principles in an argument, intuitionism means that the premise or principles of a position are not capable of being proved objectively--that the premise is known intuitively. First principles or premises are said to be not capable of proof by reasoning. In the argument below, the first statement is the premise:

Happiness is the greatest good. (This is the principle of some utilitarians.)
Telling truth produces the greatest happiness for all the people.
Therefore, individuals should tell the truth.

"First principles" are what we derive other rules from, so the first principles themselves obviously can't be derived from the other rules. This is like saying "this is the mother cat, so it can't be the daughter of the kittens."

The premise above, "Happiness is the greatest good," is incapable of objective proof. It is said to be self-evident. That literally means that no evidence is needed for its proof, from outside its self. The premise is a belief statement, similar to a religious belief.

Simone de Beauvoir's premise would be that freedom is the greatest good. That is the principle of existentialism, discussed later in this chapter. That premise too would be incapable of objective proof.

Second meaning of intuitionism: Intuitionism is a philosophy of ethics. In that sense it means that some principles are known instinctively, intuitively, without need for or being capable of proof. St. Thomas Aquinas (1225?-1274) wrote that people intuitively know good, seek to do good, and seek to avoid evil.

Rules that are known intuitively are called *prima facie* duties. These duties include repairing wrongs, seeking distribution of happiness in accord with merit, doing good to others and self, not harming, telling truth, keeping promises. Such *prima facie* duties are to be followed if there are no other overriding moral considerations. More discussion of *prima facie* and actual duties is in Chapter 6, Be True.

The objection raised to intuitionism is that not everyone "instinctively, intuitively" knows the right thing to do. For those who do know the right thing to do instinctively and intuitively, that indecision is hard to understand. But that deficit would explain why some people study "ethics" so diligently. They may seek an external, objective, written-down system or guide for behavior, because they do not have an internal intuitive one. Perhaps someday a gene for ethical behavior will be identified by science, possessed by intuitionists and not by non-intuitionists.

Contractarianism

Contractarianism is another cognitive theory. Contractarianism is advanced, as all moral theories are, to justify moral positions or statements of morality. This theory seeks to avoid the question "what is right?" (or does it seek to answer it?) by *assuming* that morality is a contract between individuals and society. Individuals are assumed to have agreed to enter a contract that defines morality.

Contractarianism is considered a cognitive theory, because people are considered to have thought about-- reasoned about--the agreement. And contractarianism (like intuitionism and naturalism) is considered a cognitive theory, because its truth or falsity can be proven by reasoning.

An example of one of the benefits of the moral "contract" is to live in a world where murder is wrong–thus it's less likely that we will be murdered. As a part of the contract, to get the benefit, we agree not to murder other people. Immediately you see that this is an ideal hypothetical contract. In the real world not all people have entered into such a contract, at least not voluntarily. The crooks have not agreed-- have not contracted--to be law-abiding.

Thomas Hobbes (see below) and John Rawls (see Chapter 5) both have philosophies that look very much like contractarianism.

Naturalism

Naturalism is another theory of ethics labeled as "cognitive." Naturalism as an ethical theory is related to the law discussed above under the topic of promiscuous homosexual behavior--a risk factor for HIV/AIDS. Adherents of naturalism theory believe the major premise or principle of an ethical argument can be measured by comparing it to "nature."

Think about it.

For example, are people "naturally" born homosexual, making that a moral behavior for them, or is their sexual preference "unnatural" and thus immoral under the theory of naturalism?

Careful, you have just been given a forced choice. Is it possible that neither choice is correct?

Naturalists argue that what is natural is right. Facts about the world, and facts about language, are used in this theory. An argument that homosexuality is wrong because it is unnatural, is an argument from naturalism. Of course, one could argue that homosexuality is genetically determined, making it natural.

In naturalism theory, a fact can be a definition. For example, what is right could be defined as what is pleasurable. Then whatever was determined factually to be pleasurable would be right by definition.

Think about it.

Who makes the definitions?

Who determines what is "natural"?

If it is "natural" for some people to be murderers, does that make it right? See the "naturalistic fallacy" next, an argument against naturalism.

A term used in discussions of ethics that is related to the concept of naturalism, is **naturalistic fallacy**. The fallacy or error is the assumption that whatever the moral standard <u>is</u>, also is what the moral standard <u>ought</u> to be. That is, that whatever exists, is natural. In ethics terms, this is called the "is/ ought" distinction. Critics of naturalism argue that just because a behavior or moral practice exists, it does not follow automatically that such a practice <u>should</u> be that way.

Think about it.
If a majority of people in the U.S. think abortion is moral, does that poll make it moral?
If it's lawful, does that make it moral? Law is always a lower standard of behavior than morality.

Think about it.
Some say that "men dominate women." Assume for argument that this statement is true. Does it follow that "men <u>ought to</u> dominate women" just because they now do?

The "naturalistic fallacy" idea is related to whether you think ethics is relative (changing), or absolute (unchanging). This discussion is presented in Chapter 6.

Think about it.
If slavery or female circumcision <u>is</u> the custom in some cultures, does that mean that slavery or female circumcision <u>ought</u> to be the custom in those cultures?

The naturalistic fallacy is evident in the following reasoning. The fact that free speech now <u>is</u> protected in the U.S., establishes the fact that free speech <u>ought</u> to be protected in the U.S.

Think about it.
If free speech is a universal principle of morality, who decided that it was?
Is female circumcision a universal principle of morality? If not, who decided that? Are you tempted to answer "it's not natural"?

Egoism
Egoism is another theory of ethics related to the value of autonomy. In egoism, people are said to be motivated by their self interest. Some assert that humans are physically, physiologically, psychologically, and genetically programmed to behave in this way. (You likely have noticed that your author leans toward this theory.) Egoists believe people

literally are unable to act on any other motive.

Psychological egoism

The theory of **psychological egoism**, is a theory from psychology. The word "ego" means "I" in Latin. Some reject this idea as condoning "selfishness."

Think about it.
Did Jesus recognize this self-love as a basic fact of human nature when he advised people to do unto others as you would do to yourself and to love your neighbor as you would yourself?

Psychological egoism is said to threaten morality, because it is said that morality must be impartial–without bias. In contrast, psychological egoism asserts that we must be biased--for ourselves. We have no choice, we are just made that way.

Think about it.
Is psychological egoism related to the ethical theory of naturalism?

An example of psychological egoism is the story of the Greek myth in Plato's Republic. Narrator Glaucon tells of a shepherd named Gyges who found a ring that could make him invisible whenever he wanted. (Note that the idea of an invisible man is not a 21st century invention.) Gyges used the power for selfish purposes, seducing the Queen and killing the King.

Glaucon asserted that even if there were two such rings, and the other was possessed by the most moral person on Earth, even that person would not be able to resist the temptation to behave selfishly. He'd be a psychological egoist. Socrates countered Glaucon, saying that the person who resisted such temptation would be happier because he'd be living a moral life.

Compare this attitude of egoism to the ethical theory of naturalism, that what is natural is good and right.

Think about it.
How does this relate to what you learned in Chapter 1 about women who are tested in ethical research--that they value their relationships with their own family, tribe, people, higher than any abstract idea of impartial justice?

Psychological egoists believe that no one behaves in a way that is not in their interest, however that interest is defined. For example,

Mother Theresa finds it in her interest to be saintly. A doorman (Mike Mann) who saved his money and gave it to charity is not praised, but is said to get his selfish pleasure from doing that.

Ethical egoism

In contrast to psychological egoism (a psychological theory), **ethical egoism** is said to be a theory of ethics. Ethical egoism is said to be a workable theory of ethics on a general scale, capable of universalization. That is, it can provide a guide for moral behavior, what we ought to be doing in principle. According to ethical egoism, behaving altruistically to benefit others instead of ourselves, actually is wrong. (However, people are very unlikely to behave totally altruistically.)

Ethical egoism is like psychological egoism in that it seems to be adverse to the concept that to be moral is to be unbiased. Ethical egoism too requires that we be biased, for ourselves. If you argue that acting in one's self-interest is good, because the good of the <u>whole</u> thereby will be enhanced, then you are making a universal argument. That is ethical egoism, and that is the difference from psychological egoism.

For example, Bernard Mandeville, French writer of the 1600's, asserts that it is absolutely a virtue to engage in whatever vice one wishes. (Mandeville uses the word "vice" in an older sense, a vice being more like gluttony, not a crime today's vice squad would investigate.) He says that in a free market the freely chosen action--even if a "vice," ultimately will benefit everyone.

Think about it.
Does buying clothes made in sweat shops, at least gives the sweaters a little wage?

But if the premise of psychological egoism is true, that people actually do act only in their own self-interest, all the time, then ethical egoism will be irrelevant. There will be no need for a universal theory of ethics of any kind, because the nature of people is not to be ethical but to be selfish.

Thomas Hobbes (English, 1588-1679) can be classed as an ethical egoist. Hobbes asserted that people act in their own interest, but at the same time they accept some altruistic rules from a social contract.

The logical problem with ethical egoism is its premise that people ought to maximize their own interest. The theory can't be a universal principle unless sometimes they do act for others, when they follow non-selfish rules set up for the whole group of people.

The answer: Following some "unselfish" rules is beneficial for the whole society, and thus also in the interest of the selfish individual who lives in the society. An ethical egoist would refrain from an act, not because it was wrong or immoral, but because he might get caught.

Think about it.

Is the ethical egoist, moral, immoral, or amoral?

If he acts according to his own theory of morality, is that acting morally?

Can the ethical egoist really can assert his premise, "everyone should act for his own good all the time"?

What is good for the egoist is not always good for someone else. If he's competing for a promotion, the ethical egoist acts for his own good. His ethical premise says his competitor also should act for her own good. But that conflicts with his own objective, to get the job.

The difference between ethical egoism and utilitarianism is this. Utilitarianism requires action for the greatest good for the greatest number of people–a collectivist attitude. Ethical egoism seeks the greatest good for one person–an individualist attitude.

Think about it.

Could an ethical egoist be trusted to act in another's interest, because he's always acting in his own interest?

Even you, the ethical egoist clinician?

Do any professionals really act in another's interest?

Or do they act in their own interest as professionals, doing a good job, for pay, for their own good opinion of themselves, for return visits if they fulfill the patient's trust?

It's said that psychological egoists sometimes act contrary to their own interest, only because they don't know the act is contrary to their interest. For example, they might lie if they didn't know they would be caught. Or they lie because in the long run it will be in their interest, knowing will not be punished even if caught.

R.L. Holmes believes psychological egoism would be refuted merely by showing that sometimes people act in other than their own interest. If they ever act out of something other than self-love, then self-love is not the only motivator of human behavior. The foundation of psychological egoism would be refuted.

Perhaps the definition of "self-love" and "self-interest" need broadening. Defining "interest" broadly, Aristotle said it was impossible for a person to act in other than his own interest.

Ethicists say that ethical egoism threatens a main tenet of morality, the concept of impartiality.

Think about it.
Before you read this chapter, did you know that "impartiality"was a main tenet of morality?
Are women who are partial to their own families more than to impartial justice--immoral?

The writing of ethicists reveals that most of them value groups of people (society) over individuals. This preference or bias may cause their distaste for ethical egoism. Ethicists react strongly against the idea that self-interest is the main motivator of people. They say accepting such a theory would "destroy" morality. If ethical egoism did destroy morality, the ethicist would then be out of a job.

Think about it.
Are the ethicists themselves acting as psychological egoists, speaking against the theory of psychological egoism out of their own career self interest?

Existentialism

Another idea related to autonomy is **existentialism.** This ethical theory or philosophy is best known by its proponents, Jean-Paul Sartre (French, 1905-1980) and his friend, Simone de Beauvoir (French, 1908-1986). De Beauvoir and Sartre believed that all we can know is that humans exist--hence the name of the philosophy, existentialism. Sartre and de Beauvoir were atheists. They did not believe that morals arose from God or nature, nor did they believe that morals arise from reason, as Kant and the utilitarians did. Existentialists believe that humans can create their own morals--that they have free will to do so.

Existentialists carry on the tradition of the French revolution of 1789, whose rebels believed that an entirely new world could be created in any way that humans could imagine it. The French revolutionists believed that human behavior is completely malleable. If you're interested in that time and that thinking, read some works by Comte, father of modern sociology, who held similar beliefs.

De Beauvoir

De Beauvoir believed that the freedom to create their own morals is inherent in humans. She placed heavy reliance on human autonomy. She said that people must work to develop, and keep, their freedom. She believed that freedom brings responsibility to use it, so freedom is burdensome and not completely a benefit. She thought that if we truly have freedom--the highest value for existentialists--then we have no excuses for what happens to us. No one, nothing, made you do anything other than yourself. All our actions are the result of voluntary choice.

De Beauvoir distinguished between free will, that is possessed by all people, and creative freedom--that people either can accept or reject. She called people who accept and use their creative freedom, "serious" people. Such people are distinguished from those who do not accept and use freedom. The latter are "infantile" persons, for example, are slaves and some women. The infantile person can stay, or become, childlike--avoiding responsibility for herself. The person who would be considered a "serious person" accepts the responsibility that freedom brings.

Sartre

Sartre too believed people have free will. He noted that people may have conflicting duties that they must prioritize and reconcile. For example, you might have a conflict between a duty to fight for your country in the military, and at the same time a duty to support your family. A true proponent of free will would encourage the person with such a dilemma to think of even another course of action. The existentialist believes you are absolutely free, not bound to do either duty.

Sartre insisted that people have absolutely free will, and that they can establish their own morality. But he said you never can know what is right, because there isn't any external absolute standard. People ultimately are responsible for themselves.

Structuralism, deconstructivism

Two other 20th century French philosophies you might hear about are structuralism and deconstructivism.

Structuralism is a method of analysis practiced in 20th-century social sciences and humanities, proposing that all things and ideas are structured into systems. Structuralism examines the relations and functions of the smallest constituent elements of larger systems--ranging from human languages and cultural practices to folktales and literary texts.

Like Marxism and Freudians, structuralism furthered the ongoing modern diminishment of the individual. It portrayed the individual largely as a construction and consequence of impersonal systems. Individuals neither originate nor control the codes and conventions of their social existence, mental life, or linguistic experience.

As a result of its demotion of the person, or subject, structuralism was widely regarded as "antihumanistic." The term *semiotics* has gradually replaced structuralism.

In the United States, schools of thought criticizing structuralism were lumped together and labeled post structuralism   The reaction to structuralism followed, called **deconstructivism**.

Deconstructivist philosophy assumes that nothing is structured, that everything that appears to have structure is being propped up in a false manner and that the falsity must be exposed by tearing everything down that appears to be structured. You can see that the French have a lot of time to think about philosophy.

REFERENCES

Ackerman F. The significance of a wish. *Hastings Center Report*, 1991; 21(4):27, 28.

Cruzan v. Director, Missouri Dept. of Health, 110 S.Ct. 2841, 111 L.Ed.2d 224 (1990).

Danis M, *et al., A* prospective study of advance directives for life-sustaining care. *New England Journal of Medicine,* 1991; 324:882-888.

Elder Abuse Act, RSMo. §404.872 (2000) (L. 1992 S.B. 573 & 634 § 7) .

Hadley EH. Nurses and prescriptive authority: A legal and economic analysis. *American Journal of Law & Medicine,* 1989; 15(2-3):245-299.

Hall JK. Analysis of nurse practitioner state licensure laws. *Nurse practitioner,* 1993; 18(8):31-34.

Helft PR, Siegler M, Lantos J. The rise and fall of the futility movement. *New England Journal of Medicine,* 2000;343(21):293-6, Comments, 1575-77.

Hirsh HL. Medico-legal considerations in the use of physician extenders. *Legal Medicine,* 1991;127-205.

HIV/STD rules seek two tests for pregnant women. *Action*, October 2000, p. 2.

In re Helga Wanglie, Fourth Judicial District (District Court, Probate Division) PX 91-283, Minnesota, Hennepin County,1991.

Nevauex v. Park Place Hospital, 656 S.W.2d 923 (Tex. App.--Beaumont 1983, writ ref'd n.r.e)

Nurse claims he was fired because he has AIDS. *Amarillo Globe-Times*, 2/18/99, p.6A.

Owen S. Practice question and answer. *RN Update*, 2000;32(4):8.

Padian NS, *et al.* Female-to-male transmission of human immunodeficiency virus. *Journal of the American Medical Association,* 1991; 266:1664-1667.

Prophylactic mastectomy--the price of fear. *New England Journal of Medicine*, 1999;340(2):137.

Schmidt WE. Death of Briton denied operation fires health care debate. *New York Times, 21* August 1993, p 4.

Sehgal A, *et al.* How strictly do dialysis patients want their advance directives followed? *Journal of the American Medical Association,* 1992; 267:59-63.

Stewart GT. The epidemiology and transmission of AIDS: A hypothesis linking behavior and biological determinants to time, person and place. *Genetica,* 1995; 95(1-3):173-193.

Stiffman AR et al. Changes in AIDS-related risk behavior after adolescence: Relationships to knowledge and experience concerning HIV infection. *Pediatrics,* 1992; 89:950-956.

Texas Health and Safety Code Ch. 166 (Vernon Supp. 2001). (See http://www.capitol.state.tx.us/statutes/he/he016600.html#he001.166.001.)

Urban v. Spohn Hospital, 869 S.W. 2d 450 (Tex. App.--Corpus Christi 1993, writ den'd).

Chapter 5: Be Fair.

"No, no!" said the Queen. "Sentence first--verdict afterwards."
LEWIS CARROLL, *Alice's Adventures in Wonderland*

CONTENTS

Distribution and re-distribution
    Procedural justice?
Rights
    Correlativity thesis
    Inalienable rights
Discrimination
    Plessy v. Ferguson
    Brown v. Board of Education
    Affirmative action
    Regents of the University of California v. Bakke
    Smith v. Board of Education of Mobile
Medical economics and justice

REFERENCES

Key concepts

justice	employee	conventional rights
social or	original position	infringement
distributive	veil of ignorance	violation
justice	rights	equal opportunity
demand	positive rights	affirmative action
supply	negative rights	reverse
cost	entitlements	discrimination
due process	natural rights	desert
labor law	correlativity thesis	
at will	inalienable rights	
independent	legal rights	
contractors	moral rights	

Fairness

Fairness is one of the earliest taught, basic ethical concepts.

Think about it.
Remember when your parents, your teachers, even your classmates, said "Play fair?"
Did we know all we needed to know about ethics (and law) by the end of kindergarten?

Another word used for fairness is **justice**. The statue of Justice is prominent in many US courthouses (and on the cover of this book). She wears a blindfold that symbolizes that Justice treats all people the same-- that she is blind to superficial differences in color, origin, or wealth.

She carries a scale that symbolizes the weight of the evidence, of real differences between people, between their cases. The outcome of the weighing will not be equal--one side of the scale will be heavier and thus one side will win, one will lose. In her other hand Justice holds a sword, symbolizing the force of law. As you read in Chapter 1, without the potential of force there is no law, only suggestion.

Justice is not the same as law

The words justice and law often are used interchangeably, but they do not mean the same thing. Justice is only one of the values that the tool of law should enforce, just as law enforces the other values that are stressed in this book. As seen throughout the book, the minimum of law enforces all the values, not only the value Justice. Laws enforce justice, but they also enforce, as you have seen, the clinician's duty to do good, not to harm, to honor freedom.

Laws enforce the other values in addition to justice. They protect Freedom and enforce Being True--as in Keeping Promises, Keeping Secrets, and Telling Truth. Laws also enforce the protection of Life-- punishing murder, for example--and enforce the minimal ethic of the right of people to their property, the results of their work. Laws that enforce fairness in work are discussed in this chapter, under Labor Law.

The words law and justice usually are indexed together, often used together, and even philosophers mistakenly discuss them synonymously. But there is danger in equating the tool of law exactly with the higher ethical value of justice. It is dangerous to assume that all laws are fair (a higher standard) merely because they are laws. Ethical behavior almost always exceeds the lower level of lawful behavior, and merely lawful behavior does not always rise to the higher standard of being just.

"If law and justice are identified [treated as identical], if only a just order is called law, a social order which is presented as law is-at the same time-presented as just; and that means it is morally justified. The tendency to identify [treat as identical] law and justice is the tendency to justify [call just] a given social order." [Material in brackets added] (Kelsen, 1945)

That is, to treat law and justice as meaning the same thing, leads to this error in thinking: Merely because a society has laws, therefore those laws are just.

In the abstract, there is not much controversy or conflict about the value of fairness. All would agree, at least in theory, that being fair is the right thing to do. The problem is in the application of the value to the real world.

Think about it.
Exactly what behavior or action is considered fair?
Is it giving everyone equal opportunity, or giving them equal goods and
   services?

Goals of fairness

The laws that enforce fairness at a minimum level, aim to prevent or to undo wrongs. They seek to restore conflicting parties to a status equal to that which existed before the wrong. In criminal law, the wrong is called a crime. People start out unharmed by each other. Then one wrongs another-- now called the victim.

The victim cannot be "unwronged," so restoring balance to the parties requires a punishment to be administered to the wrongdoer. Ideally the law will harm the wrongdoer at least as much as she or he harmed the victim. The society too is considered to have been wronged by a criminal act, so that harm to the good of the whole people may be considered in determining punishment.

In civil law, the wrong is called a tort. Parties start out unharmed by each other. Then one does a wrong to another, now called the victim. The victim may seek to be unwronged by receiving money. To make the parties equal again, the wrongdoer (now the defendant) must pay money to the victim (now the plaintiff). The wrongdoer doesn't have to be punished as for crime, because the victim is restored to his or her prior status through financial restitution.

Using law to do more than punish wrongs--for example, to do some positive good such as gaining equal outcomes in goods and services, often results in unintended consequences. This is seen in the application of social justice, below.

One sense of the word justice means equality or fairness in legal processes used in the law, not in outcomes. The goal of that definition of justice is equal opportunity in legal actions, not necessarily equal shares of a good or service.

Fairness of process under the law is guaranteed under the US Constitution in Amendments Five and Fourteen, also dealt with in Chapter 1, in Chapter 3 in the section on licensure, in Chapter 4 regarding freedom of the clinician, in this chapter, in Chapter 6 regarding covenants not to compete, and in Chapter 7 under the Fourteenth Amendment guarantee of liberty to refuse treatment.

Law also enforces fairness in the form of equality of opportunity, in laws that forbid discriminatory treatment on the basis of some status or condition that can't be changed by the individual. It is considered unfair to discriminate against people because of some characteristic they cannot change, such as sex or race (an innate or inherent condition). However, to discriminate among people on the basis of their voluntary actions is fair and even necessary. It is considered fair to discriminate on the bases of attitude, skill, and education.

Statutes at both federal and state levels forbid discrimination on the bases of specific conditions. Those conditions are not about behavior but are about ascribed conditions that people cannot change by behavior-- such as race, color, sex, ethnic origin, age, and disability. Controversy arises, however, when the line blurs between conditions and behaviors.

Think about it.
Where will you draw a line between an innate condition and a behavior?

Are some conditions freely chosen behaviors, for example, obesity, homosexuality--or are they conditions, unable to be changed?

In the United States, the ethic and law of fairness is strong against discriminating on the basis of innate conditions. If for some technical reason the court cannot invoke one of the laws against discrimination, they may use another law–see the example below of *Hall v. Bio-Medical Applications, Inc.*

PUNISHING DISCRIMINATION WITH MALPRACTICE LAW
A federal appellate court held that a clinician did not discriminate in violation of civil rights law. But it found she was negligent--that she had committed professional malpractice--in calling the patient "black son-of-a-bitch" (*Hall*, 1982).

Note that in that case, there was no specific malpractice law that the clinician could have read and followed to avoid legal problems. The court used a tenuous connection to malpractice law to punish the offender. But the clinician could have practiced good care--calling patients names is not good clinical practice. That good practice would have been ethical and would have prevented the legal problem.

Theories of fairness

Different thinkers have developed different theories of justice. Traditionally, justice has been defined as equal treatment under the law and as equality of opportunity. Now, however, some say it is justice only if each person has an equal share of some thing. Another theory of justice would give to each according to individual need, as Marx taught.

Justice also may be defined as reward according to effort expended, as exists in the voluntary free market. Or justice could be described as being achieved, if each received benefits according to her contribution to society. Or justice could be considered achieved, when people receive benefits according to merit--a meritocracy. (But someone must judge who deserves the merit.)

Think about it.

Does the scale that the statue of Justice holds, weigh which side is heavier, meaning which is right or which is guilty?

Or does the scale symbolize an attempt to make things balance, to make them even?

Does fairness mean balance in opportunities and chances to succeed, or does fairness mean outcomes or results must be equal?

Some advocate for the latter, for what is called social justice or distributive justice. Social justice is a system of doing good for people, forcing some people to give up property to share it with other people. Others say that social justice actually is not a form of justice, arguing that justice is defined as equal treatment under the law.

In many discussions of clinical practice ethics and law, the term justice does not mean the noncontroversial concept of fairness of procedure. In those discussions the word justice may be used to describe the concept of social or distributive justice.

Justice = Rights (freedom to act)
Social Justice = Goods and Services (things)

Social justice is based on the value doing good, for a group of people. When doing good is enforced in law and not done voluntarily, economic consequences result. Therefore some basic laws of economics are described later in this chapter.

Sir Friedrich Hayek, economist and philosopher, dislikes the substitution of the concept of social justice for the original meaning of justice: "[Social justice] is an abuse of the word [justice] which threatens to destroy the conception of law which made it the safeguard of individual freedom" [material in brackets added] (Hayek, 1976).

Social justice applied

Social justice usually is mentioned in any discussion of the economics of illness care. As noted, social justice actually should be classed under the value of doing good--beneficence--in a system. of illness care. Here distributive justice can be seen in its most appealing form. It is wished that all people have an equal share of a good or service–some thing, for example illness care. When people don't all get the same illness care, that is seen as unfair treatment.

An old saying that exemplifies social justice is "The end justifies the means." If the desired outcome or end is obtained, then whatever means or process was used to get it, is justified. See the example:

From a first grade reader: Jane has two cookies. At the end of the day, Jane has one cookie and Dick has the other. Distributive justice has been achieved. However, it was achieved when Dick knocked Jane down and took a cookie. To Dick, the end justifies the means.

Think about it.
Is the story better if Big Mother took the cookie from Jane for Dick?
Does the outcome justify the process?
Do ends justify means?

Suppose Dick and Jane both have the same opportunity to bake cookies and Jane chooses not to. In this scenario, both have access to a process.

Think about it.
If the process is fair, can the outcome be unfair?

What if Dick has baked two cookies and chooses not to share them. He feels it's his right to keep cookies produced by his own labor. Suppose we interfere with Dick's possession of two cookies in the name of equal outcomes.

Think about it.
Is that equivalent to stealing from him? Is it unjust?

Dick would have performed a desirable ethical act--doing good--if he made two cookies and gave one to Jane. But as it stands, the minimum of the law does not mandate that he do good to Jane.

Think about it.
When social or distributive justice is mandated in law, does the law force people to do good at the expense of their freedom?
To do good at the expense of their right to earn and keep property?
Is that limit on freedom necessary, in order to achieve social justice?

Economics of clinical practice law

Most clinicians don't study economics in their professional education. The ethics and law of clinical practice are affected by economics all the same. There are three factors in the economics of your practice –and in the economics of everything else as well. They are **demand** for care by the patient, **supply** of care by the clinician (time, technology, quality) and **cost** of the care.

Economic factor	In clinical practice terms
Demand	the care the patient wants or needs
Supply	how much and what kind of care is available
Cost	what the care costs

Demand.

1. DEMAND by the patient also is called access to care. The concept of patient demand for care includes both how many patients want care and what kind of care they want. In the United States, demand often is determined by what is paid for by some third party, either government or insurer. That is because most people do not expect to pay out of pocket for their care.

People generally have "access" to care in the ordinary meaning of the word, because clinicians are located within reasonable distance of most people. Using the real meaning of the word access, to have access to care means that care is available to buy, not that the person will be able to, or want to, pay for the care. Some people don't have the money, or don't want to spend the money, to pay for some services.

Supply.

2. SUPPLY by the clinician. Supply in health care also implies quality of care and level of care. Clinician time may be substituted for part of the term "supply." The level of care really means how much time is spent, or how much technology is available, not the quality of the care.

The measurement of quality of care necessarily is subjective. So to measure the supply of care, factors are chosen that can be measured, such as hours of clinician time, numbers of procedures, or other things that are measurable in numbers.

Cost.

3. COST--the work/money. The cost for illness care is the amount of work, money, time, and energy to be spent for care. The cost usually is measured in money.

A change in any of these three factors invariably affects the other two. In a system that guaranteed equal "access" to services (that is, free care for some), demand is increased. The cost of care would go up if the supply of care remained the same.

If supply the went up (as it would, for example, if more clinicians entered the labor market because licensure was less restrictive) then cost of care would go down. Salaries (cost of care) would go down if demand for care stayed the same.

If cost of care goes up, then demand for care goes down, *if the patient paid for the care.* However, demand for care does not go down when the government and insurers supply money to the industry by paying for care. The patient doesn't pay the bill, so he never has incentive to use less care.

A continuing ethical question is whether illness care should be considered an entitlement, such as the entitlement to a minimal level of food to prevent starvation. Mandating clinical services as a legal entitlement would have economic consequences. Some believe this might eventually result in provision of all care by the government. To examine the issue from an economic point of view, in the following scenario substitute the words *bread* with the words *clinical service.*

I have a right to (really, an entitlement to) bread.

If having bread were considered an entitlement, paid for by the taxpayer through taxes or enforced premiums, the economic results can be predicted:

1. There would be no limit to the demand for bread. Bread sales would skyrocket. The price of bread would skyrocket, too. The government pays for all the bread, so people don't care what it costs. From the suppliers point of view, there's no incentive to keep prices low to get people to buy.

Think about it.
Was this the condition of costs early under Medicare, before Diagnostic Related Groups (DRGs) limited payment to a set amount for each diagnosis?

2. To keep the national budget from being eaten (literally?), the legislature passes laws to limit the amount of bread people can have. Or they could limit the price the government pays for bread. (The illness care analogy: Under the Medicare program, DRGs limited the price that the government would pay for Medicare patients.)

    a) If the amount of free bread that people can have is limited, some bakers go out of business because the price is mandated low and so is the amount of bread they can make. The supply of bread continues to decrease. (Illness care analogy: Provider jobs decrease as organizations downsize staff due to reduced revenues from government payment.)

b) If the price of bread is limited, the quality of bread goes down because good bakers will not stay in business if their wages or profits are too low. (Illness care analogy: clinicians and hospitals are increasingly reluctant to take Medicare/Medicaid patients because of the low rates of reimbursement.)

3. But people want free bread (in this hypothetical they're *entitled* to the bread), so some private bakers are subsidized by government to stay in business. (Illness care analogy: The providers of illness care must be subsidized by the government.)

4. Finally, the government itself must bake bread. The quality, the efficiency, and the choice will be like other government enterprises. (Illness care analogy: The only provider of illness care eventually would be the government.)

Giving all people an entitlement--a "right" to free bread, sounds good, but it will have economic, ethical and legal consequences. What the government pays for, the government eventually must control (Durante, 1991).

Think about it.
Did government create the "bread crisis"?
Will removal of the government money (the entitlement to free bread) get the demand and the prices back down?
Is the only cure, to end government payment?

Substitute "care" for "bread" and see how it comes out. Check out the very different outcome that would result if payment for care were made by patients with Medical Savings Accounts, described in Chapter 6.

Myths about illness care economics

Myth: Health care is the same thing as health. A quick analysis shows that using the term health care, fosters the idea that health care is needed to make one healthy. It sounds as if a person would die without health care. In this sense, patient care or illness care is the better phrase. Illness care informs the listener what we're talking about (the care of a person who is ill), without using the word health. A person without illness care may or may not die--depending on the underlying illness.

Myth: The number of uninsured is 37 million or 42 million or (pick any number). The figure is extrapolated from much smaller sample and subject to error.

Think about it.
Does the number change according to its intended use?

Myth: Uninsured is the same as unhealthy or uncared for.
"Uninsured" means merely that a person's care is not paid for by insurance. The person without coverage may or may not be unhealthy. It is true that many people without insurance are less healthy--but lack of insurance cannot be said to have made the person sicken. Lack of insurance does not mean lack of care. Uninsured people go to doctors and hospitals at the same or higher rates than people who have insurance.

Think about it.
Does the presence of insurance guarantee health?
In countries with free care--national health insurance--does the incidence of illness go down? Are people actually healthier in countries with socialized medicine?

Myth: More insurance will solve the problem of cost of care.
Third-party payment by government and private insurers has created an enormous inflation of cost in the illness care industry. This is due to the perception that the paid-for care was free, and neither patients nor clinicians had reason to use it wisely.

Think about it.
Would more insurance, of still more people, solve or exacerbate the problem of costly care?

Myth: Too much money is spent on the patient's last year/last illness.

Think about it.
Just which one is going to be the patient's last year?

Whether her present illness will cause the patient's death usually cannot be determined prospectively, but only in a retrospective analysis. A retrospective analysis doesn't help save money. Even if you could determine in advance that this is the person's last year or final illness of life, studies show that relatively little would be saved if all treatment were stopped. See discussion in Chapter 7.

Myth: The portion of the US Gross Domestic Product (GDP) for illness care is too high. The GDP for illness care is the estimated total dollar amount of what is produced and provided in all forms of illness care. In the United States, illness care comprises a higher percentage of the nation's overall GDP than in other industrialized countries. In the other countries, the percentage of GDP comprised by illness care is growing, too. The assessment that the amount is "too high," necessarily is a value judgment.

For example, people usually don't think the percentage of overall GDP represented by the auto industry is too high. They have a choice about how much of the auto industry they support. They don't resent the 90-year-old using his own money to buy a new car, but they may resent paying taxes to fund his bypass surgery.

Think about it.
Does the illness care part of the GDP seem too high to people, because they have decreasing choices about paying for care? Can that be contrasted with the choice they have about paying for other things?

Laws that enforce fairness

Laws that enforce the ethical value of fairness include due process, antidiscrimination laws, and labor laws.

Due process

Several kinds of law enforce the minimum of the ethic of fairness. One kind of law that does so is **due process**. Translated to modern English, due process means appropriate procedure. Appropriate procedure must be followed before the government can take your life, liberty, or property. The guarantee is written in the Fifth and Fourteenth Amendments to the US Constitution, and in many state constitutions as well. You can see what your own state's constitution says about due process, by looking at your branch library's set of statutes or on the Internet. (Remember that the limit is on acts by governments, not on actions by private individuals or employers.)

Due process is important when your state-regulated credential to practice is threatened. The credential is considered to be a liberty right–it is your freedom to practice. In addition, your license is a property right because it is of economic value. Your rights to liberty and your property are protected by the Constitution in the Fifth and Fourteenth Amendments–so important they also are discussed in Chapters 1, 3, 4, 6, and 7.

> No person shall . . . be deprived of life, liberty or property without due process of law . . .   (Amendment V, US Constitution–limits the federales).
>
> No state shall . . . deprive any person of life, liberty or property without due process of law . . .   (Amendment XIV, US Constitution–limits the states).

Because of those Amendments, the state credentialing bureau or board or agency cannot interfere with your license, except by using due process--appropriate procedure. Due process means that you must be given notice of the charges against you, you must be given the right to defend yourself against the charges, and you must be given decision makers who are unbiased.

Antidiscrimination

The ethical value that people should be fair, is enforced by antidiscrimination law. These laws usually are statutes made by legislators, many at the federal level. Many laws prohibiting discrimination are enforced by the federal Equal Employment Opportunity Commission (EEOC). Your state too may have a similar agency. If the EEOC does not have jurisdiction over a particular act, their staff can guide you to the appropriate agency that does.

Think about it.
Is discrimination always bad?

You discriminate every day, in what kind of foods you eat, which job you take, which worker you hire, which house you buy. If we didn't discriminate in favor of things good for us, we would in<u>discriminate</u>ly choose things that are bad for us. The bad connotation of the word discrimination, comes from discrimination against people because of characteristics they can't change.

For example, it is <u>not</u> unethical or illegal to discriminate and refuse to hire someone who is lazy, or to discriminate and fire someone who steals or harms patients. It <u>is</u> considered unethical, and so it also is unlawful, to discriminate on the basis of color of skin, or sex, or any characteristic people have that they can't change by their own choice. As suggested earlier in the chapter, it is questioned whether some people have a choice in determining their condition or lifestyle--for example, people who are obese, who are drug addicts, or homosexual.

Several laws enforce this minimum of the ethic of fairness, and some require fairness in employment. Many of these laws are included below under labor law. For example, the Americans with Disabilities Act prohibits discrimination in the workplace against people with disabilities. (The word used formerly for "disabled" was "crippled," then it was changed to "handicapped," and now some use the word "challenged.")

Think about it.
Do you think changing the word we use to describe such conditions or people, changes the way people think about them?

Laws called civil rights laws prohibit discrimination on the basis of race, color, religion, and sex. (Sex is the better word to describe differences between male and female. Gender is the better word to describe pronouns such as "him" and "her.") Sexual harassment is considered to be discrimination on the basis of sex, and therefore it is unlawful. Other laws make it unlawful to discriminate on the basis of pregnancy, age, and other conditions. Some are described below.

Labor law

In addition to the ADA, other laws that enforce a minimum of the value of fairness are in labor laws written by Congress and the state legislatures. These laws protect workers in several ways. For example, they protect the right to organize into unions (National Labor Relations Act), to be safe on the job (Occupational Safety and Health Act), to certain rights earned toward a pension (Equality in Retirement Income Security Act), to keep the job when on leave for certain reasons (Family Medical Leave Act), to compensation when injured on the job (Worker's Compensation), and to a minimum wage. Labor laws could protect the worker in any way that the legislator can imagine she needs protecting.

People who do activities such as hiring, firing, or discipline of employees can and should find out specifics of the discrimination laws, from the agencies that enforce them. You can get the specifics of the laws from the agencies in the phone book under "labor," from your state or federal legislator, or from the Internet as described in Chapter 1.

The shorthand or shortcut to being lawful is--as always--to behave at a higher level. Be fair (ethical) with people who work with you or for you, and you practically can guarantee that your actions will be lawful too.

"At will" employment

Most employees do not work under a formal written contract.

Instead, their employer-employee relationship is called an "**at will**" relationship. That means the employer can discharge the employee "at will" and the employee can quit "at her will," meaning for any or no reason other than she wants to do so. The "at will" law in many states has been changed by statute or by case law, to require that some cause for firing be established before the employee is fired. Also, firing cannot be on the basis of any of the reasons prohibited in the federal labor law statutes– not for sex, race, disability, and so on.

Independent contractor or employee?

It matters whether you work as an independent contractor or an **employee**. For example, as an employee you may have malpractice insurance coverage by your employer's policy, and many labor laws apply to people who are employees, but not to independent contractors.

Clinicians who are **independent contractors** and not employees have less ethical demand on the employer and thus less law to mandate fairness of the employer. That decreased security may be given in exchange for more money or more freedom than is given to the clinician who is an employee.

Different agencies and different laws use different factors to determine whether the clinician is an employee or an independent contractor. No one factor is determinative, but control over one's own work is one of the most important.

Some factors used in determining employee status are
1) whether you have control over your work, or whether your work is closely directed by a supervisor;
2) whether you work for other organizations or only one;
3) whether you have and bring your own tools (usually not applicable to the clinician);
4) whether you are paid by the "job" (more likely independent) or by the hour (employee); and
5) the pattern existing in the industry.

The last is an important factor in illness care--for example, physical therapists traditionally have been independent contractors in nursing homes.

FOR WORK-RELATED WRONGS, CONTACT by phone or by Website:

Your personal attorney.
Your state professional association or specialty clinician organization.
Equal Employment Opportunity Commission, state (information

directory, state capital) or federal (phone book, U.S. government).
State occupational safety and health agencies.

Federal Occupational Safety and Health Administration (OSHA), US
Department of Labor, Washington, D.C.

OSHA Regional Offices in Atlanta, Boston, Chicago, Dallas, Denver,
Kansas City, New York City, Philadelphia, San Francisco, and
Seattle.

Unfair labor practices–applies wherever two or more are gathered about
work problems: NLRB, Washington, D.C., and in 34 regional
offices; in the phone book under U.S. Government, or try any
agency with Labor in the name.

State employee labor problems: phone number from state capital
information for any agency with "labor" or "work" in the name.

Federal employees labor problems: Federal Labor Relations Authority,
Washington, D.C.; in the phone book under US Government, try
any agency with Labor in the name.

Or search the Internet for any of the above agencies–many have
Websites.

Fair Labor Standards Act

This act enforces several areas of minimum fairness, including
number of hours in the usual workweek, number of hours that may be
worked before overtime is paid, and so on. Many clinicians are exempt
from the legal requirements of the Fair Labor Standards Act (FLSA)
because they are salaried professional employees. Clinicians who are
guaranteed a salary and who are either executives or administrators, also
are exempt.

Some court decisions have found that a worker who is exempt under
one of the above categories may be considered an hourly employee, if
the worker's pay is docked or accrued leave is taken away for partial-day
absences. The employee may be eligible for back pay based on hours of
overtime.

Spread over an agency's entire salaried work force, such policy can
result in liability for an enormous amount of money. Employers may
avoid liability by not deducting the partial-day absences from accrued
leave, and not docking for partial-day absences of professional or
salaried employees.

Employees who are exempt from the overtime pay provisions of the
federal FLSA-- for example, because they are professionals– might still
be covered under state labor law protections. State laws may require pay
for all hours worked, may specify how often workers must be paid, and
in what form the pay is made, and may mandate when the worker's last

pay must be made after discharge. The index of statutes at the library will list headings for Labor or Work, or information at the state capital will list a number for the agency that administers labor law. Or go to the Internet.

Drug testing and polygraph testing

Federal law enforces the ethic of fairness to employees in drug testing (Employee, 1988). In general, private employers can require testing before or during employment. Employers who are tax-supported entities such as federal, state or local government, however, cannot freely test because it violates the right of privacy found in the US Constitution by the Supreme Court.

If you are involved in administering drug tests or polygraph tests to employees, or you as an employee are required to undergo either kind of test, remember the rule. Adherence to the ethical standards–protecting patients from impaired clinicians, intruding minimally on the employee's life and privacy, and giving advance notice that testing is a condition of the job, results in action that is lawful too. Because the law is the minimum ethic, adhering to ethical standards should exceed the standard of the law.

Americans with Disabilities Act

In general, the Americans with Disabilities Act (ADA) provides as follows:

No qualified individual with a disability shall, by reason of such disability, be excluded from participation in or be denied the benefits of the services, programs, or activities of a public entity, or be subjected to discrimination by any such entity.

Further, no qualified individual with a disability shall, by reason of such disability, be excluded from participation or be denied the benefits of the services, programs, or activities of a public entity, or be subjected to discrimination by any such entity.

One who is disabled is defined as anyone who has a record of, or is perceived as, having a mental or physical impairment that substantially limits at least one major life activity. That phrase "is perceived as having . . . impairment" is very important. The person needn't be disabled to be covered by the Act--only be *perceived* as being disabled. Among other things, the ADA mandates that people with disabilities should be integrated as much as possible into the mainstream of the work force. Specifically for the workplace, a shorthand version of the ADA follows:

"If you can fix it so a disabled person can do a job, fix it unless it's a real problem or dangerous."

The ADA applies to all areas of life, not just work, and includes the right of people to obtain illness care regardless of disability. An important development in ADA law is its use by patients and their physicians against HMOs.

In one case disabled patients and their physician clinician sued under the ADA, and alleged that they had been discriminated against because they were encouraged to seek care elsewhere to minimize expensive treatments and maximize profits. The clinician alleged that he had been fired by the HMO for insisting on expensive tests and referrals for the patients. The HMO settled (*Zamora*, 2000).

In yet another area of protecting worker rights with the ADA, the EEOC has sued employers who require genetic testing, alleging violation of the ADA (Toppo, 2001). An earlier version of the ADA was the Rehabilitation Act of 1974.

Civil Rights--Title VII

Title VII of the 1964 Civil Rights Act protects people from discrimination for reasons of race, color, national origin, sex, and religion. The prohibition of discrimination on those bases obviously enforces the value of fairness.

The protection in that law against discrimination based on sex, is the basis for prohibition against sexual harassment. Sexual harassment can be an overt demand, for exchange of sex for job privileges. This is termed *quid pro quo*--in Latin, "this for that." Or, sexual harassment can be activity that results in a hostile work environment--for example, dirty jokes, remarks, pin-up calendars.

The plaintiff alleging sexual harassment does not have to prove psychological injury. Employers can be liable for the acts of their employees, if supervisors knew of the conduct and did not address it. As a guide: Being fair to employees (the ethical standard) results in not harassing them sexually (the lower legal standard).

Discrimination on the basis of religion also violates Title VII. For example, such discrimination could be charged when employees must work on their holy day. The employer of a Seventh Day Adventist whose religion requires she not work on a Saturday may have a duty to offer her other days of work rather than firing her.

Some agencies of the federal government go further than the statute, their policies saying: "This program or activity will be conducted on a nondiscriminatory basis without regard to race, color, religion, national origin, age, sex, marital status, disability, sexual orientation, Vietnam era veteran status, etc." People who are not behaving ethically can think of virtually endless bases for discrimination, that then may need remedy in law.

Again note that discrimination itself is not the evil. The evil is discrimination based on a condition that does not affect the person's ability to perform a job. Even if it were lawful to discriminate against a good worker with ability, it is not good ethics or good business.

Civil Rights Act of 1991

The 1991 Civil Rights Act clarified the standard of proof necessary for a person to prove discrimination. Employer groups believe the law made it easier for people to sue employers, and the burden of proof has shifted back to the employer. The employer whose work force is not of the same racial proportion as the community has the burden of proving that the work force is not the result of discrimination.

Pregnancy Discrimination Act

The Pregnancy Discrimination Act (PDA) of 1978 prohibits sex discrimination as defined in Title VII of the Civil Rights Act of 1964, discussed above.

By a vote of 9-0 in what is called the Johnson Controls case, the Supreme Court said that neither potential legal liability nor protecting the woman's potential fetus were sufficient reason to discriminate on the basis of sex.

"Congress mandated that decisions about the welfare of future children be left to the parents who conceive, bear, support, and raise them, and concerns about the next generation were not part of the essence of the employer's business" (*International Union*, 1991).

That case is specifically about the statutory protection against discrimination in employment, against potentially pregnant women. The decision shows that discrimination based on a woman's potential for pregnancy is, on its face, discrimination because of her sex. The employer's potential for tort liability for possible fetal injuries, and the employer's increased cost in employing fertile women, do not justify discriminating against women.

The Court in Johnson Controls said that if the employer fully informs the woman of the risk, and if the employer has not acted negligently, the basis for holding an employer liable for injury to the fetus seems remote at best. If the employer cannot comply both with state regulation and federal law, federal law preempts state law. The extra cost of employing members of one sex does not provide a defense for a discriminatory refusal to hire members of that sex.

Employers said they felt trapped between possible liability to a child born damaged from its mother's work, and the requirement under the federal law to allow women to do such work. The employer's interest in avoiding liability, however, was secondary to the ethical value of justice--a woman's having an equal chance at a job of her choice. And in that case the value of protecting potential life also was considered secondary to the value of justice to women.

The decision forbids employers from instituting fetal protection policies that are sex-specific. Clinical service organizations may not prohibit women from working in areas that are considered dangerous to pregnant women, such as anesthesia and radiology. The argument is made that the value of doing good for the child or protecting her from harm, was a shield for paternalism--for keeping women out of higher-paying jobs.

Age Discrimination in Employment Act

The Age Discrimination in Employment Act (ADEA) prohibits job discrimination done solely because of age (against people aged 40 to 70). The chief of cardiology who makes derogatory remarks about the average (advanced) age of clinicians in the ICU may open the hospital to a lawsuit for discrimination, if one of those old clinicians is reassigned or fired unfairly. The ADEA protects people from job discrimination. It does not, however, apply to discrimination in provision of illness care, so this law does not prevent the 90-year-old being refused a bypass on the grounds he is too old.

Equality in Retirement Income Security Act

The federal pension law is the Equality in Retirement Income Security Act (ERISA). ERISA enforces the ethical values of fairness in retirement plans and in other company-funded insurance such as health insurance. In general, the law enforces the minimum ethic that employees should not arbitrarily be denied promised pensions or other employee benefits.

Complying with the federal law allows employers to avoid state laws that require insurance coverage for specific procedures or conditions. Enforcement of the law is quite complex.

ERISA became an important issue in health insurance reform,

because as a federal law, it preempts (overrules) any state laws that might conflict. Courts have ruled that self-insurance plans for health care fall under the jurisdiction of ERISA, meaning that companies that self-insure their employees' health plans are not subject to state regulation and taxes.

Under ERISA, plans can limit coverage for people with big health risks. Based on the ERISA exemption, the Supreme Court let stand a lower court ruling that allowed self-insured companies to reduce coverage for workers with AIDS (*Greenberg, 1992*). In other cases, however, coverage has been mandated for employees with AIDS.

The federal preemption by ERISA exempts self-insured employers from state laws that require insurance coverage in group health plans for many expensive procedures such as in vitro fertilization. The ERISA exemption for self-insured plans is a catalyst for more business to self-insure. The trend is growing in small and medium-size firms, because it allows firms to keep closer control of employee expenses.

Problem: If the self-insured company goes out of business, the employee with bills for illness may be stuck with them. If the company doesn't purchase catastrophic insurance, the total bills of the employees may exceed the company's ability to pay.

The ERISA preemption causes problems with state health-reform plans. Many state legislatures mandate that insurers pay for specific kinds of care, such as psychiatry and substance abuse. As noted above, self-insured companies are exempt from those state law requirements because they are regulated under federal law. Change in federal law would be needed to allow states to mandate health benefits on companies whose self-insurance plans are covered by ERISA. Opponents of such change say that the cost of health coverage would rise as a result.

Most employers began providing such insurance in the World War II years, as a way to avoid wage controls and attract scarce workers. Employers have been limiting illness care coverage ever since they began providing it, for example, limiting coverage for polio in the 1950s, and now limiting coverages for mental health, substance abuse, infertility, and experimental surgery.

Think about it.

If employers must pay for big expenses--for example, if Congress requires benefits that employers must cover--then might more employers refuse to pay for any insurance benefits at all?

If so, what is the next suggestion for those who want to mandate certain benefits?

Right, that the law mandate employers to provide insurance to cover all benefits.

National Labor Relations Act

The National Labor Relations Act (NLRA) governs collective bargaining between employee groups and their managers and employers. The NLRA was passed in 1935 because strikers and owners were killing each other during labor disputes.

Not-for-profit health care institutions have been covered under the law since 1974. (Note that the institutions covered in 1974 were not called non-profit, because all organizations must make some excess of income over expenses--profit--to operate. Except the federal government, which can print money.)

People organized themselves into unions for a long time before the 1930s, and employers opposed that strength in their employees. The process was not always peaceful, but some resolution of differences always came. The intent of the NLRA was to promote peaceful collective bargaining. It was yet another law to enforce a minimum of a higher ethic, that people do the right thing by one another--that they be fair.

One provision of the NLRA allows union and management to mandate employees to join the union or pay union fees. The person who does not pay, loses her job and has no remedy. This provision is prohibited in what are called right-to-work states. In those states, union membership cannot be mandated by the employer's contract with the union.

Whether you think the national labor law has succeeded, probably depends on whether you are pro-union or pro-management. People in labor disputes seldom shoot each other nowadays.

Think about it.
Does mandating union membership or fees, violate the individual's freedom?
Or is it only fair that the person pay for what she got, even if she didn't ask for it?
Should the resulting union strength, the collective good, be measured against the loss of freedom to the individual?
Do you think employer and employee again might shoot each other, without the labor law to protect worker organizing?

Anti-trust law (the Sherman Act)

ANTI-TRUST LAW (The Sherman Act, 1901)
"Every contract, combination in the form of trust or otherwise, or conspiracy, in restraint of trade or commerce among the several States, or with foreign nations, is declared to be illegal." 15 U.S.C. 1, *et seq.*

Anti-trust law was created to enforce the ethic that groups of businesses should not combine to restrain trade. In other words, business are prohibited from unfairly reducing their competition. Anti-trust law is invoked when private enterprises get too big, or too effective at competition. One value expressed in anti-trust law is to do good for the consumer (for example, clinical service at lower prices), so the law affects clinical practice and clinicians.

The anti-trust law also enforces the ethic of being fair to the clinician or competing business. The goal of the law is equal opportunity to compete, not equal outcome of business. The law also enforces the value of autonomy-- autonomy for the consumer to be free to buy what he wants, and for the entrepreneur clinician to be able to compete freely.

Anti-<u>trust</u> is the term used, because in the old days such a combination in restraint of trade was called a trust. Free competition was and is valued, because it results in lower prices for the consumer. It is thought that a monopoly of the free market could raise prices. However, some economists believe that a private monopoly cannot exist--that no monopoly will survive unless the government maintains it (as it does in clinician credentialing).

Clinicians can use anti-trust law to prevent groups of other clinicians or organizations from combining to the detriment of the clinicians' economic interest. Non-physician clinicians have used these laws to challenge physicians who kept them from getting staff privileges in hospitals. Physicians have used them to challenge their peers who do the same. Physicians have used the laws to challenge accrediting bodies who arbitrarily limit exams only to clinicians who have qualified in a standardized program.

Texas physician clinicians who practice independently have gained a limited exemption from the anti-trust law, for example allowing them to join together to negotiate jointly on contracts with HMO's.

When used by clinicians to contest denial of hospital staff privileges, antitrust actions must meet Sherman Act requirement Section 1: They must prove that the clinician and another person or entity together unlawfully conspired to exclude the clinician. It takes two to tango and two to conspire.

The follow-on anti-trust law, passed in 1915, is known as the Clayton Act. That law provides for treble damages, three times the loss actually suffered–for example, a year's income times three. It also allows the plaintiff to seek an injunction. In the clinician example, you might get an injunction to forbid the organization from excluding you from staff, or the injunction might order the organization to admit you to the staff. These remedies were declared available to private plaintiffs in civil lawsuits, in addition to being enforceable under the criminal law by the government.

The anti-trust law applies to organizations that are in interstate commerce. For many years, that was not a problem–the Supreme Court usually held that almost any connection of the organization to interstate commerce gave Congress the power to regulate the organization. But in 1995 the Supreme Court reversed a 60-year trend, and now laws that are said to be based on the Constitution's grant of power to Congress to regulate commerce, are not automatically assumed to be in interstate commerce.

Family and Medical Leave Act

Clinicians who need to stop work for some time may be able to take advantage of the Family and Medical Leave Act. If you must stop work for birth and/or care of a child, for adoption or placement of a child from foster care, to care for a spouse, child or parent who has a serious health condition, or if you are unable to perform the functions of the position due to a serious health condition, you may meet one of the requirements for coverage under the Act. You may take up to 12 weeks per year of unpaid leave, or paid leave if you have earned it. The employer can require you first to use earned leave.

Many clinicians can't afford to take unpaid leave, so the law doesn't help them. People who can benefit are higher-income two-job professional partners who can afford to miss the income, and so can take advantage of the law's power to preserve their job.

If you can foresee the need for the leave, the law requires you to give 30 days advance notice. The employer can require a medical certification of need from you. The employer must maintain your health insurance coverage under any existing group health plan and must return you to your original or equivalent position without loss of benefits. Enforcement is under the US Department of Labor.

Proposals have been made in Congress to require employers to provide paid leave, instead of unpaid leave.

As with all labor statutes, the laws do not apply to all workers. Coverage depends on the numbers of employees of the employer, and on the number of hours you work. But even if you are exempt as management under the wage and hour laws that require pay for overtime, you still may be covered under this law.

Employers engaged in commerce with 50 or more employees are subject to the law, as is any public agency such as state and local government. The employee must be covered if she has worked for at least 13 months and has worked 1,250 hours during the 12 months (at least half-time). The details of the law are amended frequently, so if you need it check your human relations office or the language of the statute on the Internet.

Occupational Safety and Health Act

The Occupational Safety and Health Act (OSHA) requires employers to pay attention to employee safety, to keep records on employee safety, and to report employee injury or illness or death due to work-related causes. The ethics underlying the law are that (as much as possible) the employer should prevent harm to the employee.

This federal law covers nearly all workers. Depending on the number of employees, even employees in outpatient clinics or offices are covered. Complaints filed under OSHA are kept anonymous and the names of the files are not released, demonstrating enforcement of the minimum ethic of confidentiality.

The rules that require Universal Precautions in clinical practice organizations to prevent transmission of HIV are made by the administrative agency that enforces OSHA. Congress often adds new OSHA protections for workers, one example being the Needlestick Safety and Prevention Act of 2000.

The OSHA administration itself writes new regulations, for example, the Ergonomics Standard issued in 2000 that affected workers in clinical practice who experience overexertion injuries from lifting patients and equipment. Resistance to implementation of the rules was based on studies that found no evidence that repetitive motion involving physical strength harms workers (Pond, 2001). The newly elected Bush administration delayed implementation of the standards pending analysis, and members of Congress were opposed to the standards.

Worker compensation

Worker compensation laws, formerly known as Workmen's Compensation, are made at the state level. The laws provide damages (compensation) to workers for injuries they sustain as a result of their work. In return for a fair compensation that is certain, workers give up the right to sue the employer for damages they have sustained.

Source for labor law information

Many other laws governing working conditions are made at the state level. Sometimes those labor laws are more favorable to the employee than laws made by the federal government. You can get a listing and copies of those laws for your state, by calling the agency in your state that deals with labor and employment. The phone book, under Government, State, Labor, or Health, should have a listing for that agency. Or check the Internet law sources for the same headings in your state.

Your personnel office--now called "human resources"--has details of any and all these laws and how they affect clinicians in their work. The people in that office administer and assure compliance with the law within the organization, so usually they are expert on the details. If you need more information, look in the phone book for the listing, "US Government, Labor" for a phone number to call for assistance or referral. The agencies listed at the beginning of this section also will have information, as does the Internet.

The rule

Instead of learning all the separate laws governing employees and their employers, clinicians and employers can stay lawful by remembering the underlying ethic is to treat other people the way they personally would want to be treated, Dountoothers (see Chapter 1). The value enforced in labor laws is fairness.

You should expect treatment from others toward you, that you would expect to give to others. If you adhere to the value of justice, you will do the right and legal things without knowing all the details in the statutes.

A counter to that easy assertion: The further lawmakers stray from enforcing a minimum ethic, and the more the law is delegated to rule makers to write details, the harder it is for you or your employer to anticipate the content of the statute or regulation from knowing the ethic that underlies it.

For example, from your knowledge that you should be fair to your employees, you would not automatically predict that accident records must be kept--an OSHA requirement. But if you are fair to your employees, you would make their workplace as safe as possible--a more important OSHA requirement. Technical violations of the law, such as violations of record keeping, are far less serious than substantive violations such as having dangerous conditions for workers.

If you do the right thing--treat other people as you would want to be treated--you likely will never be sued nor penalized by an administrative agency. If that small possibility occurs, you probably (but not certainly) will win your case. There is no certainty in this life. However, if you are fair with the people who work with and for you, you may sleep better and may be content with your actions. Good practice--with co-workers, patients and employees--is lawful and right.

If you need more ethics theory than Dountoothers

(If you want to read more about, or by, the authors mentioned in this section, you may be able to find books or articles by them in your library, or in the references listed in Chapter 1.)

Justice and impartiality

The formal principle of justice states that like cases should be treated alike, and unlike cases should be treated unlike.

That is, if your case is like someone else's, you both should be treated alike. If your case is different, you should be treated differently. Being consistent in treating cases is said to be important. This principle leaves many questions to be answered.

Think about it.
Who should do the "treating"?
Who decides whether cases are like or unlike?
Who is the judge?

Ethicists say that the concept of **impartiality** is central to being moral. Remember from Chapter 4, that ethicists regard psychological egoism with distaste because it violates the ethical principle of impartiality. The tricky part is translating that principle into actual practice, in real cases.

When we are confused by a statement such as "One must be impartial to be moral," it often helps to look at the root of the word. Partial is rooted in a Latin word meaning to be a *part* of something. Humans are *part* of a group of people. To be impartial, in contrast, is to be separate, not part of the group.

There are arguments against this assertion by ethicists, that we must be impartial to be moral. The reality is that it is human nature to be partial to each other. In most behavior, it is certainly moral to be partial. Mothers and fathers are partial, to each other and to their children.

Children are partial to their parents and most agree that they should be. Professionals exhibit partiality or partisanship toward our patients--we are partial to them, they are part of us, of our group.

The time when impartiality is most called for, is not at the higher moral level of behavior, but at the lower law level. Judges indeed must be impartial, or the law won't work. People will not turn over their disputes to a third person who is partial--to a judge or jury who are going to operate as part of the other guy's group.

In an open society where people from different "tribes" must cooperate, we also sometimes ask private people to act impartially at a level higher than law. For example, we ask them to not be partial to their group when employing people--we ask black employers not to be partial to blacks, white employers not to be partial to whites.

This expectation of impartiality at a higher level than law, is true in certain public situations--for example in government actions and in employment and in commerce. But we must remember that we are asking people voluntarily to do something that is does not seem automatic in human nature. We should not be surprised when such impartiality must be enforced in law. The long list of labor and antidiscrimination laws listed above were needed, to enforce impartiality.
.

Rawls and the original position

John Rawls' book on the theory of social justice was on a list of the 100 worst books of the 20th century, but it is beloved by ethicists and often quoted by them (Rawls, 1971). In Rawls' ideal world, people who will live together as a group imagine what the laws of their society should be, by taking what he calls the **original position**.

Rawls' imaginary people decide what is justice, between and among themselves. They do this from the original position, meaning they do it before entering into an agreement that they then will be bound by--similar to contractarianism. Rawls assumed that the people would make laws to benefit all, and not to benefit themselves personally.

He would ask the people of the group making laws for their society, to imagine they work behind a **veil of ignorance**. The veil keeps the lawmakers from knowing their place or rank in society. Rawls believed that from behind such a veil, the lawmaker would make laws that indeed benefit everyone. That is because the lawmaker would worry that after the veil of ignorance is lifted, he might discover he is one of the people in the lower rank.

Think about it.
Did Rawls assume that people operate on the basis of self-interest, of

partiality?
If he thought lawmakers in the real world could be impartial, why the
need for the veil of ignorance?

Rawls suggests that people in their original position, behind a veil of ignorance, would make laws to enforce the principle that no one could work to get more of anything than another had, unless the work also benefitted the lowest member of society. Remember, his theoretical legislator believes that he might be in the bottom rank when the veil of ignorance is lifted, so the legislator would adopt such a principle out of self-interest.

Rawls theory assumes that zero-sum game exists, a situation that makes advancing one's self-interest detrimental to others. This is in contrast to the idea that people who cooperate, all advance their individual self-interests at the same time, making it an underlimited-sum game. Rawls also assumes that a clearly defined, hierarchical and stable class system exists, as do the Marxians.

This assumption is contrary to much evidence that people in US society move freely, and often, up and down in social standing or at least income. Rawls also apparently assumes that lawmakers who are not behind a veil of ignorance, pass laws that benefit only their class.

Think about it.
Do you share Rawls' assumptions about the world, that people stay in
the class they were born into, and that lawmakers pass laws that
benefit only themselves?

Rawls believed that differences in people and situations can allow some people to have more things than others, with a caveat. The caveat is that they can have more, if at the same time their actions tend toward helping the least advantaged in the society and thus the society as a whole.

This is an egalitarian position, but not radical egalitarianism because he does not call for exactly equal outcomes. For Rawls, the principle of justice that takes precedence is the people's liberty, to the extent that their liberty does not infringe on others.

Rawls' theory is deontological, not consequentialist (teleological). Chapter 2 describes the differences between those two concepts. (A shorthand summary: the deontologists set rules to live by and measure whether actions are good against those rules. Consequentialists measure whether actions are good, by looking to whether the consequences of the actions meet their goals.)

Rawls is a deontologist because he believes that once the original rules are set, people should live by them. They should not continue to evaluate actions for the value of their consequences, as utilitarians do.

Remember from the discussion of utilitarianism in Chapter 2, that enforcing the value justice is not always of utility to the whole society. For example, giving an accused murderer many avenues to appeal is not particularly useful to the whole group. Remember also that Mill answers this criticism of utilitarianism, by asserting that rights and justice for individuals in some way promotes the whole, the general utility.

Clinicians and the window of knowledge

Instead of using Rawls's veil of ignorance--making rules while ignorant of your position in society--clinicians can use the Window of Knowledge. You know (there's the *Knowledge* part) by looking to the future, that some day you will be someone's else's patient. You work now to benefit patients because later, that someone else will work to benefit you. If we are fair to patients, we increase the odds that later we will be treated fairly, too.

Being fair in all our dealings with other people increases the odds that we personally will be treated fairly in return. A system that is fair, keeps conflict to a minimum. Conflict is messy, costly, and possibly painful. Every individual seeks to be treated fairly, and people who consistently are treated unfairly, eventually will take to the streets.

Clinicians see clearly as though through a window to the future (there's the *Window* part), that the surest way to obtain fairness for ourselves is to support and participate in a system that provides justice for all. That way, you also will receive justice when you need it someday. The Window of Knowledge is a realistic, practical concept. In contrast, Rawls' social or distributive justice ideal is a utopian vision in which everyone works to the benefit of the least advantaged.

Distribution and re-distribution

The concept of distributive justice and social justice are not justice, in the sense of the formal principle of impartiality stated above. Instead they are variations of systems of government--socialism and communism.

In a discussion of justice, some texts immediately start discussing how society distributes goods to people. Some make analogies to parents and children.

Think about it.
Does distributive justice imply that the society or government is the parent, and the citizens are docile children waiting for their share?

258 ❧ LAW & ETHICS FOR CLINICIANS

When speaking about distribution of goods in context of justice, an assumption is made--that the government somehow produced the goods or services to be distributed. In reality, some individual person or group of individual people produced them. Systems of distribution usually are discussed when a shortage of goods or services is perceived. Rationing is a system of forced control of distribution of goods or services, if such goods or services are in short supply.

In discussions of distributive justice, another assumption made is that goods and services have not yet been distributed. In reality, all the goods already are distributed. The question to ask in the real world is about redistribution. That is, how to take goods from people who have them, and give goods to people who do not have them.

Think about it.
Who gets to take what, from whom, and who decides which group gets the stuff that is given away?

R.L. Holmes discusses three questions about distributive justice:
1) what are benefits and burdens to be distributed,
2) who are the people to get the benefits and burdens, and
3) what is the procedure for distributing the benefits and burdens.

Note that Holmes begs a question–in other words, he assumes the answer to the question. That question is, realizing that some individuals have already made the goods or developed the services, who is to supply these benefits (goods and services) to be redistributed in the first place?

Procedural justice?
Distributive justice measures outcomes--either the outcome is equal or it is not. In contrast, procedural justice assesses the process, emphasizing equality in the means, not the ends.

John Rawls described three ways or means to distribute goods, calling them imperfect, perfect, and pure.

First he described **imperfect justice**--that is, having a good procedure in place with no guarantee of equal outcome. This most nearly resembles the procedural justice we hope is seen in US law.

Second he described **perfect justice**. Perfect justice occurs when the outcome is guaranteed, as in the situation of people behind the veil of ignorance, or in the similar situation in which two children will share a cookie, one cutting it in half and the other choosing which half he wants.

Third, Rawls described **pure justice**, in which the outcome is irrelevant, as long as the process is <u>guaranteed</u> fair. Such perfection is hard to come by in the real world.

People have different ideas of how redistribution should be done. Some even call this "procedural justice," in the sense that it is a procedure for re-distribution. Distributive justice can be done on the basis of merit, or on equal shares, or on the basis of need--Marxian. Or, distribution can be on the principle of desert (more below)--that is, who deserves or earns the most. Or, distribution can be on the basis of who contributes more to society.

Think about it.
Is it just, that you should be graded on your score on the test? Or should you be graded for your effort in studying?
Should people be paid according to how hard they work (how much effort they expend), or on how effective they are?
On how smart they are? On how many kids they have?

No matter what definition of justice is selected for re-distribution, the problem is that the system needed to ensure the re-distribution would be very cumbersome. The socialist system of the Soviet Union was based on redistribution according to need and to equal shares. It eventually failed. Some argue, however, that socialism or communism was not given a fair trial during the 70 years that the Soviet Union existed. Other ongoing trials of communism continue in China, Cuba, and North Korea.

Robert Nozick endorses capitalism as the only procedure for distribution that allows freedom, and that works. Capitalism works, if "works" is defined as at least producing enough food for the people. Procedures for re-distribution in socialist countries of the Eastern bloc failed even to produce adequate food for their citizens. Nozick is a libertarian, believing that fewer laws and less government is best. He criticizes Rawls as imagining that goods are some ideal manna being distributed from heaven, when in reality a physical person produces the good or service that is to be redistributed.

Think about it.
What would happen if all the goods <u>could</u> be redistributed equally to all the people?
Would that equilibrium situation last more than a few seconds?
How would the state keep the people equal in goods and services--with a big police force and bureaucracy?

As noted above, the attempt to keep people equal in goods and services failed in the 20th century, in communist and socialist countries. In contrast, libertarians assert that people should be rewarded in proportion to how much they contribute, as determined in the free market.

Think about it.

Might this reward for contribution be considered unfair if some people are born wealthier, get better educations, or have more contacts?
If they are smarter, stronger, or better basketball players?
Is the desire for justice, wrongly confused with the desire for equality?
Or do you believe Justice requires equality, of goods and services for all?

Nozick's concept of justice also was held by leaders of the 1980's Margaret Thatcher, Prime Minister of Britain, and Ronald Reagan, President of the U.S. They, however, were accused of being "social Darwinists" who advocated a societal survival of the fittest.

As efforts at redistribution, enforcement of affirmative action laws may produce questionable justice. For example, AT&T was forced pay compensation to women and minorities, though evidence showed that the company hired and employed people from those two groups in greater percentage than in the population as a whole.

Some argue that justice has nothing to do with a procedure for re-distribution of goods and wealth, whether through socialism or capitalism. They assert that justice is fairness in treatment of the person who enters the criminal or civil legal system.

Think about it.

Since God or nature or evolution created people unequal, is this inherently (naturally?) an unequal imperfect world?
Is that fact an excuse to quit working to make it equal and perfect?
If you seek the perfection of equality, whose idea of perfection (equality) should be sought or imposed?

Rights

Rights are discussed here with justice, and also in other sections under various other theories and topics. Think of the various way the word is used. Much morality talk is about whether an act or a person does "right." Another meaning of the word is the right--or demand, power, or obligation--of people to be treated right or fairly.

The word right is from Anglo-Saxon *reht*, meaning direct or straight. The word is applied to the hand that usually is dominant in humans--right handed contrasted to left handed. The right hand usually is more powerful. Perhaps the fact that most of the human population is right-handed, causes us to equate the right with the good.

The issues here are whether strength equals right, whether being in the majority equals being right, whether might makes right. Some even question whether a discussion of rights should be a part of ethics, or is a separate issue. Some say that rights may be legal concepts, instead of ethical concepts, or that rights are equivalent to powers. However, the person who is said to have a right to do something, may not have the power to exercise it.

Rights are said by some to be equivalent to interests. But the person who has a right to speak may not have an interest in doing so. Or, a person with an interest in traveling to Paris may not have the right to do so.

Some writers assert that rights are valid claims or entitlements to things--goods and services--that others are obliged to fulfill. They call those **positive rights**. Others disagree, maintaining that rights are the power to demand that we be left alone, or that we be allowed to do an action without interference--**negative rights**. The Bill of Rights in the US Constitution is a list of negative rights.

These first ten amendments to the Constitution limit the power of government to pass laws that restrict the actions of individuals. Governments are limited in passing laws that restrict the citizen's speech, worship, assembling, writing, and bearing arms (having guns).

The Bill of Rights limits governments that would impose burdens on citizens, such as housing soldiers, undergoing unfair trials, experiencing unreasonable searches and seizures, incriminating themselves, and curtailing their life, liberty, and property rights without proper procedure.

These negative rights in the US Constitution are characterized as **natural rights,** that are assumed to attach to all humans. They are the right not to be interfered with--liberty rights. In contrast, positive rights are added by the French Revolution's Declaration of the Rights of Man and the UN's Declaration of Human Rights.'

Those documents list not only rights to act and to be free of government intrusion, but add rights to material things and services such as housing, food, medical care and so on. These rights to goods and services more properly may be called **entitlements**, the word originating in a "title" that implies ownership of a thing.

Thinkers such as St. Thomas Aquinas wrote about natural rights.

The discussion of natural law in Chapter 1 is similar. It is asserted that natural rights can be discerned by reason, but it appears that different people reason differently, because they find different rights. Natural rights are said to attach to all people, just because they are human.

The UN's "International Covenant on Civil and Political Rights" says it guarantees freedom of religion, expression, assembly and association. But then it warns that such freedoms may be restricted by law. In contrast, the US Constitution says flatly, "Congress shall make no law . . . [that violates the listed rights]." Material in brackets added.

Think about it.
Is a right really a right, if it can be restricted by law?
Are all rights relative, not absolute?
Do we have only the rights that lawmakers, the temporary majority, say we have?
Or is the Constitution written to guarantee the rights listed, even though the majority might change their minds and make laws to the contrary?

Correlativity thesis

The **correlativity thesis** questions whether rights and obligations correlate. The issue is whether a right gives rise to a corresponding obligation or duty--on whether a right on the part of one person produces a corresponding correlative obligation on the part of another. For example, if a charity has the right to your donation, you would have a correlative obligation to give money to charity.

Or, the charity may have no right, only a privilege to ask for the donation. If there is no correlative obligation to feed someone, then they would have no "right" to free food. It is said that obligations arise only when they can be met. That is, you have no obligation to give to charity if you have no money.

Think about it.
Does the fetus's right to life entail a correlative obligation on her mother to undergo a pregnancy for nine months?
If the woman is physically able to go through the pregnancy? If she's not?

Rights proliferate. If a right implies an obligation on someone else to do something or to refrain from doing it, a right confers enormous power on the person who has it. A right to housing may produce a correlative demand that someone else (taxpayers) pay for it.

Think about it.

If the patient does have the right to die, does that produce a correlative obligation on the part of the clinician to kill or assist with suicide? (In practice, the right to die usually is the right to be left alone, to stop treatment--different from the right to be killed.)

Does a right to care produce a correlative obligation on the clinician to give the care?

Does a right to an education produce a correlative obligation to teach?

Many of these obligations translate into an obligation of the taxpayer to pay the provider of the service.

A related question is whether the obligation stays at the level of an ethical obligation with no mandated or enforced action--merely moral pressure--or whether it is a legal obligation. If it is a legal obligation, the power of the state through the police, literally can force some person to meet the obligation. He will be punished if he doesn't-- as happens when you fail to or refuse to pay taxes.

Related to correlativity, in *Slouching toward Gomorrah* Robert Bork (1997) describes the development of 1) radical individualism that says the individual is all-important, and 2) radical egalitarianism which says all individuals should have absolute equality in all things, regardless of personal differences. Bork says that together, the two concepts have made rights into something resembling a religion. The rights of the individual, have replaced any duty the individual has.

Bork believes we have moved from the world view of a duty-based ethic, in which people are seen to owe duties to others--for example, the duty to be moral. He says we now have a rights-based ethic in which people are owed duties (rights), from others.

Abortion is an example in which the emphasis is on the woman's rights, not her duties. It is argued by some that even if the fetus is a person with a right to life, that right is not as important as the right of its mother to be free of it.

Inalienable rights

Inalienable rights are defined as those that cannot be alienated-- that is, rights that cannot be sold, or separated from the person. Such rights are those of life and liberty. "Inalienable" implies also that the person himself cannot voluntarily dispose of the rights or waive them. Other rights that are considered less important, can be waived--for example, the right to a jury trial, or the right to information before consenting to a particular surgery. Even then the waiver must be made knowingly--the person must be aware of the right and the consequences of the waiver, and freely agree to waive the right.

In the U.S., freedom is considered an inalienable right. The person cannot sell himself into slavery or sell his right to keep his body parts. That is because the consequences of slavery and selling body parts are repugnant to us. However, by your actions, you voluntarily can forfeit your rights. For example, by doing criminal acts you may forfeit your right to liberty and perhaps even to life itself.

Legal rights are those written into and protected by law. Because laws vary depending on the jurisdiction, so do legal rights. **Moral rights** are those understood to be established by morality, but not protected by law. See the information in Chapter 1 of the text about the relationship of morals and ethics to law.

Conventional rights are those obtained from conventions or customs set out by groups, associations, unions, and so on. Such rights do not rise to the level of moral rights, which are by consensus agreed to be good. Nor do conventional rights have the same status as legal rights enforced by law. Examples of such conventional rights are the American Hospital Association's Bill of Rights for patients.

In 2001, Congress considered a "Bill of Rights" for patients, especially for the patients of managed care organizations. If passed by Congress these rights would be law, so such a "Patient Bill of Rights" would be considered legal rights, not conventional rights.

Rights may be *prima facie* valid--the Latin words mean "on their face." Still, *prima facie* rights might be overridden for good reason. They are not absolute, because absolute rights could absolutely never be overridden. If there is a good reason for overriding a right, doing so is called **infringement**. If there is not a good reason for overriding the right, doing so is called a **violation** of the right.

Utilitarians agree that rights can be overridden if there is a good consequence to be obtained. That simplistic examination of rights changes, if evil consequences eventually might result from the consistent violation of rights.

Discrimination

When considering the value justice, consideration must be given to equal opportunity for people who historically have been discriminated against such as women and people of color. Note that the term **equal opportunity** has its base in the limitation on state lawmakers found in the Fourteenth Amendment to the U.S. Constitution. What is called the "equal protection" clause says

Fourteenth Amendment Equal Protection Clause:

"No state shall make or enforce any law which shall . . . deny to any person within its jurisdiction the equal protection of the laws."

This amendment essentially provides a negative right. The state cannot pass laws that deny equal protection of the law to any person.

Despite the clear mandate that states cannot make laws that deny equal protection, for years after ratification of the Fourteenth Amendment states did so, and the Supreme Court held those laws to be constitutional (see *Plessy v. Ferguson,* below). Others assert equal protection of the law is denied now, when reverse discrimination is sanctioned by the state.

Women are a majority of the population in numbers, so use of the term "minorities" for them is not mathematically correct. In the *Bakke* case (see below) Justice Powell observed that even among the white majority there are many subgroups of minorities. Some of the people now considered part of the majority have been discriminated against in times past–for example, Jewish people, Polish people, Irish people, and Serbian people.

Almost all of us agree that it's unethical to discriminate against people because of a condition that is genetically determined--such as race, color, sex, and place of birth. So the argument has been made that homosexuality is not a freely chosen behavior but a genetic condition, though scientific studies on the subject are contradictory. Note that discrimination against women is condemned, because they are people with a condition not freely chosen.

Remember that the word discrimination can mean merely to distinguish. Through discrimination for a wrong reason, the word gets a negative connotation in all usage.

Laws dealing with discrimination have a long and varied history in this country. From the founding of the country slavery was lawful, ending only with a bitter civil war in the 1860's. Many still assert that the war was not only about slavery but was fought against illegitimate federal power over states and individuals. After that war, amendments to the US Constitution abolished slavery (13th), guaranteed due process of law and gave equal protection of the law to former slaves and to all of us (14th), and gave former slaves the right to vote (15th).

Plessy v. Ferguson

After the Civil War, Southern legislatures passed what are called

Jim Crow laws that established legal segregation of the races. (Jim Crow was a popular song of the time, about a black man.) The US Supreme Court upheld the laws under what is called the "separate but equal" doctrine. In 1896 in *Plessy v. Ferguson*, the Supreme Court upheld a Louisiana law denying Mr. Plessy the ability to sit in a railroad coach designated for whites only (*Plessy*, 1896).

By 1936, however, in *Brown v. Mississippi*, the Court considered the case of three black man who were sentenced to death after a forced confession. One man was hung by the neck from a tree, lowered and confessed. None had a lawyer. The Court found the men had been denied due process (*Brown*, 1936).

Brown v. Board of Education

In 1954, the Supreme Court in *Brown v. Board of Education* held that the separate but equal doctrine in the area of education was unconstitutional. The National Association for the Advancement of Colored People (NAACP) brought the case--their lawyer was Thurgood Marshall, later appointed to the Supreme Court.

In that *Brown* decision, the Court said that education was of paramount importance to the people and society and that separate was inherently unequal. They held that the effect of segregated schools violated the Fourteenth Amendment by denying equal protection of the law to Negroes (*Brown*, 1954).

Jews are another minority that has suffered discrimination. In a letter to Harvard College in 1922, Judge Learned Hand argued against Harvard's quota that limited the number of Jewish students who could enroll at Harvard. Judge Hand said that if the goal of the institution was to produce scholars, then the only ethical basis for discrimination was merit--that is, ability.

Think about it.
Are maximum quotas for Jews similar to affirmative action minimum targets (see below), established for Americans of color or women?
Can you identify another minority--stupid (intellectually challenged) people? Or are we the majority?

Richard Wasserstrom asserted that racism and sexism now exist in society. He argued that although diversity and tolerance of differences are espoused by some, the ideal society would have people completely be assimilated--not different and diverse. Then agencies and institutions would not differentiate on any condition, any more than they now do on eye color. Some think Wasserstrom's ideal world would look dull--

beige and unisex.

Wasserstrom notes that <u>looking</u> black is different from <u>being</u> black. To some, a person with dark skin who does not hold politically correct "black" ideas is not really "black." During the early part of the 1900's, people with African ancestry sometimes passed for Caucasians--that is, they were assumed to be white. Some leaders in the African-American community today appear very Caucasian, but they espouse the correct "black" ideas.

Think about it.
Are these people passing as black because of their ideas, when in reality (race) they are white?
Or are the people "passing," those whose skin is black but have conservative ideas (in reality <u>they</u> are white)?
Are the distinctions valid?

Wasserstrom notes that racism differs from sexism. Sexism is based at least in part on perceived biological differences, so he believes it may be more pervasive and durable.

On the other hand, Iris Marion Young criticizes Wasserstrom's ideal of assimilation. Her ideal is a "relational" society with groups that are not assimilated but that have relations with each other. She believes the politics of difference is the best way to achieve it. She defends groups that employ political action instead of relying on a neutral law to achieve equality.

Affirmative action

Affirmative action is the phrase used to describe programs that seek to increase the numbers of a minority who participate in a workplace, school, or other institution. The term first was used by President Kennedy in 1962, in an Executive Order requiring government contractors to ensure that applicants are employed without regard to their race, creed, color, or national origin. This language is similar to the 1964 Civil Rights Act, passed after Kennedy's assassination. It was part of President Johnson's Great Society program.

Originally, affirmative action was race neutral. Sometimes it was called passive nondiscrimination. Later affirmative action came to signify an active push toward recruitment of minorities into jobs and schools. Still later it required preference for minorities, with goals of specific numbers of minorities to be aided, and time limits set for achievement of the goals.

Discriminating against the candidate of the majority race or sex in favor of the minority race or sex for a job or position, is called **reverse discrimination**. Many agree on the goals (ends) of affirmative action, but the actual processes--the means used--are controversial. Here is another disagreement between those who focus on the means or process used to achieve a goal, versus those whose main concern is the goal or ends.

Think about it.
If impartiality is essential to morality, is impartiality better attained by affirmative action, or by preferences in hiring, or by reverse discrimination, or by fair opportunity?

Some defend reverse discrimination, saying it is just. For example, James Rachels says that the goals of equalizing the playing field are worth the cost in unequal process. He compares reverse discrimination to a horse race, in which a handicapped horse comes in second but is awarded first place because he would have won without the handicap (extra weight).

Think about it.
In human reverse discrimination, who decides the race was unfair?
Who decides which person was handicapped?

This analogy could not have been written by a track aficionado. In real horse races, sometimes the faster horses deliberately are handicapped with more weight to carry. The race is run, and the first horse across the finish line is the winner, regardless of the weight carried. This extra weight is the original meaning of the word, *handicap*.

Think about it.
Could we do that with people--handicap them with extra weight?
Give the best and brightest people extra burdens so the slower people can catch up/ keep up?
Could we require the average students to complete 120 hours for a degree, require only 80 hours of the slower students, and require 150 hours of the smarter students?

Some justify affirmative action by saying it's fair to discriminate now, to make up for past discrimination. This defends the practice by looking backward, some version of **desert**. (See discussion below). But the persons who benefit from reverse discrimination, and those who lose from it, are not the people who were parties to the original discrimination. They are not the people who actually deserve the compensation for a wrong done to them personally, nor are they the people who deserve punishment for a wrong they personally did.

In contrast, the forward-looking defense of affirmative action focuses on the future. Those people project that a better society will result if people who are discriminated against, the minority, are fully assimilated into the larger society. This is so, even if some individuals of the majority are hurt.

Think about it.
What theory of ethics is this? (Hint, the word starts with "U".)

The result desired is a more harmonious and peaceful society, because it's assumed the minority then would have no further cause of contention. This social utility argument is the classic assertion that the end--an ideal society--justifies the means used to attain that ideal. This is asserted to be fair, even if it requires discriminating against a person because of a condition she cannot change--the color of her skin.

Think about it.
Do you believe that any group of people ever will be content, regardless of how well they are treated?

James Rachels argues also that people with some qualifications--looks, intelligence, ability--may not have earned them. They do not deserve them--the concept is **desert**. (Not dessert). He says that giving rewards to people with unearned genetic qualifications, violates the ethical principle of justice--desert.

In contrast, the utilitarian cares about fairness only if present and future fairness contributes to the good society. Utilitarians will not look back at past injustice for desert, to make things fair to individuals or groups. No valuing the ideal of justice here, just outcome assessment.

Think about it.
Should a woman with naturally large breasts be denied the job as a stripper (because she did not earn her qualifications), in favor of a woman with silicone implants? Admittedly, the implants are more "earned" through effort.
Did the person who works hard, "earn" that ability to work, or was it genetically transmitted from your parents?
What would the utilitarian think of the idea of paying reparations to

Americans of color (paying the descendants of slaves for wrongs done to their ancestors)?

Regents of the University of California v. Bakke

The U.S. Supreme Court considered the issue of actual set-asides for minorities in the case of *Regents of the University of California v. Bakke* (1978). An applicant for medical school at U.C. Davis was denied admission, though his GPA and score on the MCAT were much higher than the average of the 16 minority students who had places set aside for them to be admitted. (Bakke's Medical College Aptitude Test [MCAT] score was on the 97th percentile. The average MCAT of the 16 people who got set-aside places because they were from a minority group, was on the 30th percentile.)

The Supreme Court decided that Bakke's rights were violated. Some justices voted on the basis that the 1964 Civil Rights Act outlaws discriminating against persons because of their race.

Charles Murray argues that preferences for Americans of color in fact contributes to racism. He believes that people who are given preferences are seen by society as having gotten them because they are inherently inferior. This is similar to having a qualification without desert.

Murray makes his arguments on the basis of social utility. He says that the outcome of affirmative action is bad because it contributes to racism. But if utility is the criterion, then the possible good effects of affirmative action must be considered too--such as a more peaceful, diverse society. Murray also argues on the basis of justice--that preferences and reverse discrimination are unjust, no matter against which group.

Affirmative action is proposed as compensation for past injustice or for past unequal opportunity. Accepting this idea completely would require payment of **reparation**--a version of distributive justice. But reparation violates a principle of utilitarianism, in which today's and tomorrow's utility counts, not past debts or wrongs. If the compensation would be useful now--for example, to prevent racial violence--it might be justified. Under utilitarian philosophy, compensation would not be justified on the grounds that persons discriminated against in past were owed anything.

In another sense of justice, compensation for discrimination may be unjust, unless the individual discriminated against is compensated by the individual who discriminated. That means it is not just either, to force the great-great grandchildren of discriminators to compensate the great-great grandchildren of people who were discriminated against.

Related to treatment of minorities is the idea of outlawing "hate crimes." These laws impose an extra penalty for a crime committed because of certain reasons--for example, because the victim was of a racial minority or was homosexual.

Think about it.

If the act (assault and battery, murder, etc.) is already a crime, do hate crimes punish the assailant extra, just for his or her thinking?

Does that make it illegal to have certain politically incorrect thoughts?

Is it reverse discrimination if we punish crimes committed against homosexuals more than we punish crimes committed against heterosexuals?

Also related to treatment of minorities--and to free speech--is the issue of multiculturalism. Discussed under that heading are topics of whether America has a culture, whether the basis of that culture is Western civilization, and whether that culture is superior to others. Some consider whether Western civilization should be taught and perpetuated, or taught along with learning from other cultures, or not taught at all–because it is believed to perpetuate wrong values and actions such as white or male supremacy.

Amy Gutmann argues that people she calls essentialists are wrong to defend Western culture at all costs. She says they oppose adding non-Western, women and minority writings to literature curricula, and she says that essentialists believe the literary classics have "Truth" on every subject. On the other hand, she says that deconstructivists who claim that Western culture teaches sexism, racism, and Eurocentrism, and those who assert the non-existence of any absolute truth--are just as wrong. They deny the existence of intellectual standards.

She advocates a shared moral vocabulary and believes we should respect, not just tolerate, all views. She appears to be as much an advocate of free speech as J.S. Mill. Since her views would influence curriculum taught to students, and not just speech codes, they would have even more impact.

Smith v. Board of Education of Mobile

Religious people are said to be another minority, depending on whether the definition of minority considers numbers or discriminatory treatment. This topic also is related to the issue of free speech and freedom of religion. Judge Brevard Hand defined religion, described its characteristics, and found that "secular humanism" met that definition and exhibited those characteristics. He then determined that in the case before him, the textbooks required by the state of Alabama taught that religion.

Secular humanism is a theory in which humans and their wishes are seen as the highest authority in the universe. Judge Hand said that such teaching of religion in the schoolbooks was contrary to the First Amendment's establishment clause, that prohibits the government from establishing a state religion. The case later was overturned.

Think about it.

Applying Gutmann's description of essentialist and deconstructivist noted above, are the people who advocate the teaching secular humanism--in particular, the theory of evolution--in the position of essentialists? Or are they deconstructivists?

Does the answer merely turn on what has been taught before--what is traditional, versus what is new?

Medical economics and justice

Medical economic issues of justice did not receive much attention from ethicists until the latter half of the 20th century. At that point, new technology and widespread availability of medical treatment began to cause some ethical controversies. The technology and pervasiveness of treatment, in turn had been caused by the indirect system of payment.

Beginning in the 1940's, employers began to pay for their employee's health insurance. Benefits such as insurance were offered because WWII wage and price controls prevented employers from competing for scarce workers with more money. Then in the 1960's, the taxpayer-financed Medicare program began to pay for medical care for all people over 65, and for a considerable number who were disabled.

Taxpayer-paid Medicaid for poor people, and privately paid insurance, both increased the amount of indirect, third-party payment. By 1990, only 20% of care was paid directly by the patient.

The effect of third-party paid care removed the link that existed in both the patient's and clinician's mind, from the use of care to the cost of care. Before, the patient's perception was that use of the medical service led to some cost for the service--as it did at the grocery store or at the auto mechanic's. With third-party payment, there was no feedback--the care appeared to be free. Consequently there was nothing to inhibit increased demand for service. The use and technology and invasive nature of the care increased.

These increases caused the perception that too much care was given, too much technology used, that people were not being allowed to die and were being kept alive with machines. Added to those myths was the misperception that people are getting older and older (see Chapter 7 for correction). The correct perception is that people (taxpayers) now are forced to pay for the care of increasing numbers of others. As of the end of the 20th century, about half of the cost of all illness care in the U.S. was paid for by taxpayers. All these factors have effect on ethics and the law it spawns.

REFERENCES

Bork R. *Slouching toward Gomorrah.* New York: HarperCollins, 1997

Brown v. Mississippi, 297 U.S. 278 (1936).

Brown v. Board of Education of Topeka, Kansas, 347 U.S. 483 (1954).

Durante DL, Durante SJ. National health care: Prescription for a fool's paradise. *Freeman.* New York: Foundation for Economic Education Inc., 1991.

Employee Polygraph Testing Act of 1988, 19 U.S.C. 2001 *et seq.*

Greenberg v. H & H Music Co., Inc., 113 S.Ct. 482 (1992).

Hall v. Bio-Medical Applications, Inc., 671 F.2d 300 (8th Cir. 1982)

Hayek F. *Law, legislation and liberty: the mirage of social justice.* Chicago: University of Chicago Press, 1976.

International Union v. Johnson Controls, 499 U.S. 187 (1991).

Kelsen H. *General Theory of Law and State,* translated by A. Wedberg. Cambridge: Harvard University Press, 1945; pp. 5-6.

Plessy v. Ferguson, 163 U.S. 537 (1896)

Pond C. OSHA faces obstacles. *NurseWeek,* January 8, 2001, p. 13.

Regents of the University of California v. Bakke, 438 U.S. 265 (1978)

Rawls J. *A theory of justice.* Cambridge: Harvard University Press, 1971.

Toppo G. EEOC sues railroad over genetic testing. *Sunday Amarillo*

Globe-News, Feb. 22, 2001 p. 6A. (AP, Washington)

Zamora-Quezada v. HealthTexas Medical Group of San Antonio, 2000, US Dist. Ct., W.D. Texas, Civil Action SA-97-CA-726-FB. 34 Fed. Supp. 433, 1998

Chapter 6: Be True.

"Who shall give a lover any law? Love is a greater law than man has ever given to earthly man."
GEOFFREY CHAUCER, *Canterbury Tales*

CONTENTS

Key concepts

fidelity
confidentiality
loyalty
veracity
contracts
consideration
covenant not to
    compete
quasi-contract
unjust enrichment
Statute of Frauds
employment at will
public policy
    exception
promissory

estoppel
capitation
fee-for-service
managed care
fiduciary duty
whistle-blower
qui tam
divine command
intelligent design
moral legalism
moral
    particularism
duties and
    obligations
actual duties

prima facie duty
ethical relativism
subjectivism
objectivists
extreme relativists
cultural relativists
ethical relativist
ethical universalist
ethical
    conditionalist
ethical absolutist
dependency thesis

The value, fidelity

The Latin based word for being true is **fidelity**. In Latin, *fide* means to be faithful, to be true. True is a word used in several ways in ethics and law. Incorporated into the value of Being True are the concepts of Keeping Promises (Loyalty), Keeping Secrets (Confidentiality), and Telling Truth (Veracity).

The ethical values discussed in this chapter all are based on being true to someone, in some sense of the word. The value is expressed in many ways: Be true to your school. Be true to yourself. Be true to your ideals. Be true to me, says the lover.

This value may be the first and most basic of all values. Being loyal seems hereditary--it is present in wolf packs, in marriages, and in relationships between parents and children. To be loyal is to be partial, the concept discussed in Chapter 5.

True means faithful, and true also means telling the truth. To be faithful to another means keeping promises to her and keeping secrets she has confided. To be faithful to the patient involves telling him the truth. Being unfaithful includes lying to someone and revealing secrets about him. These be true values are learned very early. Some minimum level of the value seems innate in being human.

Laws enforce the value of being true as they enforce the values of other chapters. Contract law and employment law are derived from the concept of keeping promises (loyalty). At a minimum level, laws about whistle-blowing enforce the values of keeping promises and telling the truth (veracity). The ethic of telling the truth is enforced in the "informed" requirement in consent law. A minimum enforcement of the value of keeping secrets are the laws of confidentiality and of privileged communication between clinician and patient.

Being true means being loyal. You can be loyal to the patient, loyal to your employer, or loyal to the managed care company you work for or contract with. But clinicians are taught especially to be patient advocates, and the law enforces that ethical teaching. Advocating for the patient rests on the value of loyalty of clinician to the patient--and when necessary, putting that loyalty above some other loyalty or other value the clinician holds.

Keeping promises: loyalty

Humans grew up in tribes, being loyal to each other, keeping promises to each other. In essence, the family is a small tribe. Humans value themselves, their family, friends, organization, their own profession. By extension, clinicians value their own patients. When professionals and employers are in conflict, the underlying value being tested may be **loyalty**--loyalty to the employer tribe versus loyalty to the patient. Or loyalty to your own profession's tribe, instead of to another profession's tribe.

Think about it.
Can technicians perform some care as well as professional clinicians?

Do professionals objectively look at patient outcomes when deciding who should do care, or is your first reaction, "They're not professionals--we are"?

The union movement and professional associations are built on the value of fidelity--loyalty to the union, to the cause, to the sisterhood. This loyalty to profession, however, can conflict with loyalty to the patient, or employer, or the law. The words used in loyalty disagreements are loaded with emotion--for example, betray, treason, tattle, rat, lie.

Keeping secrets: confidentiality

Confidentiality sometimes is listed as a separate value, but confidentiality is related to the larger idea of fidelity. The words have similar origin--*con* means with, and *fide* means loyal or faithful--as in, fidelity. The patient has confidence in you, and in a whole system--to be true, faithful, to be on his side.

Being true means keeping confidences--keeping secrets the patient has told you. Almost everything the patient tells you can be classed as a secret. The things he tells you and that you learn about him, are things not even his family or his neighbors know. It is of utmost importance that you keep those secrets, not only to be ethical but also to avoid the legal consequences of violating that trust.

Your self-interest in being true to others is elemental, derived from long ago. People take care of their own. For a long time in human history and prehistory, strangers were unusual--and usually they were dangerous.

The world has changed from the time when humans developed some of their values. People now must deal with strangers daily. Clinicians must care for people without fear or hate, as if patients were one of their own. Clinicians cope with a society that is open and plural. They now must work not to hate and distrust the strangers.

Perhaps people also must now be less loyal to their small group--less partial. The German word for nationalism, extreme loyalty to the nation, is *Nazialismus*--from which came *Nazi*. Perhaps people must sacrifice even some patriotism to live in a small world in peace.

Think about it.
If we keep strong feeling for our "own people" and stay loyal to us, can we still love the stranger?

Telling truth: veracity

Being true also means telling the truth to the patient. The Latin-based word for telling true facts to the patient is **veracity** (*vera* is Latin for truth). Telling the truth to the patient about procedures to be done, is being true. One legal enforcement of the value of being true is the law of informed consent. If the patient doesn't have the truth--if he isn't truly informed--then he hasn't truly consented to the procedure with whatever risks it carries.

In the past, clinicians could be paternalistic. They could act as a father--*pater* in Latin--to the patient. That meant that the clinician decided what the patient should know. More recently, the patient is recognized to have the right to know whatever the you know about his condition.

This ethical value of being true is enforced at a lower level by law. One example of such law is the statute that requires clinicians to furnish patients with copies of their medical records. The details vary from state to state, but in general, the patient has a right to know the truth of what is in his own record. You the clinician, or your employer organization, actually own the physical paper or computer record, but the patient must be given the information if he asks.

Very rarely, you may need to withhold information (usually temporarily) if in your judgment it will be detrimental to the patient–for example, delaying the result of an HIV test until you have time to counsel the patient.

The patient's right to information does not extend to a right of his family or friends to information about the patient, unless they have legal responsibility for him. An example of the latter is the situation in which the patient is incompetent. Then, the person legally responsible may have information about the patient's condition that is needed to make a decision on his behalf.

In relation to managed care, your first loyalty as clinician is to the patient. This loyalty requires telling your patients the truth, for example when and if care is needed but not available, because of limits set by their managed care plan. If patients have truth, if they are given accurate information, they can correct managed care constraints that limit their care. They can do this either by individual lawsuit, or by political action. If they don't have the true information from you, they'll never know if they may be harmed.

Law that enforces the value, be true
Keeping promises (loyalty law)

The value of loyalty (keeping promises) is enforced at a minimum level by employment law. The employment relationship is an implicit promise by both parties, to be loyal to the other.

In a job relationship, you make an implicit promise to be loyal, to advance the employer's interest as well as your own, to work on her behalf. The employer promises to pay and to be fair--that is, to have some degree of loyalty--to the employee.

This work for pay grew out of the medieval system of fealty, of making an oath or promise to be loyal to a lord or lady--that itself originated in tribal systems. The lord or lady in return promised to be loyal to the yeoman or serf, meaning they would provide opportunity to work on land, protection, and other benefits of the relationship.

Employment law remains based on that value of loyalty and it is an area of legal concern for most clinicians, because most of us are employees.

Employment law can be divided into (1) contract law and (2) related labor law, both enforcing the ethical values of loyalty. You saw antidiscrimination law, another kind of employment law, enforcing the minimum ethic of fairness discussed in Chapter 5.

Contracts

Free advice from a lawyer: Dealing with people who keep promises without being forced to do so in court, is better than writing the best contract.

Contract law enforces (at a minimal level) the higher ethical value of Being True, by forcing people to keep promises they have made to each other. One of the oldest, most basic concepts of law is contract, in which a promise two people made to each other is enforced.

Clinicians enter into contracts as do all citizens. For example, you may have a contract for work with your employer. The lease between landlord and tenant is a form of contract, about property. Some clinicians are independent contractors with insurance companies or managed care companies or hospitals. A contract is simply an agreement between two parties.

To be enforceable in court, a contract must meet two basic conditions. First, the people making the contract must be able to make a contract--both at least adult and competent. Second, the parties must exchange **consideration**, something of value. This can be either a benefit to one party, or a detriment to the other.

REQUIREMENTS FOR AN ENFORCEABLE CONTRACT

1. The agreement must be between two people who are able to make a contract. These must be people with legal capacity--not minors nor people declared incompetent. In the process of making the agreement, one party makes an offer, and the other accepts the offer. Volumes of law are written on exactly what constitutes an offer and an acceptance. If any question about that arises, you need a lawyer.
2. Some payment or consideration is required for the promise or performance. The payment--called consideration-- can be a detriment to one party, or a benefit to the other.

For example, the employment agreement or contract is the promise of the clinician to work, and the promise of the employer to pay. Most clinicians work without written contracts, under agreements that are unenforceable in court. That employment agreement is discussed under employment at will in Chapter 5 and also below.

Covenants not to compete

Frequent cause for concern to clinicians who make a contract for work is the **covenant not to compete** in the contract. This clause seeks to limit the employee's power to compete with the employer after leaving employment. Such clauses must be for a reasonable duration, for a reasonable scope of activity (or example, the clause must not forbid all work), and for a reasonable area of restriction. If such a clause is proposed, you may change it through negotiation.

The details vary, but such clauses usually prohibit the professional from working at her occupation within a designated area near the present employer, for a designated amount of time. If the clause doesn't specify a reasonable area and a reasonable time of noncompetition, the court may either supply such a reasonable clause or may choose not to enforce that noncompete clause at all. Other similar clauses are covenants not to disclose the employer organization's trade secrets (Garcia, 2001).

Depending on how many years and within how many miles competition is forbidden, the clause might be held by a court to be against public policy. The public policy upheld is the liberty to work--a value specifically guaranteed in the Fifth and Fourteenth Amendments to the US Constitution (as in, the right to life, liberty, and property).

No person shall . . . be deprived of life, liberty or property without due process of law . . . (Amendment V, US Constitution–limits the federales).

No state shall ... deprive any person of life, liberty or property without due process of law . . . (Amendment XIV, US Constitution–limits the states).

Work is both a liberty right and a property right. These values are weighed by the court against the value of loyalty to the employer by not competing, and against the desirability of holding someone to a voluntarily made agreement.

Variations on the noncompete theme also include the employer who seeks to punish employees who leave an organization by fining them for doing so. For example, contracts have been written that say that the clinician resigning from a managed care organization must pay $700 for each patient who follows the clinician to his new position.

The clinician-patient relationship is important, and contracts such as this interfere with the patient's right to choose her own providers. The balancing question for the court: Is the profession a business--in which almost any clause in a voluntarily agreed contract is acceptable, or is access to one's chosen provider a right that a contract may not violate? Any reform or managed care system that restricts the patient's right to choose his own clinician may encounter this issue. Courts might see their role as protecting the patient's freedom to choose their clinician, in preference to upholding the freedom of organizations and individuals to contract with each other.

Legislatures in several states have written statutes that enforce the value of patient freedom to choose clinicians, by prohibiting many kinds of restrictive clauses in clinician contracts. But in most states covenants not to compete are upheld, as long as they are for a reasonable duration, scope of activity and area of restriction.

The courts analyzing a covenant not to compete also will weigh public-interest concerns--for example, the effect of such contract clauses on the public in a given area or in a time of shortage. For example, if clinicians who leave a managed care organization cannot set up independent practices, the public in a particular locale may be left with only one managed care group as a provider.

If the employment contract is not enforceable in the first place, of course the noncompete clause it contains is unenforceable also. For example, if an independent contractor is not guaranteed any work, nor obliged to take any work offered, the court might find that such language did not create a contract at all. In order to be enforceable, contracts should guarantee either that some work will be offered by the employer, or that some work will be accepted by the clinician. Clinicians who contemplate a contract either as an employee or an independent contractor, should have legal advice from a lawyer knowledgeable about labor law in that state.

Quasi-contract

Quasi-contract (half-contract) and unjust enrichment are legal theories that courts use to prevent one party from benefitting at the expense of another--who has no enforceable contract.

Even without the requirements of a written contract, a court can find that an "implied" contract was made--in legal terms, a quasi-(half-) contract. If goods or services are provided for someone without a formal agreement being made, the provider may still be able to enforce payment for the benefit (value) that the other person gained.

Similarly, if one person performs a service for a second person, or relies on the promise to her detriment, the court may prevent "**unjust enrichment**" of the second person by making the second person keep the promise. A legal fiction is created, that the "enriched" person actually did contract for the service or good she received. ("Legal fiction" means that the court made up a theory of law to get to the result the court wanted.)

Agreements that are not written might not be enforceable in court. The **Statute of Frauds** is old English law, still enforced in the United

States. The law requires a contract to be written if it is about property, or if is for a longer duration than a year--otherwise the contract will not be enforced.

Leases are contracts about property, and a lease for longer than a year should be written. Your state legislature may have modified this area of landlord-tenant law, however.

Spoken agreements for employment are assumed to be agreements to employ for longer than one year. Therefore employment agreements must be written to be enforceable.

Spoken testimony about a contract is suspect because the witness's memory of what was said or done may change, while the writing won't. Such testimony is similar to the situation of testifying about clinical practice instead of having written notes. Thus spoken testimony about what was said in order to modify a written contract (called parol evidence) may not be admissible in court.

Employment at will

Employment at will is a relationship (a promise) that can be terminated at the will of either party. The promise is that the employer will pay you as long as you work, and your promise is that you will work as long as she pays. This at-will concept is discussed also in Chapter 5, Be Fair, in the context of labor law that enforces fairness at a minimal level.

Employment law upholding that freedom to act is based on the value of autonomy for both employer and employee. Some states modify the "at will" relationship by establishing a requirement of good faith or fair dealing on the employer who fires an employee.

Personnel policy handbooks saying that employees may be fired only for "just cause" may establish a cause of action for wrongful discharge, even for at will employees. The promises in employee handbooks (personnel policies), plus verbal promises made by managers, may be held to create a contract. This is the theory of **promissory estoppel**--the words mean that the management has created a promise and is "stopped" from denying it. Thus the law enforces the promise made--the higher ethical value is Keeping Promises.

Clinicians who report employer violations of law (not mere violations of guidelines) may be protected under what is called the **public policy exception** to the at will doctrine. This exception upholds the public policy of protecting the public from harm--above the employer's freedom to fire at will.

The public policy that the clinician upholds must be written as law. Remember that you distinguish law from non-law, in that law is written, by people with authority to make law. Law is always in the form of a statute, a regulation, or a court case. A writing from other than those sources is a guide, not a law, and the public policy protection may not apply.

For example, a nurse who revealed JCAHO violations by her employer may be fired and the firing be upheld, because JCAHO guidelines are not law. Thus her actions would not qualify for the public policy exception to the at will doctrine (Cushing, 1992)

Employees may file lawsuits for harm caused by the employer in the course of termination--such as suit for slander. Punitive damages may be awarded to punish the employer and to deter future bad conduct (see discussion of slander in Chapter 3 Don't Harm). These lawsuits also enforce the higher ideal of keeping promises.

Collective bargaining

Collective bargaining agreements are a special kind of contract, and a small percentage of clinicians work under such agreements. If you work under a collective bargaining contract, or if you would like to, or if you don't want to be forced to, your union or professional association or management are sources of advice. The National Labor Relations Board (NLRB) administers the federal law that regulates collective bargaining, discussed in Chapter 5 Be Fair.

Terminating the relationship with the patient

The clinician's relationship with the patient contains some elements of contract law. When there is no third-party payment by insurance or government, there can be a direct "contract" between clinician and patient. The patient promises to pay, and the clinician promises to give service.

"Contract" with the patient:

Patient ☞$
Clinician ☞Care to Patient

Even with third-party payment (3PP), you still retain an indirect contract with the patient:

With third-party payment (3PP) from insurance or government):

Patient ☞$ to

THE MIDDLE MAN--3PP ☞$ to
Clinician ☞Care to Patient

Part of your relationship, your duty to the patient, is not to abandon him, discussed in Chapter 4 Be Free. Because of that duty, you must be careful in terminating your relationship with the patient if that becomes necessary. First, don't use the word "fire." The patient is not your employee, and no one wants to be fired.

The "contract" with the patient may not be written, and it may not be enforced in a court. But you implicitly promise (the loyalty value) that you will do your best to help the patient, and she promises that she will cooperate with your care. If either of you can't keep that promise, you may need to terminate your care of the patient.

Specific steps should be followed to terminate your relationship with the patient. Consult your management or lawyer as to the exact procedure that is best to use under your state's laws. Patients can understand that in some situations you can't effectively help them, and that they would be better served by another clinician. In such situations it is better to consider this a transfer or referral to another clinician. That suggestion should be made before any formal legal termination of the relationship is initiated.

If the patient declines your informal suggestion of referral to another clinician, you should give notice to the patient that you cannot continue to be her clinician. If she needs care immediately, give care until you arrange for care from another clinician.

Specific steps will be suggested by your management or attorney-- perhaps a written letter, sent by certified mail. Whatever the procedure, remember the *rule*, to treat the patient with the consideration you would want to receive in such a situation.

The relationship probably is being terminated because you see some problem or potential problem with the patient's care. The way the termination is done either can exacerbate or diminish the chances of a lawsuit against you. Your writer has seen a malpractice suit that was filed for one reason only: because of the rude way the termination of the relationship was done. The patient did not have a valid case of malpractice so the clinician owed no damages, but the lawsuit and much aggravation could have been avoided if the patient had been shown simple courtesy when the relationship was terminated.

Loyalty to the managed care patient
Managed care simply is <u>limited</u> care.

Who pays?	How? $$$$$$	For what?
Patient	Directly, out of her pocket	Fee for each service (FFS)
Government (3PP)	Indirectly, with taxpayer's money	Medicare, Medicaid, etc., usually prospective
Insurance (3PP)–either traditional (FFS) or managed care (HMO, PPO, etc.)	Indirectly, with premiums from patients	FFS or capitation (one payment to provider, per patient per year)

This is not a new situation--care always is limited, by how much care is available, how much care can be paid for, how much care will do good for the patient. The difference now is in who limits the care. Before, the patient and clinician jointly decided if care should be limited and for what reason. Now, a third party payer likely is involved in the decision.

Managed care is a system of payment for care that limits the payment in some way. Often this is done by the patient paying a set fee for insurance premium, and the managed care organization setting a cap on the amount of money that can be spent for the patient's care. Health maintenance organizations (HMOs) are managed care organizations. HMOs were started with the premise that keeping people healthy by providing preventive care, would keep down costs overall.

Contrasted with managed care is payment by **fee for service**, in which the clinician is paid a fee for each service. The fee might be paid by the patient, or by the insurer.

Under managed care, payment to clinicians may be limited to one payment per patient per year. (This is payment per head, called **capitation** from the Latin word for head, *caput*.) Or the clinician in the managed care group may be rewarded at the end of the year with bonuses for limiting costs.

If that is the case, fewer referrals to specialists and fewer admissions to hospital mean less cost to the managed care company and more money to the clinician. Some law cases enforcing the values loyalty and veracity, mention the legal duty of the clinician to inform the patient of payment arrangements such as this, that might increase clinician income at the expense of patient care.

Lawsuits against managed care organizations such as HMOs and their contracting clinicians, have charged breach of **fiduciary duty** (the clinician's duty to act for the patient's interest) (Rice, 1999). Note the Latin basis of fiduciary-- *fid*, same origin as fidelity. This charge of breach of fiduciary duty can be brought even without damage to the patient, if the clinician fails to disclose a financial advantage such as a bonus or other increase in payment that might result from choices made in the patient's care. Any time the clinician's decision on a patient's treatment might benefit her economic bottom line, this suit is a potential liability.

However, physicians who actually operate HMOs do not have the kind of fiduciary duty that allows them to be sued under the federal ERISA law (*Pegram*, 2000).

Critics of fee-for-service payment say that paying a fee for each service that is given to the patient, encourages clinicians to give more service--possibly unnecessary service. On the other hand, the danger in managed care is that the clinician's loyalty to the payer--the managed care company--will be in conflict with her loyalty to the patient. Some cases indicate that clinician loyalty must extend to advocating for the patient with the managed care company.

Regardless of who pays, the law enforces a minimum loyalty to the patient. In this situation, the law that would enforce the loyalty value would be malpractice law. If you failed to care for the patient as a reasonable prudent clinician, regardless of the pressure of a managed care contract, you would be liable for damages you caused the patient.

Same rule: treat the patient, even managed care patients, as you'd want to be treated.

In this century, payment by the individual out of his own pocket is projected to increase. This will reverse a trend that started in 1965 with the passage of Medicare, providing nearly free health care for the old and disabled. The resulting perception, that care was "free" because it was paid for by insurance or by taxpayers, caused great inflation in the cost of care.

A trend reversing that erroneous perception is the popular idea of Medical Savings Accounts (MSAs). As an example of how this can work, patients will pay for the first $3000 of their care yearly, out of money that their employer has put in an account for that purpose. If the $3000 is spent, a catastrophic insurance policy with a $3000 deductible will pay (at that point the deductible already will have been met).

If the employee doesn't spend the whole $3000 during the year, he or she keeps the rest. Another $3000 is put into the MSA account for the next year. Under this system of payment, patients are more careful-- they're now spending their own money for the first time since insurance became popular.

The effect of MSAs on clinicians is that they are more likely to be paid by the patient, not the insurer. This will reduce paperwork and claims denied. The control will be back with the patient, newly empowered with cash, now a true partner in his care. The clinician's tendency to be loyal to the person who pays, now is appropriate as it is the patient who pays.

Keeping secrets (confidentiality law)

The value of confidentiality is part of the more encompassing value of fidelity--of being true. Confidentiality is needed because information about the patient gives the clinician great potential to harm the patient. The patient may not have given such information to any other stranger. Disclosing of the information could embarrass or even harm the patient.

Good clinicians always have held to the ethical value of confidentiality. They keep secret (confidential) the information they learn in the course of their practice. One practical reason for you to value keeping secrets of patients is that when you do, patients then are more likely to give you all information necessary to their care. If the patient thinks you will not keep his secrets, he will be less likely to confide the information you need to care for him safely and well.

The economic result of telling secrets that are learned in the clinician- patient relationship, costs the clinician who does it in lost patients, lost jobs. Codes of ethics and laws merely reinforce what can be learned first from the marketplace.

> **All that may come to my knowledge in the exercise of my profession or in daily commerce with men, which ought not to be spread abroad, I will keep secret and never reveal.**

---Oath of Hippocrates

Above is the "be true" confidentiality clause of the Hippocratic Oath for physician clinicians. No doubt the duty was recognized long before the Oath was written over 2000 years ago (and not by Hippocrates, by the way). Notice that there is a big exception to keeping patient secrets in this clause. Things "that ought not to be spread abroad" are to be kept secret, but that implies that there are things that <u>ought to</u> be told. More about that in the section on Telling Truth.

As noted above, neither the patient nor her surrogate owns the chart, but in most circumstances they have right to access to the information in the chart. The good news about patient records: New technology makes compilation of data and access to data easier. The bad news: technology can cause violations of patient privacy and confidentiality, with potential ethical and legal problems, can allow possibly inaccurate comparison of your performance with other clinicians, and can allow comparison of performance among organizations.

Another area of concern for confidentiality of clinician actions and status is the National Practitioner Data Bank (NPDB), discussed in Chapter 3 under credentialing. The intent of the NPDB law is to protect patients from harm by identifying bad clinicians. Before the passage of the NPDB, such people could move to another state and practice there undetected.

The NPDB compiles and keeps a file on all clinicians who have been reported as having been disciplined by their state's credentialing board, or who have paid out money after being sued for malpractice. Not all clinicians are covered--see the NPDB Website at http://bhpr.hrsa.gov/dqa/DataBanks.htm

In some states, the credentialing board might discipline you and report to the NPDB for a malpractice suit filing or a late renewal of license. If the clinician or her insurer pays out money in a malpractice case--even a small amount, a nuisance claim--that payment must be reported and will be recorded by the data bank. Those data are available to any state board where you apply for credentials, and to any organization where you apply for a job. The law's intended consequence is good--to protect patients from bad clinicians. But as always, the law has some unintended consequences--it may harm a good clinician whose insurance company settles a small nuisance lawsuit.

The 1993 Clinton health reform plan would have made NPDB data available to the general public, so patients or neighbors would have been able to check on you. Proposals continue to be made that all complaints to NPDB and to credentialing boards be made public, even if the complaints were made anonymously and determined to be unfounded.

Think about it.
Do you think the protection of the public is worth the potential violation of the clinician's confidentiality?
If everyone knows everything about everyone, will that reduce bad behavior?

The quasi-intentional tort of invasion of privacy--public disclosure of private fact--is discussed in Chapter 3, Don't Harm. These cases also are examples of the law punishing someone for telling something they knew but shouldn't have told, for violating confidentiality. Such invasion of privacy situations enforce the value of non-maleficence and also of confidentiality. Keeping the patient's physical and psychological person private, is good practice and lawful and right.

Many states have statutes that enforce the value of keeping patient confidences, and violation of those may produce criminal penalties or civil suits for violation of the law (for example, Tex. Rev. Civ. Stat. Ann. art. 4495b, §5.08 (1999)

In late 2000, the federal Department of Health and Human Services issued regulations under the federal law, the Healthcare Insurance Portability and Accountability Act (HIPAA) of 1996. The purpose of the regulations was to protect the privacy (confidentiality) of patient records. These standards apply to all patients, whether privately insured, uninsured, or insured by Medicare or Medicaid. One change is that there are fines of up to $50,000 and sentences of up to a year in prison for intentional disclosure of a patient's private information, in violation of the regulation.

The regulations were opposed by some in that they allow more access to patient records by government agents. You can find the 4000+ pages of regulations published in the *Federal Register*. Or, you can apply the value of confidentiality and you will comply with the substance of the regulation, if not the detail. Protect your patient's confidences unless she asks you to reveal them, or revealing them is necessary to protect her health or the health of the public.

Privileged communication

In some situations, the patient who is in court has the right to declare communication with her clinician as privileged. That means that the patient can prevent you from testifying in legal proceedings, about private conversations between the two of you. Many exceptions to the privilege exist, such as criminal proceedings, malpractice cases brought by the patient, and so on. A good rule to follow is to assume that conversations with your patient can be ordered to be divulged in court. Following that rule will keep you conversations professional, accurate and conservative.

Telling truth (veracity law)

The truth telling (veracity) component of being true is mentioned less often in law and ethics, because most people now agree that patients should be told the truth. In the past patients might not be told of their diagnosis--for example, of a terminal illness.

The ethical value, telling the truth, is enforced in law in the Constitution's First Amendment that protects freedom of speech, and by civil and criminal laws with penalties for lying. Veracity is enforced in law because the truth gives us more information about reality, and reality is the basis of better decisions. We ask patients to tell us the truth, and in return we clinicians have a duty to be truthful to patients. For example, the patient's consent is assumed to be valid only because we assume the patient was told the truth before agreeing to a procedure.

However, some risk is inherent in veracity. The patient takes some risk by telling you the truth--you might misuse the information. And you the clinician take a risk when telling the truth–you might be fired for telling a patient about unsafe staffing levels in the organization, or of another clinician's error.

For example, the 2001 John Conley Ethics Essay Contest for Medical Students, mentions a report of medical errors by the Institute of Medicine and asks entrants to consider the following question (adapted for this text).

Think about it.
In the operating suite, you observe an error during a procedure. The patient does not die, but is required to extend her stay in the hospital several days and has more post-op pain than otherwise. The clinician told the patient there was a complication but doesn't explain the error. The patient later asks you what happened. What do you say?

(2001 John Conley Ethics Essay Contest for Medical Students, 2000). Another example of risk that results from telling the truth: Clinicians in the old days gave injections of saline, producing a placebo effect (research shows the placebo effect helps symptoms in upwards of 70% of patients, depending on the condition or symptom). But now we don't "lie" to the patient by giving placebos. Instead of saline, they are given injections of steroids and other drugs. In some cases these drugs produce dangerous or at least unanticipated side effects, certainly more dangerous than saline.

Required reporting

Legal exceptions to the mandate for keeping patient secrets, enforce the value of telling the truth for someone else's good. A major case in psychiatric malpractice law that enforced this value of veracity, and was an exception to the value of confidentiality, was *Tarasoff v. Regents of the University of California.* In that case a therapist and employer were found liable for the death of a patient's girlfriend, because she had not been informed of threats the patient had made against her (*Tarasoff*, 1976).

Statutes mandate that certain information that you may learn in the course of practice must be reported to the appropriate authority. The statutes enforce the ethical value of non-maleficence and uphold the value of being true, either to the patient or to the public.

Such required reporting may conflict with the mandate to keep the patient's confidence. Ethics and the law say you must not keep confidences that cause harm to the patient or to other people. If mandatory reporting is required, you must report only to the proper authority specified in your state's statute.

Certain laws mandate that clinicians inform some other person about the patient's condition. For example, infectious diseases that would endanger the public (AIDS, TB), must be reported to the state health department.

Some states require that the partners of HIV infected persons be told of that diagnosis. Law may require injuries that result from illegal acts to be reported, such as evidence of violence (as in gunshot wounds), animal bites, and neglect or abuse of the young, the old, or the disabled or otherwise vulnerable patient. These required reports are discussed also in Chapter 3 because they enforce the value of not harming the patient.

Because there are 50 different states with many different variations of reporting laws that enforce veracity, it is impossible to list all the laws here. Your organization's risk manager, your state credentialing board, the public health department, the police department, or the Internet all are sources to find out the specifics of the law in your state. As usual, a good shorthand for knowing the specifics of the law is to treat others-- in this case the public--as you'd want to be treated in the same situation. This time you may be revealing a patient secret, but you are treating the public, who might be harmed by keeping the secret, as you'd want to be treated.

If obeying the law is counter to your ethic, you must decide whether to obey the law or your conscience. For example, the law enforcing the value of veracity might require you to report a colleague who uses alcohol, or require you to counsel patients about the availability of assisted suicide, or require you to refer them to someone who would perform an abortion. In such a case, you may consider your ethic much higher than the minimum level of the law. You must know your personal ethical values, know the laws that apply, and be aware of the consequences of not following the law if that is your decision.

Fraud, fiduciary duty, reporting malpractice

Criminal law enforces the value of veracity when it punishes people who lie deliberately in order to take property from another person--civil fraud. Some fraud is punished by criminal law, for example lying to the Medicare system. Clinicians who know of such fraud are encouraged to report it by the potential of large awards in whistle-blower lawsuits, described below.

In addition, a growing number of cases punish clinicians who do not reveal that they make more money by giving less care to their patients. This is the situation in which clinicians who work for or contract with HMOs or other managed care organizations, get more money if their patients' care costs the organization less. See the discussion of fiduciary duty, above.

Of course, the clinician who gets paid a fee for each service will get more money for giving more care, so she has an ethical duty as well. You have a fiduciary duty to act in your patient's interest. If this duty might be compromised by the profit motive of the managed care organization, or your own profit motive, you have a duty to reveal that to the patient (to tell her the truth).

If the decision is yours to make, you would put your patient's interest in good care above your interest in making more money. For example, you would not recommend invasive cardiac imaging merely because you would make a fee from its performance.

Some contracts between clinicians and managed care organizations (MCOs) have contained what are called "gag clauses" in which the clinician agrees not to tell the patient when some policy of the MCO might compromise his care. The clinician's ethical mandate is to tell the patient the truth, and some clinicians will not sign contracts with such clauses. Some states have outlawed them.

Some advocate that clinicians uphold the higher ethical value of telling the truth even in situations in which malpractice may have occurred. This usually is a higher duty than the law requires. Some urge clinicians to tell patients when errors have been made that injured the patient, even if the patient might sue for such an injury and be able to recover damages. At least one VA hospital has a policy of revealing such situations to patients (Kraman, 1999; Johnson, 2000).

The management of the hospital asserts that this policy has reduced the number and amount of settlements in malpractice cases in their facility. Several differences make the VA a special situation, however. Clinicians who work for the VA are not personally liable for malpractice, there is a cap on most damage awards, and the government can offer a special settlement to the injured patient. That offer can be a status as "disabled because of a service-related injury"--entitling the patient to a lifetime pension. All those factors make smaller settlements more likely in the VA than in the private sector.

Though clinicians in the VA are not personally liable for malpractice judgments, their errors may be reported to their credentialing board or the National Practitioner Data Bank just as are clinicians in the private sector.

There is a case to be made for revealing errors to patients. First, if more entities like the VA noted above do so, the policy will begin to be seen as the standard of practice. If enough organizations do what now is considered ethical behavior--not required by minimum of the law-- eventually the practice will be made the law. Ethics is the mother of law, and if the public sees revealing errors as right behavior, they likely will insist that lawmakers mandate such behavior at a minimum level.

Second reason to reveal errors to the patient: under current law, if patients are injured by an error and it deliberately is covered up, the statute of limitations for malpractice never will begin to run until the patient discovers the error that caused the injury. It might even be alleged that the error was fraudulently concealed, giving the patient an intentional tort of fraud to sue for, in addition to malpractice.

The JCAHO and some state statutes enforce the ethic of telling truth by requiring a report of certain sentinel events that are related to an error (occurrences such as death, brain or spinal damage to a patient, surgery on the wrong patient, wrong site, or wrong procedure) (Hospital, 2000). In addition, JCAHO requires that patients too be told about it when they have been injured by an error (http://www.jcaho.org/news_frm.html).

Whistle-blowing

The ethical duty and legal mandate to report--**blow the whistle**--in the patient's best interest, is required in ethical codes of several professions. As noted above, blowing the whistle may produce risk with your employer, but in a few cases it also can be financially rewarding. For example, the employee who believes the government is being defrauded may file a lawsuit called a *qui tam* suit, provided under the federal False Claims Act.

Qui tam means "who as well" or "who also" in Latin. In Spanish the words are similar, *quien también*. These words are used because the plaintiff is a private individual who brings the suit on behalf of another party, "who also" is alleged to be defrauded. In health care, this usually is the government paying Medicare or Medicaid money.

The person bringing the suit usually alleges that the government is being defrauded by false billings. If this found to be true, the whistle-blower can recover a percentage of the money the government is owed, sometimes amounting to millions of dollars. This is a perfect example of the advice below.

The best security for the fidelity of men is to make their interest coincide with their duty.
        --ALEXANDER HAMILTON

Even if the employee does not have grounds for a *qui tam* suit, she may have a lawsuit for damages against an employer who retaliates because she filed a lawful claim of discrimination or other violation of law.

When taxpayer-paid programs pay for care (instead of the patient paying), some clinicians experience a conflict with telling truth. Clinicians may lie in order to help the patient stay in the taxpayer-paid program, for the patient's benefit <u>and</u> for the clinician's benefit.   For example, home health care clinicians may be faced with a conflict between 1) documenting the patient's needs and care in such a way as to get payment for the work done--or 2) telling the truth and losing the patient the care and the organization the revenue.

In another example, some clinicians amend their diagnosis to one that the patient's insurer will pay for--considered by some to be a lie, to benefit the patient and clinician. This conflict will increase as managed care payment for care may cause the clinician either to limit care or lie.

Think about it.
Does the desired end--obtaining care for the patient--<u>justify</u> the means used, lying?
Does the desired end--obtaining care for the patient–<u>never</u> justify the means used, lying?
Does the desired end--obtaining care for the patient–<u>always</u> justify the means used, lying?
Does the desired end--obtaining care for the patient–<u>ever</u> justify the means used, lying?
Do your answers tell you anything about your ethics, your philosophy?
Or do you not consider such action "lying?" In that case, what is your definition of lying?

Informed consent

An obvious law enforcement of the ethical value of telling truth is the requirement of informed consent. Clinicians have an obligation to be as truthful to the patient, as the patient was asked to be to them. That truthfulness is implied in consent, making it unnecessary to add the word *informed* to *consent*. The topic of informed consent is elaborated in the law of the value of autonomy (Chapter 4), but the law of informed consent also enforces the minimum of value of veracity discussed in this chapter.

The best ethics lesson on veracity your writer ever had was in law school. Not during the course on professional responsibility, a long semester of learning rules, but in the response of the professor of civil procedure to a student. The student asked, "If I do this (bad thing that cannot be found out), who'll know?"

"You'll know," answered Professor Ross.

He didn't add it, but it was obvious who would be hurt most by unethical behavior. In the clinical practice context it is not always the patient, and not always the organization that is hurt the most--it is the clinician's opinion of herself.

You must weigh the harm to your patients if you don't tell the truth, against the harm that might come to your or your organization if you do tell the truth. Don't forget to factor in the harm to your own view of yourself if you don't tell the truth.

If you need more ethics theory than Dountoothers
(If you want to read more about or by the authors mentioned in this section, you may be able to find books or articles by them in your library, or in the references listed in Chapter 1.)

Faithfulness
Religion

Some would assert that belief in one's religion is a form of fidelity--being faithful or loyal to one's own God or religion. Some even use the phrase "faith traditions" instead of the word religion. Faith is one of the three virtues Christians added to virtue ethics--faith, hope, and charity. (The pre-Christian virtues of the Greeks were fortitude, prudence, courage, and justice.) Material about ethical theories based on religion, faith, logically is included in this chapter on being true.

The idea that people behave morally because their religion orders them to do so has been labeled by ethicists as **divine command**. You may ask why the phrase divine command is used, instead of religion or God.

Think about it.
Does the word "command" have implications, perhaps that religious

*people are more like automatons mindlessly obeying orders,
contrasted with nonreligious people who believe they reason and
decide for themselves the right thing to do?*

*Might the use of the phrase divine command, instead of God, reveal the
ethicists' discomfort with the concept of God--a supreme, non-
human, authority?*

Some ethicists question whether or not religion has anything to do
with morality. Asking the question itself may expose ignorance or bias
on the part of the questioner. For many people, the source of guidance
for their morality is their religion. Most religions incorporate some idea
of an all-powerful, all-knowing being or beings--a god or gods.

It has been argued that religion is not necessary to have a moral
society, and it has been argued that a religious society is not necessarily
a moral one. Ethicists never assert, however, that a society that is
completely without some morality can survive long, because its members
would destroy each other.

Some theorists in ethics write as though they believe that
religion--what they call the divine command theory--teaches this: What
God says is right, is right regardless of any other consideration. They
write that religions teach their adherents, that right is what God
commands--not that right is what is good. The ethicist's view of the
situation: the divine command theory says that

**what God permits is permissive, what God prohibits is wrong,
and what God commands is obligatory.**

On the other hand, a respected early writer on ethics, Saint Thomas
Aquinas, argued that God would not command something that was
wrong, because God is good. Further, if God commanded a thing it
would not be wrong anymore. For example, in the Old Testament God
commanded Abraham to sacrifice his son Isaac as a test of Abraham's
love for God. Abraham was prepared to do it when God commanded
him to stop.

Think about it.

*Did God know all along that he would give Abraham the command to
not kill his son, because God is omniscient?*

*Did Abraham agree to the sacrifice, knowing that God would stop him
because God is good?*

Ethicists worry a lot about whether morality is independent of God.
If God says an act is right, because the act is right in the first place--

before God said it-- then morality is independent of God. God didn't make the act right--something else did. God merely recognized the rightness of the act and commanded it.

Some ethicists believe that morality does not need God to command it. They cite Plato, who quotes Socrates that the gods love holiness because it is holy. Holiness does not become holy, just because the gods love it.

The idea of **intelligent design** may challenge the thinking of some people about the place of religion in the world. Some scientists and mathematicians see evidence that the universe could not have evolved its present state of complexity without some intelligent being or beings having been involved. Despite criticism that they are creationists (people who believe the earth was created only about 6000 years ago), these mathematicians continue their research.

Contractariansim

John Dewey's theory of social ethics is something like contractarianism. Look back at Chapter 4--it's one of the cognitive theories. Contractarianism assumes that people have made a contract to behave ethically. Dewey postulates that ethics originates in the relationships of people to one another. He believes that the origin of the human conscience is in the question, "How would other people view what I am doing?"   Countering that, paraphrasing Oklahoma Congressman JC Watts,

morality is what you do when <u>no one</u> is looking.

Think about it.
Did you ever hear anyone say "What would your parent think if she or he saw you do that?"
Have you ever thought that to yourself?

Dewey's philosophy is relevant to fidelity, in that the people who participate in the social contract are making a promise to behave in certain ways. They agree to be true to their promise, to each other, to the society. According to Dewey, ethics arises as a contract between people, not between God and people.

This philosophy is consistent with a kind of moral legalism (see below), in which the enforcement of laws is considered moral because people are assumed to have agreed to obey them. The people of the society are considered parties to the social contract, though they may never have volunteered personally, individually, to be bound by any such contract or societal mandate.

If the foundations of ethics are social–that is, if morals are contracts between people--then we must question the origin of ethical treatment of animals or babies or incompetent people. They have no ability to make a contract, and they have no great ability to reason that would make them worthy, for example, of Kant's respect.

Think about it.
Are some humans naturally, genetically, hormonally, sympathetic to dependents such as babies, the sick, the old?

When confronted by the first time by an atheist, a friend who had been religious all her life said, "But if he doesn't believe in God, he could do anything! He would have no reason not to be evil!" Certainly, if religion is the only basis for morality, then there is no morality without religion. The argument can be made, however, that the reverse is true, that morality actually is the basis for religion. If that is the case, then perhaps people intuitively or genetically are programmed for morality, and then invent religions to justify and enforce it.

Non-believers question the ethics of divine command, asking whether one can be sure the command is from God, whether God can command something evil, or whether the believer should do something God commands, even if it is evil. The believer can answer with the certainty of faith-- I know. I believe.

Think about it.
Is this certainty of the believer similar to the philosophy of intuitionism (Chapter 4), a gut feeling that something is right?

Moral legalism

Moral legalism is a method to determine right and wrong by reference to specific rules or laws. It is discussed here because all the ethical theories that a fall under this concept are rule-based, and therefore they require fidelity or faithfulness to rules or a system of morality. The person is bound by--is loyal to, promises to live by--these rules. The theories that are considered to be classed under moral legalism determine what is moral by their rules, not by the consequences of actions as do consequentialist philosophies such as utilitarianism (but wait--see below). These moral legalism theories include some you have seen before:

Ethical egoism, the rule being to always act for your own good, because the good of all will result. Because this is considered to be extended to all with resulting good for all, it is considered an ethical theory and not a psychological theory such as psychological egoism.

Discussed in Chapter 4 Be Free.

Divine command, the rule being to always act as God has commanded. This is assumed to be the rule of most formal religions. Discussed in Chapter 6 Be True.

Kantianism, the rule being to always act according to the categorical imperative--the way you wish other people would act--obeying laws that are universal. Discussed in Chapter 3 Don't Harm.

Utilitarianism, surprise, there's a rule here--the rule being always act to attain the greatest good for the greatest number. Remember that *rule* utilitarians adhere to this rule, but *act* utilitarians are more like moral particularists (see below). Discussed in Chapter 2 Do Good.

Justice, the rule being always treat like cases alike, unlike cases unalike. Discussed in Chapter 5 Be Fair.

Moral legalism is said to be either monistic, using only one of the theories above, or pluralistic, using two or more of them. These rule-based theories all can be called non-consequentialist. Next you see the ultimate in consequentialist reasoning–moral particularism.

Moral particularism differs from moral legalism, in that whether an act is right or wrong depends on the particular situation. There are no universal rules at all. Whether an act is moral depends on whether it will obtain the consequences you want. Only you decide what you want--and if you want it, however you get it is "moral."

Think about it.
Using that word moral in that last sentence, did we just step onto a metaethical, definitional slippery slope?
Are we heading toward a morass of "What is the definition of 'moral'?" or "It depends on what the meaning of the word 'is' is?"

It is suggested that one could take a middle ground between moral legalism and moral particularism, using rules from moral legalism unless they seemed not to apply. If they did not apply, one could then use moral particularism.

Think about it.
Could this be called making up any morality you want? Ethics a la carte? Are you losing all respect for ethical theorists?
Or are we just getting more realistic, down to how real people decide what is moral?

Duties and obligations

Back to the reality of fidelity, to one's family or patient or tribe. Now we consider the concepts of duties and obligations. **Duties and** obligations include *prima facie* **duties** that are said to be known without further evidence or proof of their validity, intuitively. The theory of intuitionism was one of the cognitive theories discussed in Chapter 4 on autonomy.

Prima facie is Latin, for "first, on their face." Such intuitively known duties are primary, without anything further than their being stated. *Prima facie* duties are distinguished from **actual duties**. The prima facie duty is to be followed, if there is no other moral duty higher. One *prima facie* duty is to keep promises–the topic of this chapter.

But, for example, a promise to one's dying mother to finish college might be superseded if a conflicting actual duty was more important. The daughter's duty to work to feed her little sister might come before keeping the college promise–then the **actual duty** would be to go to work. The *prima facie* duties are listed as repairing wrongs, seeking distribution of happiness in accord with merit, doing good to others and self, not harming, telling truth, keeping promises. These are familiar, similar to the values used in clinical ethics and as chapters in this text-- being fair, doing good, doing no harm, being true (Hall, 1996).

For example, the clinician's *prima facie* duty is to care for her patient with an infectious disease–to do good for the patient. But if that duty conflicted with what she might see as a higher duty, for example to protect her children from risk of infection from an unknown organism that might kill them, then her actual duty might be to her children instead. Obviously this is a judgment call, in which the clinician would have to weigh the patient's needs, against the degree of danger to herself and/or her family.

Ethical relativism

Next we discuss the concept in ethical theory that is most visible and applicable in your own life, in the early 21st century, as a clinician in clinical practice. The 20th century mantra of "I'm okay, you're okay" is a shorthand version. **Ethical relativism** is the term used when discussing whether any theory of morality is real or true. Relativism itself is a theory that there is no truth, no reality–that everything is relative, everything depends on the circumstances. Whether killing is wrong depends on the circumstances. Whether it is true that there was a holocaust in World War II depends on your belief. Whether there was a World War II depends on whether you believe there was.

Part of the discussion of ethical relativism is **subjectivism**. Subjectivists take the position that standards of moral behavior generally are subjective, measured from inside, not objectively in which situation two or more people can agree on the truth. Subjectivists argue that what is right behavior--the moral standards, customs, practices, and rules--

vary from society to society, from culture to culture, time to time. **Objectivists** would take the contrary view to subjectivists. They believe that the right thing to do can be determined objectively, from outside the person and the culture.

An **ethical relativist** believes that what is right, good, or moral depends on what the culture believes. For more extreme relativists, what is right may vary even more--from person to person.

Extreme relativists believe that what is moral is within each person and possibly different for each person. There are no objective standards whatsoever by which to measure individual behavior. People who are extreme relativists can be persuaded that some practice is wrong--perhaps female circumcision. But they must be persuaded on their own set of values, what they personally believe. Perhaps they would be convinced on practical grounds–such as increased female deaths from infections. For them, there is no universal moral ground–such as the assertion that the practice violates the girl's autonomy.

Subjectivists who believe that the standard--the measuring--of morality is found within the society, are called **cultural relativists.** Cultural relativists concede that some objective determination of morality can be made outside the individual's personal standards, but their standard of right is whatever the culture or society believes. For example, if the culture's standard allows or mandates female circumcision, then it's moral.

Related to that thinking, an **ethical conditionalist** believes that certain conditions cause morals. The idea that morality is dependent on certain conditions in the culture or environment, is called the **dependency thesis**.

You may believe that some basic principles of morality are universal--or should be universal--for all individuals and cultures. An **ethical universalist** will agree that the practices differ among cultures, but what is right, the real morality, does not.

If you believe that there is one set of absolute morals and values in the universe that apply absolutely to all peoples and all cultures and times, you may be considered an **ethical absolutist**. Absolutists automatically are universalists. Whatever is absolutely correct in one place, would be correct universally in all places. But universalists are not necessarily absolutists.

Ethical universalists believe that what is right everywhere may change, though the new right would still be universal everywhere. Of course, ethical relativists are not considered to be absolutists–they do not believe there is one right moral code. Nor are ethical relativists considered to be universalists–they do not believe the same ethic should apply everywhere.

SUMMARY OF RELATIVISM:

Ethical relativist--what is right is relative--not universal nor absolute.
Extreme relativist-- what is right is relative--varies from person to person.
Cultural relativist --what is right is relative--varies from culture to culture.
Ethical conditionalist--what is right is relative--depends on the conditions present
Ethical universalist--what is right is *not* relative--it's universal everywhere, though it may change.
Ethical absolutist--what is right is *not* relative--it's universal, and unchanging.

Think about it.
Are you an ethical relativist, extreme relativist, cultural relativist, ethical conditionalist, ethical universalist, or ethical absolutist?
Or none of the above?

Do realize that this universalist-relativist debate is about metaethical theories, a subdivision of non-normative theories of ethics. (Look back at the algorithm about ethics in Chapter 1 to clarify that distinction.) The disagreement between relativism and universalism is about the nature of ethics--whether any morals are universal to all humans, or whether they depend on the culture.

The disagreement is not about which behavior is the right behavior. The debate is whether <u>any</u> behavior is right universally, or whether right is different in different cultures.

Whether morality is relative or absolute, matters in your life. If ethics are relative, then for example the treatment of women in any society is totally a matter of that society's concern. Depending on the society's ethics, girls might have no right to refuse circumcision. If morality is relative, the Samurai were acting morally when they followed the custom in early Japan of trying out a new sword on travelers they encountered.

On the other hand, if ethics are universal and absolute, then America might be justified in imposing its values on other countries and societies--by force--for or against abortion, or contraceptives, or gun rights, or democracy. Or, another country would be justified in imposing its universal and absolute values on us.

If ethics are relative and vary from individual to individual, then laws that enforce any morality are wrong. If ethics are absolute, then laws mandating at least a minimum level of morality are justified. Certain rights are enforced in the US Constitution, demonstrating that some morality is not considered relative. Some rights are considered universal and absolute--in America, regarding those specific freedoms to act.

A rights-based approach to morality provides standards by which actions can be judged. This is true in the U.S. and could be applied internationally.

Think about it.

Should the U.S. impose rights for citizens in other countries whose governments do not agree to those rights?

When we impose sanctions on other countries for violations of human rights, are we asserting that some ethics are universal and absolute?

Some argue that a rights-based ethic of rights for individuals applies only to societies in which the individual is most important. Such an ethic would not be applicable in many traditional cultures, in which the family or tribe are more important than the individual. Those include many African and Asian cultures.

Suppose ethics are relative, depending on the conditions of the society. Then it can be argued that slavery was right (or at least not immoral) for the time of its existence in the U.S. Then the Aztecs were right to eat their enemies. Then some Hindus were or are right, to urge widows to throw themselves on the funeral pyre of their husbands.

If morality is relative and not absolute, then I may believe abortion is wrong. But I also must concede it is right for you to believe abortion is moral. If morality is relative and not absolute, I must accept that you are not immoral even if you believe that slavery still is right.

If ethical relativists are correct, then arguments based on moral reasons are useless. If no morality is better or more nearly true than another, then any and all morality is equally valid. We still can disagree on actions, but we can't use morality as a reason for our own actions or for disagreeing with others' actions. This discussion about ethical relativity is a variation of the post-modern, deconstructivist movement to tear down all versions of certainty, truth, standards and structure in society.

Think about it.

Are ethical discussions a new thing?

Is ethical relativism a recent phenomenon, since we became more diverse and tolerant of each other?

Have some people always believed the ethics of their own culture are right, regardless of what they happen to be?

Socrates was killed--given Hemlock to drink--in 399 B.C. He taught ethical universalism/ absolutism--that right was right no matter what the culture said. The majority of his society thought ethical relativism was correct and had him killed for his teaching.

> Socrates: [O]ught we to follow the opinion of the many and fear that, or the opinion of the one ...who understands these matters...?

Socrates taught that right is right, even if it is believed by a minority of only one person. So much for the new practice of determining ethics by poll-taking.

REFERENCES

2001 John Conley Ethics Essay Contest for Medical Students. *Journal of the American Medical Association*, 2000; 284(9):1145.

Cushing M. The right to fire v. the public interest. *American Journal of Nursing,* 1992; 92(12):18,20.

Garcia EC, Helms FA. Covenants not to compete and not to disclose. *Texas Bar Journal,* 2001;64(1):32-43.

Hall JK. *Nursing Ethics and Law.* Philadelphia: W.B. Saunders, 1996.

Hospital risk management and incident reporting: the duty and effect of self reporting. *The Florida Nurse*, June 2000, p. 27.

Johnson C. We made a mistake: Caregivers and administrators bring medication errors out in the open--especially with patients. *Nursing Management*, 2000; 32(4):22-23.

Kraman S, Hamm G. Risk management: extreme honesty may be the best policy. *Annals of Internal Medicine*, 1999;131(12):963-967. Comment 970-972.

Pegram vs. Herdrich, No. 98-1949, US Supreme Court (June 12, 2000).

Rice B. Invitation to a lawsuit: financial incentives to limit care. *Medical Economics*, November 22, 1999, pp 144-157.

Tarasoff v. Regents of the University of California, 551 P2d 334 (1976).

Tex.Rev.Civ.Stat.Ann.art. 4495b, §5.08 (Vernon Pamp. Supp. 2000)

Chapter 7: Life.

"For every thing, there is a season. . a time to be born and a time to die"
ECCLESIASTES 3:1-2, *Old Testament*

CONTENTS

Misconception: life expectancy vs. life span
Misconception: risk probability, association, causation, and
   significance
Quality of life
Competency/capacity
   Decisional capacity
CPR/DNR
   DNR orders
Withdrawing vs. withholding
Double effect
Dehydration
Cases: the right to die
   Standards of evidence
   Cruzan
   The Fourteenth Amendment and the right to refuse treatment
   Busalacchi
   Other cases
Definition of death
Analysis of actions that cause death by degree of intent
Other-killing: euthanasia
   Nazi euthanasia
Self-killing
   Self-killing, helping: assisted suicide
The Holland experience
Pain control

REFERENCES

Key concepts

life	moral patient	competent
artificial	moral standing	incapacitated
insemination	moral relationships	decisional capacity
in vitro fertilization	agism	double effect
human pluripotent	life expectancy	best interest
stem cells	life span	substituted
eugenics	group probability	judgment
surrogate mother	case probability	beyond a
contraception	association	reasonable
Roe v. Wade	causation	doubt
sensitivity	statistical	clear and
specificity	significance	convincing
genealogical theory	confidence interval	preponderance
moral agency	Quality Adjusted	definition of death
	Life Years	euthanasia

assisted suicide

General discussion of the value, life

All of the work, ethics, and law of clinical practice are founded on the value of **life**. Valuing life is the foundation underlying the ethics and law of these last two topics in the book--being born and dying.

In some other texts and papers on the ethics and law of clinical practice, life is not even mentioned as a separate value. Those authors might explain that the value of life is implicit in all the other values. But among such writers there also is a tendency to emphasize other values-- such as the patient's autonomy or the autonomy of her surrogate, or of doing good to the patient and not doing harm to her--in preference to valuing the individual patient's life.

You may see the value life labeled as "sanctity of life" because many religions teach that life is sacred, blessed by God. Some writers characterize religious people as valuing life absolutely, whatever the condition or quality. They label the valuing of life as "vitalism."

Related to the topic of this chapter is the term quality of life. The implication of assessing someone's quality of life is that lives have different qualities, are of different value. Quality of life is discussed in the second part of this chapter, under A Time to Die.

Think about it.
Is life more valued to one person, than to another?
Are the last, dying days of a patient less valuable to that person, than the first few days of an infant's life are to her?
Can a number be put on the value or quality of life? For yourself, or for someone else's life?
What is a human life worth?

This chapter on the value life, could be organized in other ways than by time period. For example, the chapter could be organized by issues, or by whose interests are affected. But because humans have a limited, finite lifespan, marked by two physical changes--birth and death--this chapter organizes the issues surrounding the value life into "A time to be born," and "A time to die." The earlier chapters of this book relate to the legal and ethical issues encountered during the span of life between those two physical markers, birth and death.

The specific topics of these two times are different. However, you will recognize that the philosophical and ethical and legal questions are much the same for the issues surrounding both birth and death--questions such as the following.

Think about it.

What is a person?

When does a person begin to exist, or cease to exist?

What is the value of life compared to other values, especially compared to the value of money?

Whose interests prevail when the interests of people conflict--as in whose baby, whose fertilized ova, whose insurance money, whose life, whose death, whose choice, prevails?

This chapter differs from other chapters in that the law and ethics are discussed together under a given topic. The law and ethics are not separate sections in this chapter as they are in other chapters. As is true always, the laws that govern the events around birth and death continue to change, but the ethics (the value of life) remains constant.

A time to be born . . .

Most of the work that clinicians do should be called illness care rather than health care. However, care at the time of life around birth deserves the description "health" care better than other kinds of clinical practice. Even here, though, clinicians work to prevent illness and complications and to deal with them if they occur. A professional clinician is needed at the birth of a healthy baby to a healthy woman, only to deal with what might go wrong.

Midwives and other clinicians who work with mothers and babies do not make things go right--they don't make people healthy. But they may help people who are healthy, to keep from getting sick. An example is giving immunizations to a well baby. Note that none of the topics described for this section is about the usual sequence of events.

Some of the topics discussed under this first section, A time to be born, may be practice issues only for clinicians who work specifically with those patients. But the topics are concerns of all citizens *including* clinicians, and are part of the ethics of all clinical practice. Clinicians should be leaders among the citizens who shape the ethics and law in these areas, and to do that you must know about the issues.

Terms used

The reproductive cell produced by the woman is an ovum or oocyte (plural: ova). The reproductive cell produced by the man is a sperm or spermatocyte (plural, sperm), and the word for both kinds of cell is gametes. After the cells unite (fertilization), the result is a zygote.

When further developed and implanted in the uterus, the word used by most clinicians is embryo. When the clinician can see her with ultrasound at eight weeks, or hear her heartbeat with a Doppler stethoscope at ten weeks, the term used is fetus, until the time of delivery, at which time it is a newborn child (baby, infant, neonate). All these terms are misused at times, either by mistake or for a desired effect (perhaps even in this book!)

This chapter generally uses the pronoun "her" to refer to the fetus, because the fetus is human and the sex has been determined from the moment of fertilization. In lay speech, people talk about the "baby" in utero, but the word baby is loaded with connotations, such as person and human being. Its use is not favored by advocates on one side of the issue.

Artificial insemination

As generally understood, artificial is something that humans cause-- something that does not occur without human action. Using the artificial versus natural distinction often is unhelpful. You can see that "artificial" insemination requires human action--but so does natural insemination..

With **artificial insemination** (AI), sperm in semen are delivered to the cervix by artificial means (that is, other than sexual intercourse). AI uses either the husband's sperm, a donor's sperm, or donor and husband's sperm. Each year about 30,000 babies are born as a result of AI. Clinics run by ethical people use one donor for only ten women, to reduce the odds of half-brothers and half-sisters unknowingly meeting, marrying, and reproducing. Such practice recognizes an old human fear of breaking the incest taboo.

Incest--sex between members of the same family--violates virtually all known ethical codes. (In the royal families of ancient Egypt, brothers and sisters did marry each other because they were considered immortal and had to marry in their own family, the only other gods.) Incest increases the odds of genetic defects of the offspring because mothers and fathers who are related have similar genes. The odds are greater that recessive genes carrying defects will be inherited from both parents and produce the defect in the baby.

The ethical and resulting legal responsibility of the organization providing semen for AI is to check the semen donor to be sure he is free of HIV, hepatitis, and other infections. He should be rechecked after several months to verify that he was not latently infected at the time of the first check.

Many clinics test for HIV, syphilis, hepatitis, cytomegalovirus (CMV), and some test for herpes. CMV transmission from donor sperm can produce legal liability. As is true also in adoption cases, clinics must obtain personal information about the donor's family, health history, and possible genetic diseases.

Once semen is donated, it is frozen and stored in a sperm bank.

Sperm can be stored that may carry specific genetic traits. A sperm bank of Nobel Prize winners is seen by some as an attempt to do eugenics (more discussion below). One goal of Germany's National Socialist government of the 1930's was to produce a superhuman--a super race-- through eugenics.

Think about it.

Would using a superman's sperm for multiple inseminations be good for society?

What if a supply of John Kennedy's sperm were available, and many people wanted to have him as their child's father? Martin Luther King? Ronald Reagan?

AI is more expensive than natural insemination--and AI may need to be repeated many times to produce a pregnancy. It is an elective procedure, not necessary to the physical health of the potential mother or father. Some health insurance policies voluntarily pay for AI, and some states have mandated that insurance companies include AI whenever group coverage is offered.

If a particular health insurance pays for AI, other members of the insurance pool pay increased premiums for what some would consider unnecessary care. A couple with six children pay premiums for insurance, for a service they are not likely to need.

Think about it.

Should a single woman past menopause be mandated to share the cost of a young couples' attempt to have a child through AI?

In states where such insurance coverage is mandated--where all pay premiums for it--is the conception of children by at least one natural parent considered to be an important social good?

In the future, if all are mandated to buy health insurance, should AI be covered in a basic benefits package for reproductive health care?

Such a mandate is not a new idea. Tax law mandates that all pay for clinical service of the poor, the elderly, and certain other groups.

Think about it.

What if AI is not in a package of basic benefits, and a future global cap on spending for care limits the amount that can be spent totally for such care in the United States?

Then, even individuals who can pay for AI out of pocket might be prohibited from buying the service, thereby limiting their freedom. Under a global expenditure cap, people who are allowed to buy AI will reduce the amount of money that can be spent elsewhere, on other people and other illnesses.

Think about it.
Is it fair for some to spend money on AI, not necessary to life or physical health, in order to satisfy a desire to propagate one partner's genes-- when there are children of other parents available to adopt?

Some religions see procreation as the main reason for sexual intercourse in marriage, and thus they opposes artificial insemination on the grounds that AI removes the sex act from procreation. The technology of artificial insemination gives single women the power to conceive without having heterosexual sex and without having to deal with the father of a resulting child.

Think about it.
Should one partner of a lesbian couple have the right to conceive a baby and raise a child?
Is it fair to the child, to grow up in a household without the benefit of a father?
In a lesbian relationship?
Would the child be better off not to have been born at all?

If artificial insemination is available for a price, and not paid for by mandatory insurance schemes, then some poor people will be denied reproductive opportunity. At least two levels of opportunity may result. On the other hand, prohibiting artificial insemination involves government in private affairs again.

Think about it.
Do people have a right to seek to have their own genetic child or a perfect child?
Do they have a right to spend their own money on that attempt?
Do they have a right to force other people to help pay for it, through state-mandated insurance coverage?

In vitro fertilization

In vitro fertilization (IVF) first was developed in the late 1970's. In Latin, in *vitro* means in glass, and IVF literally occurs in a glass container. (In *vivo* means "in life.") To accomplish IVF, ova are flushed from the woman's ovaries with doses of fertility drugs that cause several ova to mature at the same time. The ova are retrieved and placed in containers where sperm are introduced, resulting in hoped-for fertilization.

The same fertility drugs are used to stimulate ovulation in infertile women. That process often results in multiple births. Millions of women have taken such fertility drugs since their development. Originally the only side effects known were temporary bloating and mood swings. However, studies have raised the possibility that women who took the drugs even decades before, show a greater risk of ovarian cancer than women who did not. The risk was greater if the drugs were taken and conception did not occur. The risk of ovarian cancer is low, whether the drugs are used or not.

About 15 percent of attempted IVFs result in pregnancies-- interestingly, that is about the same rate of pregnancy success as when not using IVF. In a related procedure, gamete intrafallopian transfer, ova and sperm are introduced into the fallopian tube through a laparoscope. That procedure is said to be successful about 26 times out of 100 efforts.

IVF is an even more expensive procedure than AI because of the drugs used, the procedure needed to retrieve several eggs, the fertilization procedure, and the implanting procedure. The same arguments arise about the ethics of mandating insurance coverage for IVF. Those arguments are about forcing others to pay for the process, or preventing individuals from spending their own money for it.

Some religions and some other groups oppose in vitro fertilization techniques on moral grounds. In order to get at least one viable fertilized ovum (zygote), usually four are fertilized. Opponents of IVF say that several human lives then exist in the dish,. To increase the odds that fertilization will take place, all of the zygotes may be implanted in the uterus.

If all survive implantation they now are embryos. There will be a multiple birth unless a selective abortion is done, of all but one embryo. That procedure can cause loss of all the embryos. Destroying zygotes, whether they have been implanted or still are in the dish, raises the same issues as abortion.

Think about it.
Can it be argued that it is better to have at least one baby born as a result of IVF, even though other embryos were destroyed to accomplish it?
Is it a good argument that no babies would have been born, had the procedure not been done?
Does the argument rest on whether one believes it to be God's will that people have children--and whether the creation and birth of one child justifies the destruction of others?
Does the good of society deserve any consideration?

Are more children born, good or bad for US society? For the Earth? Says who?

Fertilized ova (zygotes) can be frozen, thawed, and later used with no apparent damage. If a couple freezes zygotes and later they separate or divorce, the issue may be who gets custody of such fertilized ova.

Think about it.
Should the ova be considered children, with the attendant legal rules and procedures, or should they be classed as property, to be divided according to those laws?

In a Tennessee divorce proceeding, zygotes fertilized in 1988 were sought by their father. He didn't want his ex-wife to have them implanted. The state Supreme Court gave the zygotes to the ex-husband (*Davis*, 1992). According to news reports, he then had the zygotes destroyed (Woo, 1993).

Regardless of which parent got custody (or ownership), the other parent theoretically could be made a parent years after donating the cells. Legal cases deciding the issue have differed. Because the technology hasn't been available for long, the law still is being made. This is the status of many other issues where ethics (thus law) interfaces with technology in clinical practice. This is one reason we consider the ethics and law together in this chapter.

Think about it.
After having consented to contribute half of a person, may one contributor withdraw consent?
Does the act of having unprotected sex voluntarily, constitute implied consent to be a parent?

Perhaps some sort of advance directive can be made, incorporated in a prenuptial or pre-pregnancy agreement: "If we divorce, then the following should happen to my zygotes." The same conditions can be imposed on adoption, precluding a biological parent from later reversing consent and wanting the child back. Even the unwed father has rights attendant to his child when the mother of the child gives the child up for adoption.

Think about it.
Could the same conditions also be imposed, relative to an abortion decision?

Once the conditions for pregnancy are set up (for example, voluntary unprotected intercourse), a person could be deemed to have consented to be pregnant, and prohibited from reversing the consent. Women who did not consent to sexual intercourse, and thus did not consent to risk creating a pregnancy, still might have an abortion option.

Some consider pregnancy to be similar to a legal servitude (condition of slavery) of the woman's body. Whether the servitude is voluntary or not is arguable, depending on the circumstances of the intercourse that risked the pregnancy.

In the frozen zygote situation, the parent with custody or ownership doesn't require anyone to become pregnant because a surrogate mother can be used. But the noncustodial person still could be made a biological mother or a father.

Other ethical and legal issues are possible if a woman can't produce her own ova (oocytes). Donation of oocytes from another woman produces a situation similar to AI, but the donation process is more difficult than sperm donation. Added to the legal and ethical tangles the procedures have produced, are allegations that some clinics stole fertilized ova from couples in their care, and implanted them in other women.

hPSCs

The use of fetal body parts for transplant to fetuses, infants and old sick people is increasing, as is research using embryonic stem cells.

Human pluripotent stem cells (hPSCs) (called stem cells in the lay press) are obtained from grinding up embryos (technically, the word for this entity is *zygote*). The resulting cells are considered capable of developing into virtually any body tissue–endoderm, mesoderm, or ectoderm. Stem cell research is attractive to those of a consequentialist utilitarian philosophy. They might provide therapy for a plethora of chronic diseases experienced by aging baby boomers. Because stem cells are obtained by destroying embryos (zygotes), this is another ethical and legal issue classed under "a time to be born."

Fetal tissue research and transplantation are regulated by statute and rules. In general this law prohibits profit from such practice and mandates that pregnant women not be encouraged to abort by the knowledge of potential use of their fetuses for such research.

Some have commented on the apparent contradiction that embryos have more protection from research, than fetuses have protection from abortion. That apparent contradiction can be explained by a societal attitude that it is better to be aborted as a fetus, than to be born disabled as a result of experimentation on an embryo.   That attitude exists because the public is unaware that a high proportion of births in the normal population--between 3%-8%--have congenital anomalies that produce disabilities.

An issue related to research on fetuses is "in utero human gene therapy" (IUHGT)–transplanting genes into fetuses in utero. But therapy is not the same as IUHG<u>TE</u>, adding the "E" for experimentation. The current state of the art is research, not therapy. The problem that can be foreseen is that of informed consent.

Think about it.

Though the pregnant woman can consent for herself and give permission for gene transfers to her fetus, can she give valid consent for future generations that might be affected by gene therapy?

Some worry that in effect this is an intergenerational permission, and they ask how follow-up will be assured to see if the germ line has changed.

Some argue that the law is taking a direction that denies moral standing to the embryo and fetus. They cite federal approval of fetal tissue research, and federal approval of destruction of embryos to obtain embryonic stem cells. The ethics and law of conducting embryonic stem cell research and using fetal tissue and organs for transplant to other fetuses and infants and to old sick people, logically will follow what the people believe is the moral standing of the embryo and fetus. See the discussion about moral standing, below.

Eugenics

Eugenics is the systematic attempt to improve the whole human race by improving the "breeding stock." The Latin origin of the word is *eu* meaning true, and *genics* meaning genetics or origin. Some people already try to improve their own particular babies by testing their zygotes for genetic defects.

For example, zygotes from couples at high risk for cystic fibrosis can be tested, and researchers can identify the zygotes from the group that do not carry CF. Other genetic defects, such as Duchenne's muscular dystrophy, sickle cell disease, hemophilia A, and Tay-Sachs disease--also could be detected.

The procedure is expensive. The prenatal (pre-pregnancy) exam costs in the five figures, on zygotes of eight cells or fewer.

Think about it.

Is this better timing than testing after pregnancy commences, when the fetus is 11 to 16 weeks old? At that point, a positive test for CF could produce a difficult decision about abortion.

Will women and men with inheritable defects be more willing to risk

parenthood if testing can be done early before implantation?
Or are we merely changing the stage at which abortion or infanticide is done?

If the technology improves, prospective parents who want to be sure their baby has no defects could routinely do IVF and have DNA testing, even if they could conceive without it. Defective zygotes could be weeded out before implantation.

Think about it.
In future, will only the poor have defective children?
In future, will the baby who is born with a defect be considered lucky to at least be born, compared to the usual zygote with a defect who is not implanted or who is aborted?
Will it be a more nearly perfect world, with more nearly perfect, healthier, taller, happier people? (Blonde, blue-eyed? Brown, brown-eyed?)

If so, future generations will be able to tell who was born to poor or careless parents. That will be anyone born with a disease that could have been detected in the embryo stage. Embryos with disabilities whose parents are rich, will be destroyed. Embryos with disabilities whose parents are poor people, will be born.

Think about it.
Does that change the concept of "disadvantaged"?
Or do you believe it an advantage to be aborted, if otherwise you will be born with a defect?

A related issue is genetic testing for disease in persons who already are born. Some voice concern about potential or actual discrimination against people who are found to have genetic tendency toward certain disease. Though very few genes are simply and directly related to the individual's risk of illness or death, this information could be used by employers and by insurers to deny employment or limit coverage to individuals who are more likely to become ill or disabled in the future.

For example, people with a family history of Huntington's disease are said to find it difficult or impossible to get life insurance. See the potential for such people to use the Americans with Disabilities Act, Chapter 5.

If insurers are not allowed to use genetic test results, however, persons who know from tests that they are at risk for death could insure themselves for large amounts. They then could reap the benefit for their survivors, or for themselves using viatical insurance. People with good genetics might choose not to join the insurance pool with others who had worse risk of disease and death. This issue will gain greater urgency in the future as more genetic tests are available to calculate risks (Testing, 2000). Before you worry too much about risks, read the section on that subject below.

Cloning

Scientists have succeeded in transferring a human somatic cell nucleus into a human or animal egg. This creates a zygote or proto-embryo and potentially clones the person--giving new meaning to the term "born again." Federal guidelines in the U.S. prohibit taxpayer funding for such research, but private funding could sponsor research to clone a class of "human" beings who could be used for certain dangerous or dirty work--such as is done with embryos used for research on stem cells. The Parliament in Britain has legalized public funding for cloning of human embryos (Webster, 2000).

Cloned zygotes could be used to help infertile couples who have difficulty in obtaining ova to fertilize, or to help couples whose sperm infrequently fertilizes an ovum. One ovum could be fertilized, and then many copies cloned to implant. But many identical babies will result unless the rest are aborted.

Cloning could replace a child who has died--the parents could use cells taken from that child to clone an identical baby. Scientists can grow sperm in a laboratory, so cloning would allow infertile men to have their own genetic offspring. Male cells will be able to be programmed to produce eggs, so that both men and women can either "father" or "mother" children, allowing homosexual couples to have a child created who is genetically related to both of them (Norton, 2000).

Such techniques can be used to create people who are taller, or better relief pitchers, or even people who like to clean toilets.

Think about it.
If some very great people are identified, and the technology exists to clone them from a cell--should it be done?
Is this a form of immortality?
Is a clone of George W. Bush, another George W. Bush? Or is he a twin?
Will he still become President if he grows up in Queens instead of in Midland?

Surrogate motherhood and adoption

A woman who deliberately conceives and delivers a baby knowing that she will give it to a specified other couple or person, is called a **surrogate mother**. Some even drop the word "mother" in her description.

Think about it.

Why is the term surrogate mother not applied to women who have babies they give up for adoption to an unknown person?

Such women are called birth mother, biological mother, or natural mother--to distinguish them from adoptive mother. You may remember from psychology courses, the phrase "surrogate mother" was used to identify the wire forms that simulated monkey mothers, in Harlow's experiments on the effects of non-nurturing.

Various arrangements of surrogate motherhood are possible. The mother can be artificially inseminated with the sperm of the man who eventually will obtain the child, in which case it's his genetic child. Or a zygote from a couple can be implanted, the zygote being their genetic child

Think about it.

Can the couple be characterized as renting the surrogate's uterus?
Or be seen as buying the baby, or buying the woman's time and risk?

"Womb" is the emotion-loaded motherhood word used by opponents of the procedure, instead of the word uterus. The use of "womb" harkens back to a time only about 100 years ago when many thought the sperm contained the whole of the genetic material. Then, the woman was seen as the mere bearer of the man's seed that contained all of the material of the baby. People used to say "she bore him a child."

Think about it.

Does surrogacy exploit poor women for the benefit of those who can afford to pay?
Are surrogates different from other people who rent their body or mind for work?

Some people wish the state to stay out of the private areas of sexuality and reproduction but also oppose surrogate motherhood. Laws regulating surrogacy, however, are government intervention in that arena. Opponents of surrogacy worry about the sanctity of motherhood, the relation of the mother to child, and the mental health of such women who give up their babies.

Think about it.
Are these the same issues that concern opponents of abortion?

The issue remains unresolved as to what happens when the resulting baby has an anomaly (3-8% do, remember). If neither the couple nor the mother wants the child, the baby may be given up for adoption. If the baby can't be adopted, the state (taxpayers) might pay for the care. Perhaps the surrogate mother and potential parents should contribute to the cost of care.

If that reasoning were carried into adoption generally, a woman who puts a baby out for adoption might be obligated to pay for the baby's care if the baby were not adopted. Because the mother started the baby and carried it to term, she's responsible. It could be reasoned that she lawfully could have had an abortion instead, and could be assumed that she benefitted her personal moral values in not aborting the baby.

Major legal and ethical difficulties surface when the surrogate mother decides to keep the baby. As a result of those problems, legislation was written in several states to bar or restrict contracts for commercial surrogate births. Such laws may forbid surrogate motherhood, or forbid it for pay, or forbid the rights of the people who paid for the care of the woman during pregnancy.

For example, in Virginia prospective parents can present the surrogacy contract to a judge, and obtain court orders declaring the paternity (and maternity?) of the baby to be born. Florida and New Hampshire screen would-be parents and surrogates.

State statutes may forbid paying a woman to bear a child for another person. Laws forbid her selling a child of her own, but the Internet makes this contact between parent and wannabe parent easier than in the past. Some instances of sales are said to have occurred. For an example of this purchasing of infants from 2400 years ago, read Aristophanes (Greek, 445-380 B.C.) whose play "The Thesmophoriazusae" chastised women of the time for buying babies.

Think about it.
Is this buying of babies, different from paying costs for adoption?
Is this different from selling body parts?
Is this different from selling yourself into slavery for profit?
Why do we forbid these ultimate freedoms?
What might be some consequences if we allowed them?

Look back at Chapter 4, Be Free, for some reasons to limit autonomy, and think about your own reactions.

Court cases on surrogacy

Some highly publicized court cases have explored the issues of who gets custody of the surrogate's baby. In some cases, the baby has been given to the genetic father and his wife over the genetic, surrogate mother. Genetic parents have been awarded custody over the surrogate mother who was not related to the baby, under the legal theory that intentions matter. In some cases the baby has been awarded to the surrogate mother. Usually some kind of joint custody is arranged, and visitation rights are given to all parties.

Think about it.
What would happen if Solomon were the judge?

> Faced with two mothers, each arguing the child was hers, Judge Solomon of the Old Testament ordered the baby cut in two--one half for each woman. The thief agreed with that solution. The real mother was identified when she asked that the baby be given to the thief, to save the baby's life. Solomon gave the child to her, revealed as the real mother because she had the child's best interest in her heart (Kings).

Preliminary studies show that the couples and women involved in surrogacy are happy with the arrangement. They seem to be mentally normal people--as much as can be measured by tests-- before and after the event. Several of the surrogate mothers express an altruistic motivation, and enjoyment of the pregnant state and the feeling of giving life. Most of the women studied are Caucasian.

Adoption and best interest of the child

The ethical issues and interests of the parties to adoption are similar to those of surrogacy, and the law is developing in similar ways. The courts struggle with a familiar question of the relative importance of genetics versus environment--the nature-nurture debate. Questions include the best interests of babies raised by parents of another race or by gay couples.

Regarding the best interest of the child, technology now makes it possible for women past menopause to be pregnant with a donated ovum. Some question whether that origin is fair to such children, who at 21 years of age may have a mother who is 80. Some assert that children have a right to parents of a certain age range, and to have parents of certain attitudes.

Think about it.
Is the same issue raised when a man over 50 fathers a child by a younger

woman?

Why are questions usually not raised when mixed-race parentage results in abortion, or when a lesbian woman is pregnant and aborts, or when a 49-year-old inconveniently conceives and aborts?

Is a lack of controversy revealing, on the situations that result in abortion, and not in birth of the child?

Is it the assumption that life with such parents would be such a problem, that death for the child is preferable?

Surrogacy, adoption, and pregnancy by old mothers are not new phenomena. Women have given away their babies for millennia. In the Old Testament, Rachel has her handmaiden Bil'hah become pregnant by husband Jacob (his name means Heel), and then Rachel "bears" the child when Bil'hah delivers. The sperm is considered the whole child--the female merely carries.

> .. she [Bil'hah] shall bear upon my knees, that I [Rachel] shall have children by her (Genesis).

In earlier times in the United States, a childless couple might be given a baby to raise by a relative who had several children--an arrangement beneficial to both families. But people now usually do not live in small groups and families. Technology both separates and unites all. Things that worked informally when people knew each other in small groups (tribes, families) become both complicated and contentious when they are strangers. People rely more on formal laws, instead of ethics, to make them do the right thing.

Contraception, fertility control, and technology

Ethical and legal questions about contraception continue regarding
1)   the use of technology and its effect on attitudes toward children, and
2)   about differential fertility--the controversy that some groups have too many children, relative to other groups.

Contraception is a shortened form of the two words: contra (against) and conception. Some feminists and some others oppose the entire technology of reproduction and believe the problem is contraception technology. For others, contraception itself is an ethical issue. Both versions of the issue are about <u>artificial</u> contraception. Abstinence from sexual intercourse is contra-conception, in a <u>natural</u> sense (watch that concept of "natural" however).

Ethical conflict about contraception arose in the latter 1800's and early 1900's with a movement called eugenics, designed to improve the human race. Some people of that time worried that the poor, disadvantaged, under classes were overpopulating.

A respected nursing ethics book, published in the 1940s, stated:

"Many people are ignorant of this danger to our social stock and the expense to the state in supporting defectives whether in or out of institutions" (Densford, 1946).

Early promoters of contraceptive freedom, especially for poor women, included Margaret Sanger, the founder of Planned Parenthood. One intended consequence of that freedom was to reduce the numbers of babies born to that assumed inferior class of people.

Overpopulation may seem of less concern in the United States and other developed countries. Market forces and better economic conditions in those countries have resulted in a voluntary decrease in the birth rate. The theory is that as people get richer and more secure, they have less need to have children who will work to support them in their old age.

However, in many countries in the world birth rates are far in excess of that in developed countries. Population control--fertility decrease--may be desired in those countries. The whole Earth now has a population of over six billion and environmentalists question how many people can be supported without seriously damaging our ability to survive.

Think about it.
How many people can the earth sustain?
Is there any limit to the carrying capacity of the planet?
*Even if your country or you personally can afford many children, is there
    any ethical responsibility to limit the number of children one
    produces?*
If so, should there also be legal limits, as in China?

Later estimates are that the population of the earth will peak at about the year 2050 and begin to level off or even decline after that.

When working on aggregate fertility of whole populations, the fact of differential fertility rates of different groups is obvious. Some groups of people are more fertile than others. This consideration may be unstated, but it often underlies political decisions made about contraception, population policy, and control of fertility.

Examples of differential fertility follow: Hispanics in the United States have a higher fertility rate than Caucasians; Israelis have a high birth rate, perhaps because the Arab birth rate is high (note the irony of that position in the story of Moses, below); Serbs excused killing Muslims in Bosnia, some say, on grounds that the Muslims are outbreeding them; in the Kosovo, Albanians had a higher birth rate than the Serbs; Christians in Lebanon were said to fear that their country had a Muslim majority, so they wouldn't allow a census to confirm it; Nigeria feared the results of a census because of differential growth of different groups; and Singapore's initial eugenics policy failed because of resentment by less educated and poorer groups, the majority being Malay.

Pronatalist (pro-birth) policies have existed in France, East Germany, Russia, Japan, and other countries with a below replacement fertility rate (about 2.1 offspring per woman). A party in power in India, ruling the second most-populous country in the world, had concerns that Muslim populations were growing faster than Hindus because Hindus are more likely to practice family planning. In the United States, the population control organization Zero Population Growth (ZPG) has addressed the problem of differential fertility.

Many of the developed countries face declining birth rates, including Japan, Europe, Australia and Canada. Projections are that fewer children will mature in those countries to support nonworkers, such as the aged and welfare recipients who have been guaranteed payments.

Think about it.
Is there a human right to reproduce?

Yes, according to the United Nations Universal Declaration of Human Rights (1948), Articles 16 I and 16 III. Others say there is no right, at least not without some concomitant duties and responsibilities.

In seeking differential fertility control, poor and non-Caucasian women often are targeted. As noted, the birth control movement in the United States before WWII coincided with the eugenics movement. Contraception for poor and minority women was said to be a way to improve the quality of the population.

The experience of differential population control done by the Germans under their National Socialist government of the 1930's and 40's made people in other countries wary of such policy. Their policy of differential population control was carried out eventually with a program of euthanasia of groups of people deemed inferior–the mentally ill, the developmentally disabled, people of Jewish descent, and many others.

Think about it.
Is it discrimination to target contraception programs toward certain groups such as people of color, Hispanics, poor people, or people of second world countries?
Or is it discrimination, not to afford them the power over their reproduction?.

Fear of technology

Technology allows both contraception and abortion to be done relatively easily and safely for the woman. Some argue that the technologies of contraception, AI, IVF, and abortion may cause a money value to be put on children. Technology allows having children when one can afford and in numbers one can afford.

Think about it.
Is it fair that the rich are able to have more children than the poor?
If children are seen as a burden, is it fair for some people to be able to have fewer children?

People who oppose all technology, echo long-existent feelings that technology is both wonderful and threatening. Ted Kaczynski, the radical left-wing Unabomber who killed several scientists with letter bombs, was only one of the latest of a long line. Much earlier, a man named Ned Lud gave his name to a whole group (see below).

Luddite . . . One of a band of workmen (1811-16) who tried to prevent the use of labor-saving machinery by breaking it, burning factories, etc.—said to have been so called after Ned Lud, a half-witted man who about 1779 broke up stocking frames (Webster's, 1934).

Even ancient people were ambivalent toward technology. In a Greek myth, Icarus invented wings made of feathers and wax--high tech. He then flew too high--another lesson-- melted the wax and crashed.

Some feminists worry that contraceptive technology separates sex from procreation and allows choice about when and if to have children. The argument echoes the opposition of some religions to artificial contraception.

The argument of some feminists is that a woman using the technology of IVF cannot be certain that the baby is really hers. There might have been a mixup, accidental or deliberate. By creating the same uncertainty about paternity (maternity) that men always have endured, it is asserted that women will, like men, develop the need to dominate. (This argument assumes that men do intentionally dominate, and that women do not, and also assumes that reproductive uncertainty is the cause of the domination.)

Another feminist argument against technology in reproduction is that separating a woman from procreation separates her from her original and elemental power of life. Feminists argue that such separation gives men the power to reproduce that they have always wanted. Technology in reproduction makes children into products, with different prices and different values to society.

Think about it.
Is this the case now with abortion of fetuses, especially of those that would be born with anomalies?

Religious and other groups now question whether early sex without the potential consequences of conception, is detrimental to young people who engage in it. The ability to avoid conception with drugs that prevent ovulation, does not protect the participant from other consequences of early and casual sex--particularly sexually transmitted diseases including HIV/AIDS. Some argue that sex without the possibility of conception diminishes women from their former status as conduit of the life force, to the status of mere sex aide.

Abortion

The moral and legal issues encountered in the debate about abortion are fully relevant to other ethical and legal issues, for example the issue of withdrawing or withholding care, euthanasia, and assisted suicide--later in this chapter. Like those issues, abortion is a very close and personal debate. The issue could affect you, or your family or friends. Many texts urge readers to be as <u>un</u>emotional as possible about such issues. They suggest we examine them as rationally and non-passionately as possible.

This advice ignores research that shows that thinking cannot be done without emotion. Neurologists and psychiatrists do have patients who think without emotion--they are neurologically damaged and/or diagnosed as sociopathic.

Thinking without an emotional component is defective. Indeed, the philosophies of intuitionism and emotivism require a quick, emotional, gut reaction. Neurological research shows emotions are an integral part of thinking. The labels used in the abortion debate are used for both their emotional and non-emotional effect. (See below.)

Think about it.
Can you think critically about these issues that are personal to each of us, without acknowledging your emotions?

Abortion always has been a controversial practice, but it has become more an ethical and legal issue since improved technology made the procedure cheaper, safer for the woman, and more accessible. Abortion ethics and law illustrate that the law is a minimum and not the highest ethic. The procedure is lawful, but many believe abortion is not at the higher level of being ethical. Clinicians who perform and assist with abortion doubtless have engaged in assessment of their personal values.

Abortions had become lawful in 14 US states before 1973. That year the *Roe v. Wade* decision of the US Supreme Court ruled that abortion could not be restricted by any state law during the first three months of pregnancy (*Roe*, 1973). After that ruling, the numbers of abortions increased. But even before the effect of that decision, in 1973, 744,600 lawful abortions were reported in the United States.

In 1985, there were 1,588,600 abortions. In 1973, 19 percent of pregnancies ended in abortion; in 1985, 30 percent of pregnancies were aborted. The numbers of abortions have decreased somewhat, but at a minimum the cause of death in one of every four fetuses is abortion.

Like all other law, abortion law is a minimal standard of behavior. Thus, while it is law for all, it may not rise to the level of behavior that is ethical. Refer back to the continuum of ethics to law in Chapter 1. In every case, some people will find some law (or the absence of it) to be unethical. The current law that prohibits states from restricting abortion in the first trimester (first third) of pregnancy, is a good example.

Abortion for any reason--abortion on demand--is lawful in the United States up until the 40th week of pregnancy, until all of the fetus is delivered from the birth canal except the very top of the scalp. Surveys indicate that a majority of people believe the law should be different. People who believe this law to be unethical, wish to make the law conform to their ethics. When and if they succeed, the law then will seem unethical to other people, who favor keeping abortion on demand lawful.

Words used for effect

Words are especially important in law. Under the US Constitution, live human beings, whether called fetuses or babies, have no rights unless they are deemed persons. Under the Supreme Court's decisions, the fetus does not become a person until somewhere between becoming viable (able to live outside the uterus) and being born.

Other courts and statutes recognize personhood earlier, and thus provide remedies for injury to the fetus. For example, in some states lawsuits can be brought for manslaughter, damages, and/or criminal acts to viable fetuses. Federal law has been proposed making it a crime to kill of a fetus by means other than abortion, for example, with a gun.

History of abortion law

Some induced abortions have been performed throughout human

history, as has infanticide. English common law punished aborting a "quick" child. The child was considered quick from the time the mother felt the child's movement. US state statutes from the mid-1800s prohibited abortion, in order to protect women from the dangers of the procedure. In the early 1970s, several states in the U.S. were in process of changing statutes to allow for abortions under some conditions. As noted above, in 1973 the US Supreme Court declared abortion to be included in a fundamental right of privacy and prohibited states from interfering with abortion during the first trimester. The decision allowed states to regulate abortions during the second trimester to protect the woman, and to regulate abortions during the third trimester to protect the fetus (See *Roe*, below).

In later rulings, the Supreme Court let stand a Missouri statute that prohibited abortions after viability. The Court rejected the rigid trimester framework while keeping the essence of *Roe*--that states cannot completely prohibit abortions. The court struck down a state statute that forbad partial birth abortion (see techniques, below) saying it was too vague. The decision said the language of the statute might be invoked to prohibit any abortion, not only partial birth abortions.

To determine when a fetus becomes a person, some have proposed a symmetric definition of life and death. They would use the same criterion for when life begins and when life ends. The fetus might become a person when brain activity begins, and the person is dead when brain activity ends (brain death). Or, the fetus might begin to be a person when higher brain activity begins (when the cerebrum is functioning well). By the same criterion, the person would be considered dead when the cerebrum ceases to function well (as it does in Alzheimers) (this concept also is discussed in A time to die).

Roe v. Wade and sequelae

The 1973, the *Roe* decision found the Texas statute unconstitutional that prohibited abortion, saying the law violated personal, marital, familial, and sexual privacy. The Supreme Court found that the right of privacy was not written specifically in the Constitution, but existed in the penumbra (poor light of a shadow) of all the rights written in the Bill of Rights.

The *Roe* decision did not find an unqualified right to abortion in the Constitution. The Court did say that privacy includes abortion and so it is a fundamental right. That means that a state would have to have a compelling interest in order to pass a law restricting abortion in the first trimester, the first three months.

The state would have to prove that it passed such a restriction only because there was no less restrictive way to achieve its compelling interest. In constitution talk, this means that the state can't pass a law restricting abortion in the first three months of pregnancy--because there is virtually no state interest that compelling. And if there were, almost always some less restrictive way could be found to achieve whatever was the state's interest.

The state's interest in protecting human life begins to be compelling at viability. The issue rests not on when life begins, but on personhood as a legal definition under the Constitution. Because fetuses are not considered persons, they are not protected under the Fifth and Fourteenth Amendments' rights to life, liberty and property. (As an analogy, slaves were not considered persons with rights either, until after the Civil War of the 1860s.)

No *person* shall . . . be deprived of life, liberty or property without due process of law . . . (Amendment V, US Constitution–limits the federales).

No state shall . . . deprive any *person* of life, liberty or property without due process of law . . . (Amendment XIV, US Constitution–limits the states). [emphases added]

Roe said the state could regulate abortions in the interest of the mother's health in the second trimester (second three months). For example, the state can require abortions be done by a physician clinician, and in a hospital. In the final trimester, the state can consider the fetus's interest. See the *Roe* box below for the shorthand.

Roe v. Wade
First trimester: No state interest.
Second trimester: State can protect mother's [health] interest (require standards for the procedure).
Third trimester: State can protect fetus or baby's interest.

Through the years, decisions on laws subsequent to *Roe* have changed the prohibitions outlined in that case. State statutes have restricted where abortions can be done, required procedures to notify parents and husbands, required some delays, required explanations be given of the development of the fetus and required information be given on alternatives to abortion.

Some states have prohibited what is called partial birth abortion. This procedure is to deliver all of the fetus out of the birth canal except for the scalp, to insert a cannula into the base of the fetus's skull and suction out the contents, collapsing the skull and killing the fetus. As noted above, one statute making that a crime has been held by the Court to be unconstitutionally vague, but others remain to be considered.

Present status

Among the industrialized countries, only the United States allows abortion on demand during the first trimester. Most other countries require certification by a physician that the abortion is for a reason other than birth control. Some countries forbid abortion after the first trimester. Some require delay and furnishing information to the woman seeking the abortion.

The United States has another abortion law distinction: This is the only country in which abortion on demand was made lawful by judicial decision, not by legislative vote with the usual legislative process of compromise.

A problem is seen by some proponents of the woman's right to choose to abort. Because state laws vary, women will be able to get abortions freely in some states and not in others. People who are unable to get an abortion in their own state, may not be able to afford travel to another state. Court decisions will not change that situation. In some states now, women have little or no access to abortion because few clinics in their state do the procedure.

No matter what the outcome at the Supreme Court level, people still will disagree about the abortion issue. The *Roe* decision did not stop the disagreement, and the continued reducing of its scope or even its overturn will not stop the disagreement either. The issues must be debated, and compromise reached, if any law is to be accepted.

The law is a minimum ethic, and not the full text of ethical behavior. People could agree that abortion is wrong ethically, but the law might not punish abortion at some early stages of pregnancy, and/ or for some reasons such as rape or incest. People who believe that it is unethical to abort at any stage for any reason could adhere to that belief, because ethics is always about how people should behave, not how they must behave.

More focus could be placed on the immorality of abortion, leaving it lawful at some stages and for some reasons. Remember the argument from Chapter 1, that equating immoral behavior exactly with illegal behavior is dangerous, because then some will see behavior that is merely lawful as fully moral behavior.

Law is the minimum behavior and ethics is the ideal. Compromising on the law is the difficult, painful, unsatisfying, democratic process. Nobody gets to win it all (as one side does in court). Everybody gets to win a little (as all do when they don't go to court). They can agree on a solution even if it's not exactly what each side wants.

Abortion technique

The current ethical and legal issue and debates about abortion resulted from technological changes in medicine. In an earlier era when abortion was dangerous, it was less likely to be done even if it had been lawful. One rationale for outlawing abortion was its danger--to protect the life of the mother. The safety and comfort of anesthesia, and the sterile techniques developed for other procedures, allowed abortion to be done safely (safely for the woman).

The technology affects the ethics and law of many procedures, including abortion. For example, many people see the ethics of abortion differently depending on whether the procedure is done early or late in the pregnancy, whether it is perceived to cause pain to the fetus, or whether it is done with a pill that makes it difficult to regulate.

The physical techniques of abortion limit the timing of abortion. The technique commonly used early in pregnancy is dilating the cervix and suctioning out the contents of the uterus. Later abortion must be done by dilatation and curettage--French words for dilating the cervix and using a curette to scrape out the contents of the uterus.

Still later, the fetus is too large to dissect with instruments and remove through the minimally dilated cervix. Instead, a solution is injected into the uterus through the cervix. Labor is induced, causing the fetus to be delivered vaginally. Or as described above, the fetus can be extracted from the birth canal except for the head, which is penetrated and decompressed by suction and then delivered. All these procedures require some anesthesia, sterile equipment, and skilled clinicians.

Statutes requiring an abortion to be done in a hospital have the effect of limiting the availability of abortions, say opponents of such laws. Fewer places for abortion are available, with the result being fewer abortions done. Advocates of such laws say that women deserve the protection of abortion procedures done under strict standards of care.

A drug is available to accomplish early abortion without the necessity of invasive techniques. The medical abortifacient mifepristone (initially known as RU486) is taken orally to prevent the production of the progesterone that is used by the uterus to nourish the fertilized egg. After the mifepristone is taken, a form of prostaglandin (misoprostol, Cytotec) is administered, causing the uterus (womb?) to contract and expel its contents.

The drugs must be given under supervision, as complications are possible but not usual. Some women report emotional difficulty in taking the pills to cause abortion. They say the act of taking the pills makes them realize it is the woman, not the abortion clinician, who is terminating the pregnancy (language from the pro-choice side) or killing her baby (from the pro-life side).

Think about it.
Do you predict there will be less controversy about abortion when it can be done in a clinician's office or in the home, instead of in a clinic or hospital?

Use of aborted fetuses in research

Another ethical and legal issue in the area of being born, is the issue of experiments on abortuses. This issue also is related to the issue of experiments using hPSCs, discussed above.

Think about it.
Why might some use the word abortus instead of aborted baby or aborted fetus?
Does that decrease the emotional reaction?

Research using fetal tissue transplants has expanded possible treatment options for several traumatic and degenerative neurologic disorders such as Parkinson's disease. However, the expectations of therapeutic benefit to be gained from these methods have been challenged, and it has been asserted that adult tissue is more effective. (These are the same arguments against stem cell research.)

The issues of abortion, physical autonomy, and the principle of harm are raised about the issue of continuing research on, and the use of, fetal tissue transplants. The issues of supply and sources of fetal tissue are unresolved. As with abortion, clinicians working in this area will have clarified their values and ethical position before working in situations in which fetal tissue transplants are used.

In 1988 the administration of then President George Bush wrote a rule banning the use of tissue from fetuses in research and transplants that receive federal money. The ban was reversed by President Clinton in 1993. President George W. Bush, elected in 2000, may reinstate the ban. The issue is the use of tissue from fetuses killed by elective abortions.

People who are anti-abortion (pro-life) believe that the use of the tissue is immoral. They believe it is wrong to benefit some, from the deliberately-caused death of others. If women are informed about the use of their fetuses for research or transplant, they may be more inclined to decide to abort. But if they are not informed of the possible use of the fetus, in order <u>not</u> to influence them toward abortion, then their consent to the abortion is not truly informed.

Reports of benefits from the use of fetal tissue in research on diseases such as Parkinson's, Huntington's, and diabetes, has caused some to cite the benefit to individuals and the whole of society from use of the tissue. As researchers gain more information about genetic problems in utero, there may be more pressure to have aborted fetuses available for use in transplanting genes.

Think about it.

Then, might women become pregnant and abort for economic reasons, to sell genes to rich parents for their own babies?

Are the issues the same as prohibiting the sale of organs for transplant?

But here, the organs do not belong to the woman. Or do they?

Does the sale of ova, or of embryos, raise the same issue?

Scientists are working on the possibility of using ova from fetuses (and from corpses and from women in PVS) to use as donor ova, for women who need ova for use in IVF. Ethical questions have been raised about the effect on children who would later know that their biological mother had never been born, or that they were conceived after she died, or that she was a vegetable (lay language for persistent vegetative state). Countries where the sale of ova is discouraged (for example, Great Britain) come to the U.S. to buy them.

Experts on the ethics of abortion

Judith Jarvis Thomson does not argue that the fetus is not alive, nor that it is not a person, nor that killing it does it harm. Even if all these thing are true, Thomson argues simply that the woman has a right to be free of the fetus. Further, she argues that the fetus has no claim on the mother--no right to require her to be hostess for the nine months from conception to birth.

Thomson makes the analogy that neither does a person dying of kidney disease have any right to claim a kidney, nor a right to some time using another's kidney. She says that even if the fetus has a right to life it still does not have a right to be carried to term by the woman whose womb it happens to inhabit.

A good Samaritan may voluntarily do such carrying, but there's no duty on her to do so. In the Biblical story, the good Samaritan-- distinguished from the usual Samaritans, a rival gang-- helped a man who had been mugged on the road to Jericho. The good Samaritan had no obligation to do so. (See more in Chapter 2).

Thomson discusses several degrees of Samaritan, up to Splendid

Samaritan. She asserts that there is no duty raised merely by the fact that the woman biologically is related to the fetus, nor by the fact that she had sex (if she took precautions not to conceive). Compare and contrast this argument with the discussion of Duties, Rights and Obligations in Chapter 6.

Think about it.
What might be the Kantian attitude toward abortion?
The utilitarian attitude?

Baruch Brody opposes abortion, and distinguishes Thomson's argument about having no duty to save another's life. He points out that the person who needs a kidney, needs his life saved --he'll die without the kidney. The woman still is under no positive duty to save his life. But the fetus does not needs her life to be saved, she just needs not to be killed.

Brody believes the mother has a duty to refrain from killing her fetus-- a negative duty. In that sense, Brody distinguishes direct killing (abortion) from indirectly letting someone die (for example, by not donating the kidney). Brody does believe it is justifiable to take an innocent person's life in self-defense, but only if one's own life is at risk. This is not the case in an abortion situation, unless the mother's life is at risk.

Mary Ann Warren discusses Thomson's position on abortion as well, but believes it is too narrow a justification. That is, it puts too high a requirement on the woman to maintain the pregnancy, unless she has some compelling reason to end it. Different from Thomson, Warren believes the moral status of the fetus is very important to the argument as to whether abortion is moral. Warren admits the fetus is a biological human being of the species *homo sapiens sapiens*. But she says the fetus is not a member of the moral community--not a person with full and equal moral rights.

Warren does not concede that merely having the potential to become a human gives the fetus moral status, either. She makes the analogy to a space traveler, who could bring into being many people who are now only potential people, if only he will spend some time in captivity. Warren argues that any tiny amount of the present, actual liberty of the existing person, outweighs all possible enormous amount of potential life. Thus the liberty of the woman justifies ending the potential human's life.

Think about it.
Do you see any connection to any of the writers you have studied thus far?
Which theorists believed freedom to be the ultimate good?
From the chapter on Autonomy--Beauvoir? Mill?

Neonates

The issues about neonates (people at the beginning of their lives) are similar to issues about very old people (at the end of theirs). Those issues for both kinds of people:

Think about it.
Are they are fully human (with full rights in the society)?
Should they have expensive care, that may or may not save their lives (considering the quality of their lives)?
Should mathematical models that apply to an average (a group) be used to predict outcomes or limit care to individuals?
Is life as a person who is not "normal," worth living?
Should statutes should be used to protect individuals at risk of neglect, from abuse?

More than ever, smaller and younger babies can be saved, and most of them end up healthy and normal. But some don't. Caring for tiny babies costs a lot of money. Some say that the money would be better spent on prenatal care, doing immunizations on well babies, and to prevent low birth weight (LBW) babies.

Think about it.
If it were established that more money for prenatal care worked (it hasn't been), and if the care and money could be transferred from the neonate in the Neonatal Intensive Care Unit (NICU) over to the prenatal clinic--should it be done?

As costs are cut in the clinical service industry, some ask whether newborn intensive care is cost-effective. NICUs are proven to improve the infant mortality--from 20 deaths per thousand births in 1970, down to eight deaths per thousand in 1992. Some suggest that the money should be diverted to preventive pediatrics. (However, data on immunization rates show that many parents do not get preventive care for their children even when insurance covers the cost.)

Some people advocate limiting treatment for low birth weight babies. The cost is small, relative to other expenditures for care, but it is question of priorities. Some ask whether taxpayers' dollars should be used only on those with the potential to repay society for their care.

Think about it.
Should taxpayers pay for care only for people who will live to pay enough taxes to make the care cost-effective? That is, care only for those

who will be "worth it" someday?

"If society decides that eligibility for newborn intensive care is to be governed by the potential for economic payback, software would be developed to assign every newborn, not just the very low birth weight infant, an economic quotient. After measuring weight and gestational age, a data bank of school transcripts and tax statements for the graduates of the nursery would be consulted. The minimum score to qualify for care would be adjusted annually to the budget deficit and gross national product. Of course, only infants born to families with no insurance with large copayments would undergo such economic triage. Families with good insurance will always have access to newborn intensive care. Needless to say this software will find its way to all medical contexts" (Storch, 1990).

Ethical decisions by the numbers

As NICU clinicians know, it is risky business even to predict survival probability in neonates, much less projecting quality of life for them. But mathematical models are being developed that will be used to predict mortality risk for newborns. One model was based on admission data for infants weighing 501 to 1,500 grams at birth. The data were used to identify NICUs where the observed mortality rate differed significantly from the predicted rate.

Statistical adjustment methods should be used only with caution (if at all) to rank the performance of NICUs. Models that predict mortality or quality of life are not validated, and relationships between care and outcomes are not understood.

Extreme caution is advised in using predictive models, because your real, individual, patient never is "average." Experts say that the performance of these scores does not allow clinicians to apply them to decisions on individual patients. Predictive models include the Acute Physical Assessment and Chronic Health Evaluation (APACHE), developed at George Washington University in 1985. Decisions made using these models have enormous ethical and legal implications.

APACHE has a sensitivity of 0.5, or 50%. The **sensitivity** of a test is the number of tests in a group of people who are known to be abnormal, that correctly show up as abnormal. Another way to say it is that sensitivity is the number of people who the test shows to be abnormal, in populations of people known to be abnormal.

With APACHE, the sensitivity of 50% means the percent of patients that the test predicted would die--actually died. For example, when APACHE predicted that 12 patients would die, only 6 did. Six didn't. APACHE was wrong 50% of the time. Fifty percent of the time that APACHE predicted a patient would die, the patient didn't. Using that test for predicting which patients will die in ICU was exactly as helpful as flipping a coin--it was right 50 percent of the time.

The **specificity** of the APACHE model is 0.9. Specificity indicates the number of people who the test shows to be normal, in a group of people known to be normal. That is, normal tests in a normal population. With APACHE, the specificity is the percentage of times that patients who the test predicts will not die, in reality do not die. Out of 100 patients predicted by APACHE not to die in the ICU, 90 actually do not, 10 do. As you can see, APACHE is not a good predictor with individual patients.

Normal

Unless future ethicists decide that only normal babies of average birth weight should be saved, clinicians will work to improve the lives of the low birth weight babies saved. Studies show that one program increased the IQS of low birth weight infants. Infants whose parents were better educated and had community resources, did well with or without intervention.

The researchers concluded that it is impossible to predict which low birth weight baby will have lower or higher IQ (Infant, 1990). Life indeed IS like a box of chocolates.

"Neonates"

Newborn children increasingly are being termed neonates (from the Latin word for newborn). The term may be an attempt to sound more scientific. It also has the effect, intended or not, of considering the newborn somewhat different from older children. This attitude may make it easier to deal with children who are born with anomalies.

The interest of the newborn is assumed to be in living. Some writers on the subject say that the child has no interest that should be considered, because the child has no experience and no thought process. Therefore people other than the child may evaluate its fate.

Some even say that newborn with great anomalies, such as an anencephalic, does not have an interest in living, but in dying. The newborn who has a little disability, an easily treated anomaly, also is at risk. In the Baby Doe case of the 1980s, a Down syndrome baby was born with a birth defect (esophageal atresia with a fistula into the trachea). That anomaly easily could have been corrected by surgery, and always is in babies born mentally normal.

At the parents' request, clinicians allowed Baby Doe to starve and dehydrate to death in a hospital nursery (Pless, 1983). That case prompted federal intervention by rule-making and legislation (Child Abuse Amendments of 1984).

Apparently a question still exists as to whether this might have been the right action. That exact situation was the hypothetical given to medical students in an ethics competition. Both winners of the contest took the position that surgery on Baby Doe would have been the right thing to do (Clark, 2000; Morrow, 2000).

Some insist that the family and clinician should always be able to decide whether a child is too anomalous to live--that the law should not intervene. Others disagree:

[regarding people who would make it lawful to withhold treatment of neonates with anomalies:]

"Legal immunity can too readily feed the destructive dynamic already visible in some physicians' and families' reaction even to minimally deformed children" (Burt, 1979).

As noted above, the Baby Doe situation prompted federal law that required reporting of such abuse--the Child Abuse Amendments of 1984 (42 U.S.C. 5101 *et seq.*) That federal statute mandated that states establish programs and procedures to respond to reports of medical neglect. Medical neglect is defined as withholding of medically indicated treatment from a disabled infant with a life-threatening condition.

Children have been born with congenital anomalies since children have been born (they average between 3% and 8% of births). Evidence exists of the attitudes, ethics and values of prehistoric Americans, toward such children born disabled. An archeological site in Florida (Windover) revealed a burial site with the skeleton of a carefully buried teenager. Examination by experts revealed that the teenager had been born with spina bifida, a condition that might be difficult to care for, even with the resources of today. The child had been cared for and lived several years.

In this culture, attitudes toward disabled newborns are mixed. In 1992, the parents of an anencephalic baby asked the Florida Supreme Court to allow the baby's body parts to be removed for transplant before her death. Organs taken after death are not useful for transplant. (Anencephaly is not curable and is fatal, but for a time the baby eats, moves, and breathes on her own.)

The Florida court refused, the baby died, and the court later addressed the issue. They said that declaring anencephalics dead so their body parts could be taken for transplants, could not be automatic merely because of their diagnosis (*In re. T.A.C.P,* 1992).

The position of the American Civil Liberties Union in the case was that any view of life is inherently religious, so that an attempt to establish a clear line between life and death involves improper religious judgments. By that reasoning, legislatures could not write statutes to define death.

A study was done of 75 clinicians who gave direct care to anencephalic infants in a program of potential organ donors. A majority of the clinicians were concerned about the dignity of the life of the infant. The clinicians felt that the infants had physiological responses, and were concerned about whether the infants felt pain (Van Cleve, 1993).

Clinicians feel distress when they make moral judgments that they cannot act on. This happens to clinicians who care for premature infants allowed to die without intervention, or when decisions are made not to treat children with anomalies. It also may happen when clinicians care for premature infants that the clinicians feel should not have such care.

A related issue is that an increase is noted in numbers of infants being abandoned. Some states respond by removing criminal penalties for abandonment, if it is done without harming the child. Texas has what some call a "Baby Moses" law (Baby, 2000) (In the Old Testament, the mother of baby Moses hid him in a basket at the edge of the Nile from Egyptian government agents. They had orders to kill Hebrew sons, the result of fear the increased differential fertility of that tribe. Moses was found and adopted by the Pharaoh's daughter--Exodus 2.) One group credits the law with keeping at least three infants from death (Baby Moses law is saving lives, 2001).

Genealogical theory

The **genealogical theory** of ethics is very relevant to how fetuses and newborns are treated. This is a theory of the origin of morals, best known from the writing of Friedrich Nietzsche (German, 1844-1900). Nietzsche argued that the origin of morality is not God, and that higher values are not natural to human beings. Nietzsche asserted that morals originate in human psychology. People have psychological drives that create their morals–an idea related to psychological egoism.

Nietzsche classed people either as nobles or peasants. He said that religion--specifically, the people or priests of organized religion--helps create a slave mentality to which humans are trending. He contrasted that slave mentality, to a master/ noble/ aristocratic mentality.

Nietzsche associated a master mentality with characteristics (virtues) such as pride and cruelty. He associated the slave mentality with virtues that he believed foster mediocrity--such as humility, obedience, and compassion. Nietzsche associated vengeance, rancor, and resentment (by the lower classes) with that slave mentality. (A comparison can be made between the characteristics of de Beauvoir's infantile person, and Nietzsche's slave mentality.)

He said that the values of equality, love, compassion, sympathy and obedience are creative acts of the slave mentality (the weak). In this way the weak-- always greater in number--conquer the strong, to the detriment of mankind. The weak make their own qualities seem to be the good ones, and make the qualities of the strong (the nobles, masters) seem evil.

Nietzsche said the superior person may value self-mastery above happiness. Unlike Aristotle, Nietzsche did not value happiness as the greatest good. He believed superior people are the creators of morality. Nietzsche did not believe in any absolute ethics, nor did he acknowledge the existence of God.

Nietzsche admired the "blonde Teutonic beast" of legend, though he said that the ancestor of the Germans had no genetic relationship with the German people of his time. It is not surprising that Nietzsche and his friend Wagner (composer of heroic operas) were revered by Hitler, leader of the National Socialists of 1930's Germany.

Killing neonates

Nietzsche's philosophy was used in Germany to justify killing defective newborns (some of the 3-8% of children born with genetic anomalies). Richard Brandt argues that it is moral to "terminate" such newborns. (That word may remind older readers of the euphemisms for killing used in the Viet Nam war and other conflicts--such as "terminate with extreme prejudice.")

Brandt argues that it is kinder to kill quickly than to let the infant suffer alive. He says that there are several conditions that we can project onto the baby, in which its life would not be worth living. He further argues that it would not be wrong to kill an infant without memories, because it would have no interest in continued life.

Think about it.
If memories are the criterion for interest in continued life, what other categories of people and animals have no memories?
Can we kill people in these categories because they have no interest in continued life?

Brandt proposes that medical experts, not philosophers, would be the best judge of which lives were not worth living. The consent or voluntariness of the infant to die would not be an issue. The infant would not then--nor ever, if she were killed--be worried about her life or death. She would never know that she had the power to make decisions about her life.

Determinism is a philosophy that is relevant to the issues around being born, particularly to the influence of genetics on one's life. Determinism is the idea that things are pre-determined, that they will happen a certain way no matter what the circumstances. Some religious people have this belief, and some who are not religious have it, too. This concept is raised when issues of genetics and behavior come up.

Think about it.
Are people genetically determined from their birth to be criminals? Saints? Presidents?

Moral agency, standing, patient, relationship

Particularly relevant to the ethical issues of reproduction are the ethical concepts of moral agency, moral patient, moral standing, and moral relationship. **Moral agency** is the concept that people have the capacity to act, morally. Some people (but not all) are said to be capable of acting ethically. They are **moral agents**. This use of the word "agent" in ethics is different from its use in law. In law, an agent is defined as one who acts in place of or for another. In ethical language, "agency" means the person has the ability and duty to act, for himself.

A newborn is not a moral agent. The newborn person who is the recipient of a moral act, who is capable of suffering, may be a **moral patient**. The Greek root of the word patient is *pati*, meaning to feel or to suffer A person can be a moral agent, a moral patient, or both.

Think about it.
Is a neonate a moral patient?
Is a fetus a moral patient? At what point? Ever?
Is the legal definition of personhood relevant, or is this an ethical question?
Does the fetus being aborted, suffer?
Does the discussion of abortion consider the suffering of the fetus?

In the old days, your writer assisted with circumcisions on newborn babies (neonates). They turned red, writhed and screamed during the procedure. Concerns voiced to the clinician elicited the response that babies of this age do not feel pain. "But he's screaming" said the slave mentality clinician.

"That's because you're holding him down" said the master clinician. "But he didn't scream until you started cutting the foreskin with the scalpel" noted the slave. Research eventually showed what we knew all along–newborns feel pain.

Think about it.

Might other comforting truths that are assumed, be wrong–for example, that fetuses being dissected in abortion don't suffer?

Or, that patients being dehydrated to death, are anesthetized by the procedure?

Moral standing is an ethical concept that considers whether a thing (human, dog, fetus, tree, rock, or the whole environment) has any claim to be treated morally. If it does not have moral standing, then it is not immoral to behave toward it in any way one pleases.

The analogy to legal standing may help to understand "moral standing." In US law, the only people who can ask a court to solve a conflict are those with legal standing. They must have some interest or right in the case, some reason that the conflict affects them personally. If the person has no standing, he is considered to have no rights or interests to protect.

The court will not consider him or his arguments or position in the case. He literally can't ask the court to protect him. For example, it has been ruled in the past that a priest had no legal standing to intervene in a case in which the patient was to be dehydrated to death. The priest was considered to be a stranger to the case with no interest (legal standing) of his own that would be jeopardized.

At one time, humans who were slaves did not have moral or legal standing (a time 150 years ago in America, or around the year 2001 in some African countries). At present, some argue that humans who are not yet born, do not have moral standing. Some argue that animals that are born, do have moral standing.

Think about it.

Do neonates with anomalies have moral standing?

Do healthy newborns?

Moral relations is a related ethical concept. The questions here are whether the fact that humans live in proximity to each other-- in relationships with one another--creates a morality. Related questions are why people are moral--that is, why they do the right thing. Perhaps it is because their reason tells them to be, in which case the proscription against killing would be as obvious as 2+2=4 (that is--reasoned). (Remember from Chapter 4 that intuitionism is said to be very fast reasoning.)

Or perhaps people are moral because they are naturally inclined to be moral--that is, they don't have to reason about it. Morality may be more of an emotional, passionate recognition of what is right and good. Remember the discussion of emotivism from Chapter 3. Some students of religion may detect here echoes of the argument about original sin--that is, about whether humans are naturally good, naturally evil, or neutral.

Moral relationships, the fact that humans live in proximity and in relationships to each other, is said by some to create a morality. David Hume (British, 1711-1776) believed that people by nature are inclined to be moral. Hume directly attacks rationalist, universalist, normative, Kantian and utilitarian ethics.

Hume's theory of ethical behavior is *communitarianism*. He proposes that people are creatures who must share some moral values (have moral relationships) to live together in a community (a moral community). He believes social ethics and moral philosophy are based in historical traditions and community decisions (conventionalism). Related to this concept, remember that the words *morals* and *ethics* come from the words for "customs of the people."

Interests and rights

Throughout this examination of issues surrounding the time to be born, many interests have been considered. Clinicians must consider also their own interests, both as members of society and as individuals.

We might agree that the interest of the people is in defending the lives of those without defenses. This is the original minimal law enforcement of "Do unto others." Or, we might not agree that the whole people have an interest in defense of the defenseless.

Even if we did agree on that, the question always is where to draw the line--when to have the society intervene in family life. The autonomy of the family, of the parents, of the child, are not absolute. The law prohibits child abuse, drug abuse, sometimes homosexuality, no abortions, and not contraception.

No interests are absolute. The rights of citizens are whatever the people decide them to be, subject to the innate ethical limits that people are born with as humans. (That is, if you agree that they are born with such innate human morality.)

Rights are only words. They become reality only if people are willing to tolerate, fight for, or enforce them. But a line between the minimum standard of right and wrong--the law--will be drawn somewhere. The line is redrawn by each new election, each legislative session, each rulemaking, each court case. Together and individually, people draw it anew, every year, every generation.

Draw the line.☛_____.

A time to die . . .
The values

It sounds contrarian, but the most important value in the topic of death is the value, life. All else being equal, people act to preserve life. What may change that action–what may be the unequalizer--is the importance of some other value for the patient--such as doing good to him, not harming him, or his freedom.

People want to do good (beneficence) and to do no harm (non-maleficence). People want to honor the patient's freedom (autonomy). Using those values, sometimes we can agree on the right action. For example, if the patient is competent and doesn't want treatment, his freedom is valued. If the treatment won't do good and actually will prolong pain, all may agree that not harming is valued. In that case, to die is good--dying is valued.

But we don't always agree on what to do if the patient is incompetent, or if the patient is in a coma or vegetative, or if the treatment will keep the patient alive, but won't return her to her earlier functional level. Nor do people agree on cost limits, nor what to do if the patient is competent and wants to die, but isn't dying from some natural cause.

Even before ICUs and technology and the increased cost of care, people questioned whether to treat or to limit treatment for the patient. Treating still meant a drain on resources. The drain was more personal, not abstracted to a figure such as dollars per day for the ICU bed, or percentage of GNP. The drain was how much time and effort the family could or would spend on someone who was not going to recover, or who would not be a functioning member of the family if she did recover.

In past times people couldn't get some of the treatments that are possible. Ventilators were invented to prolong breathing for people with lung disease. Tube feedings are available to provide nutrition to people who can't be fed orally. These technologies can be used, but sometimes there is a conflict over whether they should be used on the patient.

Strangers

Instead of the family who has more information about the patients' situation, strangers (clinicians) now care for the patient. Clinicians may not know that the patient was a happy, busy grandparent until the stroke two days ago. Or clinicians may not know that the patient had been lying in a nursing home without family, without cognition, for years before that stroke two days ago.

Because clinicians don't have all the information that the family would have, they tend to treat all patients nearly the same. That practice exhibits the value of being fair. But treating all patients the same may mean treating all intensively, because strangers can't judge quality of life for another stranger. Trying to be fair, clinicians may treat all patients extensively until someone says stop.

Age and death bias

All people eventually die. Old people correctly are perceived to be nearer to death, on average, than are young people. Because of that, the attitudes that people have toward dying and death, affect the attitudes that underlie the ethics and law pertaining to old people.

One attitude, a popular myth, is that most old people live in nursing homes. Wrong. Though there is a 40 % risk of needing a nursing home for a time when you are over 65, only about five percent of *all* people over 65 are dependent, in homes. At 75, 2 of 100 men and 3 of 100 women live in nursing homes. At 85, fewer than 9 of 100 men and 13 of 100 women do so. At 90, fewer than 13 of 100 men and 21 per 100 women live there.

Nursing home occupancy is declining as other less intensive care options increase (What, 2000). Many conditions associated with being old are not the result of aging, but of treatable disease.

Agism is a bias against people merely because they are old. Numerous examples of the bias are found in life in the United States. Look at network television programs and commercials for just one evening. Count the total number of characters that you see, and note how many of them clearly are old. Further, notice how the few old characters are portrayed–as active, fun, healthy, or not. (Don't count the baby boomers who look about 55 years old, advertising remedies for impotence and hair loss).

In US society, the periods of dying and dying people are avoided. Even the words death and dying are avoided--the term "end of life" often is used instead of dying. To some, end of life implies that people can choose to end their lives when they wish, and can avoid the dying process. Of course one can only choose to end life in one direction--*earlier* than natural, not later.

Related to the bias against the aged and dying is the cost of their care. A myth about money is that "too much money is spent on the patient's last illness, on his last year of life." That assertion assumes several things.

One, it assumes that the money spent on illness should be distributed evenly across the individual's life span. It might even foolishly assume that more money should be spent on the healthier/ younger years of an individual than on her sicker/ older years.

The myth also assumes that if the money were not spent or last year of illness, that large savings in illness would result. The assertion that too much is spent on the last illness, last year, assumes that the last illness and last year can be determined in advance of its completion--death. In particular, these last two assumptions are false (Emanuel, 1994, 1996).

Think about it.

*If they are not forced to help pay for it, do people object when a very sick
old man spends his own money on a fancy car?*

*Are people unhappy to spend significant amounts of money on someone's
last illness/ last year because they are forced to spend the money
through taxes?*

*If that's not the reason for objecting to care of the old, what do you
believe the reason is? Is it because people just don't want to spend
money on old people?*

If so, is this attitude indicative of ageism?

Lies, damn lies, and statistics
Misconception: life expectancy vs. life span

The public's knowledge about aging and death affects their attitude,
and their attitude determines the ethics and law of those topics. So the
difference between life span and life expectancy are important to ethics
and law. You would think **life expectancy** is how long a baby born today
is expected to live. The words seem to say that, but the number actually
is the population's <u>present average age at death</u>.

That life expectancy number is determined by averaging the ages at
death, of people who have died during the last three years. High rates of
infant mortality will lower the life expectancy number. More small
numbers–the ages of the infants who die--will be averaged in with the
fewer large age numbers of adults who die old.

The average age at death is determined by writing down the ages of
all the people who died during the last three years, adding up the numbers,
and dividing the answer by the number of people who died. For an
example, see below titled "What's the life expectancy?"

WHAT'S THE LIFE EXPECTANCY?

If a total of two people in a population died during the last three
years, one being 98, and the other being two years old, you would add: 98
(the old guy's age) + 2 (the baby's age) = 100, and divide 100 by the
number of people who died--two. $100 \div 2 = 50$. The life expectancy
number for that population would be ___. Right. 50 years.

Around the start of the 20th century the life expectancy number was
50 years. More people died as infants then, than do now, and some
people died as old people. But even when the life expectancy number was
50, *most people did not die at 50*--either as infants or as elderly. Some
gynecologists actually say out loud (*wrongly*) that because life expectancy

was 50, women of that era did not live to experience menopause!

Because fewer babies now die as infants, the life expectancy--the average age at death-- has lengthened. Fewer babies die in infancy now, largely because of better economics (better sanitation, housing, and food) and not primarily because of improvements in medical care.

The percentage of the population who are old *is* increasing, because more people live through infancy and live to become old. But people who have lived to become old, do not live much longer today than old people did in earlier times.

Counter to another common (mis) perception, other developed countries are projected to have a larger percentage of old people in 2010 than the U.S. Those countries include Japan, Italy, Germany, Greece, Belgium, Spain, Britain, France, Netherlands, Czech Republic, Australia, and Canada (Getting, 2000). Our birth rate is down, but we have more young immigrants.

The misperception that people are living to be older and older, contributes to bias against the old and against care for them. A better concept to use is **life span**, representing the actual years lived by the average person who does not die as an infant, and who does not have some increased risk factor for illness or accident. The average life span now is 85, and it has increased very little if any during the past century.

Another myth exploded: Men whose lifestyles are comparable to women's lifestyles, live as long as women do. That is, when the data for men are adjusted for smoking, alcoholism, and accidental death, they live as long as women. So much for any inherent physical superiority of women.

Misconception: risk probability, association, causation, and significance

Risk probability numbers are used in ethical and legal conflicts about which groups of people or disease should get more money. Risk probability numbers relate to populations and are used by planners and policy makers--they have little relevance to individual patients.

For example, a group can have a risk probability of 50%. Saying that 50 of 100 people in a group will have cancer, is the **group probability**. But an *individual* in such a group can't have a cancer risk probability of 50%. The individual is either one of the 50 that will have cancer–a 100% risk for her individually–or one of the 50 who will not have cancer—a 0 % risk for her individually. Her personal **case probability** risk is either 100%–she will have cancer, or 0%–she will not (Mills, 2000).

In particular, statistics about cancer are used to mislead. A group that lobbies for cancer money says that a one in eight women will get breast cancer. That would be true only *if all women, including those who die earlier of other diseases, somehow lived beyond age 90.* But the reality is that of all 30 year old women, only 1 in 256 will develop breast cancer within the next 10 years (Many, 2000).

> "Breast cancer is much more common at older ages, but the risk of breast cancer in any given decade of life never exceeds 1 in 34" (Putting, 1999)

Further, the old advice is false that screening for breast cancer by breast self-examination and mammograms reduces mortality. In Sweden, screening with mammograms has been done since 1984 and deaths from breast cancer *have not decreased* (Gotzsche, 2000).

Screening for breast cancer does increase the numbers of false positives with resulting morbidity and mortality (Sox, 1998). The data show that among women who have 10 screening mammograms over the years, about half will experience a false positive finding. That usually results in biopsy and significant anxiety, though the woman does not have cancer.

False information from studies can cause clinicians to make bad decisions about ethics and law, because the decisions are not based on reality. One example of false information is the belief is that finding some **association** in a study, is the same as finding **causation**. Association of two factors in a study does not mean causation. That is, association does not mean that the one factor caused the other factor. For example, suicide is associated with smoking, but no one is suggesting that smoking <u>causes</u> suicide.

Meaningless associations often (even usually) are made when large amounts of data are accessible by computer. Such research almost certainly will produce some association between factors, but the association usually is not causative and rarely is even informative.

The term **statistical significance** in scientific studies is a mathematical term only, and it does not mean that the finding is significant as we use the word in ordinary conversation. Statistical significance does not automatically mean the finding is important, or useful, or helpful, or causative, or meaningful. A finding is statistically significant if it is more likely than not that the finding is not just luck.

Using poor statistical analyses can completely negate the value of a study. For example, using a lower **confidence interval** to analyze studies will decrease the value of a study to your practice. A 95 percent confidence interval--the usual standard of good studies--means that 95 times out of 100 (19 of 20), the numbers and conclusion reached by the study would not be an accident. A 90 percent confidence interval, however, means there is one chance in ten that the finding was an accident, and that other findings might be the reality.

For example, a 90% confidence interval was used to "prove" that passive smoke causes lung cancer. Because the researchers used a 90 percent confidence interval, it is possible that data about passive smoking may actually prove the opposite of what the researchers wanted to show-- there's one chance in 10 that passive smoking actually reduces the risk of lung cancer.

Quality of life

Quality of life is considered to be a subjective judgment made by the person experiencing the life, contrasting his own life to what he imagines it would be like to be dead. Assessing the quality of one's own life is a subjective activity, not an objective activity, so you may want to review the discussion of subjectivism. This was part of the discussion of ethical relativism in Chapter 6, about the law and ethics of fidelity.

As you think about this discussion on quality of life, decide for yourself whether quality of life can be determined by anyone other than the person whose life quality is being assessed. Many of the tools used in determining quality of life seek to make it appear to be measured by objective standards--outside the person, not subjectively.

Think about it.
Does the subjectivist--probably also a cultural relativist--support the idea that the society cannot determine the quality of another's life?
Would the objectivist support the idea that society can determine the quality of an individual life? Which are you?

One tool used to determine quality of life is the **Quality Adjusted Life Years** (QALYs) system. This tool combines the expected length of life that the average person of that age has remaining, with a quality of life assessed by one person for another. In a historic example of assessing quality of life for others, the Germans under National Socialism in the 1930s and 40s assessed some people's lives for them. They found some of their people had *LebensunwertenLeben* (lives not worth living), and killed them to spare them a poor quality of life (Friedlander, 1995).

People who are younger and healthier will have higher scores under the QALYs system, and whenever that system is used to allot care they will get better or more treatment. Rating systems such as health-Related Quality of Life (HRQOL) and Acute Physical Assessment and Chronic Health Evaluation (APACHE) are used to assess and to predict outcomes of therapy and ICU treatment. These systems are based on the imaginary average patient and so they are useful for planning for groups of patients. Such systems are inappropriate to use to make practice decisions in individual patients.

Studies show that patients who have had a catastrophic illness estimate their quality of life to be better than researchers and clinicians would have predicted (Hallan, 1999). Subjective measures of quality of life are more accurate than objective measures-- and with competent patients they are the only measures ethically possible to make.

Competency/capacity

Ethical conflicts about dying, however, usually are about incompetent or incapacitated people. Competent people are assumed to be making decisions in their own best interest, either choosing life or not as it is best for them. As noted in Chapter 4, freedom is not absolute for any person, but autonomy is that much more restricted for incompetent or incapacitated people.

Some distinguish between legal incompetency and functional incompetency or incapacity, but there is no legal basis for such distinction. Either the patient is legally **competent**, or he is not. Some state statutes have changed the word "incompetent" to the word **incapacitated**--the same legal condition. This has been done in order to decrease the stigma attached to the condition (!).

For the individual, being declared legally incompetent is the ultimate loss of freedom short of death. The person found incompetent becomes the **ward** of his appointed **guardian**. From then on the guardian has legal authority to make all decisions for the ward--what to eat, what to wear, where to live, all life decisions.

Decisional capacity

Another phrase for competent is **decisional capacity**. Note again the use of the word capacity as a preferred term for competent. The steps to determine competency or decisional capacity of the patient come down to some commonsense questions. This information also is discussed in Chapter 4, Be Free.

Questions to determine decisional capacity:

1. Is the patient able to receive and understand information about her condition, the treatment recommended, and the alternatives--in order to make a decision?
2. Is the patient able to consider (feel and reason about) the information given, able to make the decision, and able to communicate the decision?
3. Does the patient understand the consequences of her decision?

If the patient can't understand what the clinician is saying (Criterion # 1), she doesn't have capacity to decide. If the patient can't consider and decide and tell you of her decision somehow, she may not have decisional capacity (Criterion #2).

For example, if she says she just can't decide, and she denies that her indecision will be fatal (and if it's probable to you that her indecision <u>will</u> be fatal) then she may lack capacity. But in some cases, not to decide is to choose the consequences of not deciding. If she can't decide and she admits that her indecision will be fatal, she may be competent and actually choosing that consequence.

If the patient doesn't know the consequences of her decision or denies the consequences after being told of what might happen (Criterion #3), then she isn't competent to decide. For example, if she won't eat, but says that refusing food won't cause her death, the patient is not competent.

Questions about whether the patient understands the consequences of her decision can be tricky. Sometimes clinicians are mistakenly sure that the patient will die without treatment. A better assessment is whether the patient understands that lack of treatment <u>might</u> cause death.

You probably can't be sure that any decision will cause any other specific outcome, except that refusing food and water will cause death. It always has until now, at least.

CPR/DNR

The value underlying cardiopulmonary resuscitation (CPR) is life. The value underlying the refusal of CPR--the Do Not Resuscitate (DNR) decision--is autonomy. CPR originally was to be used with witnessed arrests, sudden death in the young, drowning, and predictable arrests such as with anesthesia and cardioversion. Since then, CPR has been applied to all deaths in acute care settings, necessitating a DNR order to avoid it.

Slow codes or partial codes are fraudulent to the extent they are used to mislead the patient's family that more care is being given than actually is done. Partial codes are acceptable if their limits are communicated–that is, if the clinician tells the truth to the family and to others.

CPR is much less likely to succeed than patients and family believe, especially on very old or very sick patients. Only 15% of resuscitation attempts on all patients were successful worldwide, from 1959 to 1992 (Winslow, 2001). Patients and families should be made aware of that fact if it can be predicted that CPR will be needed for the patient

Clinicians who work in emergency care may be (and probably should be) expected to resuscitate first and look at limits such as DNR orders-- later. Their primary task is to revive. Without obvious evidence to the contrary, they may assume that their full services were requested and consented to when they were called.

Many states are writing statutes such as an "out of hospital" DNR order, that allow orders to specify what actions to take in such situations. You can find your state's statute in the usual places (see Chapter 1). Because such orders are an enforcement of the patient's autonomy, more discussion about them is in Chapter 4: Be Free.

DNR orders

Whether the patient has a DNR order depends on the patient and the disease. Such orders are not consistently applied to patients with the same expected life span. For example, some patients with cancer have the same probable life expectancy as some patients with heart failure, but the cancer patients are more likely to have a DNR order.

The presence of a living will on the patient's record does not justify an automatic DNR order. DNR does not mean DNT (do not treat), but to some clinicians a DNR order gives rise to that presumption.

A DNR should be written when either 1) the patient refuses CPR, or 2) the clinician assesses that CPR would not be successful and should not be attempted. In the latter circumstance, the patient and or family should be informed of that assessment. The clinician must be careful to limit her decision to whether the patient cannot be resuscitated--that the attempt would be medically futile--in which case resuscitation should not be tried. The clinician's decision should not rest on whether the patient's *life* is futile.

Along with all other orders, in most organizations the DNR order may be suspended when the patient undergoes an operation. The trend is to educate the patient to this policy, and allow more autonomy in such situations.

Resuscitating all patients who die in the institution is bound to fail in some or even most cases. But a broad no-CPR policy in an organization would be as unpersonalized as is an all-CPR policy.

Think about it.
Could a policy work, that required that CPR be discussed with the patient, consented to, and ordered by the clinician, except when the patient requires CPR before that process?

Some suggest changing the "DNR" order to "DNAR," the acronym symbolizing "do not *attempt* resuscitation." The suggestion is that saying "do not resuscitate" assumes that the patient could be resuscitated but deliberately is not. (Winslow, 2001).

Withdrawing vs. withholding

The issue of withholding or withdrawing treatment concerns every clinician and potential patient. You are both.

GENERAL CONSERVATIVE RULES FOR WITHHOLDING OR WITHDRAWING TREATMENT

If the course to follow is not clear, be conservative.
Follow your ethical instincts.
If there's any doubt, *treat* because:
> Treatment can be withdrawn later but
> Treating later won't help if the patient has died from withholding treatment.
> The clinician owes a duty to the patient, not the system.
> If an error might be made, err initially on the side of life.

Most people in the United States die in a hospital or nursing home. At least 70 percent of those deaths occur without CPR being done. Statements that people are allowed to die without extraordinary efforts means that patients die without CPR–that is, with a DNR order. It does not mean that the deaths are caused by withholding water and food or by shutting off a ventilator.

In law, withholding treatment is not different from withdrawing treatment. However, people actually doing the withdrawing and withholding do report a real emotional difference. They say it is harder to withdraw than to withhold.

The practical difference between the two is that withholding treatment usually causes or allows death before much analysis can be made, while withdrawing treatment may be done after a decision process. The better distinction is between treating fully and limiting treatment.

Correcting myths about terminating life support: correct statements of the law about dying

An act that is not specifically permitted by law, is not necessarily prohibited. Just because the law doesn't say you can, doesn't mean you can't.

Terminating life support is not necessarily murder or suicide, if the patient is dying and the life support is not medically indicated.

Patients needn't be terminally ill in order for treatment to be terminated.
> The criterion is whether treatment is medically indicated. Giving food and water is indicated if the patient is not dying, unless it causes

harm to the patient.

When it is not medically indicated, ordinary or extraordinary treatment may be terminated.

In law, withholding may be the same as withdrawing treatment but it does feel different in practice–it's harder to withdraw. In law, tube feedings are not different--they may be withdrawn if that is indicated. Ethical concerns are raised, however, if food and water are withdrawn from a patient who is not dying, intending to cause the patient's death. This intent can be inferred from failure to attempt to retrain the patient to eat orally.

A court order is not necessary to terminate life support, when the treatment is not indicated.

Some acts that are lawful are not myths at the higher ethical level. Examples: abortion on demand for any reason is lawful, but many believe it is unethical. Withdrawing food and water may be lawful if the surrogate authorizes it, but it may be unethical. For many, the minimum ethic of the law is much lower than the higher ethical behavior.

Double effect

Related to the idea of treating fully or limiting treatment is the ethical concept of **double effect**. Double effect is the idea that people are morally responsible only for the consequences they intend. Thus they are not morally responsible for bad unintended consequences that happen as an accompaniment to achieving the good effect sought. The concept of double effect would hold that if the person's primary intent is good, the unintended other effect, the "double" effect, can be excused. (Remember that this is a concept from ethics, not from law. As seen in earlier chapters, you may be *legally* responsible for consequences that you can foresee, whether you intend them or not.)

Double effect is an excuse for an unintended effect, because the person intended to do good. How valid the excuse is, may depend on how foreseeable is the unintended bad effect. The evil effect of starving to death is absolutely foreseeable if tube feedings are removed from a patient who is not able to take food orally. This degree of foreseeability is high, compared to, for example, a mere possibility of the bad effect of death from respiratory depression as a side effect of an indicated dose of morphine.

Or, the validity of the excuse of double effect may depend on how severe the unintended effect is. For example, the intent to get bread at the grocery may produce the mild unintended effect of getting wet when it is raining. This is hardly comparable to the evil "unintended" effect of starving the patient to death while intending to remove a burden of tube feeding.

Or the validity of the double effect excuse may depend on the degree of importance of the intended good effect. For example, the patient may decide that the good effect of pain relief is enormously important, compared even to the possibility of the evil effect of unintended earlier death.

Dehydration

The legal and ethical issue of dehydrating patients has arisen since the technology became available to provide food for patients by means other than by mouth. In prior times, patients who were unable to feed themselves were fed by others until they could not swallow, and then they died.

Because enteral feedings now are available, some patients get them for economic factors. Higher reimbursement is available for the care, and in some cases the tube feedings may be done at lower labor cost. Research shows that up to one-half of patients on tube feedings may be retrained to eat by mouth (Leff, 1994).

If the dying patient requests it, dehydration may be considered medically appropriate and ethical, and so it is lawful. Some even advocate dehydration as an alternative to assisted suicide, that is easier on the clinician if not the patient (Miller, 1998). For patients who are not dying or who are not competent to request dehydration, the ethics and law are less clear. Some court orders have allowed it, some have not.

Clinicians who participate in causing death by this method in patients who did not volunteer, potentially are liable for licensure violations and malpractice. For example, if your state statute has a conscience clause that protects your right to refuse to participate, and if you participate in killing a patient by dehydration you will not have the defense that your employer "made you do it."

Think about it.

Would regular participation in by clinicians in causing patient death, possibly jeopardize public trust in the profession?

If society wishes to hasten the death of such patients, might the solution be to allow the families to do the care at home, likely resulting in earlier death from infection, malnutrition, or some other complication?

Would asking families to pay for their loved one's care in place of the government, achieve this result indirectly?

> "[D]enial of nutrition may in the long run become the only effective way to make certain that a large number of biologically tenacious patients actually die. Given the increasingly large pool of superannuated, chronically ill, physically marginal elderly, it could well become the nontreatment of choice" (Callahan, 1983)

Cases: the right to die

In order for a case labeled "right to die" to get to court, a conflict about withholding or withdrawing treatment or care must exist. Treatment supporting life is withheld every day. If there is no conflict between clinicians and patient or family, no one will ask a court's opinion.

Considering that millions of people die without obtaining permission from a court, relatively few cases about such issues have been decided. Some law cases on the "right to die" are designated as refusal of treatment, although in virtually all such cases the refusal is by a surrogate and not by the patient personally.

In such cases, the court may use standards such as best interest or substituted judgment. The test of what is in the **best interest** of the patient in reality is the same test as the **substituted judgment** of the surrogate, for the patient. The patient would have always made the judgment in his or her own best interest, and so should the substitute or surrogate.

A family member or loved one of the patient is preferred as substitute decision maker. This is not because that person knows better what the patient wanted–research shows otherwise. Instead, the family or loved one is preferred because they are assumed to love the patient and want her best interest, and because the patient's life or death usually affects that decision maker too.

Surrogates are allowed to make decisions, but only for those patients who are believed by their clinicians to be unlikely to improve. In these patients, either the patient's life is considered not valuable to her, or her life is considered a burden to her. Families are not allowed to decide the fate of patients whose lives are considered valuable to them. For example, the parents of potentially healthy children are not allowed to refuse care that might save the child's life.

Standards of evidence

In court cases, including those about terminating care, three levels or standards of evidence are used. The standards are 1) evidence beyond a reasonable doubt, 2) clear and convincing evidence, and 3) preponderance of the evidence.

Evidence beyond a reasonable doubt is the highest level of evidence, the most difficult to attain or prove. This is the level of evidence needed to convict in criminal trials. That standard of evidence must exist before the person's life or liberty is taken. Though her life was at stake, this standard was not the test of the evidence for Nancy Cruzan. Nancy was the subject of US Supreme Court case that approved the Missouri standard for withdrawing care, noted below.

Clear and convincing evidence is a second and lower level of evidence used for various kinds of cases. In some states this standard of evidence must be met before punitive (punishing) damages can be awarded in a civil negligence case. In Missouri and several other states including New York, the clear and convincing standard of evidence must exist before a person's life support (including food and water) can be withheld.

Such states require evidence from the time before the patient became incompetent, that the patient would refuse treatment--food and water included. A judge will decide if the evidence is clear and convincing.

Preponderance of the evidence is the lowest legal standard of evidence. It is the standard used in civil court cases such as those that establish liability in a malpractice lawsuit. For example, if the clinician testifies that the bedrails were up, and the patient testifies they were down, and if there is a little more evidence for the clinician (perhaps the chart states that fact too), then that's a preponderance for the clinician. Anything judged to be over 50 percent is a preponderance, and the decision at the trial court level will stand up on appeal.

Cruzan

In *Cruzan*, the US Supreme Court found that the Missouri court could require clear and convincing evidence of what the patient wanted before approving the withdrawal of her food and water. Or, the Court said, the state could adopt a lower standard through their legislature (*Cruzan v. Director*, 1990).

Nancy Cruzan had been in a neurologically damaged state since her car wreck in 1972. Her father and mother wanted her clinicians to withdraw her tube feeding. They refused, and the case went all the way to the highest US court. The Court held that Missouri could require clear and convincing evidence of what Nancy would have wanted.

After the Supreme Court decision, witnesses were found who then testified that Cruzan either had stated, or didn't disagree with someone's statement, about a condition similar to the one she came to be in. The statement was that Nancy "wouldn't want to live like that." The same trial court judge who originally ordered the feedings stopped, found this evidence to be clear and convincing evidence of Nancy's wishes.

He again ordered the feedings stopped (*Cruzan v Harmon*, 1990). This time the state, in the person of the attorney general of Missouri, did not appeal the decision. Nancy Cruzan's tube feedings were stopped and she died of dehydration 14 days later.

A higher standard of evidence than clear and convincing is necessary to convict a guilty person before they are executed Even if guilty, the convicted would not be executed if she were incompetent.

Think about it.
Will you be more careful in telling your friends of what conditions you'd rather be dead than be in, or would you want them to help you die in such circumstances?
Remember this question as you age.
Is your answer changing? Which way?

The Fourteenth Amendment and the right to refuse treatment

In *Cruzan,* many believe the Court established a constitutional right to refuse treatment based on the Fourteenth Amendment to the U.S. Constitution. No state can deny life, liberty, or property without due process of law. The liberty interest protects individuals from state courts, legislatures, and majorities that would limit their right to refuse treatment or to consent to it. But the Fourteenth Amendment does not give patients a right to demand treatment.

Before *Cruzan* the right to refuse treatment was established by judge-made law (common law), state by state. No federal constitutional right had been declared. New York case law had been the standard for many years, and had been adopted in all other states in some form. See below for text.

Every human being of adult years and sound mind has a right to determine what shall be one with his own body . . . (Justice Cardozo in *Schloendorff,* 1914).

That case established the right to sue for battery when unauthorized surgery was done.

As long as the right to refuse treatment was merely a common law right established by state judges, or a statute made by state legislatures, states could interfere with and restrict the right as they chose. For example, many "advance directive" laws operate only when patients are terminally ill, and don't allow patients to refuse food and water in their advance directives.

After the Supreme Court in *Cruzan* recognized a constitutional right to refuse treatment, states may not be able to restrict that right. Competent patients probably can refuse whatever treatment they specify and under whatever conditions they choose, through their advance directives.

The US Supreme Court in *Cruzan* did not differentiate between levels of treatment. Food and water can be withheld if the advance directive requires it. And the Court indicated that advance directives would constitute clear and convincing evidence in a case such as Cruzan's.

Busalacchi

A later Missouri case is that of Christine Busalacchi, residing just down the hall from Nancy Cruzan in the same facility. Christine had not expressed any earlier statement about her treatment in the event of such a condition. Her nurses and some of her doctors disagreed that she was in a persistent vegetative state (see below for discussion).

Being in close proximity, Busalacchi's father noted the success of the Cruzan family in having their daughter's treatment stopped. (In both situations, questions were raised about motives of the family for seeking death of the daughter.)   Mr. Busalacchi sought to move his daughter to Minnesota for diagnosis of PVS by neurologist Dr. Ronald Cranford (an advocate of dehydrating patients in PVS), and subsequent removal of her feeding tube.

Several groups, including nurses who had cared for the patient for several years (some the same nurses who had cared for Nancy Cruzan), protested the causing of death in their patient (Wolfe, 1992). They believed it inhumane to cause death in a person by a method that is illegal to use in animals and that is never chosen as a method for suicide by people who are competent (nor is it a method ever used to execute criminals).

Further, they objected to the use of clinicians as agents to cause death by withdrawing care. They asserted that the provision of nutrition is an indispensable function in the care of patients able to take such nutrition, and who are not dying. They objected that the clinicians giving care were not consulted nor believed when they asserted their assessment of the condition of the patient (as not being in PVS). The court relied instead on the statements of neurologists who had spent little time with the patient.

The clinicians and other employees of Mt. Vernon Rehabilitation

Center consistently asserted that this patient was able to take fluids by mouth, able to express emotion appropriately, to make purposeful movements, and to feel pain.

The case had been appealed to the Supreme Court of Missouri, whose newly elected state Attorney General Jay Nixon had run on a platform of not denying patients the "right to die" in such cases. Predictably, the day he was sworn into office, he withdrew the state's objections to her dehydration. Christine Busalacchi was dehydrated to death at Barnes Hospital in St. Louis, Missouri, dying finally on 11 March 1993.

Other cases
Mrs. O'Connor--another clear and convincing

In New York, the guardian of Mrs. O'Connor, diagnosed with senile dementia (she was not asserted to be in PVS), sought to have her dehydrated. Note that efforts to dehydrate patients are not limited only to patients in a persistent vegetative state. The New York court said the patient should keep the feeding tube when there is no *clear and convincing evidence* of the patient's wishes (*In re. O'Connor,* 1988).

Claire Conroy, also not in PVS

Claire Conroy, 84, was a nursing home patient with senile dementia (her diagnosis was made before it became common to extend the diagnosis "Alzheimer's disease" to old people). Her caretakers wished her to be dehydrated. Again, note that dehydration is not limited to patients with PVS. The court decided that the substituted judgment or best interest standard should be used to decide if the her feeding tube should be removed. The court also ordered a state ombudsman, plus a guardian, be appointed to decide the fate of such people (*In re Matter of Claire C. Conroy,* 1985).

Reason for the clear and convincing

These conditions are sometimes reversible. Examples are seen of patients who were comatose for long periods, "awakening." Such examples confuse the wish to believe that such people want to, and should be, dehydrated.

Withdrawing care is not murder

In another case, the worst fears of physicians were realized. Care was withdrawn from a comatose patient, with the consent and desire of the family---or so the doctor thought. A complaint led to a murder charge filed by the prosecutor, but later withdrawn. Testimony revealed that the family was not so clearly committed to the patient's death as the doctor had thought or wished. Lesson? Know the patient and family well enough to ascertain their wishes, even if delay in terminating treatment is necessary (Lo,1984).

Competent patients and the right to be dehydrated

Very few cases considered by the courts have been about competent patients who personally wish to be dehydrated to death. Elizabeth Bouvia, a young woman with cerebral palsy and a quadriplegic, but not terminally ill, sought the right to refuse food and water in order to be allowed to die with hospital care (*Bouvia,* 1986). She was granted that right by a court, but chose to live on in another hospital.

Hector Rojas, another quadriplegic, also petitioned a court to allow him to dehydrate while under hospital care. The court granted his wish, and he died after 14 days, having requested and been administered morphine for the discomfort of dehydration (*Rojas,* 1987).

Wendland--not in PVS

Robert Wendland had an accident that left him conscious yet severely disabled, both mentally and physically, and dependent on artificial nutrition and nutrition. His wife and conservator (legally similar to a guardian) proposed to direct his physician to remove his feeding tube and allow him to die. His mother and his sister objected to the decision, the matter finally being decided by the California Supreme Court after Wendland died of pneumonia. The court said there was not clear and convincing evidence that he would want to die in such a situation (he was not in PVS) (*Conservatorship,* 2001).

Definition of death

The change in law to redefine death from the thousand-year-old **definition of death** as "cessation of pulse and respiration" to "brain death" was done so that harvesting body parts for transplant would not result in a charge of murder.

The diagnosis of brain death will not be necessary unless patients are to be used to donate body parts. Brain dead patients will die within a few hours or days, even with artificial ventilation. But if they die before body parts are taken, organs cannot be used for transplant.

Some experts have called for another redefinition of death, to higher brain death. This definition would define people as dead when the cortex of their brain no longer functions well. Patients could be declared dead who are in persistent vegetative state (PVS), or who have Alzheimer's or senile dementia.

PVS is a diagnosis used since the 1970's to describe patients who have severe neurological damage and are not conscious. The patients seem to have sleep-wake periods and other evidence of higher brain activity.   Depending on the etiology of PVS, some patients are more likely to recover–such as those patients who are young, with trauma etiology. Patients unlikely to recover are those patients who are old, with other than with trauma etiology (Celesia, 1993). Some PVS patients who have been in vegetative state for years have regained consciousness

(Arrillaga, 2000).

In time past, other diseased people were labeled as dead--for example, people with leprosy. That diagnosis, however, did not cause them to be actually killed as the PVS diagnosis has done to people so diagnosed. PVS patients in some cases have not been formally labeled as "brain dead," but their feeding has been stopped, killing them by dehydration within about 14 days.

As suggested in A time to be born, one definition of death comes from the theory of symmetry, applied to life's beginning and ending. This theory would use similar neurological tests on both the beginning and ending of life or personhood. Personhood would begin--a fetus would become a baby--when brain stem function starts at 4 weeks. Symmetrically, personhood would end when brain stem function stops (as when spontaneous breathing stops).

Or personhood could begin when brain cortex function starts at 6-10 weeks. Symmetrically, personhood would end--one would lose her personhood though still alive--when cortex function stops as in Alzheimers, PVS, or senile dementia.

Analysis of actions that cause death by degree of intent

(Criminal Law Starts to Punish about Here)

☜More intent ↘ Less intent ☞

Suicide, Murder, Euthanasia, Assisted Suicide, Reckless, Negligence, Disease

(Note: Suicide is not punished by criminal law in any state. Suicide assisted by a physician is not punished in Oregon. Euthanasia might not be punished, if done with permission.)

From Hall JK. *Nursing ethics and law*. Philadelphia: WB Saunders, 1996

The causation of death can be divided into non-human causes--natural causes, act of God, or disease--and human causes. Further, the actions by humans that cause death can be separated into those intended to cause death--suicide, murder, assisted suicide, and euthanasia. The other causes of death are those that are not intended to cause death such as a reckless act, negligence, or increase in pain medication.

Other-killing: euthanasia

Other-killing is killing done by a person other than the one who is killed. Other-killing includes all the forms of ending one person's life by another, excluding only suicide. Examples of other-killing are negligence (unlawful killing, usually not a crime) murder (unlawful killing, a crime), abortion (lawful killing if done with permission of the mother) and euthanasia (technically unlawful killing, but not often prosecuted).

Euthanasia is other-killing done intentionally. Euthanasia comes from the Greek words *eu* for well (happy, good) and *thanatos* for dying (death). Thus, euthanasia means a well or good death. As originally used around the beginning of the 1900's, the word meant bearing death bravely and with good spirit. Euthanasia has come to mean that someone else kills the patient, with good intentions.

The patient can volunteer to be killed, but consent is not necessary to the definition of euthanasia. Euthanasia is called voluntary when the patient requests it. When the patient does not request it, it is called involuntary. When the patient's surrogate makes the request for the patient, some call that nonvoluntary euthanasia, of one who cannot request it.

Distinctions are made as above, regarding whether the patient volunteers for death. In addition, there may be discussion about whether the act of euthanasia is direct or indirect, for example whether a poison is injected (direct) or whether his ventilator is terminated (indirect). Other discussion regards whether the act is active--characterized also by some injection. Or the euthanasia might be called passive--for example, by not initiating treatment for a condition that could be treated such as antibiotic for pneumonia.

At first glance euthanasia by dehydration appears to be passive euthanasia, because the patient appears to be allowed to die "naturally."

Think about it.
Remember the discussion of naturalism in Chapter 4. If the patient dies naturally, is that automatically moral?
Do we allow animals or convicted felons to die "naturally" by withholding water from them?
Or is that considered cruel?

Clinicians who are asked to withdraw treatments (for example, ventilators or tube feedings) should be clear about their authority to do so--the law--and their motive--the ethic. If you are certain that the withdrawal will cause the patient's death, the conservative course before complying is to discuss the situation with the patient if possible, the family, the supervisor, the risk manager, and anyone else you need, for advice.   If you do not feel the act is the appropriate action to take, you have a right and possibly an obligation to refuse. You were a human with ethics before you were a clinician or an employee. For bad examples of people who forgot that, see the next topic.

Nazi euthanasia

Euthanasia gained a negative image from the National Socialists who used it in Germany in the 1930s and 40s. That period culminated in what now is termed the holocaust. German clinicians and their professional organizations were actively involved in killing of millions of people in that era, performing euthanasia and other kinds of killing (Steppe, 1992).

"Whatever proportions [National Socialist] crimes finally assumed, it became evident to all who investigated them that they had started from small beginnings. The beginnings at first were merely a subtle shift in emphasis in the basic attitude of the physicians."

"It started with the acceptance of the attitude, basic in the euthanasia movement, that there is such a thing as life not worthy to be lived. This attitude in its early stages concerned itself merely with the severely and chronically sick. Gradually the sphere of those to be included in this category was enlarged to encompass the socially unproductive, the ideologically unwanted, the racially unwanted, and finally all non-Germans."

"But it is important to realize that the infinitely small wedged-in lever from which this entire trend of mind received its impetus was the attitude toward the nonrehabilitable sick" (Alexander, 1949)

This activity was not unique in history, nor was the attitude that degenerated into euthanasia limited to Germany. A sizable number of people today in the U.S., believe that people who have incurable disease or some degree of disability would be better off dead.

Integral to the discussion of euthanasia are the actions of self killing-- suicide and assisted suicide.

Self-killing

In order to think clearly about the law and ethics of assisted suicide, you must know your attitude toward suicide itself.

Think about it.
Do you believe it is acceptable for people to kill themselves?
Is it the ultimate in autonomy, or are they mentally ill, or depressed?
Should such people be helped to live, or to die?
Or does your attitude depend on their physical condition?

Whether assisted suicide is right depends on whether suicide itself is right. In other societies and in times past, suicide has been seen sometimes as positive, sometimes as negative. Surveys show that many in this society, now, support suicide for patients who are old and ill.

People object to the cost of caring for the old and terminally ill with increasing costs that are mandated through taxes. Some prosecutors share that belief, and are reluctant to prosecute clinicians who perform euthanasia or who assist suicide (Meisel, 1999).

The fact that the public does not support suicide for young and healthy people is good evidence of the underlying utilitarian values. The issue is not the quality of the patient's life, to himself as an individual, but the utility (actually the *dis*utility) of his life, to the greater society.

Research reveals data that is surprising to many people, and contrary to what is projected onto persons who are diagnosed as being terminally ill. People diagnosed with terminal illness, even those in pain, rarely want assisted suicide. The only persons who are terminally ill and who say they want to die, are those who are depressed (Hall, 1998). Good treatment is available for depression.

Think about it.
Would treatment for depression be given to a young healthy patient who
    wanted suicide--even involuntary treatment? Should it be?
Why or why not?

Self-killing, helping: assisted suicide

In the context of clinical practice, **assisted suicide** care may be defined as "prescribing drugs for patients to kill themselves." If you do more than provide the poison or gun to the patient you are not helping the patient to self-kill, instead you actually are doing the killing. Clinicians who are not physicians face as much ethical and potential legal pain regarding assisted suicide or euthanasia as do physician clinicians. That is because such work invariably will be delegated.

Suicide is not unlawful in any state, but assisted suicide is unlawful in all states except Oregon. In 1994, Oregon voters passed a law allowing physician clinicians to prescribe drugs to patients for their use in killing themselves. In earlier years in Washington and California, such an issue had been defeated at the polls.

In 1997, the US Supreme Court considered whether patients have a constitutional right to assistance in suicide. The issue was whether the Constitution limits the power of states to make the act of assisting suicide a crime. One argument asserted in that case against state laws that make assisting suicide a crime, was that the Fourteenth Amendment guaranteed the liberty of the individual. In this case the liberty asserted was the liberty to choose death with help. The liberty arguments echoed those of the abortion cases–for example, *Roe v. Wade.* The liberty arguments were made also in the withdrawal of treatment case, *Cruzan v. Director, Missouri Department of Health.*

The other argument against state laws that criminalize assisting suicide relied on the Fourteenth Amendment also. This argument rested on the Amendment's guarantee of equal protection of the law (seen in Chapter 5). It was asserted that people who refuse treatment and then die, in effect have killed themselves. This was said to be a right that was unfairly denied to people who wouldn't die with passive withdrawal of treatment–people who thus needed their clinicians to help them kill themselves.

The Supreme Court disagreed. They distinguished the right to refuse treatment, from an entitlement to have someone assist with suicide. The Court did not, however, require states to make assisted suicide unlawful (*Washington,*1997).

The Oregon assisted suicide law went into effect in 1997. Early on, few patients were reported to have killed themselves with physician prescriptions. Much of the early experience with the law regarding reasons the patients chose suicide and the adequacy of their care at death, was kept from public inquiry (Oregon, 2000). Officials in Oregon cited the need for the privacy of the patients who chose suicide. Only 19% of the patients who had clinician help to kill themselves in 2000, received any psychological evaluation, compared to 37% in 1999. In 1999, 26% of the suicide patients said they more feared being a burden on others than experience of pain, but in 2000, 63% of the 27 suicide patients gave that reason for wanting to die (Will, 2001)

American oncologists have decreased their already tepid support for assisted suicide and euthanasia. Their support dropped from 45.5% down to 22.5% who support assisted suicide, and from 22.7% down to 6.5% who support euthanasia (Emanuel, 2000).

The Holland experience

Physicians in Holland have been protected from prosecution for to euthanizing their patients since the mid-1980's. Several putative criteria are required, such as the patient having intractable suffering, being competent, making repeated requests, and having two doctors agree on the appropriateness of the killing. Euthanasia had not been legalized in Holland by their Parliament, but it was not prosecuted as a crime. In 2000, their Parliament made it officially lawful.

The Dutch law now makes it lawful to euthanize minor children over 16 at their request after their parents are consulted, and children between 12 and 16 may be killed if their parents agree with the request. Advance directives delegating the decision about euthanasia to a physician are authorized. The patient need not be terminally ill, merely to have "lasting and unbearable suffering."

Dutch physicians have been acquitted for killing patients who "suffered from life itself" (Dutch court, 2000). Another was not punished for murdering an 84-year-old woman who had not asked for euthanasia and who had said she did not want to die (Dutch GP, 2001). Evidence from Holland has been published that patients are killed without the even the law's minimal criteria being satisfied, and without the deaths being reported as euthanasia (Dutch court, 2000).

In 2000, Dutch doctors succeeded in having the euthanasia law extended to assisted suicide--prescribing poisons for patients to use to self-kill. The reason given for the change was said to be because the act of killing patients actively was becoming distressing to the profession (Dutch Parliament, 2000).

Pain control

A related issue to assisted suicide and euthanasia is pain control. Some patients are thought to request death because pain relief is inadequate, but evidence from experience with dying patients and in places where they are intentionally killed such as Oregon and Holland, refutes the idea that pain is the reason patients want death. Instead, people say they want to die to avoid loss of control, and because they do not want to be a burden.

Clinicians continue to seek ways to meet pain control needs of their patients, short of killing them. Hospice clinicians have said they have never had a patient express a wish to die--with or without help--who was free of pain and who felt wanted. Clinicians can help effect both of those conditions.

The US Congress considered federal legislation that would have facilitated pain control for patients, while forbidding the use of federally controlled deadly drugs in killing patients. The law, called the Pain Relief Promotion Act, was under consideration in 2000 (Pain, 2000), but was believed to be unnecessary. Attorney General Ashcroft was expected to reverse the former Attorney General's permissive stance, that allowed Oregon doctors to prescribe federally controlled substances to patients for use in killing themselves.

The JCAHO issued standards for pain management in an effort to improve pain management for patients, available from their Website (JCAHO, 2000). Some state clinician boards have issued guidelines for pain management as well. If your state has such guidelines they would be available at your state credentialing board's Website.

Clinicians recognize that their patients die, and that they need care while dying as much and more than they do in getting well. Clinicians can be sure of practicing ethically and lawfully if they practice with the guide that dying patients are as valuable as those who will get well. The goal is that patients die as comfortably as possible, knowing to the end of their lives that they are valued as human beings.

Clinicians will practice ethically and lawfully if they remember that we cure sometimes, relieve often, comfort always. Good practice is comforting the patient by controlling his pain. As always, good practice is lawful and right.

REFERENCES

Alexander L. Medical science under dictatorship. *New England Journal of Medicine,* 1949; 241(2):39-47.

Arrillaga P. Woman returns from 16-year coma. AP, Downey, CA, *Amarillo Daily News,* 3/11/2000, p. 11A.

Baby Moses law is saving lives. *Texas Accent*, 2001;20(3):5.

Baby Moses law will help abandoned infants. *Medical Board Report*, Fall 2000, p.9.

Bouvia v. Superior Court for Los Angeles County, 225 Cal. Rptr. 297,307 (Ct. App. 1986).

Burt R. *Taking Care of Strangers: The Rule of Law in Doctor-Patient Relations.* New York: The Free Press, 1979.

Callahan D. On feeding the dying. *Hastings Center Report,* 1983; 13(5):22.

Celesia GG. Persistent vegetative state. *Neurology,* 1993; 43:1457-1458.

Child Abuse Amendments of 1984, 42 U.S.C. 5101, 45 C.F.R. 1340.14 *et seq.*

Clark RT. Baby Jose. *Journal of the American Medical Association,* 2000; 284(9):1144-45.

*Conservatorship of Wendland,*accessed at http://www.courtinfo.ca.gov/cgi-bin/opinions.cgi, August 25, 2001

Cruzan v. Director, Missouri Department of Health, 497 U.S. 261 (1990).

Cruzan v Harmon, No. CV 384-9P, Circuit Court of Missouri (Mo. Cir. Ct. Jasper County Dec. 14, 1990) (Teel J.).

Davis v. Davis, 842 S.W. 2d 588 (Tenn. 1992)

Densford K, Everett, M. *Ethics for modern nurses.* Philadelphia: W.B. Saunders Company, 1946; p. 93

Dutch Parliament 'legalizes' euthanasia. *Life at Risk, A Chronicle of Euthanasia Trends in America,* 2000; 10(6):2.

Dutch court allows physician-assisted suicide without a medical disorder. *The Lancet,* 2000; 356:1666.

Dutch GP found guilt of murder faces no penalty. *British Medical Journal,* 2001; 322:509.

Emanuel EJ, Emanuel LL. The economics of dying: The illusion of cost savings at the end of life. *New England Journal of Medicine,* 1994; 330(8):540-544.

Emanuel EJ. Cost savings at the end of life. What do the data show? *Journal of the American Medical Association,* 1996; 275(24):1907.

Emanuel EJ, et al. Attitudes and practices of U.S. oncologists regarding euthanasia and physician-assisted suicide. *Annals of Internal Medicine,* 2000;133(7):527.

Exodus 2, Old Testament.

Friedlander H. *The origins of Nazi genocide.* Chapel Hill: The University of North Carolina Press,1995.

Genesis 30, Old Testament, King James Version.

Getting older. *The Economist,* March 1, 2000, p. 108.

Gotzsche PC, Olsen O. Is screening for breast cancer with mammography justifiable? *The Lancet,* 2000;335:9198.

Hall JK and Sicola V. I wouldn't want to live': the myth about attitudes of terminal patients. *Journal of Nursing Law,* 1998; 4(4):31-43.

Hallan S, *et al.* Quality of life after cerebrovascular stroke: a systematic study of patients' preferences for different functional outcomes. *Journal of Internal Medicine,* 1999; 246:309-316.

In re. O'Connor, 53 NE 2d 607 (NY 1988).

In re. matter of Claire C. Conroy, 486 A 2d 1209 (N.J. 1985).

In re. T.A.C.P, 609 So.2d 588 (Fla. 1992)..

Infant Health and Development Program. Enhancing the outcomes of low birth weight, premature infants. *Journal of the American Medical Association,* 1990; 263:3035-3042.

JCAHO. *Pain assessment and management: an organizational approach.* Accessed at: http://www.jcaho.org.

Kings 3, Old Testament.

Leff B, Cheuvront N, Russell W. Discontinuing feeding tubes in a community nursing home. *Gerontologist* 1994; 34(1):130-133.

Lo B. The death of Clarence Herbert: withdrawing care is not murder. *Archives of Internal Medicine,* 1984; 101:248-251.

Many C. Putting your risk in perspective. *Ladies Home Journal,* May 2000, p. 162.

Meisel JD, *et al.* Prosecutors and end-of-life decision making. *Archives of Internal Medicine* 1999; 159:1089-1095.

Miller FG, Meier DE. Voluntary death: a comparison of terminal dehydration and physician-assisted suicide. *Annals of Internal Medicine,* 1998;128:559-562.

Mills GB. Understanding risk: A prerequisite for making informed decisions. *Oncolog,* 2000; 45(5):8.

Morrow J. Making mortal decisions at the beginning of life: The case of impaired and imperiled infants. *Journal of the American Medical Association,* 2000;284(9):1146-47.

Norton C, Rogers, L. Clone scientists can grow sperm in laboratory. *The Sunday Times,* 12/31/00, http://www.sunday-times.co.uk/news/pages/sti/2000/12/31/stifgnfar01003.html.

Oregon: "botched" suicides, flawed report. *Life at Risk,* 2000, 10(2):1.

Pain Relief Promotion Act: floor debate set for September. *Physicians for Compassionate Care,* 2000; 3(2):5,8.

Pless JE. The story of Baby Doe. *New England Journal of Medicine* 1983;309:664.

Putting the risk of breast cancer in perspective. *New England Journal of Medicine*, 1999;340(2):141.

Roe v. Wade, 40 U.S. 113 (1973).

Rojas v. District Attorney Erkenbrack, Civil Action No. 973V142. Filed January 20, 1987, District Court, Mesa County.

Schloendorff v. Society of New York Hospital, 105 N.E. 92, 93 (N.Y. 1914).

Sox HC. Benefit and harm associated with screening for breast cancer. *New England Journal of Medicine*, 1998; 338:1145.

Steppe H. Nursing in Nazi Germany. *Western Journal of Nursing Research*, 1992; 14(6), 744-753.

Storch T. Editorial board speaks: The unkindest cut. *American Journal of Diseases of Children*, 1990; 144:533.

Testing times. *The Economist*, October 21, 2000, pp 93-94.

Van Cleve L. Nurses' experience caring for anencephalic infants who are potential organ donors. *Journal of Pediatric Nursing*, 1993; 8(2):79-84.

Washington v. Glucksberg, 521 U. S. 702 (1997); *Vacco v. Quill*, 117 S.Ct. 2293, 138 L.Ed.2d (1997).

Webster P, Hurst G. MPs give go ahead for embryo research. *The Times*, 12/20/00, http://www.thetimes.co.uk/article/0,,2-53953,00.html.

Webster's New International Dictionary, Second Edition, Northampton, MA: G. & C. Merriam, 1934.

What are the odds of needing care. *U.S. News & World Report*, June 5, 2000, p. 85.

Will Oregon law's third year be its last? *Life at Risk*, 2002;11(1):1.

Winslow EH, Beall J. Code blue: what makes a difference? *American Journal of Nursing*, 2001; 101(1):24m, 24p.

Wolfe JE. Nurses' groups join court debate in right-to-die case. *Joplin Globe*, 25 August 1992.

Woo J. Embryo custody fight. *Wall Street Journal*, 16 June 1993, B6.

GLOSSARY

A priori knowledge is gained through reasoning, not just by experience

A posteriori knowledge is gained after observing the fact of experience.

Abuse is intentionally maltreating another, often defined in statute as harm to a dependent person.

Act utilitarianism strictly analyzes the goodness of an act, without evaluation of rights or rules.

Actual duties are duties to be followed if there is a higher moral duty than the *prima facie* duty.

Administrative law is made by the executive branch of government, to carry out the aims of the statute law made by legislators.

Advance directives are directives made in advance of the person becoming incompetent and unable to consent or refuse treatment for herself.

Affirmative action describes an active program that seeks to increase the numbers of a minority participating in a workplace, school, or other organization.

Agent is the employee or independent contractor who works on behalf of the principal.

Agism is having a bias against people merely because they are old.

Alternative Dispute Resolution (ADR) includes ways to solve conflicts outside of court.

Annotated statute is one with dates of enactment and amendments to the statute and with the history of the legislation.

Apparent or ostensible agency is possessed by one who appears to act on behalf of the organization.

Applied ethics is the application of ethical theory to actual practice.

Arbitration is a form of dispute resolution in which the parties agree to binding decision by judge-like decider.

Artificial insemination is the procedure in which sperm in semen is delivered to the cervix by means other than sexual intercourse.

Assault in civil law is defined as fear of immediate harm from a battery.

Assisted suicide in a clinical practice context can be defined as "prescribing drugs for patients to poison themselves."

Association in a study is a finding that two factors are associated.

At will employment is without a written contract, in which the employer can discharge the employee "at will" and the employee can quit "at his will" meaning for any or no reason.

Autonomy requires that actions taken should be those that are freely chosen. In Greek, *autos* means self; and *nomos* means governance or control, similar ideas being power, liberty, and choice.

Axiological ethics determine whether an act is right or wrong, by the value of the consequences of the act.

Battery is defined as harmful or offensive contact to the person, with intent to contact, and caused by the person who is the defendant in the lawsuit.

Belmont Report is an ethical standard for medical research issued after ethical violations committed under research by the US Public Health Service in Tuskegee Alabama.

Beneficence is the value underlying malpractice law, the Latin root meaning to do good or make good.

Best interest is a test of what is in the best interest of the incompetent patient.

Borrowed servant is one who the physician clinician was considered to have "borrowed" from the actual employer.

Breach of the standard of care is one factor necessary to establish malpractice.

But for is the legal test of what is the proximate (close) cause of the patient's injury.

Capitation from the Latin word for head, *caput,* limits payment to one per patient per year or similar type of payment.

Captain of the Ship is a doctrine used to find physician clinician liability for negligence committed by an employee of others.

Case probability is the risk that an individual will experience an event.

Case law is one of the three sources of law, written by judges in deciding appeals of lawsuits.

Casuistry is conducting ethics for clinical practice on a case-by-case basis.

Categorical Imperative is the idea that you should judge every act you do by whether you would choose the same behavior for everyone in the world.

Causation is established if the clinician's breach resulted in patient injury, a finding that one factor caused another.

Civil law is the division of law in which the individual is considered to have wronged another private individual or organization, distinguished from criminal law.

Claims made malpractice insurance covers the clinician for claims that are made while the policy is kept in force.

Clear and convincing evidence is the middle level of evidence, used for various kinds of cases–for example, in some withdrawal of treatment cases.

Code of behavior is a series of statements about what behavior is expected of a person in that occupation.

Code of Federal Regulations is the compilation of rules made at the federal level into a code of law.

Codes of ethics are a series of statements about what ideals are expected of a person in that occupation.

Cognitive theories of ethics are those that use reasoning to determine right behavior--including intuitionism, contractarianism, and naturalism. These theories assume that ethics is based on the cognitive abilities of human beings.

Compact licensure states make a compact (an agreement) to license clinicians from each of the other members of the compact.

Comparative negligence reduces the plaintiff's damages, proportionate to his own percentage of fault.

Competence measures ability in advance–an example is the licensure test.

Competent means able to manage one's affairs.

Confidence interval in statistics are the odds that the conclusion reached by the study was not an accident. A 90% confidence interval means the odds the conclusion is meaningless are 1 in 10. A 95% confidence interval means the odds the conclusion is meaningless are 1 in 20.

Confidentiality (keeping secrets) has similar origin with fidelity--*con* means with, and *fide* means loyal or faithful.

Consent by proxy is evidenced by verbal or written expression--by one who gives consent for another.

Consent is derived from two Latin words, *con* meaning "with" and *sentire* meaning "feeling"--permission to perform an act.

Consideration is something of value exchanged by the parties to a contract.

Contingency basis is payment for malpractice lawyers with a percentage of the damages, contingent on the plaintiff's winning the case.

Contraception is a shortened form of the two words: contra (against) and conception.

Contractarianism, a cognitive theory, assumes that morality is a contract between individuals and society.

Contracts are agreements that can be legally enforced.

Contribution allows a codefendant who has paid more than the correct share of the judgment to seek fair payment from the other(s).

Contributory negligence is a defense to a malpractice lawsuit, asserting that the patient contributed to her own injury.

Conventional rights are obtained from conventions or customs set out by groups.

Conversion is the intentional tort defined as acting to exercise dominion and control over another's chattel.

Corporate liability is a theory of liability for corporate acts.

Correlativity thesis is the idea that rights and obligations correlate, that is, a right gives rise to a corresponding obligation or duty.

Cost of care for the patient is one of the factors that determine the economics of clinical practice.

Covenant not to compete is a contract clause that seeks to limit the employee's power to compete with the employer after leaving employment by forbidding work of a certain kind within a certain area for a certain time.

Criminal law is the division of law in which the individual is considered to have wronged the whole public.

Cruzan v. Director was the case decided by the Supreme Court that gave the right to refuse treatment a constitutional basis.

Cultural relativists have as their standard of right, whatever the culture or society believes.

Damages are the injuries of the patient that were caused by the breach of the standard of care by the professional.

Decisional capacity means capable of making decisions.

Deconstructivism was a reaction to structuralism, asserting that nothing was structured and everything needed to be destructed to show that there was no structure.

Defamation is an injury to the person's reputation that results from an untrue statement made to a third person.

Definition of death was "cessation of pulse and respiration" and now is defined in most state statutes as "brain death."

Demand for care by the patient is one of three factors of clinical practice economics.

Deontological theories of ethics decide what is right by reference to a duty, rule or principle, contrasted with teleological theories of ethics, that decide whether an act is right by the outcome of the act.

Dependency thesis advances the idea that morality is dependent on certain conditions in the culture or environment–related to ethical conditionalism.

Descriptive ethics is the study and description of ethical beliefs of various cultures.

Desert is the concept of giving rewards only to people who have earned them, not to those genetically advantaged or those whose ancestors were wronged.

Discipline of the license is a penalty such as warning, probation, suspension, termination, or non-renewal.

Divine command is the idea that people behave morally because their religion orders them to do so.

Documentation standard is that charting should be an accurate and complete record of the patient's condition and care.

Double effect is the idea that people are morally responsible only for the consequences of their acts that they intend. This does not excuse clinicians from liability for malpractice if they can foresee the consequences of their act.

Due process means that appropriate procedure must be followed before the government can take your life, liberty, or property.

Durable power of attorney designates a person to consent or refuse treatment for the person if, and after, they become incompetent.

Duties and obligations include *prima facie* duties and actual duties.

Duty is the legal concept that the professional in a relationship owes an obligation to the patient.

Egoism is an ethical concept that assumes that people are motivated by their self interest.

Emancipated minors usually are married, or have a child, or live independently, or are in the military, and thus can consent for themselves.

Emotivism is a non-cognitive theory, in which emotion is said to be the base of deciding right and wrong, and that seeks to explain intuitionism in less rational, more simplistic terms.

Employee is a person engaged to work for an employer, having certain rights under many labor laws.

Employment at will is an employment relationship that can be terminated at the will of either party.

Endorsement is the process of having the clinician's original state endorse her application for licensure in a new state.

Enterprise liability is a proposed reform of malpractice law that would make the organization liable for lawsuit instead of the clinician.

Entitlements originated in the word "title" that implies ownership of a thing or claims on others.

Equal opportunity is a passive program based on the Fourteenth Amendment equal protection clause, that seeks to increase opportunity without specifically requiring increased numbers of minority participation.

Ethical absolutist believes that what is moral is absolute and unchanging.

Ethical conditionalist believes that what is moral depends on the conditions that exist.

Ethical decision making is the technique used for making decisions about ethical conflicts.

Ethical egoism is a theory of ethics that asserts that people are motivated by their self interest, said to be capable of universalization.

Ethical practice is ethical action--distinguished from moral reasoning.

Ethical relativism is the term used when discussing whether any morality is real or true. People who use this ethical theory believe that what is moral is relative, not absolute.

Ethical universalists believe that what is moral is universal across cultures.

Ethics can be defined as being the customs of ideal behavior that people should follow.

Ethics committees in an organization write bylaws and procedures, may set policy for staff to use in situations of ethical conflict, educate staff and the public about ethics, and decide cases.

Eudaemonia as described by Aristotle is the happiness achieved by acting in the area of the golden mean.

Eugenics is the attempt to improve the human race by improving the genetics of the people.

Euthanasia means a well or good death--originally it meant bearing death bravely. But it has come to mean killing the patient with good intent.

Evidence beyond a reasonable doubt is the highest level of evidence, needed to convict in criminal trials.

Existentialism asserts that all humans can know is that they <u>exist</u> –hence the name of the philosophy.

Express consent is consent made by writing or speaking.

Extreme relativists believe that what is moral is within each person and possibly is different for each person.

Extrinsic values are relational qualities of a thing, what makes it valuable for us and our needs–for example, that the car goes fast.

False imprisonment is defined as confining a person to a bound area by force, without good reason.

Federal Register is a daily publication in which US federal agency rules are published.

Federal law is made at the national level, by federal lawmakers--statutes, regulations, and cases.

Fee-for-service pays the provider a fee for each service that is given to the patient.

Fidelity originates in Latin, *fide* meaning to be faithful, to be true. The value incorporates Keeping Promises (Loyalty), Keeping Secrets (Confidentiality), and Telling Truth (Veracity).

Fiduciary duty is the clinician's duty to act for the patient's interest--the basis of fiduciary being *fid*, similar to the word fidelity.

Foreseeability is the legal requirement in a malpractice case that harm could be anticipated from the breach of the standard of care.

Futility is care that is asserted to be not warranted in the situation.

Usually the term is invoked when care is given to incompetent patients with a poor quality of life who will die without the care.

Genealogical theory of ethics says that the origin of morals originate in human psychology.

General normative ethics are the theories of ethics that prescribe some rules for ethical action.

General intent can be presumed from the fact that you did the act, and that you knew in advance what the result of your act would be.

Golden mean is the area of action between extremes, recommended by Aristotle.

Good Samaritan laws make rescuers immune from liability for ordinary negligence, usually not for gross negligence.

Good will was thought by Kant to be a good mind set--a good intent.

Governmental immunity provides immunity from suit for taxpayer-supported organizations of local, state, or federal governments.

Group probability is the risk that a certain percentage of the group will experience an event.

Guardian is the person who is made responsible for the ward.

Harm limits autonomy on the basis that the act might harm another.

Hedonism considers pleasure as the highest good.

Heteronomy is the condition of a person who is said to be a slave to desire and not reason–contrasted to a person with autonomy.

Human pluripotent stem cells are obtained from embryos and are considered capable of developing into endoderm, mesoderm, or ectoderm tissue.

Implied consent is not expressly spoken or written out, but may be implied by the patient's condition or by the patient's act.

In vitro fertilization is the union of sperm and ova outside the human body, literally occurring *in vitro*, in a glass container.

Inalienable rights cannot be alienated–that is, cannot be sold, or separated from the person.

Incapacitated people legally are the same as those who are incompetent.

Incompetent patients are considered unable to make rational decisions in their best interest. Generally they cannot lawfully consent to or refuse treatment for themselves.

Indemnity allows one who paid a judgment to sue the party actually responsible for damages.

Independent contractors are people who work in a "contract" relationship, not as employees.

Infringement is the word used if a right is overridden for a good reason.

Institutional Review Boards (IRBs) oversee research that has federal funding, to protect subjects.

Intelligent design is the speculation by scientists that the universe could not have evolved this complexity without some intelligent being or beings having been involved in the design.

Intent is <u>what</u> you meant to do, contrasted to motive, <u>why</u> you did it.

Intentional misrepresentation is the intentional tort of deliberate lying in order to effect some gain.

Intentional infliction of emotional distress is intentional outrageous conduct that makes another person experience severe emotional distress.

Internet is the world wide web, a source of information accessible at home or at the office or at a public library.

Intrinsic values are the inherent qualities of a thing–for example, that the car is red.

Intuitionism is a cognitive theory that asserts some principles are known instinctively, intuitively, with very fast logic, without need for or being capable of proof.

Invasion of privacy is a quasi-intentional tort that includes 1) using your face or name for advertising without permission, and 2) disclosure of private facts.

Joint and several liability holds all tortfeasors equally liable to pay any or all damages.

Justice is a value or principle commonly described as fairness.

Land ethic advocates believe that ecosystem integrity is the criterion for moral standing.

Law is a minimum behavior standard written by people with authority. It enforces at a low level the higher behavior standard, the ethics.

Legal rights are those written into, and protected by, law.

Legal moralism limits autonomy to prevent immoral behavior.

Libel is written defamation.

Licensure is legally enforced credentialing that limits certain practices to licensed clinicians only .

Life is the value upon which all of the work, ethics, and law of clinical practice are founded.

Life expectancy is the present average age at death, determined by averaging the ages at death of people who have died over the last three years.

Life span represents the actual years lived by average humans who do not die as infants and whose genetic and environmental risk factors are average.

Living will says what the person wants if he becomes incompetent and ill, and cannot give or withhold consent for himself.

Loyalty is part of the value fidelity, and requires keeping promises.

Malicious prosecution is an intentional tort, prosecution of a civil lawsuit with malicious reason for bringing the suit.

Malpractice is the term for some negligent practice by a professional, that causes injury to the patient or client.

Malpractice insurance covers clinicians for losses from malpractice.

Managed care is a system of payment for care that manages the case or limits the payment in some way.

Mandatory continuing education requires a minimum amount of continuing education be obtained for a clinician to be relicensed.

Maxims are subjective principles that people establish for themselves before an encounter with an ethical problem, to guide their behavior.

Mediation is one form of dispute resolution in which parties voluntarily try to settle their conflict with a mediator's help.

Medical savings accounts are set up with funds to pay medical expenses, plus an insurance policy with a deductible for the amount of the account. If the employee uses all the account on expenses, the insurance kicks in to pay the bills. If he doesn't use all the account, he keeps the surplus.

Mental health directive is a consent to mental health treatment given in advance of incompetence.

Metaethics is the philosophy of ethics.

Minor is the term for person under 18 who usually cannot consent for herself.

Moral agency is the concept that certain people have the capacity to act, morally.

Moral development is the idea that people develop morally, as they learn from education and life.

Moral legalism is a method of determine right and wrong by reference to specific rules or laws.

Moral judgments are judgments about whether behavior is moral or not--right or wrong.

Moral patient is the recipient of a moral act, who is capable of suffering.

Moral particularism assumes that whether an act is right or wrong depends on the particular situation.

Moral reasoning is moral thinking, distinguished from ethical practice or action.

Moral relationships create a morality from the fact that humans live in relationships with one another.

Moral rights are established by morality, but not protected by law.

Moral standing considers whether a thing has any claim to be treated morally.

Motive is why you did what you did, contrasted with intent--what you intended to do.

Narrative ethics is a technique of narrating or telling stories about ethics and analyzing them, using paradigm cases.

Natural rights are assumed to attach to all humans, merely by their status as humans.

Natural law is a philosophy of law that focuses on what law ought to be, with reference to ethics and morality.

Naturalism is cognitive theory that asserts that the major premise or principle of an ethical argument can be defended by measuring it against "nature."

Naturalistic fallacy assumes that whatever the moral standard <u>is</u>, also is what the moral standard <u>ought</u> to be. Thus, whatever exists is natural and is ethical.

Necessity limits autonomy on the basis that the limit is necessary.

Negative rights are the power to demand that people be left alone, or be allowed to do an action without interference.

Neglect is a form of abuse, failure to provide the necessities of life for a dependent person.

Negligence *per se* is violation of a statute that prescribes a certain behavior that is intended to protect the class of person who has been harmed.

Negligent infliction of emotional distress is negligent conduct that makes another person experience severe emotional distress.

Nihilists are those who absolutely deny that an act can be judged right or wrong.

Non-maleficence is the Latin term for the value Don't Harm. Non means "not," mal means "bad," and ficence, means to "do or make."

Non-cognitive moral theories are those that do not use reasoning to determine right behavior--including prescriptivism and emotivism.

Non-normative approaches to ethics include descriptive ethics and metaethics.

Nonmoral judgments are judgments that do not have a moral context-- for example, those that identify good or bad wine, not right or wrong behavior.

Normative judgments apply a norm to judge something.

Nuremberg Code is an ethical standard for medical research issued after ethical violations committed under the National Socialist (Nazi) regime.

Objectivists believe that the right thing to do can be determined objectively, from outside the person and the culture.

Occurrence malpractice insurance covers the clinician for any event that occurred while the policy is in force.

Offense to others is a principle for limiting autonomy if the act offends others.

Original position is Rawls' imaginary place that people occupy before they agree to form a society.

Out-of-hospital DNR is an order to prehospital clinicians who give emergency care, not to give certain care (usually resuscitation).

Paradigm case is one that purports to set the standard in narrative ethics.

Paternalism justifies the restriction of liberty of some, in order to limit or prevent harm to the person himself.

Patient Self Determination Act (PSDA) mandates that the organization have a policy to inform patients of their right to refuse treatment and requires the organization to decide whether it will honor advance directives. This federal law (also called the Danforth Amendment) encourages the use of advance directives.

Performance is a term for measurement of the ongoing assessment of ability.

Positive law is a philosophy of law that focuses on what law is as written, arguing that law can be determined and studied and enforced without reference to ethics and morality.

Positive rights are claims or entitlements that others are obliged to fulfill, contrasted to negative rights, the right to be left alone.

Preponderance of the evidence is the lowest legal standard of evidence, the standard used in civil court cases such as malpractice--anything over 50% majority.

Prescriptive judgments prescribe what people should or should not do.

Prescriptivism is a non-cognitive theory of ethics, in which moral language is said to prescribe--either commend or condemn some action.

Prima facie duties are known on their face, intuitively, without further evidence or proof of their validity. They include repairing wrongs, seeking distribution of happiness in accord with merit, doing good to others and self, not harming, telling truth, keeping promises.

Primum non nocere (pronounced "preemum non no-cherry") is Latin for "first, do no harm" (non-maleficence).

Principal is the person or entity who is represented by an agent or attorney in fact. The terms are used in a durable power of attorney for health care.

Procedural due process is fairness (appropriate procedure) in law making and in law enforcing.

Profession is a concept in which the members of an occupation exhibit at least three qualities: organization, learning, and altruism.

Promissory estoppel is a theory of contract law used to avoid one party losing, by the legal fiction that one party has made a promise (in essence, a contract) and is stopped (estopped) from denying it.

Psychological egoism is not an ethical theory, but a theory from psychology–that asserts that people are motivated only by self interest.

Public policy exception modifies the at will doctrine in employment law, by protecting employees without a contract from firing if they are acting to enforce a law that protects the public.

Punitive damages are assessed to punish the wrongdoer, by giving extra penalty to people who do harm with a large degree of recklessness or even intent.

Qualified immunity provides immunity from legal liability when acting to protect the patient or another.

Quality Adjusted Life Years combines the patients average expected length of life with a quality of life number, to determine quality of life.

Quasi-intentional torts exhibit a degree of intent between intentional torts and unintentional torts. They also are called injury to economics and dignity.

Quasi-contract literally means half-contract–a theory of law used when the court needs to enforce a promise that does not meet the legal conditions for a contract.

Reciprocity is used when two states have a reciprocal agreement to honor one another's licensees.

Registration laws register or title clinicians, protecting only the use of the title from non-registered clinicians.

Regulations are one of the three kinds of law, written by people in the executive branch of government that is headed by the governor of the state or by the president of the country.

Res ipsa loquitur is Latin, meaning the "thing itself speaks"–a legal theory of causation in which the injury tells its own story and proves negligence.

Respondeat superior is Latin meaning that the "superior (employer) responds"--pays for the damages caused by its employees.

Reverse discrimination is the situation when the minority race or sex is favored over the majority race or sex.

Rights are the demand, power, or obligation of people to be treated fairly. Rights also are defined as claims or entitlements that others are obliged to fulfill.

Risk probability is the concept that a certain percentage of a group will experience an event, for example the odds that part of a group will have cancer.

Roe v. Wade is the decision of the US Supreme Court ruling that abortion could not be restricted by state law during the first three months of pregnancy.

Rule utilitarianism adds some value of obeying the rule, to the equation of what is the greatest good.

Sensitivity of a test is the number or percentage of tests in a group of people known to be abnormal, that correctly show up as abnormal (abnormal tests in an abnormal population).

Sentient means capable of experiencing pain.

Skeptics as defined in ethics theory, are people who question whether an act can be objectively judged to be right or wrong.

Slander is spoken defamation.

Slander *per se* is slander that needs no proof of damages–for example, slander of another's business or professional reputation.

Social or distributive justice is based on the value doing good (for a group of people). This concept enforces equality in outcomes, not necessarily equality in opportunity or process.

Sovereign immunity is a legal theory that the king or ruler can not be sued.

Specific intent requires that you intended to accomplish the result of the act, not merely intended to do the act.

Specificity indicates the number or percentage of tests in a group of people known to be normal, that correctly show up as normal (normal tests in a normal population).

Standard of care for clinicians is to give the care that a reasonable prudent clinician would give in a similar situation.

State law is law made at the state level, by the state legislators, rulemakers, or judges.

Statistical significance is the probability that the finding of a study likely is not due to chance or luck.

Statute of Frauds is old English law that says that certain agreements that are not written, are not enforceable in court.

Statute of limitation is a statute that limits the amount of time the patient has to file a lawsuit after his injury occurs.

Statutes are one of the three sources of law--the law written by the legislative branch of government (federal, state, or local).

Strict liability torts do not require negligence or intent to be proven, only that an act is done that causes harm.

Structuralism philosophy proposed that all things and ideas are structured, of two opposite views–that individuals are merely part of much larger structures or systems.

Subjectivism advances the position that standards of moral behavior generally are subjective, measured from inside.

Substantial factor is a lower legal test of causation, established if the breach of the standard of care is even one among several factors causing the injury.

Substantive due process is fairness in the substance of the law, not just in the procedure used in administering the law. The standard for constitutionality is that the administrative agency or board or legislature must have had some rational basis for making their rule or statute.

Substituted judgment is a test in which the patient's substitute or surrogate, judges what the patient would want (usually, what is in the patient's best interest).

Supply of care by the clinician--time, technology, and quality--is one of three factors of clinical practice economics.

Surrogate mother is a woman who deliberately conceives and delivers a baby that she knows she will give to another specified couple.

Tail malpractice insurance covers claims that are made after the employment is finished, for occurrences that happened while the clinician still was employed.

Teleology means to look at things from the point of view that they are destined to become something else. The word also refers to a philosophy that looks to the outcomes of the action to determine its rightness or wrongness, as contrasted with deontological philosophy.

Transplantation is the process of removing tissue and organs from one person and grafting them into another's body.

Trespass to land is the intentional tort of entering another's property without permission.

Ultra vires is an act done outside the power that was granted by the legislators to the rule maker or rule enforcer.

Unjust enrichment is a legal theory that courts use when no enforceable contract exists, in order to prevent one party from unfairly (unjustly) getting a benefit (enrichment) at the expense of another.

Utilitarianism judges all actions by the principle of their utility (usefulness) in producing the desired effect--the greatest good for the greatest number.

Value judgments identify whether some thing or some behavior is good or bad. Value judgments can be either moral or nonmoral.

Veil of ignorance in Rawls scheme keeps the lawmakers from knowing their eventual rank in society--contrasted with the window of knowledge used by clinicians.

Veracity is part of the value fidelity and originates in Latin, *vera* meaning truth–the value requires telling the truth..

Vicarious liability enforces legal responsibility on one party, for the actions of another.

Violation is the word used if a right is overridden for a bad reason.

Virtue ethics is the ethics of character, described by Aristotle

Ward is the person who has been formally judged by a court to be legally incompetent or incapacitated.

Whistle-blower is the person who reports a violation of law, usually an employee reporting an employer.

INDEX

EPILOGUE

This book first went to print during the week after the terrorist attack on the USA. As you read it, no doubt you will apply the law and ethics described here to that event in addition to applying them to your clinical practice. The ethics described here were valid long before I wrote, and they will be long after.

Jacqulyn Kay Hall

Ordering Information

JACKHAL BOOKS
18 Nottingham Road
Amarillo, TX 79124
Phone/fax 806-353-8727

8:00 AM to 5:00 PM CST

LAW & ETHICS FOR CLINICIANS
JACQULYN KAY HALL, RN, JD

Single Copies $ 34.95 US

Plus Shipping $5.00

(Texas Residents add 8.25% sales tax)

Courses for credit, continuing education materials and study guide are available, based on this text and created to fit your specific needs.